D0443877

fP

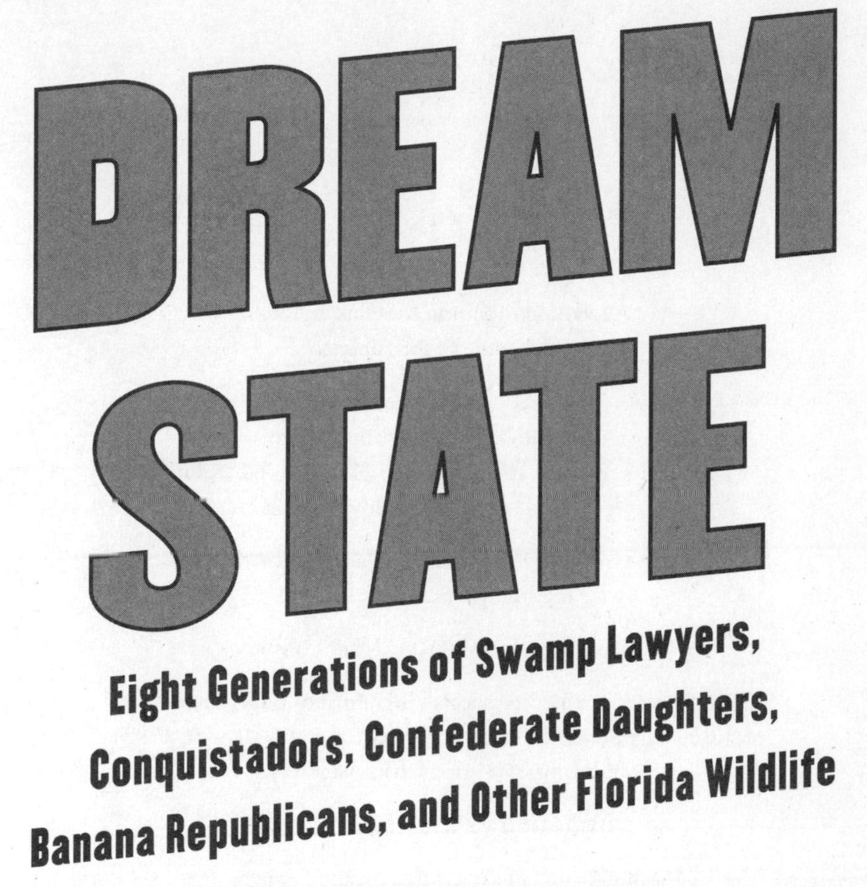

Dream State

Eight Generations of Swamp Lawyers, Conquistadors, Confederate Daughters, Banana Republicans, and Other Florida Wildlife

Diane Roberts

Free Press
NEW YORK LONDON TORONTO SYDNEY

*f*P
FREE PRESS
A Division of Simon & Schuster, Inc.
1230 Avenue of the Americas
New York, NY 10020

For information regarding special discounts for bulk purchases,
please contact Simon & Schuster Special Sales at 1-800-456-6798
or business@simonandschuster.com

DESIGNED BY PAUL DIPPOLITO

Manufactured in the United States of America

10 9 8 7 6 5 4 3 2 1

Library of Congress Cataloging-in-Publication Data
Roberts, Diane.
Dream state : Eight generations of swamp lawyers, conquistadors, Confederate daughters, banana Republicans, and other Florida wildlife
p. cm.
Includes bibliographical references and index.
1. Roberts, Diane—family. 2. Florida—History. 3. Florida—Social customs.
4. Florida—Biography.
F311 R63 2004
975.9—dc22 2004056276
ISBN 0-7432-5206-3

For Bradford Wayne Roberts

Contents

DREAM
STATE

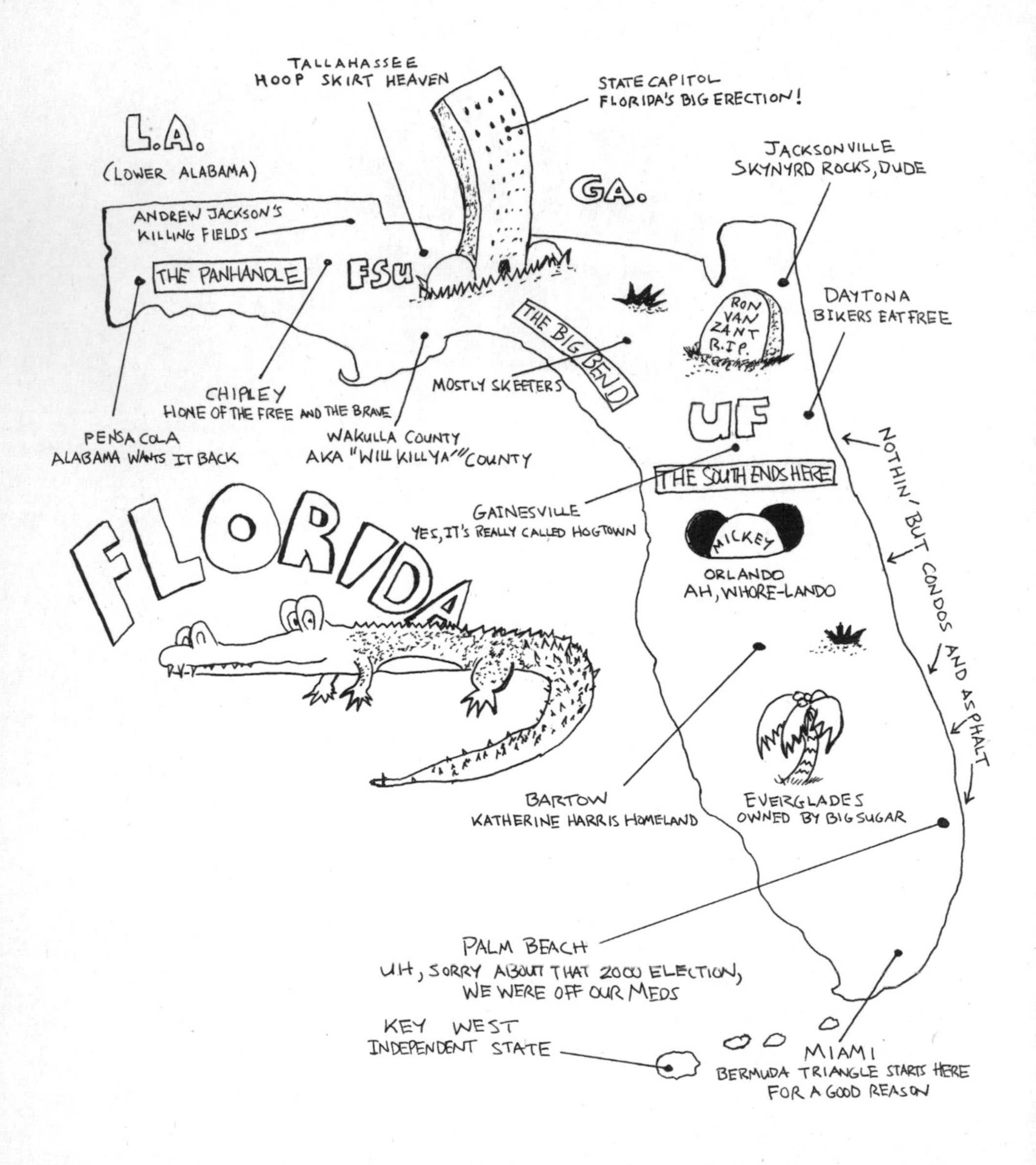
TALLAHASSEE
HOOP SKIRT HEAVEN
STATE CAPITOL
FLORIDA'S BIG ERECTION!
L.A.
(LOWER ALABAMA)
GA.
JACKSONVILLE
SKYNYRD ROCKS, DUDE
ANDREW JACKSON'S
KILLING FIELDS
THE PANHANDLE
FSU
RON
VAN
ZANT
R.I.P.
DAYTONA
BIKERS EAT FREE
THE BIG BEND
MOSTLY SKEETERS
CHIPLEY
HOME OF THE FREE AND THE BRAVE
UF
PENSACOLA
ALABAMA WANTS IT BACK
WAKULLA COUNTY
AKA "WILL KILL YA" COUNTY
NOTHIN' BUT CONDOS AND ASPHALT
THE SOUTH ENDS HERE
GAINESVILLE
YES, IT'S REALLY CALLED HOGTOWN
FLORIDA
MICKEY
ORLANDO
AH, WHORE-LANDO
BARTOW
KATHERINE HARRIS HOMELAND
EVERGLADES
OWNED BY BIG SUGAR
PALM BEACH
UH, SORRY ABOUT THAT 2000 ELECTION,
WE WERE OFF OUR MEDS
KEY WEST
INDEPENDENT STATE
MIAMI
BERMUDA TRIANGLE STARTS HERE
FOR A GOOD REASON

Prologue: Debatable Land

IT'S TALLAHASSEE. It's Friday afternoon. It's November 17, 2000, ten days after the not-election. The votes—chads dimpled, dangling, hinged, hanging, or pregnant—still sit in boxes. The Motel 6 still declares NO VACANCY. News anchors still drink Bombay Sapphire martinis in the Doubletree, bugging the bartenders: "Could I have *extra* olives? A bowl would be good." Ex–secretaries of state still eat shrimp and grits at the Cypress Restaurant. Television trucks, their satellite dishes pointed at the cold heaven, still clog Duval Street. Walgreens is still sold out of collapsible umbrellas. Home Depot is still sold out of extension cords. Florida is still the center of the universe.

I'm walking around downtown, acting like a tourist in the place I was born, hoping maybe I'll run into Jesse Jackson or Warren Christopher or Tipper Gore (incognito in Audrey Hepburn sunglasses) or just somebody who feels like sucking down a couple of cosmos at Chez Pierre. Things have gone quiet. The "Sore Loserman" sign-toting rent-a-rabble have decamped to the high ground of the Holiday Inn. The lawyers are holed up in their offices navigating stacks of statutes, Lexis printouts, briefs, and mostly empty Pizza Hut boxes. The judges have disappeared behind the silver doors of the Florida Supreme Court, pondering their next Delphic pronouncement. The whole world is watching. There's just not much to see.

I pick my way over black TV cables, thick as a convention of king snakes, behind the New Capitol, reaching past the fountain that should have water splashing over white stone except it's been broken and dry since the 1980s. The State of Florida is too cheap to fix it. But beneath my feet, down through the concrete, down below the blanket of red clay on the hill, underground rivers course through limestone passages: you wouldn't have to dig far to hit water. Make a natural fountain. The Floridan Aquifer on parade. It would even be free.

I guess the governor and the legislature have bigger mullet to fry. Aesthetics has never been much of a priority around here. Every year legislators ritually complain about the James Rosenquist mural on the ground floor of the capitol: *Why the giant orange peels? And a rock stuck to a rope? And a crab wearing a cowman's hat?*

Political sensitivity isn't much of a priority, either. Unlike Alabama, Florida still flies its Confederate flag. The Second National, also known as the Stainless Banner, flaps near the defunct fountain along with the lions and castles of León and Castile, the Fleur de Lys, the Union Jack, and the Stars and Stripes, emblems of the sovereign powers that have presided over Florida since 1513. Rumors run around Tallahassee that the governor would like to haul the Second National down and pack it off to the Museum of Florida History, where no one would notice it. A Rebel banner outside the statehouse in the year 2000 is embarrassing. The governor's had enough trouble with African American voters, too, ever since the 1994 campaign, when some reporter asked him what he planned to do for black people and he replied, "Nothing." Things went downhill from there: Nine months ago he unilaterally ended state affirmative action.

But it's an election year; he can't get rid of the thing *now*. The Sons of Confederate Veterans would have a hissy fit, white rural Republicans big on states' rights would get mad, and everybody would accuse him of sucking up to people who'd be about as likely to vote for a member of the Bush family as burst into a spontaneous rendition of "Dixie."

You can feel the governor's pain. Here in forward-looking, twenty-first-century Florida we don't like to be reminded of slavery days. Florida had plantations, sure, and Jim Crow and race riots and lynchings (lots of lynchings); Florida still has white guys with "Forget, HELL!" mud flaps and "Heritage Not Hate" bumper stickers, but

Florida isn't Alabama. We promise. Or Georgia or South Carolina or Mississippi. We are bright, hopeful, and historyless. The current unpleasantness over the presidential election is like a hurricane. An act of God. Not our fault. This hurricane has ripped off a few roofs, rearranged the lawn furniture, and brought down some big tree limbs. But it will soon be over. The clouds will clear. Then we can go back to the Florida that's about *fun,* fun and sun and money, back to the Florida that pretends very hard that the past doesn't matter.

The eternal present almost works in South Florida, where most of the population recently arrived from Michigan or New Jersey; they bulldoze the old and wild places, evidence of a pre-air-conditioned, pre-condo, pre-golf-course era. The eternal present doesn't work in North Florida, where the ghosts are in residence year-round. I walk over the crest of the hill that sweeps down to the site of the Apalachee village of Anhaica, where, in 1539, the conquistador Hernando de Soto camped on his way to die on the banks of the Mississippi. I pass the Old Capitol, where, in January 1861, Catherine Murat, princess of France and great-grandniece of George Washington, pulled a silken rope and fired the cannon that announced Florida's secession from the Union. I cross College Avenue, which used to be called Clinton Street. It wasn't named for the forty-second president, though I wish it had been. To the west is a brick castle, towers, battlements, and all, the administration building of Florida State University. In the early 1970s, *Time* or *Newsweek* (nobody in Tallahassee can ever remember which) called FSU "the Berkeley of the South." Students for a Democratic Society flourished, Nixon-hating was a religion, and a guy named "Radical Jack" Lieberman used to teach a class on "How to Make a Revolution." Before World War II, FSU was the Florida State College for Women, and before that, it was the Seminary West of the Suwannee. My great-great-grandfather Luther Tucker was a cadet in 1865 when word came that Union troops were marching up from the Gulf to take Tallahassee. He got a note from his mama (required by the college), picked up his rifle, and, along with a bunch of other teenagers, engaged the Yankees at Natural Bridge.

Monroe Street is Tallahassee's main drag, unless you count the interstate (and we don't). During the lunch-counter protests of the early 1960s, students from Florida Agricultural and Mechanical University marched up and down the sidewalk with placards citing the Golden Rule and verses from the New Testament. My mother bought her lizard-skin stilettos and matching handbags from Miller's and her cocktail dresses from the Vogue. Her wedding presents came from Moon's Jewelers, where the carpet was as thick as custard and the salesladies members of the DAR. Old Mr. Moon, who would worry bees till they stung him (he thought this helped his arthritis), is dead now. The stores are gone, replaced by law offices, lobbying firms, citrus, cattle, construction, phosphate, and banking associations, all keeping a crocodilian eye on Florida government and thus their profits. The lobbyists always outnumber the legislators; over the last few weeks, the reporters have outnumbered the lobbyists, prowling the town like frat boys in search of cheap beer.

Actually, the reporters are often literally in search of beer, though to be fair, they prefer Sam Adams to Miller Lite. And that only after they've turned in the daily on last night's court ruling and what Al Gore's lawyers said about it and what George Bush's lawyers said about it and the spin put on all of it by Warren Christopher and James Baker, or maybe the weekender or magazine piece on the white-columned houses on Calhoun Street or the Indian mounds at Lake Jackson or the Florida panthers at the Junior Museum or the judge who writes mystery novels or the lawyer who raises polled Herefords or the Spanish moss thing or the manners thing or the "y'all" thing. A piece that uses "folksy," "drawl," "quaint," "Southern," "sleepy," and/or "legendary congressman Claude Pepper" in it. A piece that expresses astonishment (while trying to disguise it) that anything in Florida is older than Disney World.

You can't blame them. It's hard not to feel (though most of the reporters have stopped saying it) that a constitutional crisis should be happening somewhere with more *gravitas:* New York or Pennsylvania, even Illinois. It's hard not to feel that the whole country's fallen down a rabbit hole. To have the presidency, the very keystone of the Great Republic, coming unglued in a state where people march around in black-felt mouse ears, a state that boasts the world's only professional clown school, a state where a good percentage of the population confuse dirty glass in Clearwater with the Virgin Mary and a small Cuban boy in Miami with Jesus Christ, is not a paradigm shift but a paradigm violation. Where's the grandeur of democracy? The clarity of the Common Law? The majesty of the Bill of Rights? Hell, where's the beach?

It's not as much fun for the reporters as you might think. Most of them arrived from somewhere else, somewhere freezing, under the impression that they were going to *Florida,* a place of tropical ease and tropical warmth. They got to Tallahassee to find it wet and cold. They had to go to Nic's Toggery and buy tweed jackets and Mister Rogers' cardigans—Nic's is now famous as the place where Warren Christopher went looking for a pair of pajamas. The reporters live out of carry-ons in beige rooms at the Doubletree or the Radisson or, if they were late getting down here, the Days Inn off Highway 19 in Thomasville, Georgia. They eat at Andrew's every day: the "Blackened Jeb-Burger," the "Bob Graham-Burger," the "Secretary of State Salad Plate." They get their underwear dry-cleaned.

The natives smile politely, though the reporters get the feeling that, instead of being interviewed for the *New York Times* or *All Things Considered,* the natives would rather be at the mall. There, with giant red bows everywhere and Santa on his throne, they can pretend that the biggest political story since Watergate isn't exploding like a truckload of cheap firecrackers in their backyard.

Still, they're friendly, the natives. As if somehow they see the whole town—maybe the whole state—as their living room and the reporters as their guests. The local lawyers for both Gore and Bush, the judges, the capital press corps, the political operatives, and the bartenders are all on multigenerational elbow-clutching terms with one another. These y'all-sayers want to make sure you've got something to drink, and have you been to Posey's at St. Marks for the smoked mullet? and have you been to Albert's Provence for the bouillabaise? and have you ridden out to Wakulla Springs and taken the Jungle Cruise to see the anhingas and the alligators and the place where they made *Creature from the Black*

Lagoon? The natives tell you the difference between camellias and sasanquas, grouper and snapper, FSU's running game last year and FSU's running game this year. People in Miami or Palm Beach or Lauderdale don't behave this way. They don't give a shit if you've made it to the Seaquarium, Domino Park, Vizcaya, or the Polo Hall of Fame; they want to talk about *it,* the vote recount, the lawsuits, the word out of Austin, the word out of Washington. South Floridians will just come out and ask: Is Jeb Bush banging Katherine Harris? Is Al Gore as big a whiny asshole as he looks on TV? Tallahasseeans, citizens of the state's capital city, want to know—God, do they want to know—but they act like they're embarrassed, preferring maybe to pretend that the world's press has descended on them to cover the annual Jingle Bell 10K Run.

The reporters see their point. After all, banana republics are calling Florida a "banana republic." Fidel Castro has offered to send "democracy educators."

I begin to worry that something big is going on somewhere and I'm the only one who doesn't know about it. Walking through the Chain of Parks, five blocks' worth of grassy rectangles canopied with live oaks that were fully grown when Thomas Jefferson was president, I consider calling the *St. Petersburg Times* bureau or going home to check CNN. Then, in Lewis Park, I come upon a reporter for an up-north newspaper. I'd met him in Waterworks the other night. Waterworks is a postmodern tiki bar on the Thomasville Road with an ingenious yet low-tech system of artfully punctured Sears garden hoses hung at the top of its picture windows so that from the inside it always looks like there's a North Florida monsoon pouring down outside. The newspaper and magazine people, the younger wire people, the BBC correspondent in the motorcycle boots, and the Agence France-Presse girl with the suspicious tan like to go there for the martinis, which come with a little pink plastic monkey hanging off the side of the glass.

A couple of nights ago a BBC radio guy and the up-north reporter made their monkeys be George W. Bush and Al Gore. The monkeys duked it for the presidency of the United States of America on a sticky tabletop as Iggy Pop's "Lust for Life" crashed out of the speakers. But now the up-north reporter is standing there on the still-verdant turf, staring at a stump.

It had been a very big oak tree, broad as a banker's desk. What's left is dry and gray as a dove. "Hey," I say. "What's going on?"

"It's dead," he says.

I look at the stump, then at the up-north reporter. "Yeah," I say, "it's dead. Struck by lightning in 1986."

"Why don't they dig it up?"

"You don't understand," I say.

He says, "Is there an election metaphor in here somewhere?"

I tell him this is—was—the May Oak, one of the holy things of Old Florida, a tree that is more than a tree, an iconic representation of who we think we are, we who came to Florida in Andrew Jackson's bloody wake. Under the May Oak's vaulted green branches more than a hundred May Queens were crowned, more than a hundred May Poles erected and beribboned to be danced around by the flower-garlanded children of considerable white people. The *Tallahassee Floridian* of 1848 declared that the May Party was "an ancient custom handed down from the days of romance and chivalry." Never mind that less than three miles away you could find wildcats and bear (or they could find you). Never mind that the considerable white people copied the May Party out of a book and that Florida had been a state for less than three years.

I tell the up-north reporter that in the late 1960s, I was one of the children singing "*Sumer is icumen in, lhude sing cuccu!*" without having a clue what the words meant and anyway concentrating on weaving a clumsy pink and green crepe paper braid around the May Pole. Mary Harmon Hunt was my May Pole partner; she was taller than me and better with the streamers. Mary Harmon's mother, Mary Cecilia, had been May Queen in 1950. She wore long white gloves up to her shoulders and a white organdy dress over a hoop. She carried a bouquet of yard flowers—Queen Elizabeth roses, pinks, sweet william, night-blooming stock, and bronze iris—made up by the ladies of the Garden Club. She sat in a huge white fan-back chair. The May Queen and her court got dressed in their crinolines in a house up the street. In 1865 a

Union general had stood on the porch of that house and read the Emancipation Proclamation.

The up-north reporter wants to know if there are still May Queens and May Poles. I tell him that the May Party, like everything else in Florida, eventually became a political problem. Once the May Court came entirely from Leon High School, which was—no shock here—entirely white. But by 1974 Leon had been integrated. What if a *black girl* got on the May Court? Tallahassee wasn't just Gwynns and Lewises and Proctors and Moors and Duvals and Hopkinses, whose mothers were all in the Garden Club together and whose fathers had been KA or SAE brothers at UF. Tallahassee was getting to be like other places: There were two malls and three McDonald's. FSU had a black homecoming queen. Some civic worthies were agitating for a spring festival that would attract tourists to Tallahassee, with a parade and an arts and crafts show. Something for the new people; something to make money. The May Party didn't make money.

In 1973 Governor Reuben Askew declared his intention to drag Florida kicking and screaming out of the Old South. He was building us a new capitol, a real skyscraper shooting above the trees and the towers of the antebellum churches. This was partly an answer to the South Florida senators who'd been agitating to move the capital to Orlando, which would be, said the senators, more central, more like "Florida," with wide highways and orange groves and Yankees moving in and Mickey Mouse moving in. What they meant was that Tallahassee seemed too hysterically historical.

Lucky for Tallahassee, the usual gang of North Florida legislators, gallus-wearing Machiavels who weren't about to let the prize porker run off downstate, killed the plan dead. Can you imagine the vote recount coverage as officials held press conferences in the Haunted Mansion, reporters from *The News Hour with Jim Lehrer* interviewing Goofy and Snow White, Pocahontas appearing on *Larry King Live,* giving her assessment of Supreme Court rulings? Askew had wanted to tear down the Old Capitol, with its plantation house porticos where tradition says slaves were bought and sold and its memories of secession fever and battle-flag-waving atavism, but the ladies of the Garden Club, along with the United Daughters of the Confederacy and half of middle-class Tallahassee, bowed up and threatened to chain themselves to the fat Doric columns in front for all the world—or at least everybody driving up Apalachee Parkway—to see.

Askew lost the Old Capitol battle but got his New Capitol, rising behind the old one, a piece of cement brutalism with miserly windows. At about the same time, the May Party died like a frostbit bud, leaving just the tree, its rheumatic limbs getting too heavy for it, and a list of queens dating back to the 1840s. The New Capitol replaced the oak as the symbol of the New Florida. Tallahasseeans call the building "Reuben's Erection." Look at it from the top of the hill a mile to the east, the shaft thrusting up twenty-two stories, flanked on either side by the domed chambers of the House of Representatives and the Senate; you'll see why.

"If you still want a metaphor," I say to the up-north reporter, "what about the New Capitol?"

"I've been to Florida lots of times," he says, "mostly the part with the palm trees and poolside cocktail service. I've covered Florida politics. But a lot of what goes on up here is people talking about who they were at law school with. And who their cousins are. And their daddies. Everybody has daddies. Are you sure this is Florida?"

"We were here first," I say.

"Okay, I've been in this town two weeks. I even like it. It's just not the ticket I thought I bought."

"Or the ballot you thought you punched."

My way-back cousin Enid Broward was May Queen in 1907. Her daddy was Governor Napoleon Bonaparte Broward, known as the Fighting Democrat. The Browards had once been big plantation people in East Florida, but they lost it all in the Civil War. Napoleon Bonaparte had to work for a living, cod fishing, captaining a tugboat, and running guns to Cuban revolutionaries. As governor, he wanted to drain the Everglades, make some money off all that land doing nothing but lying around underwater. Napoleon Bonaparte was planning on going to Washington, but about the time he was fixing to ignite his senatorial campaign he died. My great-aunt Vivienne, ruthless ruler of the

Winnie Davis Chapter of the United Daughters of the Confederacy, would say that at least he lived to see Enid enthroned under the May Oak. In 1915 the state named a new county after him, a vast lozenge of land containing much of the still-liquid eastern Everglades. Now Broward County is famous as the natural habitat of the chad that may change the world.

The up-north reporter is looking at the stump, shaking his head. "I need a beer."

It's only three in the afternoon, but what the hell. Andrew's two-for-one cheap chardonnay'll be starting soon. It's either drink or go home and watch nervous rehashes of the Volusia County totals or exegeses of circuit court opinions to make Thomas Aquinas twitch with impatience or still more footage of George W. clearing still more brush from his ranch. Or worse. CNN is an unrelenting magic mirror, reflecting Florida's secret self. Instead of Miami sunshine, there's Tallahassee rain. Instead of icing sugar sand and peacock blue water, fluorescent-lit courtrooms. Instead of Worth Avenue babes in Versace, lawyers in bow ties.

The Red Queen says, "Now *here,* you see, it takes all the running you can do to keep in the same place."

One night late, maybe 2 A.M., on rerun Headline News tape of a Katherine Harris press conference, I even saw myself. We are all the way through the looking glass now.

"It's a poor sort of memory that only works backwards," the Queen remarked.

Tallahassee's been a political town for a thousand years. At about the same time French stonemasons were building Chartres Cathedral, aboriginal Floridians were building the six great mounds on the northwestern shore of Lake Jackson. The mounds aren't graves: they probably had a ceremonial or religious function. Like the towers of Chartres, they stuck up higher than anything else around and so showed who was boss in these parts.

In 1823, two years after Spain offloaded Florida (cheap) to the

United States, territorial governor William DuVal decided it needed a new capital. So he got two solid citizens, William Simmons of St. Augustine and John Lee Williams of Pensacola, to start walking from the eastern and western extremities of the territory. Tallahassee, the "old fields" of the Apalachees, domains of a people whose ancestors had arrived ten thousand years ago, was about the midway point.

Simmons and Williams met with Mikasuki chiefs Neamathla and Chifixico to "negotiate" property rights. Not that the chiefs were fooled. Simmons tells how Chifixico grabbed up a handful of Tallahassee dirt and demanded, "Is this not my land?" You hope Simmons had the grace to look ashamed. But Tallahassee had to be the capital, even though Tallahassee was twenty-five miles from the sea and five miles from the nearest good-size river. They built Washington, D.C., in a bog. I guess some places just smell of power.

I come from a political family. Until 1976 we were, pretty much all of us, Democrats, though some belonged to the *To Kill a Mockingbird* wing of the party and others to the *Gone with the Wind* wing. Jimmy Carter caused a schism: as one of my aunts said, he was "for the *Negroes*." She voted for George Wallace. A lot of them later turned to Ronald Reagan.

During the recount I watch us on television, my cousins by blood or marriage, distant or close or just claimed. L. Clayton "Clay" Roberts, director of the State Division of Elections, the tough-jawed young man always whispering in the secretary of state's pearl-decked ear, is an eighth-generation Floridian like me. Charlie Francis, one of the judges press-ganged into hand-counting votes, is married to my cousin Brenda Roberts. Dexter Douglass, general counsel to Governor Lawton Chiles, lead local attorney for Vice President Al Gore, is some kind of relation by marriage to the Browards. And probably still poltergeisting around the State Supreme Court Building, unable to bear missing the biggest court case in Florida history, is B. K. Roberts: in life chief justice for twenty-seven years, in death the name stuck over the door of the Florida State University law school, alma mater of several lawyers on both sides of the vote recount imbroglio.

Here in North Florida, kin—however remote, however politically misguided, however many times indicted—is kin.

My great-aunts' doxology was "Remember who you are." As if I'd be allowed to forget. The first of us arrived in Florida a little more than two hundred years ago. The rest came after Jackson's ethnic cleansing campaign made the territory safe for white men with seed cotton and slaves. We've more than flirted with power. My cousin Donald Tucker, a two-term Speaker of the Florida House of Representatives, looked like he'd be a star in the national Democratic Party. Jimmy Carter nominated him for a federal post. Sadly, Donald never made it. It could be that the Carter administration eventually got around to reading some of the newspaper accounts of his high-smelling business deals. It couldn't have helped that his brother Kit—Luther Christopher Tucker, Jr.—had been indicted (though not convicted) for larceny, forgery, and uttering. My Roberts grandfather (whose mother was a Tucker) said that Kit took after his daddy.

Senator Luther Christopher Tucker, Sr., was a member of the Pork Chop Gang, a farrow of rural legislators in the '50s and '60s who took up a disproportionate amount of space at the public trough. The Lamb Choppers, the Pork Choppers' largely urban opposition, adhered to the radical notion that the legislature should pass laws for the good of the state as a whole, rather than, say, Wakulla County, population 5,467, all of whom were kin to you. Luther Tucker, glad-handing, womanizing, and bellicose, was the Pork Chopper's Pork Chopper, and nothing some pink-cocktail-drinking, white-shoe-wearing, *New York Times*–reading *Lamb Chop sumbitch* from *Miamuh* said was fixing to cut any ice with him. Tucker brought the bacon, cured, sweet, and fat, home to Wakulla County: roads, bridges, even a schoolhouse or two. When he wasn't in trouble with the law, that is.

The Boys of Old Florida

The up-north reporter wants to know if I've ever worn a hoopskirt. You should see the look on his face when I say yes.

The hoopskirt is the tribal costume of the white-girl South, I say.

He says he's still having trouble understanding that he's in the South and not Florida. Or the Florida that's the South. Or something. He's still amazed at the judges who talk like Foghorn Leghorn, the legislators with the Queen of Cotton smiles, the "honey" this and the "sugar" that. "What's a hoopskirt made of?" he says. "How do you walk in it?" He's actually writing this down.

I tell him it's constructed of concentric circles of plastic covered in cotton and tied at the waist. It holds out your dress. It feels good to wear, especially in the summer, when the way it swings around cools your legs. You do have to be careful to wriggle your hindquarters back at an angle when you sit down or else the hoop will fly up in your face and reveal your Maidenforms or your thong or whatever it is you keep under there.

"I'll tell you this much," I say. "Driving a Honda Civic in a hoopskirt is no damn joke."

My friend Stuart and I were going to this costume party, and we were too lazy to outfit ourselves as Elvis or Alice in Wonderland or a rack of toast, so, being white girls from Tallahassee, we did the belle thing. We had to get all the way over the Georgia border, and our dresses were so vast we came close to wrecking twice. For thirty miles we fought the fabric and the fabric nearly won. Once we got to the party, we shook out our ruffles, got a couple of glasses of Cuvée Napa down us, and swooped around like we inhabited these contraptions every day of our lives.

"But before we drove home," I say, "I took the thing off and stuffed it in the trunk. I didn't care who saw me, either."

There are hoops stored in attics and guest-room closets all over Tallahassee. Sorority houses keep five or six of them around for girls who get invited to Kappa Alpha Old South Weekend. I tell the up-north reporter about how, in 1978, I sashayed with my sisters out of the Sigma Kappa house between a double line of boys with upraised swords, dressed in the gray coats and yellow braid of General Lee's officers—no raggedy conscript cannon fodder in *this* Confederate Army.

At a barbecue held at some alum's pretend plantation house, we drank several quarts of cheap bourbon with limp mint leaves floating around in it. Later the girls, having switched to Tab, would spread our flounces out on the veranda steps, smoke Kools, and talk about the boys. The boys, having removed their swords, would be collapsing onto the alum's putting green or vomiting into the azaleas.

The Kappa Alphas call themselves "the last Southern gentlemen."

The up-north reporter says that he thinks he's sleeping at the Kappa Alpha house tonight. Unless it's the Pi Kap or the Kappa Sig house; he's got it written down somewhere. He's been kicked out of his hotel.

Most of the reporters have been kicked out of their hotels. This isn't a breakdown of Tallahassee's much-touted hospitality or an attack on the free press, it's a matter of priorities. There's a football game, *the* football game, Florida versus Florida State. Fifty thousand people calling themselves Gators or Seminoles, their Land Rovers and Chevy Suburbans flying window flags with the grinning Gator head of the University of Florida or the politically (and historically) incorrect profile of Florida State's Chief Osceola, fifty thousand people dressed in orange-and-blue tracksuits or garnet-and-gold sweater sets sporting buttons that say "Criminoles" or "Go to Hell, Gators," have reservations in every hotel, motel, flea-pit, rooming house, and state park campsite within a thirty-mile radius, reservations they made in 1999. The journalists, the campaign staffers, the freelancers, and the Washington power dogs have resorted to the Ramada in Americus, Georgia, the dorms at Tallahassee's Soviet-style community college, a friend of a friend's sofa, or the kindness of strangers. Some Tallahasseeans have decided to treat the recountistas as a strange class of refugee, offering them a place to sleep, a hot shower, and a full grits, eggs, biscuits, and locally made sausage breakfast for free.

FSU fraternities, on the other hand, don't want karmic credit, just money. So they are renting out their best-not-closely-inquired-into beds. The brothers can crash anywhere (girlfriends' place, library, back of the truck) and have a righteous party with what they make off the out-of-town geeks.

Most of the displaced are going quietly; others are fussing. Don't these rubes know that the government of the United States hangs in the balance? James Baker, George Bush, Sr.'s, secretary of state, George Bush, Jr.'s, Florida fixer, a man who knew several Russian premiers by their vodka-night nicknames, was told to vacate his suite at the Doubletree. It had been prebooked by a Bull Gator, a big donor to the University of Florida. Baker had to move into a rented apartment that probably doesn't even have HBO. But the sports fans, even the Republican ones, are unmoved: Presidents come and presidents go. This game is about the national championship.

Walking back toward the TV tent city, the up-north reporter and I notice town isn't as quiet as it had been. A CNN blonde in a cobalt suit is doing a stand-up by the Confederate Memorial: "Today in Tallahassee—" She looks at her cameraman. "I'll start that over. *Today* in Tallahassee, there's a pause in the legal maneuvering as this small Florida town turns its attention to football . . ." A gaggle of Seminoles and Gators in team regalia crowd around, probably ruining the shot.

"Hey," says a guy in a jacket embroidered with an alligator wearing a sweater but no pants. "Is that Greta Van Susteren? She's hot."

Outside Clyde's, the sticky-floored bar of choice for business lobbyists and their legislative protégés, the television above the door blares Fox News. They're relaying tape of George W.'s flack Ari Fleischer explaining about the Palm Beach butterfly ballot and the oddly large number of votes Pat Buchanan pulled in a place where a number of citizens still have a concentration camp number tattooed on their forearms. *"Obviously,"* says Fleischer, with a Tweedledee smile, "Palm Beach County is a Buchanan stronghold."

"Well," says the up-north reporter, "obviously a bunch of old Jews are going to vote for a guy who believes in the superiority of Christianity and Western Civilization. Obviously."

At 7:52 P.M. on November 7, John Ellis of the Fox Network Decision 2000 team called Florida for Al Gore. ABC, NBC, CBS, and CNN had already projected a win for Gore. At 7:58 P.M., John Ellis phoned his first cousin John Ellis Bush, better known as Jeb, to say he was awfully sorry, old man, but Junior was about to crash and burn in Florida. Shortly before 2:15 A.M. on November 8, John Ellis dialed the governor's mansion in Austin, Texas. Good news: Republican numbers have shot up. At 2:17 A.M., John Ellis declared Florida a win for Cousin George W. The other channels followed like sheep. Marvin Bush, the brother you've never heard of (as opposed to Neil Bush, the brother involved in the 1990 Silverado savings and loan scandal, the one that cost taxpayers one billion dollars), reportedly said to the governor of Florida, "Hey, Jebby! You can come in off the ledge now!"

Jeb Bush named his dog Marvin.

At this point on election night, I'd drunk an entire bottle of pink champagne by myself (for the Gore victory at 8 P.M.), then two shots of Lagavulin and a Snickers bar (after Gore lost at 2:18 A.M.). I was about to down a big glass of sweet tea and a Xanax on my way to bed, but for some reason I stayed on the sofa, pushing buttons on the remote. At three-something Al Gore conceded. Just before 4 A.M. he deconceded. The networks reported the conversation between George W. Bush and Al Gore:

> The Governor of Texas: "You're calling back to retract that concession?"
>
> The Vice President of the United States: "You don't have to get snippy about it."

George W. thinks he won. The Bush logic goes like this: 1. Jeb said he would win Florida; 2. Cousin John Ellis said he did win Florida; 3. On national TV, damn it.

We haven't had this much excitement in Tallahassee since the Secession Convention of 1861.

While the up-north reporter talks on his cell phone, I beat a suit with a BUSH CHENEY 2000 button on his Brooks Brothers lapel to the last outside table at Andrew's. He's a Republican fixer from D.C. He has two cell phones. He using them both, clamped to his ears, looking like the Hear-No-Evil monkey, but he's so good at multitasking he can still give me a snarly don't-you-know-who-I-am look while, no doubt, conferring with the Austin war room and making reservations at Chez Pierre. The up-north reporter hits the hang-up button. Stories are floating around like pine pollen about Republicans getting overseas military to vote late, after the postmark deadline, and send in the ballots anyway, daring Florida not to count them. The up-north reporter says, "Nobody can prove it: If you ask the Bush people, they wrap themselves in the flag and start singing the Marine Corps hymn. And the Gore people just talk about giving the benefit of the doubt to our brave fighting men and women."

"Speaking technically," I say, "this is fucked up."

When I was thirteen, I lost my faith in democracy. Lost it right there in the House of Representatives, where I was working as a page. I fetched resolutions and bills, copies of the *St. Petersburg Times* and the *Miami Herald,* Cokes and MoonPies for fat, loud white men in outfits that knew no natural fibers, while they ate, snored, joked, and smoked their way through the spring legislative session. For this I got a pit-side view of Florida democracy in action, a week off school, and $51.20.

I don't remember being obsessed by politics and the law the way my uncles and aunts and older cousins were. As a fifth-grader, I had supported Richard Nixon. I've no idea why, except the other guy had got fatally confused in my mind with Humpty Dumpty. But my week as a page in the capitol exploded the propaganda of civics class. When we weren't delivering junk food or stacks of paper to legislative desks, we sat, dressed in patent leather shoes and clip-on ties, against the wall of the House, watching our elected representatives honk chaw into their coffee cups and pat their secretaries on the fanny. During one of the many debates on open government, a bunch of West Florida Dixiecrats started fencing with cane fishing poles and giggling, not even stopping when the Speaker banged the gavel. We decided it would be good to get back to the relative decorum of the seventh grade.

We would walk over to Morrison's Cafeteria and eat nothing but coconut cream pie for lunch if we wanted. Sometimes we'd see a member there who'd look up from his meat loaf and iceberg salad, and he'd say your mamas would have a fit if they saw you pages eating nothing but dessert. But we took no notice; we knew that the really important legislators ate at the Silver Slipper or the F&T. You don't have to be in Tallahassee long to figure out that some animals are more equal than others.

Morrison's is gone now. Andrew's, where the up-north reporter and I sit with two glasses of house merlot each, occupies the old Morrison's site. Everybody comes to Andrew's. Or at least walks past. There's Tom Feeney, current Speaker of the House and Jeb Bush's running mate in his first, failed governor's race. Two pale-eyed girls with ironed blond hair walk behind, hissing into cells or writing in little books. In 1994 Feeney called for Florida to secede from the United States if the national debt topped $6 trillion.

There's Dexter Douglass, Gore's Tallahassee attorney, hired because he knows everything in the world about the Florida Constitution, what with him helping to write it. Douglass has been lawyering in Tallahassee since the Eisenhower administration. His first case was defending Martin Van Buren Tanner, the governor's butler and an unparoled convict who got caught up in a bolita sting at the local moonshiners' place. There's Barry Richard, the Democrat who's running the Republicans' Florida case, skinny as a stork with a meringue of hair. The up-north reporter has, like all the other journos within squealing distance, leapt up after these people. Feeney and Richard claim nothing much is happening. Dexter Douglass says, "Gators by seven."

"You know Barry Richard's wife writes messages in lipstick on his bathroom mirror every morning," says the up-north reporter, returning to his drink.

"Like what?" I say.

"The one I heard was 'Go get 'em, Stud.'"

I need another two-handed merlot.

One night a week or so ago I sneaked into the capitol. Students from Florida A&M were holding a sleep-in to protest the disenfranchisement of African American voters. The capitol cops were madder than wet hens. They'd been blindsided earlier by the kids, who looked like clean-cut young folks out to have a look at the seat of state government instead of dangerous radicals planning on lying down on the floor. The cops wouldn't let reporters in. The cops wouldn't let the Domino's Pizza dude in. The cops kept obsessing over the time, back that spring, when a couple of black legislators sat on the governor's sofa and wouldn't get up, protesting the governor's dismantling of affirmative action programs. There were reporters around then, too, reporters who caught the governor barking, "Kick their asses out," on camera, the governor forgetting that their asses had a right to be in a public building.

The cops weren't inclined to err on the side of constitutional liberality this time. "No, ma'am," they said, standing in the way.

But I knew there was a door on the south side that hadn't been locked since 1977. A guy from Knight Ridder, a woman from the *St. Petersburg Times,* and I got all the way down to the rotunda without getting nabbed (you stick to the staircases, don't use the elevators) and found ourselves in the middle of what looked like a slumber party with heavy security. While the cops stood glaring out at the night, FAMU students, apparently a lot of them freshmen who'd voted in their first election—or tried to—sat around playing hearts, playing with Game Boys, drinking Pepsi, and eating Chee-tos next to the Great Seal of the State of Florida, with its Indian maiden pitching orange blossoms at a Spanish galleon. One kid had a Winnie the Pooh sleeping bag.

I guess the cops decided that if you got in, they couldn't be bothered to kick you out, especially with those TV cameras peering through the glass doors. The real reporters got to work interviewing. I just took notes. A girl in a Barbie nightshirt offered me some Church's fried chicken out of her bucket. "We just want to see justice done," she said.

The *St. Petersburg Times* reporter came up and hissed in my ear. "Go into the ladies' room by the visitor information desk. Check out the graffiti in the last stall."

It was written in black grease pencil. It said:

One little hut among de Bushes,
One dat I love,
Still sadly to my memory rushes,
No matter where I Rove.

"Get the hell out of here," says the up-north reporter. "What is that, anyway?"

I tell him that it took me a couple of days, but eventually I got it: it's verse three of the state song. "Old Folks at Home" by Stephen Foster is a lament for "de ole plantation," written in de ole slave dialect.

"But 'Rove' wouldn't be capitalized," says the up-north reporter.

"Not usually," I say. "'Bushes' either. Maybe it's a sign."

Adams Street is starting to fill up, not just with eight-foot cameramen lugging battery packs like Sisyphus pushing his rock up the hill and tiny black-jacketed NPR correspondents toting digital recorders no bigger than an evening bag—they've been here for ten days—but sports fans hollering "Goooooo Gators!" or "F! S! U! F! S! U!"

This is the "Downtown Get-Down," a city-sanctioned street party held every Friday evening before a Florida State home game. Large men in orange-and-blue or garnet-and-gold satin jackets squire women with orange-and-blue bows in their hair or hats spray-painted gold with garnet streamers. Small boys in too-large University of Florida jerseys and small girls in Florida State cheerleader outfits cling to their parents' hands and demand French fries *now*.

"Well," says the up-north reporter as he gets ready to launch into the crowd and gather local color, "at least this isn't political."

Which shows what he knows. Florida State's team is called the Seminoles, after the native people dispossessed or slaughtered by Andrew Jackson's empire-making machine. When the Seminoles were nearly gone, and so safely romanticizable, Florida State chose them for its mascot. In the 1940s and '50s, the few real Seminoles left made a tourist attraction out of fighting what was assumed to be their bitterest enemy (aside from white people), the American Alligator. For a dollar, a Seminole would wrestle a live one.

The up-north reporter and I debate whether to decamp for pecan-encrusted grouper at Cypress or stay here and eat. It's getting colder. But Adams Street, smelling faintly of Bud Lite and tequila, is getting interesting. In front of Clyde's, two guys in chinos and blazers and two girls in cashmere twin sets are lined up swaying and singing "We are the boys of old Florida, F-L-O-R-I-D-A—" Somewhere over by the First Baptist Church I hear the FSU fight song: "We're gonna fight, fight, fight for FSU, we're gonna scalp 'em, Seminoles—."

UF's mascot, a guy in a green plush gator suit the color of Astroturf, starts mock-tussling with an FSU cheerleader, trying to mess with her pom-poms. More camera crews are showing up. More orange and blue. More garnet and gold. And now the signs: "Bush-whacked"; "This Is America: Count Every Vote"; and the theologically dubious "God Made George W. President." The singing-cum-spelling competition intensifies, the well-dressed young white professionals bellowing "F-L-O-R-I-D-A! Where the girls are the fairest, the boys are the squarest—" and the Seminoles, now backed by an unseen brass section, maybe part of the FSU Marching Chiefs, yowling "For FSU is on the warpath now and at the battle's end she's great! So fight fight fight fight for vic-to-ry, the Seminoles of Florida State! F-L-O-R-I-D-A S-T-A-T-E!"

A fight starts on Adams Street in front of the offices of the Florida Education Association. One staggering FSU frat boy and one staggering UF frat boy, veterans of happy hour somewhere else, each accuse the other of dissing him. Then a guy in a "Gators for Gore" T-shirt steps in to defend his fellow UF fan, who looks at his shirt and yells, "Sore Loserman!" The Gator for Gore, who put football before politics, is insulted and gives the Sore Loserman a push. A couple of the frat boys holler (not helpfully), "Are you ready to RUMBLE?" and laugh like tickled toddlers. One of the well-dressed young white professional men quits his crooning and heads in that direction, despite one of the cashmered-up girls hanging onto the sleeve of his Hugo Boss jacket and saying "Now, Peyton, now, darlin'—"

Suddenly there are a few dozen people shoving one another and yelling "Asshole Republican!" and "Go to hell, Gators!" and "You lost!" and "Gator bait!"

The headline in today's local paper said: "Officials Hope Game's Fans Behave in Front of Company."

There have always been fisticuffs between Seminoles and Gators, especially when they get liquored up. Florida State and Florida were forced to play each other in the 1950s (Florida didn't think FSU was good enough) by the governor and legislature: They threatened to pass an actual law. At the 1999 game in Gainesville, I witnessed a phosphate millionaire with senatorial ambitions punch a corporate lawyer and big contributor to the Democratic Party. Their wives didn't even try to now-Peyton-now-darlin' them, but just stood there, holding their husbands' sport coats, looking apologetically at each other.

Football, politics, bare-knuckle fights: We get them confused. Earlier this summer, a couple of Republican legislators went mano a mano in a Miami parking lot when one's daddy supposedly insulted the other one's daddy on Radio Mambi. Representative Carlos Lacasa whomped on and was, in turn, smacked upside the head by Representative Renier Diaz de la Portilla (not to be confused with his brother Senator Alex Diaz de la Portilla or Representative Mario Diaz-Balart, who's a cousin of Fidel Castro, though the Diaz-Balarts don't like to talk about that) in a matter of family honor. Martha Flores, a Radio Mambi talk show host, shrieked on air: "Hail Mary, Mother of God, the Diaz de la Portillas are out there!" She begged the listeners to call Miami PD. They did, crashing the whole 911 system.

In 1876 Florida stole a presidential election. Democrat Samuel Tilden won the popular ballot, but in Florida he and Republican Rutherford B. Hayes were within fewer than one hundred votes of each other. Hayes was about to concede, but one of his strategists, General Daniel E. Sickles, who'd recently been acquitted of murdering his wife, sent "visiting statesmen" to Tallahassee with the message "Hold your state!" The Democrats, looking to capitalize on the plantation gentry's frustration with a Reconstruction government in which *Negroes* held state cabinet posts, sent their own "visiting statesmen" to Florida. Democrats told stories of bribes to "correct" ballots. Ballots disappeared. Republicans charged Democrats with trying to impose mob rule—there were demonstrations in the streets with citizens demanding "Tilden or blood!"

We're not far off that now. "Visiting statesmen" stage "spontaneous demonstrations" now in front of courthouses across the state. Back in 1876, Susan Bradford, a distaff relation of mine (all these cousins!), witnessed the invasion of Florida by Washington political operatives. She wrote: "Fraud and corruption stalked in hideous nakedness throughout the length and breadth of the land."

The Florida Supreme Court ordered a recount that time around, too. Hayes suddenly gained votes; Tilden mysteriously lost them. Democrats cut a deal. Federal troops were withdrawn from Florida and the rest of Johnny Reb territory. White rule was restored. The state constitution disenfranchised a lot of black people by means of the poll tax and a bar on voting by anyone convicted of a felony (which could be nothing but petty larceny or sassing white folks) since, as its proponents baldly stated, ex-slaves would be most likely to commit such crimes. Susan Bradford, relieved, said, "There was a very noticeable decrease in the black hordes, which had paraded the streets so noisily a short time before."

White Southerners called this "Redemption."

The up-north reporter is standing on his chair, taking notes on the fight. It looks to me like the miniature melee, which never quite rose to the level of a first-rate brawl, is winding down. The up-north reporter asks me to translate a T-shirt for him: It's of a cartoon Seminole garrotting a cartoon alligator with a cartoon necktie. The shirt says "The Choke at Doak."

I say that it refers to the epic 1994 matchup at FSU's Doak Campbell Stadium. The Gators were beating the Seminoles like the family mule. The Seminoles, down by four touchdowns at the beginning of the fourth quarter, came from behind and scored twenty-eight points in about ten minutes. The game ended in a tie: 31–31.

"Why am I not surprised?" says the up-north reporter.

Suddenly there's a commotion nearby, and everybody packing a camera or a notebook stampedes. The great doors of the members-only (get on the waiting list), ten-bucks-a-cocktail, ice-sculpture-centerpieced Governor's Club swing open like the emerald gates of the city of Oz, and out sweeps Katherine Harris, secretary of state, the cabinet officer charged by the Florida Constitution with seeing that Florida runs a free and fair election. She wears a Hermès scarf tied jauntily around her tanned neck. She wears lipstick the color of the orange juice concentrate her citrus baron granddaddy, Ben Hill Griffin, got rich manufacturing. She wears big gold earrings with eagles clutching pearls in their talons. Her hair is stiff; her smile is stiff. She clearly hasn't noticed the big run up the side of her black stockings. She's followed by a phalanx of young men who look as if they've been polished with Johnson's Wax. I try to see if my cousin Clay Roberts is among them but he's not—I guess somebody has to run state elections.

This week's round-the-bar-stool story is that Katherine Harris thinks of herself as Queen Esther. Which is nice because J. M. "Mac the Knife" Stipanovich, the wiliest Republican coyote in town, the political consultant who's been sneaking into Harris's capitol office every day, calls her husband, a Scandinavian businessman, "the king of Sweden."

Mean old King Xerxes wanted to kill all the Jews, but Esther, the prettiest girl in the Babylon harem, came out as a Jew and begged for mercy for her people. "If I perish, I perish," she said tragically, bravely. Xerxes fell in love with her flashing dark eyes and her ability to energize the party base. He decided he'd spare the Jews after all.

During the recount, Harris has been sweeping around the capitol in invisible robes, declaring "If I perish, I perish" and gazing nobly into the middle distance, especially if anyone brings up Florida's massively screwed-up index of "ineligible" voters. The State of Florida paid a private company $4 million to identify felons on the rolls. Some of those "felons" were surprised to find themselves unable to exercise the franchise. Linda Howell, elections supervisor of Madison County, found herself branded a felon. The pastor at Leon County's House of Prayer Church found himself branded a felon. People who really *were* felons but who had had their civil rights restored were not allowed to vote. People whose names were similar to those of other people who really were felons were not allowed to vote. The state wasn't too worried about precision.

Cousin Clay said, "The decision was made to do the match in such as way as not to be terribly strict on the name." The list had some people convicted of felonies in 2007.

"'Contrariwise,' continued Tweedledee, 'if it was so, it might be; and if it were so, it would be, but as it isn't, it ain't. That's logic.'"

As Katherine Harris sails down Adams Street like the battleship *Florida,* waving to the right and left, she doesn't look worried about disenfranchising several thousand African American voters, doesn't look aware of the conflagration of politics and sports all around her. The up-north reporter, who isn't even bothering to try and get a quote this time, watches her make her way toward the capitol with something like awe. "I'll bet she knows how to wear a hoopskirt," he says. "I'll bet she knows how to do Scarlett-fucking-O'Hara and, as God is her witness, never go hungry again."

Dream State, Root and Branch

You were going to get a family tree with this book, a map to help you keep the Vauses, Tuckers, Revells, McKenzies, Bradfords, Browards, Gilberts, and Robertses of Florida straight. That was the plan.

I got a big piece of paper and started drawing, eight generations from my brother and me to the first Broward, born in 1755. When I started on my mother's people, I realized that this was fixing to get harder. The Bradfords go back at least five hundred years. I got a bigger piece of paper, this one the size of the kitchen table. It was still tough to get them all in. My great-great-grandmothers had, on average, ten children each, who then had ten children each—you see my problem. The family tree ended up covering a space so large it could be rented out as a flat in London or New York. I used different colored inks so I could tell which branch was which. When I got through, the thing had reached a level of incomprehensibility like unto the diagram of a particularly baroque multinational corporation or of a complex molecule. There were crisscrossing lines (we intermarry in the South, just as you've always suspected), arrows, blanks where we're not sure exactly what the connection is, the same names repeating over and over, generation upon generation. The publisher took one look at it and said *no*.

So you're not getting the family tree after all. You would have needed Ariadne's ball of string to find your way through it anyway. But that's okay: the book *is* the family tree, in all its wandering tangle of roots and branches. When I started writing *Dream State,* I thought it would be a pretty straightforward story of two families. I'd use them to tell the history of Florida. Then I'd start tracing a limb back and find that it was never one but multiple, as vast and tangled as a briar patch. The Bradfords led me to Susan, the Dixie diarist, and Roxanne, the teenaged bride who became the mother of thirteen children; the Robertses led me to Richard, the man of mystery wounded over and over in the Civil War yet refused to lie down and die; the Browards led me to Jane, who left the luxuries of her East Florida plantation to live in the swamp, and François, who came to Florida in the first place because the king of Spain was giving away free land; the Gilberts led me to John Wesley—he may have left a wife and two children behind in Carolina; and the Tuckers led me to Mary Elizabeth, who knew how to smash up a moonshine still.

There are too many stories to tell in one book. Yet the story of my family is the story of Florida. Not the only story, of course: the descendants of Spanish land grant families, the descendants of slaves brought from Africa, and now the Cubans, Haitians, Nicaraguans, Puerto Ricans, Canadians, midwesterners, New Yorkers—they all have their own stories and their own experiences of Florida. What's different about my kin is that we are so dug in, so long-rooted. Over the past hundred years, we have been involved, for good or ill, in the shaping of this strangest of American states. We're a bit like the May Oak—holders of the deep memory of Florida.

PART I

1

Everybody's Magic Kingdom

THE STORY I WAS TOLD, the story all Florida schoolchildren were once told, was that Juan Ponce de León came to Florida to find the Fountain of Youth. Maybe Spain was full of geriatric *conquistadores,* looking for a place to unfreeze their old bones and heat up their blood once more. This made sense to us. Florida was full of old people wearing shorts in fierce gum-ball colors, old people on golf carts, old people with burnt sienna tans and parasoled cocktails and fifty-dollar manicures, all trying to feel less old. It was as if Florida were some kind of American reward: Live most of your life in a place where you have to work in the cold, walk on ice, and shovel snow, then go south, go where you can play like a child in the sun.

Nobody now buys the miraculous waters idea. Juan Ponce's obsessively detailed royal charter, his *asiento,* enumerates gold, territory, gems, souls to be converted to the True Faith, but nothing about rejuvenation. In 1511 Pietro Martire d'Anghiera, aka Peter Martyr, an Italian priest at the court of the king of Aragon, drew a ghostly map of a place called la Isla de Beimeni Parte. It lies due north of Cuba, but all the map shows is a fractured, partial coastline, shores trailing off into nothingness, a phantasmagorical land. There was some rumor about Bimini and eternal youth, maybe brought back from one of Columbus's voyages. This fountain business didn't get attached to Juan Ponce until a hundred years after his voyage to Florida, when historian Antonio de Herrera y Tordesillas picked up a line about a fountain the Indians said transformed geezers into lusty adolescents. The Bimini that's in the Bahamas, that tiny comma of land, gamely tries to wrap itself in the story. Denizens of Bimini will show you a well that's supposed to be Juan Ponce's fountain. They'll show you some ruins of Atlantis too.

In Florida fiction thrives like kudzu. We *own* the Fountain of Youth. We've got three or four Fountains of Youth. One burbles up in St. Augustine just north of the shrine of Our Lady of *La Leche*. Last time I was there it cost five bucks to get in. The water is covered by a hut with murals depicting Juan Ponce as a white-haired Don Quixote. It tastes of sulfur and smells like a basketful of rotten Easter eggs. Around the spring lie the graves of sixteenth- and seventeenth-century Timucuas, many of whom died from the smallpox and measles given them by the good Christians come to save them.

There's a Fountain of Youth in Volusia County, too, not far from the Daytona International Speedway. When John James Audubon visited in 1831, the place was called Spring Garden. Then it became Garden Springs. In the 1880s, the residents took a shot at calling it "DeSota," but the post office informed them Florida already had one of those. So they decided to capitalize on the water pushing up out of the Eocene limestone and went for DeLeon Springs. Ponce de León, a tiny hamlet that happens to have a spring (in common with 319 other places in Florida), pulled the same move. The place is two hundred miles west of the Atlantic, but why ruin a good founding myth with geographical and historical facts? Maybe Juan Ponce got farther into Florida than he's given credit for. Maybe Jesus visited England, just like the monks at Glastonbury (and William Blake) said; maybe aliens visited New Mexico, just like *The X-Files* said. Any explorer worth a damn, from Odysseus onward, heads west.

West is the direction of magic, toward the sunset, beyond the Pillars of Hercules, beyond the edge of the world. Out there you could find the Hesperides, Atlantis, Avalon. You could spread your faith, your language, your DNA, your animals, your laws, your viruses to new worlds—or worlds new to you. Out there you could find silks, jewels, tobacco, sugar, cotton, spices, space. You could build an empire.

The Spanish always get the credit for being the first Europeans to see Florida. They may not have been. The Welsh tell how Madog, a twelfth-century prince, sailed around the Keys up into the Gulf of Mexico. One of my great-uncles said the first Robertses and Tuckers met a blue-eyed, red-haired Welsh-speaking Indian.

Or there were the Vikings, who may have got blown off course for Vinland and ended up camping on Amelia Island. St. Brendan set off in an oak boat sometime in the sixth century, heading southwest from Ireland. In the Western Sea, the saint and his fourteen companions saw a tall crystal column rising out of the sky, skirted the island where Judas, reprieved from damnation on Sundays, took the form of a man-shaped cloud, and came upon a warm land with waters so clear you could see the skeletons of ancient beasts far down on a white bed, just like the mastodon at the bottom of Wakulla Springs, in Wakulla County, Florida.

Maybe it was Wakulla Springs. Brendan could have wandered into the Gulf and got entangled in the lattice of rivers and creeks until one dead-ended in a round pool of boiling cold water, iridescent blues, greens, and violets, deep as hell and beautiful as paradise, silvery bones resting on far-down sand.

Or maybe Juan Ponce de León was the first Christian to look into the depths and declare it a miracle. Old guidebooks thought so; my great-uncle Malcolm thought so. Wakulla's waters, 400,000 gallons a minute, sharp as a winter midnight, push up from a great reservoir of accumulated rain below the clay, down in the limestone chambers that emerged when Florida rose from the sea for the last time ten million years ago. Wakulla is very deep, no one knows how deep, the visible end of a whole underworld of rivers and caves, the subterranean mansions of the earth. No one has ever found the source. You take it on faith, this wonder of the swamp.

West

The story always starts this way: A man, a European man, sails away from civilization and bumps into land not marked on his *mappa mundi*. He calls it empty, even if it isn't. He records some marvels, takes some treasures. He plants a flag and a cross. The New World is discovered.

The New World is also named, as if God had just finished making it. The Genoese navigator the Castilians called Cristóbal Colón played Adam: He describes an island its own people call Guanahani, but he declares it will now be San Salvador. The next one becomes Isla Santa Maria de Concepción, then Isabella and Fernandina after his employers, and Isla Juana after their daughter, the deranged princess called "la loca" (though not to her face) who would spend a lot of her life locked up in a tower. Every place the Spanish ships make landfall, they unfurl a banner with the red lions of León and yellow castles of Castile. They proclaim the place now a possession of *los Reyes Católicos.* They move on to the next *milagro*.

For Americans, Columbus's voyage is evidence of Divine Providence. The king and queen of Spain are sitting around one day and this guy comes in with a Big Idea about a round earth and sailing west to find the East. The queen sells some of her diamonds to buy him ships. He "discovers" America, getting the ball rolling on creating the greatest country the world has ever known. And that's enough history for us.

In 1492 the Christian rulers of northern Spain finally conquered Granada, the last caliphate, ending 750 years of Moorish rule on the Iberian peninsula. Muslims and Jews were expelled or forcibly converted. This was Christ's country now. If the converts didn't seem sufficiently enthusiastic in their Catholicism, Tomás de Torquemada, the queen's confessor, would introduce them to the Inquisition. Isabella and Ferdinand meant to scour Spain clean of any un-Christian taint, even if they drew blood doing it. They occupied the Alhambra, hanging images of martyrs on Boabdil's delicately carved walls. The patron saint of Spain, the apostle whose bones the pilgrims traveled to Compostela to supplicate, was transformed into Santiago Matamoros, St. James killer of Moors, even though St. James probably never even met a Moor, much less violated the dictates of his Lord and offed one.

Columbus's voyage was an extension of the Reconquista, energized by a sort of Catholic Spanish Manifest Destiny. The farthest reaches of the globe would be embraced and purified by the envoys of Isabella and Ferdinand, vice-regents of Christ. And if there was profit to be made in the process, all the better to finance a state of perpetual crusade, dedicated to retaking the biggest prize of all, the Holy Land. The road to Jerusalem ran through Cuba, Puerto Rico, Florida. Marking these *maravillosa* islands for Spain, three thousand miles away, chopping down mangroves and palms to make crosses that Isabella and Ferdinand would never see, hammering them into alien sand—this would gain the favor of God. Columbus called it "*la gran vitoria,*" the great victory.

The Spanish could hardly have imagined they'd spend all that time and energy in the Reconquista, kicking the Jews and the heretics and the Muslims out of Spain, only to have, four hundred years later, the Jews and the heretics (by now called Protestants) and even some of the Muslims buying time-shares and condos and three-bedroom ranch houses in their old colony of Florida.

The worldwide Reconquista became a career for noblemen who found the pious court of *los Reyes Católicos* (after there were no more Moors to kill) stifling. In 1513 Juan Ponce de León went looking for the legendary Isla de Beimeni Parte. He came from an aristocratic family in Valladolid, and ever since seeing the warm wonders of the Caribbean with Columbus in 1493, he preferred New Spain to Old Spain. He had plenty of money and plenty of time; he'd been governor of the colony of Puerto Rico, one of the oldest in the "New World," but lost his job to Columbus's son Diego in a political power struggle. Ponce de León was only thirty-nine years old and ready for a few more adventures, a few more amazing sights, before he retired to the starched lace and autos-da-fé of Castile.

Juan Ponce got his *asiento,* the royal charter spelling out the goals of the Bimini mission: land and gold. Miracles were extra. He got two caravels (light, fast ships) and a bergantina. He got Antón de Alaminos, the best pilot in the Caribbean. He assembled a band of adventurers, a New World *Argo,* with young *hidalgos* bored with a Moor-free Spain, some Taíno-speaking native guides from Puerto Rico, two African freemen—Juan Gárrido and Juan González Ponce de León—even two women, Juana Jiménez and Beatriz Jiménez.

Four weeks out of Añasco Bay, on April 2, 1513, Juan Ponce sighted a strand long and smooth as a court lady's neck. Bush-headed palms and tall grasses with leaves sharp enough to cut skin met the sand, and everywhere there were flowers—sun-colored lantana and wild allamanda, milkwort and spiderwort and pink purslane, columbine and cattail, Tread Softly and Venus' looking-glass, sumac and sea daisy—such flowers it seemed a sign from God, a memorial of the Resurrection. Juan Ponce came upon this place in Easter season, after all. His three ships celebrated the holy day at sea, the calls of Allelujah! Christ is risen! singing out over the waves and mixing with the cries of the gulls.

Juan Ponce's *Argo* made landfall not far from Cape Canaveral, dropping anchor between what's now Launch Pad A and Launch Pad B at the Apollo/Saturn V Center. He rowed ashore to take possession of the new land, surely taking some men-at-arms with him, Toledo blades at the ready, maybe one of the Taínos, too, and his namesake Juan González Ponce de León. Beatriz and Juana probably waited in the boat. Still, it was a multicultural posse wading through the jade shallows of the Atlantic, a preview of the Florida to come. Instead of declaring it Bimini, Juan Ponce named it after Pascua Florida, the Easter Feast of Flowers, and claimed it for Fernando II and Jesus. The travelers stood on the sand for a while, looked at the lantana and wild allamanda, milkwort and spiderwort and pink purslane, columbine and cattail, Tread Softly and Venus' looking-glass, sumac and sea daisy. No monsters, no treasure, no golden fleece, just a beach. Juan Ponce's Argonauts went back to their ships.

They sailed farther down a curve of sand past what would become, in four hundred years, the Philippe Starck hotels and Armani bou-

y 5 pm
ups or
dual appt.

tiques, the condo gulches and Mercedes showrooms of Bal Harbor and South Beach and Key Biscayne. They were beset by uncooperative Tequesta warriors, who, perhaps having met Spanish slave expeditions before, were in no mood to share. Juan Ponce headed south and west, following a chain of elongated little islands, *cayos*. He named them Los Martires because, he said, they "seemed like men suffering." He couldn't know that, 490 years later, those *cayos,* especially the one at the end, would be full of men partying.

Juan Ponce had gone back to Spain in 1514, intending to return soon to the western seas: The king had named him governor of the island of Florida and the still-elusive Bimini. But his wife had died and his daughters were too young to be left alone with the duenna. He didn't get back to Florida until early 1521. Now his mission was to colonize the place, not just look at it.

He assembled an expedition that was more ark than *Argo,* with two hundred men and women, horses and cattle, pigs and mules, bags of seed, orange and olive saplings. They sailed from Puerto Rico on February 26. They landed, well, somewhere, most likely near the mouth of the Caloosahatchee. The soil looked promising and there was fresh water. On the minus side, the place was inhabited by Calusas—their name means "fierce people." Maybe the *adelantado* of Bimini and Florida, agent of Holy Roman Emperor Carlos V, wasn't about to let a bunch of moss-wearing heathens push him around. Maybe he went back to show the Calusas that his god was tougher than theirs. Or maybe Juan Ponce's ark didn't stop there at all but sailed up to Tampa Bay or Waccasassa Bay or Suwannee Sound or Ochlockonee Bay. Maybe they found themselves marveling at the green-roofed Wakulla River, until the Apalachees materialized out of the cypresses like ghosts.

Whichever tribe it was and wherever they were, the Spanish were perpetually harassed. The seedlings withered, the crops died. Some of the colonists died, too. Juan Ponce was wounded in the thigh. The Spanish decided it wasn't worth it. So they upped anchor and headed south, leaving their wooden crosses, which soon rotted, their unsown fields, and their cattle. Juan Ponce's wound became infected. He died in Cuba in July 1521, lost in fevered dreams of fabulous islands just beyond the horizon, the Fata Morgana Bimini just beyond the reach of his ship.

The truth is Juan Ponce had found Bimini. Florida *is* Bimini, the magical western island with the incomplete outline, as much as anywhere can be. In their New World, the Spanish expected treasure and wonder in equal measures. They saw manatees and called them mermaids. Columbus said that people from a certain part of Cuba were born with tails. They imagined they were in the fabulous Indies, where anything was possible, where fish would sing and water would make you young, the same way later Floridians imagined they had come to a land where the laws of gravity (thanks to plastic surgeons) and the laws of astronomy and the rule of the seasons were suspended, and there could be flowers in January.

Liberty County, west of Wakulla in the Panhandle, is the original Garden of Eden. It is supposedly the only place in the world where the *Torreya taxifolia,* the gopherwood tree, grows. Noah's ark was made of gopherwood; gopherwood grew in Eden. Ergo, according to E. E. Callaway, a contrary old cuss, a white NAACP lawyer who ran as a Republican for governor of Florida in 1936 when Republicans were rarer than talking serpents, Florida owns paradise.

"The Bible tells us that 'a river went out of Eden to water the Garden and became four heads,'" said Old Man Callaway. "Well, the Apalachicola is the only four-head river system in the world. The U.S. Army Corps of Engineers' map shows you that. God created the Adamic man one mile east of Bristol. Then he created the Garden of Eden just north of town."

Old Man Callaway is dead now. But many in the Full Bible, Free Will, and Pentecostal towns from the Georgia line to the Gulf still believe.

The Revolutionary

The Revolutionary was the first of us, my great-great-great-great-great-grandfather. In 1799 he crossed the St. Marys River, passing from the relative order of Georgia into the protean country to the south, where borders were drawn and discarded almost weekly; where in the streets of San Agustín you could hear English, Creole, Gaelic, Greek, Spanish, French, Italian, Hitchiti, Temne, Malinke; where there is a creek named for a massacre, an island named for the Resurrection, and a great river named for St. John, the voice crying in the wilderness.

Never mind that the protean country was, at least officially, Spanish, and the Revolutionary was French—and First Consul Bonaparte sat in the Elysée Palace lusting openly after Spain, not to mention Russia, Austria, Italy, and England. Never mind that he had fought with the American insurgents, who, having won their thirteen colonies, started eyeing a fourteenth, down there in Spanish territory. Never mind that he said he was a democrat, a freedom fighter, yet owned African slaves. The Revolutionary was protean himself.

The king of Spain was giving away land in East Florida: a hundred acres to each head of a household, plus fifty acres for each dependent and slave. The Revolutionary claimed a wife, five children, and eleven slaves. On November 6, 1800, he registered with the governor in San Agustín, declaring himself a *labrador,* a farmer, a native of *La Provincia de Perche en Francia*. He swore allegiance to the Bourbon Carlos IV. The governor's lieutenant signed his name with a crisscrossing flourish, fancy as lacing on a court dress. The Revolutionary signed his name in plain letters, easily legible two hundred years on: François Brouard.

François Brouard was born somewhere in the Perche region of Normandy in 1755. He washed up in Charleston in time to join the polyglot cavalry under Casimir Pulaski, the Polish count who got tired of fighting the Russians at home and so came to America to fight the British.

Being French, François Brouard probably needed no encouragement to go after the ancient enemy on new soil. The family story is that he soldiered in the siege of Charleston in 1779 and made a dashing raid through British lines in Savannah to bring quinine to Count Pulaski's malaria-ridden troops. He got promoted to captain. Maybe he cherished elevated ideas about reason, equality, and liberty; maybe he admired his fellow Norman the Marquis de la Fayette; maybe he had read Rousseau. Or maybe he just saw an opportunity to transform himself from farm boy to landed gentleman. Charleston was full of French made good. You could build a fine house on one of the fine squares and own a country plantation fat with rice, cotton, and indigo. You could be like Thomas Jefferson or Richard Henry Lee, at once a *seigneur* and a *revolté,* especially in the South. And still farther south, in the endlessly mutable realm of Florida, you might turn into, what—a prince? an emperor?

François Brouard became the fountainhead of a family now so absorbed into the groundwater of Florida that they barely notice their names on the maps and the buildings anymore, Big Daddy of ten generations' worth of plantation owners, poor white trash, governors, lawyers, loggers, doyennes of the Daughters of the Confederacy, soldiers who fought everybody from the Seminoles to the Viet Cong, engineers who drained the marshes and built the roads that let the rest of the world into Florida, and politicians—lots of politicians. His Roberts and Tucker descendants call him Francis Broward, forgetting (or preferring not to admit) that the first of our ancestors to become a Floridian was also a Frenchman. And likely a Roman Catholic—at least he claimed to be a Catholic when he moved to Catholic Spanish Florida. Nobody minded about him being a slaveholder.

He parked wagons, family, slaves, and mules in an enchanted forest just north of a river that would later be named for him. Some of his land was high, raisin-colored alluvial soil; some of his land was drowned; some was a cocktail of water, earth, and grass. John Bartram, botanist to His Majesty (that would be King George III), traveled to the St. Johns country in 1765 and saw what became the Broward fiefdom. Bartram tells of "monstrous grape vines," *Magnolia grandiflora* seventy feet high, oak trees six feet across. He came upon a "hammock of oak and hickory and a fine spring of clean water almost big enough to turn a mill." Bartram thought Florida would be a grand place to grow rhubarb, lychees, pistachios, and opium poppies. He also thought that the Floridian air acted as an aphrodisiac, noting solemnly that Spanish women had more babies in Florida than back in Spain, "where they are generally accounted but indifferent breeders."

John Bartram could have worked for the Duval County chamber of commerce. He swears he only saw two snakes on his whole journey and insists that Florida has fewer insects than anywhere else in

America—Florida, with the mosquitoes big as tire irons. Bartram was either myopic or a liar. Florida's best boosters have often been both.

The Spanish land grant records list the Revolutionary as "Breard," "Breward," "Broward," and sometimes even "Brevard"—which is another old Florida family entirely. François Brouard, the rebel, the immigrant, the Frenchman, began to disappear into Francis Broward the landowner, the paterfamilias, the American gentleman. He was a small-time farmer when he married Rebecca Sarah Bell, a girl from a good Scots family in Carolina, in 1784. He risked his life to detach America from its colonial master but decided to leave it for a land ruled by another colonial power, swapping one king for another. Florida had been Loyalist in the War of Independence; in 1783 Britain traded it back to Spain in exchange for the Bahamas. But then François Brouard had noticed that countries had a way of changing hands. A clever fellow could turn that to his advantage.

Sarah and François had at least five children, probably more, but only four made it out of the fatal fevers of childhood: Charles, Sarah Elizabeth, John, and Francis. Future generations of Browards would remember that they were the progeny of a revolutionary and stick their children with revolutionary handles: George Washington Broward, Montcalm Broward (after the French general who died defending Quebec against the British in 1759), Pulaski Broward, Osceola Broward, and two Napoleon Bonaparte Browards (one of whom had a sister called Josephine). But Sarah and François chose names for their own offspring that sounded as if they could have come over on the *Arbella,* instead of a rackety old ship from Brest, solid British names that would also survive in the family for two centuries, reflecting Sarah's heritage more than François's. If John was ever Jean or Francis François, there's no evidence of it. In Spanish Florida, the Brouards began to shed their Frenchness like an old skin.

It's hard to tell if François shed his Catholicism, too. In San Agustín, there were still missions with Franciscan friars in brown habits, and the mass was sung every day in a long coquina church with a New World baroque facade. Outside the city, though, in the new settlements, Protestants were becoming the majority. The Brouard lands lay in Nassau, a region in the top right-hand corner of Florida named by the British for the ancestral palatinate of the anti-Papist William III. It may be that Sarah, very likely a Presbyterian, converted him, or François wasn't Catholic, after all. There's some evidence that he may have been a Huguenot, a passenger on a boatload of 371 French Calvinists that docked in Charleston Harbor in 1764. He would have been nine years old. Many of his kin prefer that story because it better conforms to what Americans think their country is about: flight from persecution. Or he might have shifted his affiliation to suit his setting—Catholic, Protestant, whatever worked. This we know for sure: His eldest son, Charles, my great-great-great-great-grandfather, became a Methodist minister. And many of his descendants turned foot-washing Baptist in the swamp.

Maybe François Brouard was prescient in moving to Florida, figuring that the Americans eventually would conquer or finagle Florida away from the exhausted Spanish. Everybody, from Juan Ponce de León to John Bartram, gushed over Florida's trees and Florida's sunsets and Florida's seafood and Florida's flowers, but, landed with the place *again,* the Spanish felt they'd got shafted. For three hundred hard, bleeding, expensive years, they never got much of a return on their Florida investment. Still, they hung on to the peninsula despite there being no gold, no emeralds, none of the profitable commodities that made Peru and Mexico worth the trouble of killing all those people. The gaudy maps they passed around at the Spanish court—vast waters with pictures of sea serpents smiling ominously in the waves, weird configurations of terra incognita promising cities strewn with gems, countries populated by Amazons or anthropophagi or talking animals—translated into nothing more than pretty beaches and bad-tempered inhabitants with very sharp arrows.

Florida was nothing but trouble: pirates, plagues, the heat, the storms, the French, the English, the Indians, and eventually Andrew Jackson. In 1586 Francis Drake raided San Agustín, the chief Spanish city, mostly for fun and profit but also to impress upon Philip II that Elizabeth I would not tolerate any trespassing on her Atlantic ambitions. There were border skirmishes. On the logic of old maps with the land labeled "Florida" extending as far as Texas, the Spanish fought French encroachment from the west. Some of these same old maps showed "Florida" reaching up into Virginia, so the Spanish argued that the Carolinas, at least, were theirs. The British took a dim view. *They* had a proprietary grant down to the twenty-ninth parallel, below where Daytona Beach is now.

In 1794 a bunch of Georgia farmers, hopped up and giddy over the executions of Louis XVI and Marie Antoinette (death to all tyrants!), decided to invade East Florida and declare it an independent republic. They burned the fortification of San Nicolás, singing "La Marseillaise" and proclaiming that they were, in fact, French forces come to overthrow the Spanish monarchy. It took several months for the *adelantado*'s soldiers to drive the Cracker *sansculottes* back across the St. Marys.

The Spanish, threatened in Europe by real Frenchmen, their forces stretched too thin from Santa Fe to the Strait of Magellan, looked almost ready to give up. Maybe François Brouard, in addition to becoming rich and important, looked forward to outlasting them. It would leave him, the underground Frenchman, in possession of lands that had once been French, lands where much French blood had been shed.

In the spring of 1562, Jean Ribaut and a handful of would-be settlers camped by a wide river that flowed north like the Nile. Ribaut named it after the month of May and claimed this land for Catherine de Médicis, queen regent of France. The French wanted to make clear to the Spanish that they did not acknowledge that the papal donations gave Spain exclusive rights over North America. And Queen Catherine wanted somewhere to ship her troublemaking Protestants. Ribaut's band did all right for a bit. The Timucuas and the Mocamas were bemused but not hostile, even bringing grapes and maize to these overdressed, underprepared people who went around proclaiming the territory from the Atlantic to the great swamp to the Gulf and beyond to be la Nouvelle France.

Meanwhile, the Spanish got wind that not only had Frenchmen beat them to planting a colony in a corner of Nueva Hispania, the colony was full of followers of the excommunicate Luther, polluting the virgin land with outlaw doctrines. The governor of Cuba sent a ship to investigate. But by the time they got to the Riviere de Mai (the San Juan to the Spanish and the St. Johns to the rest of us), all they found was one Guillaume Rouffi. He'd been left by his turn-tail colleagues, a French consul among the Timucuas, who fed him and took care of him like a pet chicken. Havana reported back to Madrid that the French colony had failed.

Busy with spying on the French queen and trying to destabilize the English queen, the Spanish still didn't get around to establishing their own colony, and the French tried again. In 1564 René de Laudonnière brought an even bigger consignment of Protestants to Florida: nobles, peasants, men, women, children. They might have been anathema to Catholic Spain but they weren't wildly popular in Catholic France, either. They built a fort inside the mouth of the north-flowing river, a stylized triangle of a stockade that looked like a giant arrowhead. They named it Fort Caroline.

In a few months food ran short. There were mutinies and rebellions. Some of the colonists stole boats and took to Caribbean pirating. At least there was money in that. Pedro Menéndez de Avilés, named by Philip II governor of Florida—even though the Spanish had no actual settlements in Florida—attacked Fort Caroline and killed pretty much everyone. Menéndez sanctified himself before battle by celebrating the feast day of St. Augustine of Hippo, on August 28, 1565. Then he named the patch of Florida he stood on for the saint, the church father who prayed, "O Lord, give me chastity and self-control—but not yet!"

When Ribaut returned with reinforcements, they killed him, too. Anyone who didn't die in battle was hanged. Menéndez stuck signs over their heads: "I do this, not as to Frenchmen, but as to Heretics." He renamed the arrowhead-shaped fort San Mateo, after the author of the first Gospel, and called the inlet nearby Matanzas, "slaughter."

It was a holy killing, you understand. They were infidels. Menéndez considered himself a righteous man. He planned to found a school in Havana where the Jesuits could educate the children of the native people. He wanted to plant missions in the land of the Guales from St. Augustine up the Georgia coast. The Guales, whose territory he occupied, called him "Mico Santamaría," Mary's high chief.

Mary or no Mary, on Good Friday 1568, the French came looking for revenge. Dominique de Gourges, an angry French aristocrat (a Catholic, even), sailed into the mouth of the St. Johns. He burned San Mateo and hanged anybody he could find. Above the gallows he placed his own sign: "Not as to Spaniards, but as to Traitors, Robbers and Murderers." Honor satisfied, de Gourges thanked God, resupplied his ships, and headed back to Dieppe. France declared victory and never fooled with East Florida again.

There's an engraving from 1591 of this monument the French erected near the mouth of the St. Johns. It's so stylish—anyone could build a fort, but the French defied the might of England and Spain with a marble column carved with the crown of the Capets and the lilies of St. Louis. In the engraving, it's draped with flower garlands. Baskets of fruit and corn are sat around its base. A dozen long-haired, bare-breasted Timucuas in moss skirts kneel before the column, their hands uplifted. The explorer René de Laudonnière looks on, impassive (and probably very hot) in his beard, padded doublet, and lace collar.

Next to Laudonnière stands the Timucua chief. He's naked except for a breechcloth and necklaces of shells. Two panther tails are worked into his headdress. He's tall, six inches taller than Laudonnière, and muscled like a statue of Hercules. One hand rests lightly on Laudonnière's shoulder. The other gestures toward the column, the symbol of French civilization in savage lands, the marker of French possession. The nails on the chief's hand are long and filed to sharp points like arrowheads.

Lost in the Swamp

I don't know what Jane Broward looked like. If she'd stayed in East Florida, on the Broward domains, in what passed for civilization, maybe there would be a portrait or something. But François Brouard's grandchild, my great-great-great-grandmother, would be carried off to the west, to the wild places.

Jane Broward was the eldest surviving daughter of François Brouard's eldest surviving son Charles. She was born on the Broward plantation in 1814, the year the British burned Washington, the year the emperor Napoléon was exiled to a small island off the coast of Italy. Florida still belonged to Spain.

François Brouard's properties occupied what had once been Saturiwa lands, then the mission lands of Santa Maria and Santa Catalina de Guale. His sons soon expanded the family holdings. The Browards didn't own as much as Moses Levy, who bought the title to an old royal land grant of sixty thousand acres, or Zephaniah Kingsley, who lived with his Senegalese wife, a freed slave named Anna Madgigaine Jai, in a great house on Fort George Island. The Browards weren't as aristocratic as the Spanish families who went back 250 years in Florida, then another 250 years in León or Aragon. Still, Charles Broward had three hundred acres and planted Sea Island cotton; his brother John got a grant of sixteen thousand acres from José Coppinger, the last Spanish governor, and ran a sawmill on Broward River. They were rich enough. Jane Broward was a catch.

In 1824, when Jane was ten, her uncle John married Margaret Tucker, whose people planted at Black Hammock near the mouth of the Nassau River. Margaret's father, Andrew Tucker, had got his royal dispensation of land in 1804, but in 1812, when some American farmers, bored ex-soldiers and assorted no 'counts decided to "liberate" the land south of the St. Marys, the Tuckers went the other direction, back to a farm they owned in Camden County, Georgia.

Maybe the Tuckers thought Spanish land-grant plantation holders would get short shrift from these "patriots." Their flag showed a lunging infantryman, bayonet at the ready, and declared, *"Salus Populi Lex*

Suprema," Safety of the People the Supreme Law. *Which* people remained unclear. Or, perhaps demonstrating the political agility the Tuckers would display throughout the twentieth century, they just didn't want to be around when the shooting started. In any case, when President James Madison refused to recognize the revolt, the Tuckers came back to Florida. They settled back in Black Hammock as if nothing had happened.

Margaret Tucker had a little brother named Rufus, nine years younger than she. He had been born in Georgia during the territorial spat but grew up at Black Hammock. There must have been a lot of visiting between the Tucker and Broward households; they were kin now. Margaret Tucker Broward probably thought it would be a fine thing if her brother and her brother-in-law's girl got engaged. So tidy, keeping the family properties together. No doubt she gave things a shove. There would have been river picnics and suppers organized by the Big House ladies in the region. There would have been fancy balls sometimes in San Agustín, which had become, now that Florida was American, St. Augustine. The Browards might travel to the old Spanish city maybe twice a year for business and elevated entertainment. Great-Aunt Vivienne always said that Rufus and Jane danced a quadrille there in 1833, at a winter ball given by one of the old Castilian families, friends of her grandfather from the days of the *adelantados*. Jane wore a hyacinth blue satin dress with a white camellia in her hair. Great-Aunt Vivienne got that from her cousin Miss Hortense Broward. She was sure it was a quadrille.

No matter what dance or what dress or where it was, in January 1834 Rufus Tucker and Jane Broward got married. Jane's father, the Reverend Charles Broward, didn't perform the ceremony; one of her Eubanks uncles on her mother's side, a justice of the peace, pronounced them man and wife. We don't know why Jane's Methodist minister father didn't preside over his daughter's wedding. Maybe he didn't like Rufus. Maybe he didn't like the Tuckers, who might have developed a reputation, even by 1834. Maybe it was that Rufus had a notion to take Jane off to West Florida, a hundred miles away.

Rufus wasn't heir to the Black Hammock plantation, but with his father's and wife's family's help, he could have acquired land in Nassau or Duval or started a livery stable in the thriving new town of Jacksonville. Jane could have stayed near home. But Rufus was tired of home, tired of how cultivated everything and everyone was getting, tired, too, of hearing what a big deal the Browards were, hearing how Jane's cousin was going to Harvard and Jane's uncles were friends with Governor DuVal and Jane's father had met the Marquis de la Fayette. He figured he'd go to a part of Florida that was as yet unclaimed (and with good reason, said the horrified Browards), south of the capital.

A well-connected young couple like Rufus and Jane could have become part of the Beautiful People of the Red Hills—the Red Hills was what they called the plantation country to the north, east, and west of Tallahassee. The governor would have received them at Mount Aventine, the plantation he'd named for one of the seven hills of Rome. Rufus could have gone into politics or speculated in the Whig versus Democrat banking wars. Jane could have been on calling terms with the likes of Ellen White of Casa Bianca Plantation, a famous belle who inspired Edward Bulwer-Lytton to write poetry for her and who was nicknamed "Florida," as if she were the territorial mascot. Rufus and Jane could have spent a lot of time dancing quadrilles with Virginia Randolphs and Carolina Bradfords. Jane would need a lot more satin dresses.

Rufus, though, wanted to make his way in the empty lands, figuring to log and fish and farm in the river country instead of clearing hundreds of acres for cotton in the uplands, where he'd be expected to live like a planter, like his daddy, wearing a tie every day. So in 1835 Jane and Rufus packed up the wedding presents—a few pieces of silver, an old French soup tureen, a slave named Sarey—and followed the Spanish *camino real* to Tallahassee. They got to the foot of the rise on which the capitol stood and turned toward the sea.

The capitol hill isn't a hill, exactly, but the Cody Scarp, a high, long ridge, curving east to the Withlacoochee River and west to the Chipola. It's an ancient shoreline. A million years ago the waters of the Gulf of Mexico slapped at its roots. The Cody Scarp is also a dividing line. To the north the soil is the color of carnelians. Live oaks like it, roses like it, and magnolias. More important, cotton likes it, and tobacco. To the south the soil is sandy, gray, and thin—when it's dry—and full of broken shells from Pleistocene times. Turkey oaks like it, tupelos like it, and pines. To the north lay the clean fields and great houses with their poetical names; to the south it often seemed that the land was trying to return to the sea.

Jane Broward must have wondered what she was doing, stirring her coffee with a silver spoon at the bottom of America. Her children and grandchildren and great-grandchildren wondered, too, and took themselves off to the seminary in Tallahassee, battlefields in Virginia, poinciana-lined streets in Miami, law school in Gainesville. Then they'd come back to the swamp, compelled, exasperated. Their country was half water, half land, with green-black sloughs, acres of thick chartreuse grasses that would merge with the Gulf if there was a big storm, pines thin as pencils growing out of saw palmettos, brown water rivers that curled like cast-aside ribbons. There were forests where cypress, hawthorn, and sweetgum grew so thick you could only see blue shards of sky. Sometimes the ground would just open up and your house or your barn would disappear down a sinkhole.

In the mid-1830s, when Jane and Rufus set up housekeeping in a dogtrot cabin the color of the earth it sat on, most of the places didn't yet have white-people names. The British and a few of the French had been through here but didn't stay. William Bartram, son of the royal botanist, visited swamp country in 1765 with his father and met the Seminoles. They called him "Puc Puggy"—flower gatherer. The Spanish spent mosquito-bitten years there, looking for elusive riches, trying to convert the Apalachees, dying in great numbers, killing in even greater numbers. For them the place was haunted.

Panfílo de Narváez, a red-haired, one-eyed, mean son of Spain, famous for ordering the slaughter of 2,500 native people in Cuba, got the license to run Florida after Juan Ponce de León succumbed to that Calusa arrow. He brought the usual church decrees, diseases, and swords, along with settlers, slaves, and wannabe conquistadors. He also brought with him a literarily inclined Andalucian, Álvar Núñez Cabeza de Vaca. The "cow head" part of Álvar Núñez's name comes from an ancestor who, in 1212, saved Christian soldiers from the Moors by showing the way through a mountain pass using a bovine skull pointed in the right direction. "Cabeza de Vaca" is a title of honor.

Cabeza de Vaca called his Florida best seller *Naufragios,* or "Shipwrecks." This is all part of the myth: the tempest that blows you to a strange land which might be blessed or bad, home to a beautiful princess or a witch who turns men into pigs. Florida has a wealth of shipwreck stories. In 1696 a clutch of Quakers got caught in an August storm on their way from Jamaica and crashed somewhere near Jupiter. Their sheep and pigs swam ashore and escaped. The Quakers swam ashore, too, but the Indians waiting there took almost everything they had, including their clothes. There they were, naked as Adam and Eve after the Fall. They covered their shame with pages torn out of their Bibles. (Bibles were large in those days.)

Jonathan Dickinson, who wrote his own best seller about the ordeal, said that only "Protecting Providence" saved them from the "cruel devouring Jaws of the inhuman Cannibals of Florida." There is a little state park dedicated to Dickinson and the other Quakers, off Highway 1 not far from Hobe Sound.

In April 1528 Narváez landed in Tampa Bay. When the Spaniards waded ashore, somewhere near Abercrombie Park in St. Petersburg, the Tocobagas were waiting. They had already decided they didn't want to cut sugar cane for His Catholic Majesty, so they applied a little preemptive misinformation. The Tocobaga cacique assured Narváez that Florida's good stuff—the gold, the emeralds—were way up in the chiefdom of the Apalachees. Narváez, greedy, bought the story. This could be the new Peru. He could be richer than the king. He sent four ships, the ones with the women and the food and the fresh water, north to rendezvous with him at a bay the Tocobagas assured him would be so full of fish he could practically walk on the surface. Then he took off for the Apalachee capital of Aute with three hundred men, forty horses, and Cabeza de Vaca, who was taking notes.

The interior was alien, but Cabeza de Vaca calls it "wonderful to look upon" with trees of "liquid amber," trees taller than any they'd seen, but "riven from top to bottom by bolts of lightning which fell in that country of frequent storms." Cabeza de Vaca writes admiringly of Indians, assuring his readers that most of them will take to Christianity eventually. Maybe not the ones he met in North Florida, though. A decidedly un-Christian Apalachee shot a Spaniard's horse full of arrows. Armor wasn't a lot of use, since these arrows had such force they could pierce a pine. They shot a young gentleman named Avanellada clean through his neck. The Apalachees were scarily superhuman, six or eight inches taller than the Spaniards. They wore almost nothing, even on cold nights.

Narváez was looking for a river emptying out into a bay, as advertised by the Tocobagas and described in earlier expeditions. It may have been the St. Marks, it may have been the Ochlockonee. Narváez decided he would name the river after Mary Magdalen, the fallen woman redeemed by Jesus. She had red hair, too. Only the Magdalen's river was nowhere to be found. Narváez and his men got lost in boggy-bottomed, thick-canopied woods where the sun barely penetrated. Finally they tripped into a bay the color of the beads the Moors used to ward off the evil eye. The ships weren't there. Rations were almost gone. The Spaniards decided they would die if they didn't try to sail to Mexico, where there were palaces and cathedrals and apothecaries and food, plenty of food, and *los Indios* were servants.

Florida made Narváez sick. Florida made all of them sick. Cabeza de Vaca was forced to take notes on bits of bark. The Apalachees were still shooting at them from the forests at the edge of the beach. Every three days they killed a horse and ate it. They named the bay Bahía de Caballos to mark it in their misery. Or maybe to honor the horses.

None of them knew how to make a boat. But they tried. The ones who weren't half dead of dysentery managed to build rafts with young trees caulked with palmetto fiber and lashed together with ropes plaited from the dead horses' manes. They used what was left of their cambric shirts for sails. Narváez, in a fit of temper and despair, drank sea water.

He turned delirious, but in one moment of lucidity he told them, according to Cabeza de Vaca, "Each man should do what he thought best to save his own life. That's what I shall do."

Narváez died. Most of them died. Cabeza de Vaca says of the 600 who set sail from Spain, 140 died of disease and hunger. Almost 200 were killed by the Apalachees. Of the ones who left on rafts from Bahía de Caballos, fifteen lived for a while, shipwrecked somewhere between Tate's Hell and Texas, gradually shedding the shards of their armor and their European clothes, starving, thirsty. Cabeza de Vaca hints that when one died, the rest ate him.

Finally there were only four: two *hidalgos,* one African servant named Estévan, and Cabeza de Vaca, now taking notes in his head. They survived by sometimes trading with the natives or more often being their slaves. After a few years they began to be taken for shamans. They began to wear necklaces of shells. They learned some of the language of the people. When they finally got to Mexico City in 1536, eight years after sailing from Havana, Cabeza de Vaca said that he could barely wear clothes again. He preferred to sleep on the bare floor. He had become a real American.

Conquistador Hogs

Jane Broward would have known the history of the Spanish in Florida. She had lived on old mission lands among the ruins of Franciscan chapels; she had met descendants of the settlers Governor Menéndez had brought to populate his city of San Agustín, high-toned Castilians with gold crosses and long memories; she knew that her family's land came from a Spanish king. She heard the stories about the Spanish in her own neck of the swamp, thrashing around lost, hungry. Maybe she picked up a rosary bead in the grounds of the fort at St. Marks.

But the Spanish were rapidly becoming just a romantic story, a fairy story, like their own fantastic tales of the Fountains of Youth or the mermaids Columbus says he heard singing off the Atlantic coast. Jane and Rufus and their children and all those other heretic white folks would live in the swamp where the Spanish died. Nobody had to worry about the Calusas or the Ocales or the Apalachees anymore: Thousands were taken as slaves to Cuba or Puerto Rico. Many died in battle. Most died of illnesses they had no words for: measles, typhoid fever, smallpox, Old World pathogens spat out in the New World. By 1720 they were almost all gone, dead because Europeans came to Florida and breathed their air.

By the time Hernando de Soto was dispatched to Florida in 1539, the Spanish were no longer interested in miracles and wonders. This time they meant business. They wanted the place conquered, whipped, slapped around, beaten into submission, and tidily absorbed into the Spanish empire. Florida needed to make money—the Reconquista was expensive. Fighting wars with heretics was expensive. The Inquisition was expensive.

De Soto had studied Hispano-Indian relations with Francisco Pizarro in Peru as they slashed and burned their way through the early 1530s, looting the great Inca cities, piling up bodies, and piling up treasure. When he headed back to Spain in 1535, he was insanely rich and seriously ambitious. He asked Carlos V if he could have Ecuador; the king gave him Florida.

De Soto was smarter than Narváez: He left the supply ships safe in Tampa Bay, guarded by cavalry, until he sent men back with a road map and precise instructions where to meet him. He took a large, slow company into the interior, heading for Apalachee lands: soldiers, priests, horses, mules, long-legged range hogs. De Soto was no Cabeza de Vaca liberal. When the Spanish came across a Tocobaga or Ocale village, a priest would read out the *Requirimiento,* a proclamation of the necessity and supremacy of the Roman Catholic faith. The *Requirimiento* was, of course, in Spanish. The Tocobagas and the Ocales hadn't the least idea what they were hearing, but if one of them so much as looked sideways at these small, pallid people with their beards and their beads and their images of a suffering god nailed to a tree, de Soto's soldiers might cut off his nose or ear or hand, or maybe take his daughter or wife the way they had probably already taken the village's supply of corn.

De Soto and his hard-liners had waded ashore in midsummer; it was October when they got to Apalachee lands west of the Aucilla River. The Apalachees were no more accommodating than they were the last time they met a conquistador. They burned their own villages and their own corn, withdrawing inland, waiting for a chance to ambush. In December the Spanish passed through fields of winter crops, hills rising up around them and cool little streams lacing across the land. At the St. Marks River, the Spanish fought a pitched battle with the Apalachees. It was ugly. The blood soaked into the red clay of the riverbanks and spilled into the water like poison. This time the crossbows and swords of the Spaniards beat the medicine-charged arrows of the Apalachees. De Soto occupied the Apalachee town of Anhaica, where on December 25, 1539, the priests sang the Christmas mass to celebrate the birth of the Prince of Peace.

A hundred years later, Spanish soldiers had raised mud and coquina forts along the coasts. Spanish monks had strung missions along the Red Hills, each with its little pine chapel dedicated to an archangel, a saint, or a martyr. There was even one, San Martín de Tomoli, there on the Cody Scarp where one day the Americans would build a log hut and call it a capital. In the spring, if it wasn't raining, you could see all the way down to the Bay of Horses.

Two hundred years later, the Spanish forts needed repairing, and the missions were mostly just a few rickety walls covered in trumpet vine. A Carolina Scot, John McIver, built his house on what was left of San Martin de Tomoli. He said he liked the view. But the "royal road" the Spanish had made between San Agustín and Pensacola was more or less intact, if full of thigh-deep ruts. Rufus and Jane rode down it past de Soto's 1539 camp in the middle of the old capital, Anhaica, now part of the new capital, Tallahassee.

These days the site is asphalted over with offices and condominiums (the Florida curse), obscuring the ancient earth. But before the buildings went up in the late 1980s, the state archaeologist found a tiny piece of chain mail. Then a few blown glass beads. Then the iron point of a crossbow and a copper coin, a four-maravedi piece, minted when

Ferdinand and Isabella still sat on the twin thrones of Castile and Aragon. Then the jawbone of a pig.

In the uncertain lands between the Cody Scarp and the sea, kin of that pig got good at avoiding alligators in the creeks and feeding off poison ivy. Their forefathers and mothers had been hardy, resourceful range pigs from the hot scrublands of Extremadura. The Spanish abandoned Florida, but their swine never left, thriving generation upon generation in the very swamps that defeated Narváez and confounded de Soto. My Roberts grandfather—we called him Papa—would tell how his great-grandmother Jane would hear them at night, trying to get into her vegetable garden. "Great-Granddaddy Rufus would get up and try to shoot him one," said my grandfather. "Those old conquistador hogs were lean as a cat," he said. Not so tasty as domesticated, slop-fed hogs, but they cured up okay for the winter.

Down at the River, as Papa referred to our ancestral swamp, he kept a pen of respectable pigs. He'd let me help scoop out their feed, hard corn kernels yellow as mustard, and tell me about the conquistador hogs that ran in packs like wild dogs. "The old king hog, he had them living over on Mack Island." Papa would gesture out in the direction of a piece of liquid ground out there in the labyrinth of bays, landings, hammocks, marshes, and forest. Once when I was down there I saw six or seven of these wild pigs, their bloodlines going back to the Reconquista, swimming across our slough. They held their brindled snouts out of the brown water as daintily as sorority girls trying not to get their hair wet in the pool. Their eyes were hard as bone. Papa told us that a hog bite is worse than a cottonmouth bite or a rattlesnake bite. It's worse than anything except a human bite. I ran back to the car and hit the automatic lock, as if conquistador hogs would know how to open doors.

Jane Broward Tucker wrote to her father back at the Broward place that his grandson Charles Broward Tucker, born in 1842, was doing well, and that she and Rufus had a hundred acres or so now. She didn't tell him that half of it was underwater. The important thing was that once again a French Brouard had stuck it out where the Spanish had turned tail and run.

Before Port Leon got wrecked in the big hurricane of 1843, Jane and Rufus would drive down there, or to Kings Bay to buy oysters. Rufus loved oysters. Jane would walk on the beach carrying the parasol her Uncle John had brought her from Jamaica. She had heard that you could still see crosses carved in the bark by the desperate and starving Spanish, who hoped that God, at least, hadn't forgotten them in the land of the Apalachees. Some of the old people, part African, part Indian, who made potions and conjures in the swamp, said that once the white sand there had been covered with the skulls of horses.

Luther Tucker, Jane and Rufus's third son, would tell how one time Rufus and Jane took him and his brothers Charlie and Washington over to St. Marks. Franklin and Milton were too little, so they were left home with Sarey. Rufus hired a skiff from a fellow and took them up the Wakulla River (Charlie was big enough to help row) all the way to the springs. Rufus said that this was the genuine Fountain of Youth that the old Spaniard Ponce de León was looking for hundreds of years ago. Rufus told how de Soto kept going once he discovered that the Fountain of Youth didn't work and there was no city of El Dorado in Florida. "He went to Georgia and he went to the Carolinas and Tennessee and Alabama. He ran smack into the Mississippi River. Got sick as a dog and died." Rufus always repeated that part, "Got sick as a dog and died."

The remnants of de Soto's conquering Christians buried him in a secret place in the bed of the river, where maybe the catfish feasted on his mortal remains.

Rufus would tell this story at Wakulla Springs. Jane would trail her hand in the rock-cold water. They'd let the skiff drift a little in the middle of the round spring, while Rufus would show the boys the bones of a giant beast on the bottom. Papa's grandfather Luther thought it was a dragon. Luther's brother Charlie said there were no dragons, it was some old animal that had died even before the Spanish came. Jane wondered if maybe it had drowned in the Flood that covered the earth in Bible times, maybe at the very beginning of the world.

2

Red, Black, and White

DAMN, IF THAT ISN'T ANDREW JACKSON, Old Hickory himself, riding a bay gelding down Monroe Street in his gold-epauletted coat and cockaded *chapeau bas,* his Ray-Bans and his Rolex.

All right, it's really some property developer, a builder of subdivisions named after whatever was destroyed to put them there: Live Oak Estates, Heron Lakes, Clearwater Creek. But today he's the seventh president of the United States, the first governor of Florida, all dressed up for the "Springtime Tallahassee" parade.

We get a new Andrew Jackson every year, a chamber of commerce poster boy chosen by the civic-minded white folks who run the festival. He used to ride at the head of the procession, but there were complaints. Andrew Jackson despised Florida. Andrew Jackson lived in Florida less than six months. He *never* lived in Tallahassee. He practiced genocide. In the First Seminole War in 1817, he went around killing Mikasukis and burning their villages. In the Second Seminole War in 1835, when he'd become president, he ordered that Florida's remaining Native Americans be decimated or driven off—whichever was more convenient. No doubt he would have embraced the Third Seminole War in 1855, except by then he was dead. Now he's lucky to get a parade slot between Thomas County High School Marching Yellow Jacket Band and the Tallahassee Tumbling Tots.

Political correctness, mutter the Springtime Tallahassee bosses. *What do they want us to do, have slaves in head rags toting cotton sacks on the Antebellum Florida float, or get a dozen Mikasukis off the Tamiami Trail Reservation to walk alongside the Territorial Krewe wearing chains?*

Springtime Tallahassee's version of Florida history goes like this: In the sixteenth century, Spaniards in puffy britches and pointy helmets, along with their mantilla-draped girlfriends, discovered Florida and brought Jesus. Time passed, then Andrew Jackson blew in and did things we'd rather not discuss (but our destiny was manifest, obviously). In 1821 he made us an American territory. This cleared the way for top-hatted gents and belles in ruffled crinolines, who got rich and built houses grand as Greek temples, apparently without breaking a sweat. In the 1860s brother fought brother over slavery (which, no matter what some people say, Wasn't That Bad). The Civil War was romantic and tragic, but it was a Good Thing in the end because it resulted in integration, which resulted in FSU winning national championships in football. After the Civil War, the 1920s happened and flappers twirled long beads while riding in Model Ts. Jazz was played. Then NASA put a man on the moon and Disney put a mouse in Orlando. Now the gents drive Chris-Craft speedboats, the belles wear bikinis, and every day is just another day in paradise.

Andrew Jackson was born in South Carolina twelve years before the first shot was fired in the Revolution, son of an Ulsterman. His people weren't any of your posh Myddletons or Pinckneys—they were closer to being white trash. He was hard as nails (or hickory), notorious for his love of horse racing, card playing, and game cocking. He was a mythic monster of a pioneer who raised himself up from the backwoods through the law, politics, and regenerative violence. I think a lot of my kin identified with him. My Roberts grandfather told me that his great-grandfather had killed Creeks with Jackson. This may be true. In any case, he said it like he was proud of it.

Jackson invented himself as a famous soldier in the War of 1812, whipping the British in January 1815 at the Battle of New Orleans. He proclaimed that America fought "for the reestablishment of our national character." It didn't matter that the Treaty of Ghent, officially ending hostilities, had been signed on Christmas Eve, 1814. War was a good career move.

By 1816 he was looking for somebody new to kill. Just over the Georgia border in Spanish Florida, three-hundred-odd free Negroes and escaped slaves, men, women, and children, were living in an old British fortification, called the "Negro Fort," on the Apalachicola River. Jackson, a slaveholder himself, felt that a Florida prepared to harbor runaway black folks was an intolerable Florida, a threat to white womanhood and the security of the plantation South.

Moreover, the British had left a slew of munitions and military equipment in there. In May 1816 Jackson wrote to Colonel Edmund Gaines, commandant of nearby Fort Scott: "I have little doubt of the fact that this fort has been established by some villains for the purpose of rapine and plunder." Jackson didn't care that the people in the fort were living under Spanish jurisdiction, or that many of them had been freed or even born in freedom; it was the duty of the United States to "return the stolen negroes to their rightful owners." Jackson added that the fort "ought to be blown up."

Which is exactly what happened. In July 1816 Americans fired on the fort from the Apalachicola River. A lucky hot shot hit the powder magazines, and the whole place exploded. Only a few dozen people survived. Some were executed. The rest became slaves.

Wiping out the Negro Fort didn't solve the Florida problem or the Negro problem or the Indian problem. Florida, black people, and Native Americans were all tangled up together. In the early eighteenth century, the Spanish figured they'd shore up their territories against the British through an alliance with the Creeks of Georgia, inviting them to come live on the depleted lands of Florida. The Apalachees were almost gone, killed by diseases or kidnapped by the British-backed Yamasees and sold into slavery on Carolina rice plantations. There was a certain amount of intermarriage between nations, and as if this weren't complicated enough, Creeks also intermarried with the black slaves some of them owned. They spread across Florida from the Choctawhatchee River to Payne's Prairie to the St. Johns, taking over the old villages, the old sacred sites. They renamed themselves "Seminoles," the Muskogean version of the Spanish word *cimarrones*. It means "wild ones." They raided white settlements and encouraged slaves to run off from the plantations to join them. They were mongrels and proud of it. Gopher John, a Seminole interpreter, was a black man. Abraham, one of the Seminole war leaders, was part black.

The Seminoles defied the rules of race, caste, and class definition. They were always changing territories, weapons, names. Sometimes they didn't call themselves Seminoles, but went by an old name: Red Sticks.

White, in the Creek tradition, is the color of peace. Red is the color of war.

In 1817 Chief Neamathla, who reigned from Fowl Town, a Georgia village across the Flint River from Fort Scott, warned Colonel Gaines to stay on his side of the water. Gaines wasn't about to be spoken to like that by some dirty pagan, so he sent 250 U.S. soldiers to burn Neamathla's town. In retaliation, Neamathla's band opened fire on a riverboat, killing thirty-seven soldiers, six women, and four children.

It was time for regime change. Secretary of War John C. Calhoun sent Jackson to deliver some shock and awe in the First Seminole War.

Which Jackson did, with a force of 5,000 U.S. soldiers versus 1,300 Seminoles. He violated the international border between U.S. territory and Spanish, ignoring Spanish protests. At Lake Miccosukee, he destroyed Kinhajo's Town, the largest Seminole settlement in Florida. He slashed and burned his way down to the Suwannee, harrying the Seminole chief Bowlegs. He took the Spanish port of St. Marks on the Gulf of Mexico and occupied the old Spanish city of Pensacola for good measure. He ignored another whole set of international treaties when, deep inside Spanish Florida, he court-martialed two British entrepreneurs, Robert Ambrister and Alexander Arbuthnot, charging them with aiding and abetting the Indians. Ambrister was executed by firing squad; Arbuthnot was hanged from the yardarm of his own ship. The name of the ship was *The Last Chance*.

Jackson had a mind to besiege the Spanish capital at San Agustín. He'd spread democracy to the southern end of the continent, whether they wanted it or not. He wrote to Calhoun that if the cabinet gave him the high sign, he could conquer all of Florida. And if they'd send him some boats and a few more soldiers, he'd "liberate" Cuba while he was at it.

This early-nineteenth-century mission creep was starting to get embarrassing, even to a government full of Monroe Doctrinarians. Jackson didn't, in the end, invade Cuba, but his assaults had convinced the Spanish governor and the recently restored Bourbons, back in Madrid after having been booted out by Napoléon, that Florida was not strictly necessary to Spain's power and prestige. They'd take cash.

Luis de Onís, Ferdinand VII's minister, and American secretary of state John Quincy Adams quietly started negotiating. President Monroe himself spun Jackson's Florida raids to Congress as protecting the nation. Jackson huffed that he was just trying to "chastise a savage foe, combined with a lawless band of negro brigands" who prosecuted a "cruel and unprovoked war against the citizens of the United States" and posed a threat to the American Way of Life. His poll numbers shot up.

Maybe the Springtime Tallahasseeans are right and Andrew Jackson ought to lead our parades. You could argue that he is the presiding genius of the state: rootless, restless, self-made, a social Darwinist before Darwin. He was at the center of what is now the quintessential Florida disaster—not a hurricane, but a disputed presidential election. Jackson won the popular vote in 1824, but the electoral college balked at certifying him the victor. The dispute was kicked into the House of Representatives, but it was also split. Speaker Henry Clay, who had himself been running for president, refused to support Jackson. The other candidate, John Quincy Adams, a New Englander with a Famous Father, a Yankee born knowing which fork to use, moved into the White House.

Jackson sulked in his Tennessee mansion for a while, reemerging for the election of 1828, ready to kick patrician butt. The political sloganeers said the choice was between "John Quincy Adams, who can write, and Andrew Jackson, who can fight." This time fighting beat finesse. Jackson rode into Washington and laid out a philosophy of preemptive violence and a program to get rid of the Indians, especially in Florida.

The plan was this: Florida was to be a place where there were two races: whites to own the land, blacks to work it. The Seminoles, Mikasukis, Red Sticks, whatever they were calling themselves, were useless as slaves. Besides, they had guns. The Seminoles, Mikasukis, Red Sticks, whatever, had to go. There's never been enough of Florida. Everybody wants a piece—a big piece—for something: cotton, tobacco, cattle, oranges, sugar cane, phosphate, turpentine, pulp, resorts, theme parks, suburbs, golf courses, and "wilderness" where the last panthers, the last bears, the last eagles, the totem animals of the Seminoles might find a home. But you can't go wasting Florida on people who refuse to make a profit from it.

The Shape-Shifter

Osceola was the romantic one, the handsome rebel, the one they wrote newspaper articles and poems about, the one the government wanted dead or alive. During the Second Seminole War, some of the other Seminoles agreed to put their marks on an agreement with Andrew Jackson's officers, giving up land in Florida. Osceola pulled out his knife, stuck it into the paper, and said, "This is the only treaty I'll ever make with the whites."

Osceola was the embodiment of the Seminole problem—walking racial anarchy. His father was white British, a man named William Powell. His mother was a Georgia Creek. Osceola married the daughter of a chief and a mulatto slave woman. His name in Hitchiti was As-se-se-he-ho-lar or Asiyahola, which is what the Seminoles called the Black Drink, the sacramental tea brewed out of holly and yaupon leaves. In a ritual of purification going back through the Creek Nation to the mound-builders two thousand years ago, you took the Black Drink, you vomited, you were renewed to fight another day.

The Seminoles said Osceola could manipulate the atoms of his body like the famous Coacoochee—Wildcat—who shrank himself and twenty of his warriors to slip through the bars of his cell in St. Augustine. Osceola could draw out your soul: He took the soul of Indian agent Wiley Thompson before shooting him outside Fort King in 1835. Osceola was a sorcerer: he could make trails invisible or put soldiers to sleep. Osceola was a prophet, a follower of the chief Tecumseh. In 1811 Tecumseh exhorted the Creeks to throw down the plow, take up the war club and the scalping knife, and drive the whites off the sacred places.

The whites thought they'd won, thought the days of the war club and the scalping knife were pretty much over; they could push farther and farther into Florida with their slaves and their fences. For New Year's 1836, Tallahassee hoteliers had ordered extra cases of champagne, barrels of hock and port, boxes of Jordan almonds and candied fruit. The Red Hills gentry would dance all night. Andrew Jackson had taken care of the Seminoles once and for all, by God. There were treaties, the Seminoles were going to go west, or south, or somewhere, anywhere, out of the way. The remnants would be confined to reservations. They had been beaten by a superior civilization. Surely they realized that.

But the superior civilization had let the Seminoles go hungry on the reservations, where they couldn't hunt, and had encroached on their remaining lands. They lied about the Canaan beyond the Mississippi, "Indian Territory." Andrew Jackson remained their hated enemy. On December 28, 1835, 175 miles south of Tallahassee, the war leaders Jumper, Alligator, Abraham, and the old chief Micanopy, heir of Bowlegs, descendant of the high cacique Cowkeeper, led the attack on Major Francis Dade's detachment of one hundred men. The whites were all killed. The next day Osceola attacked General Duncan Clinch, stopping him from entering the Cove of the Withlacoochee, where Seminoles had taken refuge. The combustible General Edmund

Gaines, still angry at being "insulted" by Neamathla in 1817, didn't wait for orders from Washington but rounded up one thousand soldiers and headed to Florida to fight. General Winfield Scott showed up, too. For the first few months of 1836, the Wahoo Swamp seethed with generals trying to fight in water up to their boot tops, their mules drowning, razor-leaved palmettos slashing at them, half-asleep alligators in the mud (not happy to be awakened from their winter doze) snapping at them. They lost their provisions in the black bogs while the Seminoles shot at them from behind bald cypress, then faded back into the damp green darkness.

Deep in the swamp, Osceola, Micanopy, Abraham, and the other chiefs made a victory fire. Nearby on a ten-foot pole hung the scalps of American soldiers. The Second Seminole War had begun.

It lasted until 1842, a war of raids, sporadic battles, guerrilla attacks, double-crossing, and cruelty on all sides. The Seminoles had some successes, but their numbers were dwindling, pushed into the wet reaches of the Big Cypress Swamp and the Everglades, or captured and transported west. In October 1837 Major General Thomas Jesup, Jackson's man in Florida, got tired of chasing Osceola. Jesup raised a white flag of truce, as if he wanted to talk. Osceola agreed. Then Jesup seized Osceola, declaring that this uppity Indian was now a prisoner of the United States.

The army dragged Osceola off to the stockade at Fort Moultrie in South Carolina. It seemed that outside Florida Osceola couldn't or wouldn't put a sleeping spell on his guards or slip through the bars or shape-shift. He didn't even try to escape. He was sick with quinsy, a severe throat infection, and malaria.

There's an 1838 George Catlin portrait of him, often engraved and reproduced in the popular press—a dead Indian is not only a good Indian but a romantic Indian. Osceola stands there, Achilles tall, holding a long rifle, erect and arrogant, feathers in his black hair. In late January 1838 he knew he was dying. He dressed himself in his princely Seminole regalia, like Cleopatra before she embraced the asp, his bracelets and necklaces and his powder horn, beating the whites at public relations even as he breathed his last on January 31.

Osceola is buried at Fort Moultrie. All except his head. His doctor, Frederick Weedon, cut it off. There was a story that Mary Thompson Weedon, the doctor's wife, was a cousin of Wiley Thompson, the Indian agent Osceola assassinated, and demanded revenge. There's no evidence this is true. It's more likely that Dr. Weedon wanted to study Osceola's phrenology. It could be that owning the head of a celebrity gave Dr. Weedon a thrill. It could just be that he was one of those Victorian collectors who'd fill his house with everything from butterflies pinned on cards to orchids to stuffed dodos. Weedon kept the head in a case at his house until it was given to a New York medical college museum. Then Osceola's head falls out of history. Nobody knows if it was still there when the museum burned in 1865.

Osceola had asked to be buried in Florida, but the National Park Service refused to move him from South Carolina. Maybe even a dead Indian isn't quite romantic enough to get what he wants from the United States government. Or maybe they think we'll make a theme park out of him.

We have our own Osceola in Florida—just like we have an Andrew Jackson. At every FSU home football game, some frat boy puts on brick-colored greasepaint and a long black Cher wig, a "traditional" tunic, and suede boots. He mounts a horse named Renegade. He rides—bareback—onto the field, holding a burning spear. He canters Renegade from goalpost to goalpost then trots to the center and plunges the spear into the fifty-yard line. It is considered an honor to be chosen to impersonate Chief Osceola: a hero to the red, a hero to the black, and, now that he and most of his kind are safely dead, a hero to the white.

Prince Murat's Fancy Girl

My sisters and I used to sit by the graves of Prince and Princess Murat, trying to freak each other out. Our sorority house wasn't far from the old St. John's Cemetery. After dinner on sharp, early spring evenings, we'd pick our way through the graves of planters who died of gout and judges who died of old age and belles who died in childbirth and a whole family who drowned off the coast of North Carolina, triggering one of the most baroque inheritance lawsuits in Florida history, to the twin obelisques marking where the remains of Achille and Catherine Murat had long since become fertilizer for the fat green North Florida grass. We'd pass around a joint and, as night clouded in all gray and cool, tell ghost stories.

We were drawn to Princess Murat. She was Florida royalty, kind of spiritual sorority sister, a Southern girl who'd done what Southern girls were supposed to do: marry a prince. We'd tell one of the pledges that if she stood facing Princess Murat's grave with her eyes shut, counted to a hundred, then opened her eyes, she'd see the princess's ghost, dressed in white lace, hovering just off to the right by that big camellia.

It was easy to scare the shit out of a pledge.

Here's what's left of the Murats: a motel with a mostly burned out light-up crown for a sign where, in the 1960s and '70s, senators used to meet young women for intimate lobbying sessions; the prince's armchair, which smelled of wet dog (I sat in it illegally once when I was about seven and it was shoved in a corner of the old library); and a portrait of the prince on toast. The artist laid 130 pieces of toast in a square, did something to them so they wouldn't go soggy in the Tallahassee damp, and painted the disdainful face of Achille Murat in blacks, grays, and whites. The portrait hangs in the back corner of Waterworks—which is the sort of bar the prince would patronize were he alive today. I don't know if the toast is white or wheat.

Andrew Jackson gets much more notice in Florida, and it's not fair: He only lasted three months as governor. Achille Murat lived here for twenty-three years. Andrew Jackson never took to Florida; it was too hot, too buggy, too full of racially dubious Seminoles, too roiled with the ancient intrigues of its former colonial masters: the Spaniards, the French, the British. In Florida, too many rules were being broken.

On the other hand, that's why some people liked it. That's why Achille Murat liked it.

Eurotrash are attracted to Florida like cats to butter—always have been. In the sixteenth century, the younger sons of down-on-their-luck Spanish aristos came looking for gold in all the wrong places.

British grandees who'd got themselves in hot water liked to hole up in Florida till the scandal died down. In the late nineteenth century, Queen Victoria's cousin, the Duke of Sutherland, ran off with his lover, a woman called Mary Caroline Blair. They used to ride matching white horses on the beach at Clearwater. Fifty years later the Duke and Duchess of Windsor would descend like a plague of plummy locusts on the North Florida quail plantations of their rich American friends, doing a little shooting and a lot of mooching.

The Jacksonian years, the 1820s and 1830s, were the real boom times for the dubious, the titled, and the dubiously titled. You couldn't walk through the Presidio in Pensacola, down Monroe Street in Tallahassee, or past the Castillo in St. Augustine without bumping into some German *Freiherr* writing a poem. The Comte de Castelnau hung around the capital, sketching oxcarts in dirt streets and turbaned slave women wringing out washing. His Florida looks more noble than savage. There's a little drawing from 1838 of the territorial capitol that makes it look like a classical folly in the "rustic" end of a chateau garden: no poisonous snakes, no wood ticks, no Seminole bullets.

Some of these Europeans came to Florida with sentimental notions drawn from literary magazines, or an engraving displaying all the signifiers of paradise: the palm tree, the Indian princess in a state of nature, flowers in her hands, on her head, and under her feet. They came because they had read Chateaubriand and, like him, got mixed up as to which side of the Mississippi was which. America represented radical innocence, the overturning of old orders, and maybe a way to a fast franc (or *real* or crown or pound). They came because they had read the naturalist William Bartram's breathless account of touring the St. Johns country, in which he described Florida as "a glorious apartment in the sovereign palace of the Creator," making the place sound like a kind of anteroom to the halls of heaven. They came because they wanted a new life—sort of.

The ne plus ultra of Florida exotics was Charles Louis Napoléon Achille Murat, sometime Crown Prince of Naples. He descended on East Florida in 1824, twenty-three years old, looking to remake himself as an American. By the time Achille Murat was five, his uncle the emperor Napoléon had made him Duke of Berg and Cleves. By the time he was eight, he was heir to a pilfered kingdom, living in a palace under an active volcano. By the time he was fifteen, he was an exile.

Nobody was ever better prepared for the vertiginous enterprise of becoming a Floridian than Achille Murat. He was raised on a beach. Naples, Italy, exuded an in-the-marrow unreality, just like Naples, Florida. Tourists from the soberer parts of Europe traveled there to misbehave (Lord Nelson and Lady Hamilton began their illicit affair in Naples) and to gawp at the Isle of Capri and the ruins of Pompeii. Naples was a provisional place, ruled by Caesars, Arabs, Normans, princes of the Holy Roman Church, princes of the House of Bourbon, and now Bonapartes. Vesuvius could blow at any time. The whole Napoleonic project, a mix of military potency and brass-faced spin, could blow at any time.

Achille's mother, Caroline, was Napoléon's baby sister. She had married Joachim Murat, a stupid but good-looking Gascon soldier who'd impressed Napoléon with his bravery during the 1799 Egyptian campaign. In 1808 the emperor rewarded Joachim and Caroline with Naples (she had wanted Spain) as the Bonapartes divvied up Europe. But after Waterloo, all Bonaparte bets were off. The original proprietors of the various principalities, kingdoms, and provinces took them back. The Italians lined King Joachim up in front of a firing squad in 1815. He begged them to aim for his heart instead of his head: he wanted to be a handsome corpse.

Lucky for Queen Caroline, Prince Metternich, the Henry Kissinger of nineteenth-century Europe, had once been among her lovers. He offered her and her four children asylum at Frohsdorf Castle in Austria. Paris gossips swore that he wore a bracelet of her braided hair.

The Bonapartes were masters of self-invention. Originally a Corsican family of shaky gentility, Jacobin sympathies, and decidedly Italian names, they Gallicized themselves when it looked like they could end up ruling France. Giuseppe became Joseph, Girolamo became Jérôme, Annunziata became Caroline. They swept away the old kings, the old nobility, the old church, the old laws, sometimes appropriating history, sometimes indulging in amateur apotheosis. Pauline (born Paola) married Prince Borghese and had herself sculpted as a reclining Venus. Joachim and Caroline saw themselves as new Caesars. They commissioned Fidele Fischetti to paint a fresco on the ceiling of their palace of Prince Achille as a naked charioteer, a young Apollo to light up the Bonaparte pantheon.

By 1823 Achille was sick of the chilly salons of Austria. He wanted to either overthrow all the regimes of Europe or else go to America. His mother thought that, on the whole, America was a better idea. So she sold some jewelry and bought him a ticket. He packed up two boxes of books and two bags of gold and sailed for New York. He hung around his uncle Joseph's house for a while (the ex-king of Spain had chosen New Jersey for his exile), then headed south. There was something welcoming, something familiar, about the Florida territory. White people had treated Florida as if it were empty space. They created their plantations out of a landscape of Apalachee villages, sacred lakes, and forests, but they felt as if they were making their own brand-new planet. As a member of a family used to making up history as they went along, Achille could get with this program. If anyone in the 1820s could imagine Disney World, it would be Achille Murat.

Besides, real estate was cheap.

Things didn't go well on Achille's first plantation. His tobacco crop failed. St. Augustine was full of priests and stiff old Spanish families with coats of arms going back to Alfonso VI who saw the Bonapartes as a bunch of usurping peasants. They stared disapprovingly at Achille, just because he often conducted business sitting in a chair at the edge of the ocean. He liked to cool his bare feet in the Atlantic while negotiating the price of a slave. He was bored, too. "I am," he said, "cruelly deprived of all society suited to the education and habits of an accomplished man." There were no theaters, no libraries, no opera, no good dinner parties, not much fun. He complained to his mother: "We have nothing to produce the same effects but whisky."

In 1825 he sold the East Florida land and took his books, his slaves, and his pet owl inland. He bought a land on the Wacissa River about fifteen miles from the territorial capital. He named it "Lipona."

When Caroline Murat fled to Austria she took to calling herself the Countess of Lipona—an anagram of "Napoli," a cryptographic souvenir of her lost kingdom. Lipona is a pretty name, a name like a tropical flower, but it means nothing and exists nowhere. Achille had called his first Florida plantation, the one near St. Augustine, "Parthenope"—Parthenope being the old Greek name for Naples. Like his mother, Achille was reminding himself of who he used to be.

Achille reckoned he ought to get a wife. The Red Hills country teemed with young ladies whose daddies owned impressive plantations. Achille was, however, an acquired taste. He slept on a pine needle mattress. He hated bathing. He was addicted to chewing tobacco. He fucked his slaves. He was an atheist. He liked to experiment gastronomically with the local wildlife. He'd have his cook serve guests baked alligator Béarnaise, and rattlesnake en croûte on Limòges painted with the royal crest of Naples. He liked dueling. In a spat over a stolen hog, Judge David Macomb shot off half Achille's right little finger. Achille put a bullet through the judge's shirt, though not the judge himself. The shot had, said the prince, "at least scared out the lice."

On the plus side, Achille was handsome in what the local debutantes described as "an Italian sort of way." He was related to a bunch of kings, queens, and emperors—ex-kings, ex-queens, and dead emperors, anyway—and owned a thousand acres of good cotton land.

Achille first cast his eye on Marcia DuVal, the redheaded (and rich) daughter of the governor. But she looked to do better. He transferred his attentions to Catherine Willis Gray, a young widow with dark hair and dark eyes. She was the great-grandniece of George Washington, so Achille probably thought she had money. At a picnic in the ruins of the old Spanish mission of San Luís de Talimali, he boldly pulled off one of Catherine's kid slippers. He filled it with *eau de vie,* toasted her beauty, and drained it, the rake. They married in 1826, though by that time he knew that she was poor and she knew that he was a drunk. Achille expanded the house at Lipona, adding a second story and a veranda. He hung lace curtains and put a marble bust of Queen Caroline by Canova in the parlor. He bought a real bed. Catherine must have thought he was worth the ruin of a perfectly good shoe.

The Red Hills planters figured that even a prince of the down-and-out Bonapartes would lift property prices in their up-and-coming cotton empire. They'd had hopes that a more famous Frenchman, the Marquis de la Fayette, would have made Florida his home. La Fayette was a hero of the American Revolution, a hero of the French Revolution, and, by 1824, nearly broke. He toured the United States reminding the citizens that without him there would be no United States, so could they maybe show their gratitude with a bit of cash or something? Congress coughed up $200,000 and 23,000 acres in Florida, one corner of it touching the edge of Tallahassee. Everyone waited for la Fayette to descend like Zeus from Mount Olympus, as one of them said, "to gild our little society." Instead, la Fayette sent sixty wage-earning *paysans,* Prichards, Casseaux, and Barineaus, from his Norman estates. They were to start growing not cotton, not tobacco, not even sugar cane, but olives. And limes. And silkworms. Even a few vines, in the hope that one day bottles of Cuvée Apalachee would grace the sideboards of the Calls and DuVals.

Not showing up was bad. Planting strange crops was bad. But far worse was la Fayette's attitude toward chattel slavery: he thought it economically inefficient, morally wrong, and inconsistent with revolutionary ideals. The planters, raking in Yankee dollars from record harvests of cotton, corn, and tobacco, rolled their eyes: Trust a Frenchman to take the Declaration of Independence *literally*.

Achille Murat traveled to South Carolina during la Fayette's national tour, to urge him, Frenchman to Frenchman, to come down and see for himself the rich, red, beautiful soil of North Florida, soil that would grow almost anything. Except olives. Or limes. La Fayette didn't realize that in Florida meteorology is destiny. The olives and the limes froze. The silkworms got a blight. The vines rotted from too much rain. In the end, he gave up on Florida without ever setting foot in Florida. He sailed back to France to fight one more time, at seventy-three helping overthrow the last Bourbon king. All thirty-six square miles of la Fayette's broken Utopia were sold to slave-owning cotton planters. Some of the Prichards, Casseaux, and Barineaus went home to Normandy; some stayed, settling in a village near the capital *les Américains* called "French Town."

For a few years in the 1980s, there was a vineyard on some of the old la Fayette property. They made mostly muscadine wine, purple as Napoléon's coronation robes and sweet as cake. The vineyard produced one almost-dry *vin de table,* and it sold pretty well, especially to lobbyists up for the legislative session and civic boosters in the suburbs. They called it "Plantation White."

Achille Murat thought of himself as a revolutionary, too—up to a point. He was always hatching plots to overthrow the Spanish government or "liberate" Italy. He could get sentimental about 1789 and that *liberté, égalité, fraternité* business, as long as it was for, well, plantation whites. Slavery would make the New World great; slavery would make Florida great; slavery would make Achille Murat great. Africans had the bodies of mules and the minds of children. They would help build the American Empire by picking the cotton, cutting the sugar cane, and having the babies that would become the next generation of field hands. But they weren't *quite* human, were they? Look at Haiti, once the richest of France's colonies. A rabble of ex-slaves singing "La Marseillaise" and wearing gold-laced uniforms in imitation of Napoléon himself killed as many white people as they could get their hands on and expelled the rest. For Achille, it was close to home. His aunt, Empress Josephine, was born on Martinique; they said she had Negro blood. Napoléon divorced her.

The prince didn't mind sleeping with Negroes himself. Slave concubines, "fancy girls," were as essential to him as his horses and his whisky. Why pay a whore when there are all these female bodies you already own as surely as you own that chair or that cow, all these female bodies at your disposal as surely as you could smash the chair or sell the cow? Other planters had sex with their slaves; you were supposed to keep it dark. Still, everyone had heard the stories about Thomas Jefferson and that High Yellow of his, Sally Hemings. They said she was also his dead wife's half sister, but it wasn't nice to talk about it, certainly not around ladies, or in Middle Florida society, where Jefferson's grandson, the upright Francis Eppes, was intendant of the new capital.

Everyone had heard the stories about Achille Murat, too. He didn't bother being discreet. When he went to Louisiana in the 1840s to speculate in sugar, he wrote cheerfully to his sister Letizia that he had got himself an octoroon *placée* to play with, "a good woman." He figured slaves saw getting screwed by the master as a treat, not abuse. He called it "a sort of compensation for their servitude." Black women weren't hung up on virginity and chastity and the Angel in the House thing like white women: "It is in vain that the *modest blushes* of young Negresses is hidden by the color of their skin," said Achille archly.

In the yard at Lipona there must have been several children with café au lait skin and the Bonaparte nose. If Catherine felt betrayed, appalled, insulted, and hurt, she didn't say so. Ladies didn't discuss it, except maybe in whispers or in entries in their diaries or in angry coded letters. But she must have known. About the women at Lipona, the woman in New Orleans, and the one in East Florida. The one who died.

Achille bought his first plantation from Moses Levy, twelve hundred acres for $1,960. Apparently he got an erotic charge out of owning some of Levy's land, some *Arabian Nights* thrill. He wrote to his mother back in dull old Austria, recounting the delicious (but largely fabricated) story of how Moses' mother, Rachel Levy, was a teenage English girl, kidnapped by Barbary pirates and sold to Jacoub ben Youli, ruler of Fez. Ben Youli installed her in his seraglio. After a couple of years she had a child, rather pointedly named Moses. Eventually there was some sort of uprising in Morocco, giving Rachel a chance to escape with her baby to the West Indies. The Countess of Lipona must have been amused: Her son usually just wrote asking for money, which, of course, he used to set up his own seraglio.

In the spring of 1824, Achille bought a girl at the slave market in St. Augustine. She was fourteen years old and her name was Mary. He paid $500 for her. At that price, more than a quarter of what all of Parthenope cost, she must have been what the traders called a "prime article"—a virgin, pretty, with silky hair and light skin, nearly white. By autumn that year, Mary was pregnant.

While Achille was away, discussing metaphysics with Ralph Waldo Emerson (whom he had met in St. Augustine) and trying to talk the Marquis de la Fayette into relocating to Florida, Mary fell under the influence of Achille's sworn enemy, a priest whom he'd denounced as a charlatan and a fraud in a fit of Jacobin anticlericalism. The priest would ride out to Parthenope and talk to Mary about sin and expiation. He convinced her that God was punishing her for giving in to Achille's lusts—as if a slave had a choice. Raised a Christian, a Catholic, she was tormented. She was an affront to the Queen of Heaven, whose name she bore. The priest told her everyone knew that Achille was planning to sell both her and the child. The child would be even whiter than she, worth a lot of money in St. Augustine or New Orleans, especially if it was a girl. Mary knew what happened to white Negro women. Achille would use the money to buy more fancy girls, make a new harem.

As the wild plums, the oxalis, and the pink almond bloomed in the St. Johns country, Achille still wasn't back. Mary sat in the cabin at Parthenope, saying the Rosary and staring east. In early summer she gave birth. It was a girl. Mary looked at the baby once, then strangled her. A few days later Mary died. Maybe she fell sick with puerperal fever; maybe she killed herself. Nobody knows. Achille returned to Parthenope to find his lover and their baby buried in a patch reserved for slaves. He said nothing about the death of their baby, the granddaughter of a queen, the great-niece of the conqueror of half of Europe, born into slavery in Florida. He did comment on the death of his fifteen-year-old fancy girl, saying, "Had she been white, I would have written a touching novel about her."

"Parthenope" means "virgin voice." In Homer, Odysseus goes sailing by the Italian coast, near the future site of Achille's lost kingdom. Sitting on her lonely rock, the siren Parthenope sees him and falls in love with him. When Parthenope fails to lure him overboard to join her, she jumps into the sea and drowns.

Savages

In 1835 Jane Broward and Rufus Tucker went on a Christmas junket to Tallahassee. The pine and cypress house down near the Ochlockonee was just about finished, so they left it with Sarey, one of the slaves that had been Jane's wedding present. They stayed at the City Hotel, danced at a Christmas ball, and ate pickled lobster.

Jane missed conversation. The deep forest was all silence, punctuated occasionally by an hawk's cry, a hog's grunting, a woodpecker's racket, an ax blade on a tree trunk. Town, thank God, was all talk: about the railroad that would get the cotton down to the port at St. Marks, about the big house Ben Chaires was building east of town, practically a palace, they said, with thirteen rooms and ten columns and marble everywhere, about the governor's wife, Peggy O'Neale Eaton, a Washington party girl whose laugh was just a little too loud, whose décolletage just a little too low, and who had too many men friends. There was a scandal. Her husband, Secretary of War John Eaton, resigned from the cabinet, and it was thought best if they made themselves scarce. President Andrew Jackson appointed him governor of Florida.

Florida was getting a reputation as a place for people who needed a new start, people like Mrs. Eaton or Achille Murat. The prince, who liked to be called "Colonel," went around with a large, filthy St. Bernard dog that smelled like a tobacco barn. He loved his chaw, but since both Princess Murat and her snooty Virginian mother hated the stuff, he wasn't allowed to have a spittoon in the house. He used the dog instead.

Broward family lore has it that Jane was introduced to Princess Murat (addressed as "Madame") at a tea given by one of Tallahassee's political hostesses, the town's first lobbyists. It's possible. The Whigs and the Democrats competed over everything in Florida: organizing the banks, financing the railroads, parceling out the land. Over macaroons and ratafia, the ladies of the DuVal, Branch, and Gamble families made sure that the Browards and the Tuckers were on their side, politically correct on such issues as restricting the movements of free Negroes and pushing the Seminoles—who were a bad influence on all the Negroes, free and slave—off the peninsula. In other words, good Jackson Democrats.

Jane was eating sugarplums with the princess and the plantation dames and Rufus out pricing mules and slaves when word of the massacre of Major Francis Dade and his men reached Tallahassee. So much for the New Year's parties. Everyone was scared. Everyone knew about Green Chaires's wife and babies, murdered and mutilated by Seminoles. Or that poor lady up at Horsehoe Plantation. Everyone repeated what Jackson had once written to the governor of Pensacola, whipping himself into a frenzy with the hideous prospect of "helpless women massacred and the cradle crimsoned with blood." Everyone had heard that Osceola threatened he would take Tallahassee and dance the Green Corn Dance in the middle of town.

Rufus was an able-bodied fellow of twenty-six who knew his way around a rifle and a swamp. He may have joined Governor Richard Keith Call's Florida militia in 1836. But my great-aunts, though always ready to advertise the Tuckers, Robertses, and Browards (there were votes in it when one of the boys was running for office), never told a story about Rufus the Seminole Fighter. It could be that in that first rush of war, he sent Jane to stay with the Browards in East Florida, where they'd solved their Indian problem thirty years before by starving them out. Or he might have left her in the Ochlockonee house with a shotgun and a bowie knife and rode off to be heroic.

Achille Murat was certainly there, riding south with his friend Richard Keith Call toward the Cove of the Withlacoochee. Achille hoped to catch or kill one of the chiefs, Micanopy or Wildcat or, even better, the charismatic Osceola. The newspapers compared Osceola with Francis Marion, the "Swamp Fox," who fought a guerrilla war against the British in South Carolina, or even Napoléon. Achille would show them no savage compared with a Bonaparte.

Feats of arms aside, Achille fretted about what there was to eat in the wilderness. The militiamen refused to touch the wild hogs that roamed the Withlacoochee country because the hogs, indiscriminate carnivores, had been feasting on the flesh of dead Seminoles killed in skirmishes with whites. The hogs ate dead American soldiers, too. Achille blithely barbecued a pork shank on his campfire and declared it delicious. Richard Keith Call was impressed with his cold-bloodedness. Of course, Achille was also the man who tried to create a good recipe for buzzard. He gave up after several dinner-party disasters, declaring of the buzzard, "He is no good."

It seems most likely Rufus never got the chance to try the prince's cooking. Jane was pregnant, so if he ever went off to kill Seminoles, he didn't stay away long. Soon enough Seminoles became as rare as Mohicans. In 1835 there were around six thousand living in Florida. Seven years later there were only three hundred. Over four thousand were captured and deported to Arkansas. The others were killed. Though the Second Seminole War officially ended in 1842, the Seminoles never surrendered. Instead, they went underground and the U.S. government just sort of gave up. The war had cost $20 million. The last of the *cimarrones,* led by chiefs Sam Jones and Billy Bowlegs, holed up in the Big Cypress Swamp, a thick-aired, gator-plagued bog in the southwest of the territory, or else over by the Atlantic, where the soil was useless, nothing but sand, and so far down the peninsula that Christians would never covet an inch of it.

In our swamp, between the Sopchoppy River and Thousand Yard Bay, Seminoles became just a by-the-fire tale about warriors and magic, soldiers and scalpings. My father told how his grandmother told how her grandmother Jane Broward would scare the children good by describing how Osceola could turn into a bear and carry young 'uns away on his back. Sometimes at the old house on Red Lake where Granddaddy Roberts lived, they'd be fishing and see a bear come down to drink. And they'd look at each other, thinking maybe that was him, Osceola, come home to Florida.

In 1885 my great-great-grandfather's brother Milton Tucker died, according to the frankly contradictory family record, "invading an island" with his nephew George. They were either "killed by savages off the coast out from Fort Myers, Florida," or "savagely killed off the coast out from Fort Myers, Florida." Milton Tucker and George Tucker were then "put on a raft and burned in the Gulf of Mexico." My father, named for Milton Tucker, said it was Indians that killed him. He didn't say which Indians. Or which island.

There are dozens of islands near Fort Myers where the Caloosahatchee, the Myakka, and the Peace Rivers spill out into the lower Gulf: Cayo Costa, Gasparilla (named after pirate José Gaspar), Captiva, Sanibel. I'm guessing Sanibel. The Calusas ambushed Juan Ponce de León there on his first Florida trip. Several died, and in the way that the Spanish like to mark places of death on the map, Juan Ponce named the place Matanzas. It didn't stay Matanzas for long (who would want to colonize that?); somebody else called it after Santa Isabella, which morphed over time into Sanibel. Now the place is choked with high-end tourists in Tommy Bahama beach casuals, toting Wilson rackets and factor 30 sunblock. In the 1880s it was a green and silent barrier island, palms and vines in a rococo tangle in the middle, glittering sand around the edges, and clear sky all the way to the state of Vera Cruz. Fort Myers had been a stockade during the Seminole Wars and a Union stronghold during the Civil War, but, until somebody found phosphate in the Peace River in 1881, the place was a blank on the map.

The Tuckers may have been mining phosphate. Or they could have just gone fishing. The Third Seminole War had ended in 1858. Milton, Jane and Rufus's fifth and youngest son, was six at the time. It wasn't much of a war, more of a set of skirmishes, ignited in 1855 when a bunch of American soldiers hacked down Chief Billy Bowlegs's prized banana trees in the Big Cypress Swamp. Just as in the second and first wars, the Seminoles didn't surrender. What remained of them just bored ever deeper into the Everglades and the Ten Thousand Islands. But maybe there was one last renegade band living on Sanibel, one last band that had cleared a Creek Squareground, with its north, south, east, and west alignments, for dancing. They'd be drinking the holly brew still, and performing the Green Corn Dance in gourd masks, and guarding the medicine bundles with their sacred objects and objects of power. I can see Milton Tucker, who'd never been afraid of water or jungles or anything that lived there, who'd marched off with his brother Luther to the Battle of Natural Bridge, even though he was only thirteen, rowing over to Sanibel and doing something or seeing something he shouldn't have.

There's a tantalizing scrap of family legend about us being part Creek. A very, very small part, true, courtesy of Great-Great-Great-Great-Grandmother Quirta Jerusha Kirby Revell. Pretty much all Southerners claim to "have some Indian" in them: It gives us that backwoodsman, tracker-hunter-shaman cred that makes us (we think) closer to the land. Quirta Jerusha Kirby's father's kin go back to Yorkshire in the sixteenth century, yeoman farmers who eventually got rich enough to buy a coat of arms and call their place "Kirby Hall." But her mother, Margaret Brown, lived with the Qualla Creeks in Carolina as a child in the 1760s. Quirta Jerusha was born in 1796. She married Stephen Revil (the Wakulla County bunch spell it Revell) in 1812. By 1850 the Revells had almost all left the Darlington District of South Carolina for Florida, thriving on the western side of the Ochlocknonee below the Black Cat Islands and the Indian Creek Islands, just this side of Queens Bay. Margaret Maria Revell, Quirta Jerusha and Stephen's third child, had married a farmer named Ephraim Vaux or Vause (in Wakulla County it's Vause) from an old, maybe Huguenot English, family. The Revells wrote back to their Vause kin: "The dew in Florida is like the rain in Carolina. Come on down."

Margaret Maria and Ephraim Vause's daughter Harriet Jerusha married Rufus and Jane's son Luther Tucker. Harriet Jerusha and Luther Tucker's daughter Mary Elizabeth married Valarious Lafayette Roberts. Their grandson Milton was my father. When my parents lived in Miami in 1957, they'd drive out the Tamiami Trail to the "Indian Village" west of Sweetwater. My father liked the alligator wrestling, and my mother liked to watch the Seminole ladies making patchwork skirts with every color in the paintbox in them, covered in ruffles and rickrack, and so reasonably priced.

3

Still Longing for the Old Plantation

MY CHILDHOOD IS HAUNTED by houses, some seen, some just rumors.

Harwood, the last of the Lake Jackson plantations, was across the road. It was a broad, dingy, square-columned place encroached upon by wisteria and sticky vine. Harwood looked deserted, but it wasn't. Millard Caldwell, who had been governor in the late 1940s, rattled around in there with his faint-looking wife. The Caldwells were waited on by a black family who lived in a paintless cabin nearby. The black family would let me come look at their particolored chickens—bantams, Dominickers—scratching around uncooped in their precisely raked dirt yard. My father had been at Leon High School with their daughters, so the Caldwells didn't mind if I ran around their woods digging wild violets.

There were other houses left from slavery days: the Grove, huddling in a mantle of magnolias as tire dealers and furniture stores sprang up around it downtown; and Waverly, now surrounded by a subdivision of split levels and French provincials; and Goodwood, its silver door hinges tarnished and frescoes of Aesop's fables crumbling in the North Florida damp.

Then there were houses that were only memories, mine or somebody else's: Pine Hill, Verdura, Casa Bianca, burned down, torn down, paved over to make malls and "planned communities" or just abandoned to entropy, foundations of slave-made brick covered in kudzu, marble mantels stolen, timbers rotted and gone back to the wine-dark soil that had made their owners rich in the first place.

The land my father built our house on—our unromantic, uncolumned, unnamed, Miami-windowed ranch house—had once been planted in corn and Sea Island cotton by Robert Butler, a Philadelphian who had soldiered with Andrew Jackson at the Battle of New Orleans in 1815. He later became surveyor general of the Florida territory, geometer of the peninsula. His acres fanned out over the wide clay hills east to Lake Jackson where he built a showplace on the bluff. In the 1850s Colonel Butler would hold all-night parties he called "Feasts of Roses." He'd sing "My Boy Tommy" and "The Twa Corbies" while his tail-coated butler dipped apple toddy out of a tub on the porch for the gentlemen or poured glasses of champagne for the ladies. They would dance in the hall under an Irish chandelier that had traveled down by mule cart from Philadelphia, each prism wrapped in muslin. The windows were open on the colonel's flower beds one way and his citrus grove the other, the scent of Malmaisons hanging in the air like a spell. At midnight, they'd eat dinner.

Colonel Butler's fine house has disappeared as completely as Troy. The site of his flower garden is now occupied by a stuccoed minimansion with a swimming pool on a quarter acre of thick-bladed St. Augustine grass. All that's left of his cotton kingdom is an irrigation ditch his slaves dug in the 1840s along the valley of a steephead stream. The stream is lined with redbud and beech, maidenhair and Venushair ferns. You can walk along the tops of the ditches to the place where he had his gristmill. It's in the woods, not far from an Indian mound the young people liked to picnic on. They called it the Mound of

Dreams. Where once you could hear the plantation economy grinding away by day and the clink of Bohemian glass at planters' tables by night, the only sound now is the flutter of lake water and the wind in the beeches like the rustle of silk skirts across the years.

In my family, we have an invisible house of our own. It appeared and disappeared in Washington County, built by my great-great-grandfather John Wesley Gilbert for his wife, Roxanne Bradford. Their daughter Blanche—the Gilberts call her Aunt Bankie—was born there in 1860. She said it had seven or eight rooms, high rolled-glass windows, a few pieces of English silver on the sideboard, and broad heart-pine floors the color of tupelo honey. Her nephew, my grandfather Bradford Gilbert, doubted it was as fancy as all that, but it would have been what he called a "gentry house," the house of a young fellow on his way up in 1852, a young fellow with every expectation that he would make a bigger and bigger crop and buy more slaves and add on to the house, maybe a two-story portico, as the South got richer and richer and cotton topped twenty cents a pound.

The trouble is, nobody knows where the house was. There is no chimney or foundation left. There is no photograph or drawing. It is marked on no map. So the house moves around like a wandering ghost, from Orange Hill to Oakie Ridge to Davis Branch. The house had a short life, anyway; by 1866 or 1867 it was gone. But Aunt Bankie told my grandfather she remembered playing with her mother's coral beads on the floor of the bedroom. Aunt Bankie also said she remembered when Union troops came by after burning the Episcopalian church in Marianna, twenty miles away. Roxanne and the children, Mary Etta, Charles, John, Roxy, and Blanche, hid in the woods. Aunt Bankie always kept a .32 pistol under her pillow, an old naval officer's sidearm she bought at a pawn shop in Panama City. After she died in 1939, she left her nephews $5,000 in gold pieces, which she had buried in snuff cans around her house on Hard Labor Creek.

I spent summers with my Gilbert grandparents in Chipley, just up the road from Orange Hill and Gilbert's Mill. We'd take cane poles and a cup of wigglers and ride out to the farm that had belonged to Aunt

Bankie's little brother Zet—my great-grandfather—to fish. Wearing big, sweat-stained straw hats that tied under the chin, my grandmother and I would wobble into this little skiff with Great-Aunt Elia and row out into the middle of a pale green pond full of cypress knees. Aunt Elia had bad eyes and wore what looked like aviator sunglasses, even at night, but she could sure catch bream.

My grandmother and great-aunt would sit there in their flowered cotton dresses, stockings, and lace-up brogues (sometimes Grandmama wore a pair of old gloves long past their church days), baiting hooks. And I'd ask them—again—to tell me about the house, John Wesley and Roxanne's house. My grandfather and Aunt Elia and Uncle Fred, my grandfather's brother, kept changing their story. One minute the house sat where that stand of laurel oaks is now, on the rise above the millstream, or else it was a mile away on Orange Hill, either just above the little cemetery where John Wesley and Roxanne and two of the slaves are buried, or else right at the top, where on sharp November days you can almost see down to the Gulf of Mexico. The house had a fanlight over the front door, brought from Savannah, or maybe it was little squares of colored glass; the house had a deep porch or maybe dormer windows; the house had a staircase with a mahogany bannister, or, possibly, maple.

There's unanimity on the roses. John Wesley took a hand out of the field for a day to help him plant old varieties of roses, the ones that smell good, for Roxanne Bradford, who was seventeen and pregnant. John Wesley was prouder of Roxanne's ancestors than she was, proud that his children and grandchildren would be descendants of William Bradford the Pilgrim. My grandfather Bradford Gilbert would say that John Wesley had big plans.

At the end of the Civil War or just after, the house went up in flames. There are, of course, competing accounts. The house burned because the cook tumped over a pan of hot lard, which exploded; or a vengeful ex-slave lit a piece of fat wood under the house and fed the fire with the last bottle of old Madeira that George Washington Gilbert, a drinking Methodist, had brought from Carolina; or Sister Mary, who was always cold-natured, stood too close to the parlor hearth at her wedding and set her veil on fire. She survived (her hair was never the same), but the house, framed in pitch pine, went up like kindling.

Pine Hill

It's not that there was nothing. There were the abandoned cornfields and deserted villages of the Red Sticks—sometimes not so deserted. There were the ruins of the missions with their talismanic names, half Spanish, half Apalachee: Santa Maria de los Ángeles de Arapaha, San Carlos de Yatcatani, Purificación de Tama. There were the trees and the rivers and the lakes.

Still, for the on-the-up white people coming down from Virginia or over from the West Indies or across the Atlantic, Middle Florida was the chaos out of which they would create order, the abysmal darkness into which they'd bring light. They would utter, *"Fiat Arcadia!,"* and the land would be cleared and planted with cotton and worked by Africans named Caesar and Cleopatra, Pompey and Juno. Onto this green emptiness houses as awe-inspiring as the Temple of Jupiter Optimus Maximus would appear in groves of oak and yaupon. A new golden age would begin at the farthest reach of America.

The hills between the Choctawhatchee and the Suwannee birthed cash crops fast. Rich as Christmas pudding, the dirt beneath their feet allowed the emigrés—some bored with overrefined Richmond or Charleston, some younger sons with no prospects, some poor white trash looking for the big score—to write their fantasies on the tabula rasa of Florida. One minute they're hacking down a gum and scrub oak jungle, eating boiled possum and sleeping on a Spanish moss mattress in a shack with chinks big enough to let in every mosquito from Savannah to Port of Spain, the next they're ordering chandeliers and champagne from Philadelphia, eating green turtle soup at a restaurant with a genuine New Orleans Frenchman for a chef, and dressing up as Mary Queen of Scots or Harry Hotspur at a costume ball. Instant aristocracy: just add a ready source of water, banks offering limitless credit, and a bull market in textiles, tobacco, sugar, and slaves.

In 1845 the United States Congress admitted Florida to the Union. The population was nearly 58,000, split almost evenly between whites and blacks. In the governor's race that year, William Dunn Moseley, a North Carolinian, a former schoolteacher with a plantation on Lake Miccosukee, beat Richard Keith Call, a Virginian, a veteran of the Second Seminole War with plantations on Lake Jackson and near Tallahassee. At Moseley's inauguration, victorious Democrats unfurled Florida's first statehood flag. It had five horizontal stripes: blue, orange, red, white, green. On the orange stripe rests a banner reading "LET US ALONE."

For a people whose lives turned on the realities of rain and frost, boll weevils and cotton tariffs, puerperal fever and malaria, the planters did their damnedest to live a literary dream. The whitewash barely dry on their Doric columns, they fashioned for themselves a world copied out of poems about the Middle Ages and novels about the British landed gentry. Florida lacked a past, or so they thought, so they imported one, just as they imported marble fireplaces from Naples or silver knives from London. They imagined an Italy out of Byron's poetry or a Highlands out of *The Scottish Chiefs* in a state where the only ancient temples were Indian mounds and the highest land was at most three hundred feet above sea level.

There was the May Pole dancing and the dressing up as "Night" or "La Belle France" for parties. A week before Christmas, there was the Ring Tournament. The young gents would deck themselves (and their horses) out in tin armor and dyed ostrich plumes cadged from their mothers' and sisters' hats. They gave themselves noms de guerre such as "the Knight of Tuscawilla," "the Unknown Knight," or "the Knight of the Sun, Moon and Stars." They'd congregate in a valley near the Betton Plantation on the edge of Tallahassee (near the current site of the Miracle Movie Theater) and joust. Susan Bradford devotes page after gooey page to the Ring Tournament in *Through Some Eventful Years,* writing of "ladyes faire" and "Sir Knights," wishing that she had "an enchanted pen from fairyland instead of this prosaic typewriter."

The tournament was a plantation dating ritual, the boys showing off for the girls. The Red Hills debutantes, wrapped in velvet and furs, sat in carriages waving silk scarves as the boys charged with wooden lances that Uncle Ned or Old Sam, way beyond being surprised at white folks' weird notions of amusement, had planed and whittled for them back at the plantation sawmill. The object was to thrust the lance through a small ivory ring hanging from a tree branch a hundred yards away. Whoever speared the ring first chose got to choose the "Queen of Love and Beauty."

One year there was an ice storm in December, killing Colonel Robert Butler's orange crop. The red mud in the valley had a thick crust of ice, slick as polished rosewood. But the "Chivalry of Middle Florida," as Susan Bradford calls them, would not be daunted by mere weather. Everyone had already made their costumes.

Still, it was nasty out there. One of the Gamble sisters slid down the bank into a large puddle, breaking the ice that covered it, ruining the calfskin boots her father had brought her from New York. Then the strawberry roan ridden by El Cabellero de Esperanza, also known as William Moseley, Jr., son of the former governor, skidded and did a complete somersault, landing El Caballero in the freezing mud. His blue velvet outfit was ruined, and almost as bad, he lost the tournament to the Knight of the Lake, Robert Hall of Lake Hall Plantation, who got to crown Miss Dora Triplett of Lebanon Plantation Queen of Love and Beauty for 1851.

Susan Bradford never made Queen of Love and Beauty, or even Maid of Honor (the runner-up knight's pick). She was only thirteen when Florida seceded and the "knights" went off to fight for real. Susan was almost the same age as the state of Florida itself. For her birthday on March 8, 1854, she got her first diary:

> *Mother says I write well enough, so she has given me this book and Father has sharpened a pencil for me to write with.*

Two days later Susan got her first slave:

> *March 10, 1854: at first I could not believe grandpa had sent me that little girl; but he really had. I am not sure yet that I like my present but of course*

I will for did not grandpa think she was a nice present? I asked Mother what she was for and she said she would be my maid and wait on me.

Susan had just turned eight years old. Frances, her birthday present, was five.

Susan Branch Bradford was born in the Big House at Pine Hill Plantation. Her father was Edward Bradford, a doctor who brought his household (brothers, books, furniture, slaves, aunts) from North Carolina to Middle Florida in 1831. Her mother, Martha Branch, was the daughter of Governor John Branch, master of Live Oak Plantation. Susan called herself a "blue-blooded child of the Old South." She believed that people like her, people with ancestors (she was descended from William Bradford the Pilgrim, too, same as Roxanne Bradford), people who owned old Duncan Phyfe chairs, Sèvres china, and leather-bound (but much-read) copies of *The Aeneid, The Pilgrim's Progress,* and *The Complete Works of Shakespeare,* people who owned land, people who owned slaves—they were the natural ruling class. She believed that slavery was ordained by God and the Constitution. Free the slaves and the next thing you know there'll be orgies, craziness, no rules: "freedom from matrimonial bonds, then freedom from the constraints laid by the Holy Bible on the passions of human-kind."

Cousin Susan was a dramatic speechifier. As a lot of her fans in the United Daughters of the Confederacy said, she should have been in politics. If she were alive now, she'd be one of those pastel-suited ladies from the Eagle Forum who stalk the hallways of the Florida Capitol, sugar-accented, pink-smiled, lobbying in the nicest possible way against equal pay on the grounds that it's antithetical to traditional wife- and motherhood. She would talk about personal responsibility and scold black people, sweetly, for their affirmative action fecklessness. Maybe she would be Katherine Harris.

Both Susan Bradford and Katherine Harris grew up on large chunks of prime Florida real estate, both had rich granddaddies who gave them things (or, in Susan's case, people), both love "culture" (preferably European), both love Jesus, both have hides like you'd find on a hundred-year-old alligator. In 1926, when Susan published her diary, she was still insisting that the Confederacy was right and that everything was the fault of Harriet Beecher Stowe, the liberals, and ungrateful ex-slaves. In 2002, when Katherine Harris published *Center of the Storm,* her vote recount bust-up memoir, she was still insisting that the 2000 election went just fine from her end and everything was the fault of Al Gore, the liberals, and the ungrateful media.

Susan Bradford explains that 1. Florida planters were exemplary Christians; 2. therefore Florida slaves were happy; and 3. the Civil War ruined the paradise that was Florida. Katherine Harris explains that 1. George W. Bush won the 2000 election fair and square; 2. she was not political; 3. she is an exemplary Christian; and 4. the press didn't understand her—or Florida.

During the 2000 recount, reporters fell hook, line, and sinker for the easy stereotype of Katherine Harris as a Southern belle who really shouldn't be worrying her pretty little head about no silly old presidential election, Scarlett out of her depth, Talking Republican Barbie saying only what the Bushes told her to say. But if you got close enough, you could see how cold the eyes were, how focused. The Fauvist makeup everyone fixated on couldn't disguise the determined jaw, hard as alabaster. If a Yankee broke into her Tara, she'd shoot him without a second thought.

You see a similar expression in the photograph of Susan Bradford at sixteen, aloof and almost fierce, standing there in her best day dress, velvet cuffs and wide belt cinching her little waist. It's 1863. The Confederates recently won a battle at Chickamauga, but not much else. Her cousin Richard Bradford has been killed at the Battle of Santa Rosa Island. Lincoln has issued the Emancipation Proclamation. She stares at the camera, unsmiling, holding a small book—a Bible? her diary?—stiffly in one hand. She looks strangely like my grandfather Bradford Gilbert in his World War I portrait, made when he was nineteen. The kinship is far-off, indirect, but if you lined up the pictures they could be brother and sister, the same narrow eyes, the same horizontal brows, the same sternness: two young Floridians at war.

To hear Susan tell it—and she did tell it, over and over, not just in

Through Some Eventful Years, but in a volume of poetry and the semi-sociological *Negro of the Old South*—Middle Florida in the 1840s and 1850s represented the acme of slave societies, created ex nihilo by the old colonial stock of the Upper South who had, after all, two hundred years of practice being aristocrats. No one went hungry. Even lazy white trash could depend on the generosity of the gentry. Susan calls Pine Hill "God's Country," with lapis lazuli lakes and gardens full of crape myrtle and jasmine, and pastures full of Alderney cows, which, she says, "furnished the richest of cream and the yellowest of butter for the inmates of the mansion."

After the War (in which God seems, perversely, to have abandoned his country), the cream wasn't so rich or the butter so yellow. But in Susan's childhood Arcadia, at Christmas, everybody, white and black, feasted on brandy cakes, mince pies, lemon tarts, and syllabub. On the Fourth of July, everybody, white and black, went to a barbecue.

Susan had every reason to expect that she would be married at Pine Hill, wearing a pearl tiara as nice as the one her father gave her sister Margaret when she married Amos Whitehead of Mossview Plantation. Then her life would focus on her house, her husband, her children, her slaves. But until then Susan, the last Bradford daughter at Pine Hill, would be the remembrancer, the recorder, the celebrant. She would paint Florida as "fairyland." And no one was ordinary in Fairyland. That dark-eyed boy Susan liked from L'Eau Noir Plantation over on Lake Lafayette wasn't just another cadet at the West Florida Seminary, but Thomas Jefferson's great-grandson. Catherine Murat, mistress of the small cotton plantation of Bellevue, wasn't just the widow of an unhygienic, debt-laden, slave-seducing alcoholic, but a princess of France with an allowance from Napoléon III and servants in Bonaparte livery.

Even governesses were as good as romance novels. The Bradfords had hired a Miss Letitia Damer to educate Susan and her cousins. Miss Damer had a head of chestnut curls the girls envied, one big curl looped over her forehead. She had a secret, too: All these strange letters she got, letters that made her cry. But she managed to make the curriculum—*Willard's Universal History, Boyd's Rhetoric, Brewer's Science of*

Things Familiar—interesting. She showed them how to roll pine cones in flour to make them look snowy for Christmas tree decorations. She organized a Shakespeare Club so that the bright young things of the Red Hills could play Rosalind and Viola, Orlando and Orsino, Juliet and Romeo.

One day Susan and Cousin Alice got to looking at the portrait of George IV in their history book and decided that he looked just like Miss Damer. Or rather, she looked just like him, only prettier, same large Hanoverian nose, same thick hair concentrated on the forehead ("a family mark," Miss Damer had said once in her mysterious way). Confronted with the picture, Miss Damer came over all tragic and claimed that her mother was the king's daughter by Maria Fitzherbert, the Catholic he had married illegally. Susan's mother said they weren't allowed to ask what she was doing in a Florida schoolroom, four thousand miles from the nearest castle. Everyone was much impressed. Miss Damer got invited to the best houses in the county. Drinking tea with the kinfolk of Napoléon Bonaparte and Thomas Jefferson was fine; being taught algebra by a descendant of William the Conqueror was better.

The thing about Fairyland or Arcadia or Eden is that you don't get to live there forever. The place is always evanescent. Your stay is always temporary. There is always a serpent in the garden. In Middle Florida, there were Seminoles and sickness and abolitionists. Despite the grand houses and the cotton wealth that bought their pearls and their Scott and their silver and their silks, the planters' dreamworld was always in danger of demolition. During the last days of the Red Sticks, a woman called Mrs. Dorcas was scalped and left for dead in the Pine Hill woods. Susan and her cousins would ride out and look for the spot. In 1841 the Yellow Jack came, carried by the female of the *Aedes aegypti* mosquito. More than a hundred died from Port St. Joc to Madison.

In May 1843 an arsonist (they never found out who) burned Tallahassee to the ground: shops, hotels, houses, livery stables, newspaper offices, almost all the little town except the capitol and the Presbyterian church. Early that morning a girl whose father owned the Planters

Hotel told her older sister she had this nightmare: a great triangle hung in the sky over Tallahassee, like the one on the dollar bill, only in place of the All-Seeing Eye were the words "Cursed of the Lord."

There were signs and portents, all bad. In 1833 the stars fell and white people said the slaves thought it was the end of the world. The slaves said no such luck. A few years later a total eclipse of the sun made the midday sky dark as jet. Susan said the slaves thought it was the Day of Judgment. If it was the Day of Judgment, the slaves said among themselves, it would be the white folks who got judged.

The Bradfords soon had governess problems. Miss Damer inherited a fortune and took her quasi-royal self off to London. Her New England replacements kept turning out to be crypto-abolitionists. Miss Julia Parkman Young would be caught crying over the slaves (she told Susan to call it "weeping" instead of "crying"), while Miss Cornelia Platt would sneak out to midnight meetings where she exhorted the slaves to rise up and torch the plantations, including Pine Hill. The Bradfords didn't discover she was a seditionist until one of the Bradford slaves told on her—at least, that's what Susan says. Mrs. Bradford bought her a one-way ticket to New York and had her deposited at the train station under escort. Even the Frenchman who came once a week to improve the Bradford girls' accents was suspected of reading William Lloyd Garrison's *The Liberator*.

A friend brought Edward Bradford a copy of *Uncle Tom's Cabin*. He read it, then threw it in the fire. Susan writes,

> *I wanted to read that book myself but it must have ben a bad book for Father, who loves books, to have treated it that way.*

But the novel, now in its 130th edition, wouldn't leave Susan alone, nor would "Fred Douglass," as she calls him. To Susan's disgust, Harriet Beecher Stowe went to much-publicized dinner parties with duchesses in London and met princes in Paris and made thousands and thousands of dollars.

White people were getting nervous in 1856 and 1857, seeing abolitionists everywhere. Dr. Bradford went to meetings in Tallahassee. Ten-year-old Susan played with Lavinia, one of her Christmas presents. At first when Susan writes about Lavinia, you think it's a doll:

Aunt Dinah says she will take care of it for me and I can have it to play with whenever I want it. Mother says Lulu can make me a trunk full of clothes for my baby and I can keep the trunk in my doll house and when I want the baby to play with, we can get her and giver her a bath in the blue tub she has given me and dress her in the clothes from the trunk.

Then you realize Lavinia is a real child, the slave Dinah's child. Susan owns Dinah, so Susan also owns Lavinia.

In 1859 news of John Brown's raid on Harpers Ferry reached Florida. The planters thought it might be the apocalypse this time. Susan cries in her diary on October 18:

What will become of us? Will our Father in Heaven let us be destroyed? Will the people we have always loved put the torch to our homes and murder us when we seek to escape? This is what John Brown was urging them to do.

So much for Fairyland. The Bradfords' "dear black folks" suddenly seemed sinister. How many Nat Turners lurked out in the quarters? Lulu, Susan's nurse, was all right, and Dinah, but Frances, Susan's eighth birthday present, Frances, whom Susan was teaching to read (until her mother made her quit), asked Susan, "Do you understand what this is all about?"

Susan said she didn't. Frances laughed, a "crazy" laugh, according to Susan. Then Frances said, "Yes, you will; you white folks will know a heap you ain't never knowed before."

Susan had nightmares. Abolitionists with horns and cloven hooves, looking the way Uncle Aleck said the Devil looked, chased her across the cotton fields of Pine Hill. Dr. Bradford said she ate too much fruitcake.

Orange Hill

Roxanne Bradford is fifteen years old. Her sister Mary is eleven. There is no boy. There won't be; anyone can see her mother is worn out. Her father's farm made only thirty bales of cotton last season. Isaiah Bradford calls the place a plantation anyway, even though there's no paint on the house. The Bradfords over in Leon County have plantations. They have 7,500 acres, and 275 slaves, and green-shuttered houses three stories high. Roxanne's father owns 120 acres and three slaves, though Old Let is as worn out as her mother. After Old Let makes the biscuits in the morning, she sinks down in the rocker and asks Mrs. Bradford to read from I Corinthians.

Roxanne has never met the Leon County Bradfords. They are cousins removed more times than Isaiah Bradford can count, descended from the Bradfords who left Massachusetts for Virginia, then Carolina, a long time ago, more than a hundred years ago. Isaiah Bradford met Dr. Edward Bradford in Tallahassee once, and called at Pine Hill. Pa said Dr. Bradford has a house full of girls, too, four of them. And no son. One daughter's name is Rebecca, which is Roxanne's second name. A lot of Bradford women have been called Rebecca, Pa says, through Massachusetts where he was born, back to England.

He thinks it's a great thing, being a Bradford. He has a paper with the Bradford coat of arms on it, kept carefully in the back of his Bible. There's a shield with three little bucks' heads in a row and a big buck's head on top. He tells Roxanne and Mary how William Bradford's kin were farmers up in Yorkshire, a hilly, wide-skied country that looks a little like Orange Hill, back when Elizabeth was queen of England. He tells them that William Bradford and the "Saints" left on the *Mayflower,* how they had nothing to eat in the winter of 1621 except what the Indians gave them. It was a deliverance from God, he said.

Roxanne has never been to England. She has never been to Massachusetts. She has never been to Tallahassee. She asked her father if the Pine Hill Bradford girls wore silk dresses. He said he wouldn't know about that, and besides, she should turn her head away from vanity. She has never worn a silk dress.

Roxanne was born in 1835, back in Laurens County, Georgia. She doesn't remember Georgia. They left when Mary was a baby, heading down to Florida in two wagons with old quilts wrapped around the furniture. There was new land in Florida, better land. The big planters didn't have it all yet. Isaiah Bradford read William Bartram's *Travels,* an account of his trip to Florida, published in 1791. Bartram calls Florida "inexpressibly beautiful and pleasing." Florida was also cheap. And unlike Massachusetts, where the apparatus of state had been grinding along for a full two hundred years (often fueled by Bradfords), Florida was a young place, not yet part of the Union. Andrew Jackson had run off the British, the Spanish, and the Indians. Now Florida was a country for white men.

When the Bradfords moved to this high, green ground, full of springs and ponds and wild strawberries, people called it Hickory Hill. But sometime before 1850, the inhabitants got to thinking, like good Floridians, about their image. Anyone can have hickory trees. So they renamed it. The Reverends Herman and Joshua Mercer, Baptist preachers who'd started a church on the hill, favored "Mount Carmel," that being where Elijah challenged the 450 prophets of Baal and the 400 prophets of Asherah to take on *his* god and see who won. But the Methodists and Presbyterians preferred "Orange Hill," evoking perpetual sun, tropicality, plenty. Oranges were not the mundane, peon-picked, mass-market grocery staple they are now. Oranges were for Christmas. Oranges were for weddings. Oranges conjured up the Alcazar gardens of Spain or the royal orchards of Persia. Orange Hill it became. Oranges and satsumas will grow on the hill, but if there's frost and freezing rain or snow—it will snow—the citrus trees have to be tucked in blankets like children in the cold.

Roxanne and Mary go to the Orange Hill Academy, half a mile across their father's fields. The headmaster is the great Reverend Dr. John Newton, a Presbyterian minister from New England who helped found a school over in Walton County. Nobody is sure why he's here, teaching a bunch of Cracker young 'uns in a little slat-board schoolhouse. He comes to the Bradfords for Sunday dinner. He and Isaiah, children of those old text-besotted Puritans, debate the relative righteousness of John Knox and the Wesley brothers. Isaiah is a Methodist. Sometimes Roxanne will be called into the parlor to sing "Lord Randall" or recite a psalm. The Reverend Dr. Newton has taught her enough French that she can translate the Bradford family motto, *"Fier et Sage,"* Proud and Wise. He doesn't waste Latin on girls.

One day the Reverend Dr. Newton was gone, off, they said, to California. It turns out he was an abolitionist, a William Lloyd Garrison man in a West Florida where white people dream of sitting on big front porches watching their slaves picking their cotton on their broad acres, making them money, and all the while feeling clean in the eyes of the Lord.

The Washington and Jackson County planters who'd paid $8 a month tuition (plus $8 for board, $2 for washing, and 50 cents for lamps) at Orange Hill examined their children for signs of ideological pollution. Did Dr. Newton say that Africans were our brothers? Did he say that they were as good as the Anglo-Saxon race? Did he give them any pamphlets to read about Frederick Douglass or Nat Turner or Denmark Vesey? The children remember mostly the algebra and lectures on the Wars of the Roses—white for York? Roxanne doesn't care. She has met a man with hair the red-gold of ripe peaches. He's a Methodist, even.

John Wesley Gilbert has four hundred acres. He has a double-pen log house high on Orange Hill. He's from Brunswick County, North Carolina; all the Gilberts are. They'd been there since before the War of Independence. John Wesley's father and older brother arrived in Washington County in 1845, just in time for statehood. John Wesley appeared in 1848 or 1849. They were all sick of small-patch farming on the rocky Appalachian slopes. They wanted to be planters down on the gentler hills of the Promised Land of Florida, a land to be revived in, a land where even the flag said *Let Us Alone.*

John Wesley Gilbert has two mules, two leased slaves, and a saddle horse. He has a Bible, a hymnbook, and a copy of *The Pilgrim's Progress*. He has a father, William Gilbert, and a blind old-maid sister, Louisa. He has a brother, George Washington Gilbert, who owns good properties on Orange Hill and in the Holmes Valley. John Wesley also has, or so they say, a wife and two little sons back in Brunswick County. The story is that she refused to go south. She said she heard Florida was full of savages and thunderstorms and snakes and insects that took your blood. He said he'd wait for her and the boys in Asheville. He did wait, waited until the convoy of wagons he'd paid to join was ready to leave. Then he rode on without looking back.

If Old Man Gilbert or any of the Gilberts know the truth of the matter, they aren't saying. Mrs. George Washington Gilbert, whose given name is Tabitha, wears a high-crowned bonnet with a green ostrich feather on Sundays. She looks so formidable there in her pew in the Methodist Episcopal church, with her sons William, John, and George beside her, that nobody dares ask for details of the scandal about her nice-looking brother-in-law. Besides, George Washington is known to have a temper.

If Roxanne Bradford has heard the rumors, she isn't saying, either. Now, instead of the Reverend Dr. Newton, John Wesley Gilbert sometimes rides back from church with the Bradfords and stays for Sunday dinner. John Wesley and Isaiah Bradford don't talk about the distinction between predestination and salvation by faith, but seed cotton and feed, the merits of buying land up toward Blue Lake and buying slaves from a trader. Sometimes John Wesley says that even though Florida has only been in the Union for five years, it's time for Florida to leave it. They're talking secession over there in Tallahassee. And Senator Calhoun up in Washington has the right idea. California should be a slave state, all the United States should be free for slaveholding. Isn't that why we fought the British? Isn't that why we took Texas from the Mexicans? In the Bible, Abraham and those old patriarchs had their wives and their children and their flocks and their chattel. You can't go taking slaves away from a man the minute he can afford to buy some. That's not American. But those abolitionists get the churches in Boston and the Congress all stirred up about the African, when everyone knows that the African is as near an animal as anything able to walk and talk at the same time can get.

Roxanne embroiders a dresser cloth, tiny stitches to make lilies of the valley. She says nothing. She listens to her father complain about his poor crop. He's always complaining about his poor crop. He's never had a good one. These Negroes and these girls are eating him out of house and home. She tries to forget what Old Let says about red headed men. John Wesley Gilbert has given her a book of poetry, some by Lord Byron. The Reverend Dr. Newton did not think Byron was suitable for young ladies. Roxanne isn't going back to school. She is grown up.

By the summer of 1851, Roxanne Bradford and John Wesley Gilbert are married. The Reverend Porter David Everett, a Methodist Episcopalian minister, says the words over them in his own dining room. Everett is the biggest planter around and has the best house, a big white becolumned place, the sort of house the Tallahassee cousins must live in. There's a Gilbert family story that the Orange Hill Bradfords invited the Pine Hill Bradfords to the wedding. The Tallahassee cousins didn't come, but they did send a present, a little silver dish. No one knows what happened to it.

Reverend Everett's wife, Miss Bernetta, helped Roxanne with her trousseau, Roxanne's mother being almost bedridden now, turning out some of her own not-so-old lawn dresses and edging two petticoats with Nottingham lace. She gave Roxanne a real silk dress to wear at the wedding, soft pink with *point de Venise* around the neck. The wife and children in Carolina—if they ever existed—are not mentioned.

There's a wreath of orange blossoms on Roxanne's head. There's a necklace of orange-red corals around her neck. Orange and magnolia leaves decorate the mantels. All over the house, there are silver bowls and cut-glass bowls full of oranges and sugared slices of orange on the twelve-egg cake. John Wesley is telling his brother and sister-in-law about the house he's going to build for Roxanne Bradford, a house as fancy as the Everett place, with glass windows tall as she is. Maybe a name, Kenilworth, Little Egypt, or Midlothian. Roxanne would wear silk down to her skin and he would be a plantation gentleman as fine as any in Florida.

Old Folks at Home

Pine Hill is a ghost house. Fifteen years ago it was down to a few bricks tangled in double helixes of potato vines and dewberry briars. Now it's gone. The road to Georgia has been widened. There's a grocery store and a Target for the Range Rover drivers who live in the 8,000-square-foot manors on what had been the Bradford brothers' cotton fields. The Bradford dead lie in their little cemetery behind a strip mall called Plantation Centre.

Other houses live on, cherished like Loire chateaux. You wouldn't think that white columns would get Floridians all stirred up, but they do: Old times here (at least in North Florida) are no more forgotten than in the other remnants of the slave empire. I remember this party in 1966 or 1967 when I was little. I think it was a Tallahassee Garden Club Mother-Daughter Luncheon; I'm not sure. I am sure that it took place at the Grove, the house built by Richard Keith Call in the 1840s. The Grove is as plain as a pine tree, but elegant, with a tall Doric portico. It's a real live plantation house, owned by Mary Call Collins, a real live plantation aristocrat. She had silver teapots and maids in starched aprons. She had a ring made of Andrew Jackson's braided hair.

For the white ladies of Tallahassee, watching the center of the state slip away from them down the peninsula, watching "Florida" come to mean Fort Lauderdale and Biscayne Boulevard, both Mary Call and the Grove were icons of our Southernness, our not-Miaminess. She was the great-granddaughter of a governor and she was married to a governor, LeRoy Collins. The Grove was Old South, but LeRoy Collins was New South, a convert from segregationism to civil rights. He was a Tallahasseean and *one of us,* but he had also, some of the Garden Club ladies said, wrecked his political career by "having his picture made with that Reverend Martin Luther King in Selma, Alabama."

I wasn't thinking about any of this at the Garden Club Mother-Daughter Luncheon. My mother, suited, hatted, shod, and gloved in white and sherbet green, said to me in her low damn-it-I-mean-it voice that I'd better behave myself in Miss Mary Call's house. I did behave. I was in 1855. I was my great-great-grandmother Roxanne Bradford Gilbert, trailing flounced skirts across the polished floor.

We still sing this, somewhat shamefacedly, but it is our state anthem:

Way down upon de Swannee Ribber
Far, far away,
Dere's what my heart is turning ebber,
Dere's wha de old folks stay.
All up and down de whole creation
Sadly I roam,
Still longing for de old plantation
And for de old folks at home.

Stephen Foster wrote the song in 1851, the lament of a displaced slave, desperate to get back to the comforts of the cotton field. Stephen Foster never saw the Suwannee. He never even came to Florida. The original was a paean of praise to the Pee Dee River in South Carolina, but he decided that "Swannee" sounded more mellifluous than "Pee Dee." Not that it matters. Generations of white Floridians have gone all teary-eyed to "Oh, darkies, how my heart grows weary, far from de old folks at home!"

Florida got enlightened in 1978; we substituted "brothers" for "darkies." There were subsequent revisions. At Jeb Bush's second inauguration as governor in 2003, a young black woman gave a moving, nondialect rendition of "Old Folks at Home," except "still longing for the old plantation" came out "still longing for my old connection." Perhaps someone confused Stephen Foster's lyrics with a cell phone commercial.

The throng of Miamians attending the inauguration looked puzzled. What is that song *about*? And why the hell is it so cold here? (January in Tallahassee can be bitter.) Since a Bush spokesperson had asked that the inauguration be "modest," most of them had left their endangered species furs at home and, in a display of becoming simplicity, contented themselves with wearing good Republican mink coats.

The governor was sworn in, watched by his wife, Columba, who didn't want him to run for reelection; his son George P., so dentally gifted it will be a crying waste if he doesn't enter politics; his other son, Jebbie, who became a fixture of the tabloids after he and his girlfriend got caught in the mall parking lot allegedly engaging in Unnatural Practices; and his daughter, Noelle, who got busted for writing her own prescriptions. The governor said he had a dream that one day these state office buildings would be empty of workers. Abolish government. Privatize *everything*.

The minked-up Miamians went wild. The night before, they'd danced in a giant tent on FSU's intramural field at the Black Tie and Blue Jeans Ball, congratulating themselves on achieving a repeat Republican regime, a political feat unmatched since federal troops imposed military rule in Tallahassee back in 1866. Now they're headed over to the mansion for the Inaugural Carnival. The governor's official residence is a copy of Andrew Jackson's Big House, the Hermitage. The 1907 Mansion, the one Napoleon Bonaparte Broward lived in, was torn down and then rebuilt in the mid-1950s. The new one looks almost authentic. You can just imagine the porticos festooned with belles in wedding-mint-colored hoops and parasols. Now it's festooned with nothing but security guards, watching as a guy holds a two-foot alligator over his head. The alligator switches his tail like an annoyed cat, but his jaws are bound with duct tape. A metaphor for Jeb Bush's Florida.

4

The Babies Go to Battle

IN THE SPRING the old man liked to ride down to where the St. Marks River bent like a backward question mark and watch the Johnny Rebs and the Yankees shoot at each other. Sometimes I would drive him there, and we'd stand amid wild plums and dogwoods, looking. He'd seen the fight lots of times but he always enjoyed it; he said it always came out good.

The Battle of Natural Bridge was one of the last and least battles of the Civil War. It kept the capital of Florida from falling into the hands (the *fell hands,* as the great-aunts would put it) of the Federals. By 1865 that didn't really matter. Still, the old man, my grandfather, Papa—named for his daddy who was named for the French aristocrat who wanted to free the South with silkworms and olives, but nonetheless called "Lee" after the Virginia aristocrat who wanted to save the South from freedoms it wouldn't know what to do with—Edgar Lafayette "Lee" Roberts loved the battle. For him, the accountants and the insurance salesmen and the old hippies and the amateur historians and the seafood wholesalers and the IGA managers in their lumpy gray or blue uniforms and their inauthentic eyeglasses and their inauthentic haircuts firing smoky fake muskets at each other across the hot green grass, trying not to giggle when they got "killed," weren't just playing. They were performing a ritual. This is Florida, north and south, white and black, poor and rich, perpetually at war with itself.

Papa could see ghosts. Sometimes he saw two little girls in white dresses, his father's sisters, who died in 1869. They used to follow him a quarter mile down a stretch of road near Carter Branch where they were buried, then disappear into the thick lavender air of evening. Twice at Vause Branch he saw a grown lady in a long black veil—we don't know who she was. His grandfather was here at Natural Bridge on March 6, 1865, "sixteen years old," Papa would say, "a skinny young 'un with a big old head and eyes as blue as deep water." So when Papa looked over toward the sullen St. Marks, I thought he could see Luther Tucker same as he could see me.

In 1865 Luther Tucker was a cadet at the Seminary West of the Suwannee in Tallahassee. Inside College Hall, he studied astronomy, arithmetic, *The Iliad, Henry V,* Virgil's *Georgics*, geography. Outside College Hall, he drilled, marching up and down in the red mud with the other boys, rifles shouldered, flat caps smart on their heads. They were waiting for the war. The war was in Georgia and Alabama and Carolina. The war had been in Marianna and on Santa Rosa Island in West Florida and at St. Augustine and Orchard Pond in East Florida and Key West way down by Cuba. It was time the war visited them. What good was learning geography if the war stayed away?

Two of Luther Tucker's brothers met the war in Virginia. Washington Tucker joined up when he was seventeen, never mind what his daddy, Rufus Tucker, said. Charles Broward Tucker, three years older, had enlisted in "the Wakulla Tigers," Company I, the 5th Florida Regiment, in March 1862. Washington was durned if he'd let Charlie go off without him. Besides, Uncle John's boys over in Duval, their twice-over cousins Pulaski, Washington, and Montgomery Broward, had already got in the war with Marion's Light Artillery in 1861. Uncle John and Aunt Margaret's eldest son, Napoleon Bonaparte Broward, was a captain. Washington Tucker's ardor for war didn't cool even when he heard that cousin Washington Broward had died in the federal prison at Hilton Head, South Carolina. Margaret Tucker Broward sent her sister-in-law (who was also her niece) Jane Broward Tucker a letter tear-run and nib-torn with grief.

Despite clear evidence that war wasn't exactly fun, two of Jane's five sons, Charles Broward and Washington Tucker, marched north just in time for Second Manassas on August 28, 1862. Five days later Washington "fell out of ranks on march," the record said. He was sick with some disease—they never said what—and died shortly after in Middleburg, Virginia.

If he made it out of his teens, Charlie was going to be an officer, all the Browards and the Tuckers said so. Charlie had something about him. And he could fight like hell. They would say that Charlie helped Lee run the Federals out of northern Virginia at Second Manassas and pushed on to Antietam in Maryland. He survived the cold of Fredericksburg in December 1862. He wrote to his mother that the 5th Florida "ain't been whipped yet." He got promoted to corporal in March 1863. But by then it hurt to breathe. They sent him to General Hospital No. 3 in Lynchburg. He had pneumonia. He died on April 19, twenty years old. They couldn't get him home, not with the war tearing up every railway line and taking every mule cart and wagon. The 5th Florida had him buried in the Old City Cemetery in Lynchburg. Jane just wished that he could have died in the Florida Hospital in Richmond with Florida boys, boys he'd been fishing with, boys he went to Methodist Sunday School with, boys who knew the wisteria and salt smell of a spring night at Apalachicola.

On March 4, 1865, messages came over the signal stations from the coast to Tallahassee: There are gunboats at the lighthouse, a Union flotilla is trying to get up the St. Marks River, the Federals have come for Tallahassee bringing, as Susan Bradford scribbled in her diary, *colored troops*.

Everybody who could swing a shovel helped put up breastwork between the Gulf and the capital. There was no real army left. The CSA had withdrawn all but 2,500 troops by 1862—too much war everywhere else. The Florida regiments were in Virginia and Tennessee. A bunch of old men calling themselves the "Gadsden Grays" came over from Quincy. There were a few soldiers on leave, recovering from their wounds. There were a few cavalrymen. But no big divisions, no honed fighting force. There was talk of getting together a company of women who knew how to load and fire a rifle. Governor John Milton called up the Baby Corps, the schoolboys at the seminary who'd never shot at anything deadlier than a deer.

To get in the war, Luther Tucker had to get a note from his mama. All the cadets did. Even though his daddy, Rufus Tucker, was off with the Home Guard somewhere, and Charlie and Washington were dead, even though she was home alone with little Franklin and Sarey's girl Lucy, Jane Tucker said yes. Maybe she thought it was the duty of Browards and Tuckers to sacrifice themselves for Florida. Maybe she figured he'd go anyway, forge her name or something. So Luther and twenty-five other boys marched to the station and took the train for Newport on the St. Marks. His little brother and fellow cadet Milton Tucker, only twelve or thirteen at the time but already mean as a snake, may have sneaked onto the train and gone, too. The governor himself saw them off that night at the Tallahassee depot, acting, Luther said later, "like one of those crazy men in one of those plays by William Shakespeare."

The governor claimed to be a descendant of the poet John Milton, author of *Paradise Lost*. He was of a melancholic turn of mind, like the man up the tower in "Il Penseroso." He often said so himself. Governor Milton paced up and down the train platform muttering and looking like his best dog had just died. A friend of his, a doctor, said, "I think he must have been suffering from some disease of the brain."

The boys didn't care. The Yankees had finally come to Florida. At Newport the Babies met up with Colonel George Scott's cavalry and faced down Union soldiers commanded by Brigadier General John Newton, not the abolitionist schoolmaster of Orange Hill, though maybe some New England kin of his. Newton's Union Navy support, commanded by William Gibson up from Key West, had run aground in the shallows of the St. Marks, delaying their advance. Newton decided he couldn't break the Confederate line at the Newport Bridge so he moved north to Natural Bridge, where the St. Marks flowed through a series of underground passages then emerged aboveground again. The cadets, the cavalry, and everybody else on their side of the river went, too.

At dawn on March 6 the firing started. It went on all day. By evening General Newton, frustrated, decided that, now that you mention it, the blockade was more important than capturing the capital of Florida. He retreated south. The Babies marched back to Newport to counter him. When they got there, it was dinnertime and rations were nothing but corn pone. At Natural Bridge they'd had picnic hampers with ham and molasses cake and put-up peaches in syrup, packed by plantation ladies like Mrs. Edward Bradford and Mrs. Arvah Hopkins and brought down by slaves. Corn pone. The Babies were disgusted. Instead of eating it, they rolled it into pellets and threw it at one another. Papa said Luther Tucker probably started the food fight.

Newton still couldn't find a way over the river, thwarted by a bunch of old men and cocky boys. He gave up, got on his ships, and sailed back to Key West. The old geezers, the recuperating regulars, Scott's horsemen, and the Baby Corps had saved Tallahassee. The Babies got to march back to school escorting a couple dozen genuine Union prisoners while their sisters and their sisters' friends made a fuss over them.

But everybody knew—even the Baby Corps knew—that everything was changed. It's just that nobody knew what everything had been changed into. It seemed like half the blue-capped faces they stared at, aimed at, across the swampy St. Marks were black, Negroes, but soldiers same as them, from the 2nd and 99th United States Colored Troops and the 2nd Florida Cavalry. Some of them had been born in Florida; some of them were from Florida plantations, young men who had fished in the same creeks as Luther and Milton and the Broward boys. Now they'd come home to liberate Florida.

Luther wasn't scared. He'd never been scared of colored boys; he'd grown up with them, Old Sarey's sons, all the Broward and Tucker

Negroes. And he couldn't be scared of Yankees—he'd never come across one. His Broward cousins said that Yankees had blue-white skin from the cold up there and six fingers on their left hand. Charlie laughed at that and said yes, and old Aunt Harriet Beecher Stowe has a spiky tail under her petticoats.

Jane had raised her sons on stories of her father and Uncle John fighting that Scottish adventurer and inciter of Latin American revolutions Gregor MacGregor when he invaded Fernandina in 1817. Better still, she told how her grandfather François Brouard, fighting the British in Carolina, rode like one of Charlemagne's knights through enemy lines, carrying the quinine that would save Count Pulaski's soldiers in Savannah. The big Secesh men—Calhoun, Yancey, Ruffin—said this war was another American Revolution, fighting for the Constitution as planters like Washington and Jefferson imagined it. Maybe the Baby Corps thought that, too, or maybe they just thought war was more interesting than algebra and Latin—a good way to get girls.

During the late 1850s, the Browards had been red-hot for secession, what with most of their money coming from the profits of slave labor. Two months before the Florida Secession Convention, Luther's Aunt Margaret, his cousins Helen and Caroline, and various other Broward and Tucker cousins in Duval County calling themselves "the Ladies of Broward's Neck," produced a petition: "To the Politicians of Florida as to Their Present and Future Protection against Abolition Emissaries of the North." It urged the politicians of Florida to act like Real Men and "avail themselves of the means given them by God and nature" to defend the Southern Way of Life. In case they missed the point, Helen Broward presented a new state flag sewed by the "Ladies" to Governor Madison Starke Perry. The governor, cornered, called it "a bright and effulgent star by the side of South Carolina on a field of azure which I devoutly pray God may fitly represent the future serenity and cloudless sky of Southern Nationality."

Come 1860, Rufus Tucker was all for the cloudless sky of Southern nationality, but he didn't relish all the trouble it was going to take. Still, Florida belonged to him and his kind: Andy Jackson had run off the

Spanish and killed off the Seminoles. White men had taken Florida fair and square. If it took a war to keep it like they wanted it, well, all right, then. So in January 1861, when they held the convention at the Capitol, he went along to watch and took Luther, who was thirteen and just started at the seminary. He told Jane it would be as good an education in history and politicking as anything Luther could get at College Hall. Edward Bradford thought the same thing: Susan could miss French and candy-making for a few days and learn about how their future serenity, not to mention their financial status, depended on the proper operation of the Tenth Amendment.

The Bradfords had a front-row seat in the House of Representatives. The Tuckers were farther back in the throng. Thirteen-year-old Susan gushed all over her diary. Mr. Leonidas Spratt, "the ambassador from South Carolina," had a "pair of brilliant, beautiful eyes." Since South Carolina had seceded on December 20, I guess they regarded it as technically a foreign country. The imposing Judge Gwynn of Tallahassee pinned a palmetto cockade on Susan's coat. There were a lot of long Ciceronian speeches name-checking George Washington.

Papa said that his grandfather Luther mostly remembered what he called "a lot of jawing" about how it was Southern men that made the nation and, if pushed, Southern men would unmake it, and some "old boy who said that if Mrs. Harriet Beecher Stowe had died before she wrote *Uncle Tom's Cabin* this never would have happened. But she didn't, so that was that."

Everybody knew what was going to happen. Despite mighty sermons and prophesying from slaveholding Union men such as Richard Keith Call, the former governor, and Colonel George T. Ward, the vote was 62 to 7. There was a long, stretched-out silence, as when an old lady, sick for years with cancers and bronchial complaints and the general miseries, finally dies. It's a relief and a shock, a sort of moment preserved under a glass bell. Slow tears ran down old Governor Call's face. Rufus Tucker and Dr. Bradford sighed.

Then the glass moment shattered. Men cheered. Women applauded, their gloved hands giving the clapping a muted, hollow sound. But outside the Capitol, as the word raced around the broad streets and rode hell-for-leather out into the Red Hills and toward St. Augustine and Pensacola, boys whooped "War! War!" At the City Hotel and the Planters Hotel, toasts were drunk. They'd say: "Give us such men forever!" That one really referred to Washington and Lafayette, but it'd do for the secession convention, too. And after a few more glasses of Madeira or champagne they'd say, "To the Fair Daughters of Florida—all that can be wished and more than can be expressed!" What the fair daughters of Florida were going to do in a war was as yet unclear.

A bunch of torch-carrying men who subscribed to the one-Southerner-can-whip-ten-Yankees school of military strategy taunted Richard Keith Call: "Well, Governor, all right; we have done it."

He said, "And what have you done? You have opened the gates of hell, from which shall flow the curses of the damned, which shall sink you to perdition."

On January 11, 1861, the Ordinance of Secession was signed on the East Portico of the Capitol. Edward and Susan Bradford were watching. Rufus and Luther Tucker were watching. The ambassador from South Carolina was watching. Princess Murat, a widow since the prince drank himself to death in 1847, adjusted the sables she'd bought in Paris with Napoléon III's money and waited for the final signature. When the last man put down the pen, she yanked a silk cord and fired a cannon. Florida was divorced from America.

The Beefsteak Raid

My grandfather had another grandfather in the war. He's buried in the hidden cemetery of a vanished church in a grave outlined with oyster shells, cooked white as salt in the sun.

His name was Richard Roberts. He said he was born in Georgia. His family were probably Welsh, or maybe Presbyterian Irish. Papa said the story was that Richard Roberts' grandfather had come over on the boat (what boat nobody knows) before the Revolution to Charleston or maybe Savannah. Papa said he, the grandfather, "was so poor he didn't have a last name so they give him one."

If he were from North Wales, say, and spoke more Welsh than English, he could have said he was Dafydd or Huw or even Richard ap Robert, "son of Robert," and so become "Roberts." Half of the old kingdom of Gwynedd is called Roberts. Anyway, Richard Roberts appears in Florida out of nowhere—or out of Georgia, anyway—just in time to go get the hell shot out of him in Virginia.

People with nothing descended from people with nothing start to show up in the historical record only when they acquire land or join the army. Richard Roberts gets on paper when he enlists in the Florida State Troops in September 1861. His pay was $17.23 (Confederate) a month. After that he's invisible again until he volunteers for the infantry under Captain William Bloxham. It's March of 1862. He goes into training at Camp Leon, the 5th Florida's drilling ground at Six-Mile Pond in the soupy woods below the capital. For a while he's posted to Palatka on the St. Johns with the rest of the regiment to help keep Union-occupied Jacksonville quiet. They spend their days dodging alligators and their nights being eaten alive by mosquitoes. By the end of June they're back at Six-Mile Pond, dodging alligators and being eaten alive by mosquitoes. Florida, as one young lieutenant right off a Carolina farm said, is a tough row to hoe.

The Bradfords, the Eppeses, the Hopkinses, and other plantation lords and ladies send baskets down to the camp every day or so with fresh eggs and dressed chickens and pole beans and pork from the smokehouse—for the officers, at least. The privates mostly get cold hominy with a little bacon fat mixed in. By August the 5th Florida is off to Virginia, where they figure there aren't as many swamps. Or gators. Or skeeters. Just Major General John Pope and his army of 75,500 Yankee soldiers tramping out the vintage where the grapes of wrath are stored.

Winning at First Manassas in 1861, the Confederates briefly, deliriously, made the war look easy. The planter fire-eaters who had shoved Florida into the war in the first place said so what if the Confederate army was less than half the size of the Union forces, so what if 97 percent of firearms, 95 percent of munitions, 94 percent of iron, and 96 percent of railroad materials were manufactured in the North? Southern soldiers were *gentlemen*.

Second Manassas was different: 1,500 Confederates were killed, 8,000 wounded. It was a victory, yes, though not one to spin around shouting "Joy! Joy!" about, as Susan Bradford did when she heard about First Manassas. But at least everybody still had boots then, and socks. Richmond, the Confederate capital and the 5th Florida's headquarters, was still full of girls who'd hand posies to boys in uniform. Richmond was full of Floridians, too, some of them walking, some not. Mary Martha Reid, widow of territorial governor Robert Reid, established a hospital for Florida soldiers in Richmond. A lot of them died there, hallucinating their mama's face or the green Gulf of Mexico.

The war had already lasted a lot longer than the sixty days predicted by some of the Red Hills bucks, the same young men who played knights at the Ring Tournament. Back in early 1861, one of them had even boasted that he'd personally drink all the blood spilled in this little old nothing of a war.

If Richard Roberts heard that, he must have rolled his eyes. Rich boys dressing up in gray the way they'd dressed up in tin armor and feathers, playacting. Some of them worried harder about having a pretty coat than learning how to kill. Susan Bradford's cousin Charley Hopkins joined a Florida company called "Gamble's Artillery." Susan said his shirts were made out of "a beautiful piece of French opera flannel." The buttons were not "common metal buttons" but "real silver": His mother had them made by the jeweler in Tallahassee. Richard Roberts wore homespun. Soon, when the blockade choked off the fabric supply, the Knight of Tuscawilla, the Knight of the Lake, and the Knight of the Mist would be wearing homespun, too.

Even in Richmond, where the Confederate court ladies called Mrs. Jefferson Davis "Marie Antoinette" or sometimes "Empress Eugénie" (they meant this as a compliment), and gave balls and teas with champagne and cakes, supplies were running dangerously low. Molasses became a luxury. Soon there were no buttons, silver *or* base metal. Or ink. Or oats. Or coffee or salt or silk or paper or sugar or shoes.

In the spring of 1863 several hundred women rioted. They were the wives of foot soldiers or wives of men from the Tredegar Iron

Works. They were never invited to Mrs. Davis's parties. They toted knives and revolvers, some of them, and went through the city, snatching bread or whatever else they could get their emaciated hands on. A barrel of flour cost $70. Or more. When one woman, who said she had seven children to feed, asked how on earth she was supposed to pay prices like that, the shopkeeper replied, "I don't know, madam, unless you eat your children."

The 5th Florida followed Robert E. Lee to Antietam, where the Confederates lost 2,700 men and any hopes they cherished of occupying Maryland. Then they marched back to Virginia and met the Yankees at Fredericksburg, where they killed 1,300 and wounded nearly 10,000 keeping General Ambrose out. Richard Roberts got shot in the shoulder. Some time between Christmas 1862 and the run-up to Chancellorsville, Richard Roberts was admitted to General Hospital No. 9 in Richmond. They kept moving him, too, first to Chimborazo then to the Huguenot Springs Hospital. He must have been, as Papa put it, "meaner than a nest of stomped-on yellow jackets not to have just upped and died." Confederate hospitals killed Confederate soldiers almost as efficiently as Yankees did, what with the tuberculosis, staphylococcus, typhus, pneumonia, osteomyelitis, blood poisoning, peritonitis, and dysentery. If you were lucky, you didn't witness how dead bodies no one had time to bury would swell up to twice their normal size and explode. If you were lucky, they dosed you with morphine or laudanum, no matter what was wrong with you.

By early summer he was cut loose from the ward and remustered just in time for Gettysburg. Papa had this Nietzsche meets Calvin meets Faulkner theory about Richard Roberts and Gettysburg. Since he failed to die in one of the three Confederate hospitals he spent a couple of months in, he should have been one of the nearly 8,000 killed when Robert E. Lee had the bright idea of invading Yankeeland. The Florida Brigade was assigned to protect General Pickett's right flank on July 3, 1863. Out of 717 soldiers, they suffered 455 casualties.

Richard Roberts had tested Fate or Providence enough as it was. Papa would say, "I reckon by rights that old boy should have been buried there in the cemetery with Pickett's men."

Papa would then do something else for a minute, shell some peas or stake his dahlias, and say with this sly smile, "But he lived. That old boy lived right along."

Richard Roberts must have been beating some kind of odds his whole life. He was thirty-three years old when he volunteered. The war had been on for a year. Where had he been between 1828, when he was born, and 1861, when he went for a Confederate soldier in Tallahassee? He could write, we know that: He signed his own name on the regimental roll, below the Langston brothers, who would become his neighbors in Wakulla County, and right above Stephen Revell, who would be captured and imprisoned in Fortress Monroe until the end of the war, and whose great-niece would marry Richard Roberts' son.

But who was Richard Roberts before he became a foot soldier in Marse Robert's army? He must have left Georgia some time before the war, probably in the 1850s. He could have made a living carpentering or blacksmithing or fishing or logging on the coast or in the piney woods or around Tallahassee. But he appears in no census, no register, no receipt. And not much by way of stories, either. In the South, everybody's got a story, a long, elaborate, rambling, subordinate-clause-filled, bullshit-laced, possibly even entirely made-up story. For his parents and his early life, Richard Roberts didn't even fashion himself a fiction. Papa—who was born in 1903, thirteen years after Richard Roberts died—said that his father didn't say much about *his* father. Maybe he didn't know. But Papa would hint that there was a mystery.

I wonder if Richard was a true believer prepared to take his stand and live or die in Dixie, or was soldiering for the Confederacy just as a gig, a shot at three squares and some big boytalk glory. If so, he must have been disappointed—and hungry most of the time. If he hadn't joined up, he could have been drafted anyway. In April 1862 the conscription laws came into effect, allowing Confederate marshals to round up able-bodied men from eighteen to forty-five (and their definition of able-bodied was fairly elastic), handcuff them, and march them off to fight. The plantation gentry felt it was better if poor whites were given something constructive to do. Like sacrifice themselves for the Cause.

People with land and carriages and family portraits and silver and slaves in Middle Florida, from Holmes Creek in the west to the St. Johns in the east and Tampa Bay in the south, supported secession with all the Bonnie Blue flag-waving and Robert Burns–quoting and Sir Walter Scott–imitating they could muster. The dirt farmers and itinerant workers couldn't for the life of them see why they should fight to defend Big House people's slave-owning ways. They would "lay out" in some of the same swamps and woods that Osceola and the other Seminoles holed up in to conduct guerrilla campaigns from, around the Fenholloway, Apalachicola, and Suwannee Rivers. If they got caught, they could be hanged. Sometimes their wives and children were burned out of their cabins and left to starve. Susan Bradford claimed confidently that some of the conscriptees' wives were actually Yankee spies working for the blockaders. Anyway, she sniffed, these people "led lives which, in many instances, would have shamed the very beasts."

Well, Richard Roberts' life might have been one of those that would make a bear blush. Or he may have told himself he was fighting not for slavery but, as Susan Bradford declared, for "liberty of opinion and action, for principle and for HOME." No telling. What we know is that he survived the crucible of Gettysburg, then the Bristoe Campaign, then the Mine Run Campaign, then the Battle of the Wilderness, the Battle of Cold Harbor, and finally, in June 1864, the interminable battles of Petersburg.

Petersburg was this little place on the Appomattox River, twenty-three miles south of Richmond. But two railroad lines ran through it and a third was nearby. Richmond was dependent on Petersburg's staying in Confederate hands; snatch Petersburg out from under Lee, and the whole fairy-tale castle conjured up by Jefferson Davis and the cotton dukes and the Knights of Tuscawilla and the Lake and the Mist would collapse and dissipate like vapor.

The Union generals threw everything they had at Petersburg: Major General William Smith, Major General Benjamin Butler—in New

Orleans during Reconstruction they called him "Beast" Butler because he gave an order that white ladies who disrespected the Federals would be treated like whores—even Ulysses S. Grant. There were always about twice as many Union troops as Confederates, but the Confederates were dug in for the long haul. Which was just as well since the long haul turned out to be ten months.

There, at one end of the social, cultural, and sartorial scale, was Brigadier General Pierre Gustav Toutant de Beauregard, CSA, a Louisiana Frenchman, curled, feathered, talcum-powdered beneficiary of a blockade-run gold-laced uniform, married to the heiress Laure Slidell, the Chevalier de Bayard of the slaveholding South. At the other end, my great-great-grandfather Richard Roberts, CSA, a Georgia Welshman (we think) with no land, no money, no slaves, no wife, no shoes: at least, not ones that fit—he had to find just the right dead Yankee to get him some new boots. Richard Roberts must have gazed at Beauregard like a dog might gaze at a cut-glass pitcher.

When he had time to gaze at anything. Mostly the Confederates were getting shot at and charged and stormed and blown up and shot at some more. Unbeknownst to the Confederates, Union troops, lots of them ex–Pennsylvania miners, had dug tunnels under the Confederate fort and packed them with four tons of gunpowder. On July 30, the gunpowder exploded. An entire Confederate regiment was buried. But this didn't work quite as well for the Federals as it was supposed to: For some reason, the Union troops, black and white regiments, ran down into the crater. The remaining Confederates picked them off like rabbits in a pen.

Petersburg remained stubbornly besieged. One day in mid-September 1864, it's not quite clear which day, and it's not quite clear why, Richard Roberts took a bullet in the leg—added to the hole in his shoulder and the graze on his arm and the scarred lungs he had been dealing with since Antietam. As usual, nobody's sure about Richard Roberts, but Papa said he always heard his granddaddy got shot during the Beefsteak Raid.

The Confederates would kill for a decent piece of meat. They had dried pork and jerky and some sorry bacon grease sometimes, but not much else. They knew that not far away on the Blackwater River, near a Union supply base, were three thousand Yankee cattle, juicy, plump, and rich as cream pie, fed on more corn in a week than the Johnny Rebs saw in a month. They were also poorly guarded.

General Wade Hampton thought it would be an idea to go get him some beef. The Confederates hatched a plan to sneak through enemy lines, attack the men from the 1st D.C. Cavalry who stood between them and a steak dinner, and make off with the herd. Which they did. A few of Hampton's boys got hit. The cattle got through just fine. Papa said he could just see Hampton, Beauregard, and Lee, "sitting at a polished table in their tent in Petersburg, eating a big old roast." Maybe the men had roasts, too, or barbecue, or maybe somebody cooked up a fine, lean Brunswick stew with 'taters and carrots and dark winey gravy. A Georgia delicacy.

There's no proof Richard Roberts was a hero of the Beefsteak Raid. Papa just felt like it was the kind of thing a "woods fellow," used to moving quietly through trees and fields after deer or rabbits, would get picked by the general to do. And maybe Richard Roberts, the mystery man, had some special talent for cattle rustling. What we know for sure is that by September 19, a couple of days after the raid, he was laid out—again—in a hospital in Richmond on sheets that the blood would never quite wash out of, nursed by the daughters and widows and wives and mothers of Florida boys still fighting with Lee or locked up in Union prison camps at Johnson's Island or in Elmira or buried somewhere—Shiloh, Chickamauga, Fredericksburg.

This time the wound, on top of what the hospital called his "general debility," was bad enough that after a month they sent him home on furlough. Not that we know exactly where "home" was. It was in Florida, maybe Tallahassee, maybe down in the piney woods, maybe Smith Creek. Papa's sister, my aunt Vivienne, claims Richard Roberts convalesced with the Smith family, which is as good a story as any. Edwin and Sarah Norwood Smith had come down from the Darlington District of South Carolina in about 1850 with two or three young children and acquired several hundred acres on the Ochlockonee River. Some of it was high enough to plant on. A lot of it was wet enough to fish in. They named the creek after themselves.

Their son, Redden Smith, served with Richard in Company C, but in the fall of 1864 he was still at the siege of Petersburg. Richard got to use his bedroom and got to see lots of his sister Ellen Jane, too, a fair-haired, stubborn, skeptical girl. Richard told her stories about Gettysburg, Second Manassas, General Lee—Richard saw him half a dozen times, sitting there on Traveller, pointing at something, looking just like the engravings in the illustrated papers. He told her that General Beauregard wore soft lawn shirts the men said had come from Paris, France. At Petersburg, his leg shot to strips of skin and splinters of bone, General Beauregard had spoken to him. Asked him if he's from Florida. Laughed when Richard said, "Yes sir, General." Said, "That country is even hotter than my own. I hope there are pretty girls there somewhere in those swamps."

Richard Roberts told this by way of courting.

For about three weeks from the time Major General Sam Jones surrendered to Brigadier General E. M. McCook, commander of the U.S. forces at Tallahassee in April 1865, Richard was technically a prisoner of war. He was paroled in May 1865. He was married to Ellen Jane Smith in September 1866, in Tallahassee.

He wasn't the most impressive bachelor in the county, that was for sure. He was almost twenty years older than Ellen Jane. He had no people. He had no land. But there weren't a lot of men left. And Ellen Jane, nineteen and tough, would please herself—she'd please herself her whole life. After Richard died in 1890, she took up with a Mr. Stewart, a drummer with a logging company, then dumped him for a man who was a good fifteen or twenty years her junior. Her children never forgave her for remarrying. She didn't mind. She'd always made it clear that her children bored her.

But in 1866 Richard must have seemed just fine to her. Her parents deeded a parcel of land to them at Fox Branch on Smith Creek near the Methodist Church and helped them build a house. Richard Roberts figured with the big planters broken and almost as poor as everyone else, a working man might even prosper in this New South. Florida wasn't cotton-or-bust, like Mississippi or Alabama. Florida might get rich off oranges or tobacco or timber. There were miles and miles of timber up where Richard and Ellen lived. There were acres and acres of Florida that white men had never seen. There was Yankee money up north for draining and dredging and planting new crops. Richard would go around saying that the war was over, damn it, the war was over.

Only it wasn't. Not really. Richard had seen bad things, nightmare things, at Gettysburg and Petersburg, headless torsos blown up by the gunpowder, boys on the field with blood spurting out of their mouths like fountains. And in the hospitals at Chimborazo and Huguenot Springs and Richmond No. 9, boys with both legs shot off, crying for their mothers, boys choking on their own vomit. He'd lain there listening to the nurses lying, saying yes, you'll be home soon, in a week or two, and yes, she'll still love you no matter what.

And there was his body: the leg that wouldn't work right, the arm that wouldn't work right, the pain when he walked or plowed or lifted something higher than his shoulder. There were the fevers and night sweats and dreams. Ellen Jane had twins, but they died when the influenza went around Smith Creek and Sopchoppy, hardly big enough to have names, but they did anyway, Jane and Sarah. Papa said they were the two little girls he would see on the Carter Branch Road, the two that would fade like a white morning mist.

Their grandfather Smith had two tiny coffins built for them, and he and Richard dug a grave out behind the church. Ellen Jane and her mother, Sarah, lined the grave with the bottoms of colored glass bottles and oyster shells. They did the same when John, born in 1868, died. Unlike his sisters, he seemed content to rest in the sandy soil. Richard was going to have headstones made for them in Apalachicola, when there was a little more money. But there never was. Or maybe he just didn't get around to it, what with three more young 'uns coming in 1872, 1875, and 1878. The first two had fancy names, Theophilus and Valarious Lafayette. The littlest was named Edwin after Ellen Jane's father.

On June 3, Jeff Davis's birthday, the boys would watch as their father, wearing his patched and fading gray shirt and cap, paraded slowly with the others from Wakulla and Leon Counties who had been in the War and who could still more or less walk. Tuckers and Langstons and Revells and Vauses. Some had been at Natural Bridge or at Olustee or Santa Rosa Island or all those places in Virginia everyone could say by heart. Some of the men had fine coats with gold and medals, most didn't, a few talked about the War as if the South had won it after all, as if that was a secret the rest of the country would catch on to eventually.

Richard Roberts never said things like that. He rarely said anything about the War. When Theophilus asked him one time what that war had been about, Richard said, "Damned if I know, son."

The boys played Rebel soldiers down by the branch, being General Lee, General Longstreet, and General Beauregard, shooting with whittled-wood rifles at invisible Yankees hiding among the cabbage palms, huckleberries, and mayhaws, running them out of Florida for good this time.

Sons and Daughters of the Confederacy

The girls, big and small, flagged down the train at Bel Air. It was dark, the Baby Corps wanted to get back to some food that wasn't corn pone. But there were the girls, the big ones in pale dresses and sashes, coming forward to crown the Babies with wreaths made of tea olive, and little ones with bows in their hair, singing:

The young cadets were the first to go-o
To meet and drive away the foe,
Look away! Look away! Look away!
Dixieland!

Luther and Milton Tucker were heroes, all the Babies were. They had saved the capital of Florida. Governor Milton himself would thank them. Their mother would be proud. The Browards would be proud.

All the nasty parts of Natural Bridge started to recede: the scared eyes, the blood, the screaming. A boy had told Luther that a couple of "deserters" had been sentenced to death by a drumhead court. One of them looked at the firing squad and said, "I don't give a damn," but the other cried. Maybe that wasn't true. Anyway, as one of the girls stuck the tea olive leaves on his hat, she told Luther that the young ladies of Leon County were going to have a big party in the state house, a celebration of what she called their "great and gallant victory" at Natural Bridge.

And they did, the last belles of Florida's last stand. Susan Bradford's sister Martha and her cousin Jennie planned to sing a German duet, and another cousin would play "Sleeping I Dreamed Love." The girls stuffed the House of Representatives with every rose they could gather from three counties' worth of gardens. They propped up a life-size portrait of George Washington. They hung the "Ladies of Broward's Neck" secession flag. The Confederates were losing battles in South Carolina, Georgia, Virginia. They ignored that. The governor of Florida had just committed suicide. They ignored that, too.

Governor John Milton could see what the girls and the Baby Corps and even some grown men in uniform refused to believe: The South was whipped. People were starving. It was over. Nonetheless, he'd told the state legislature, all solemn and epic and grand like that other Milton's light-bearing angel before the fall, "death would be preferable to reunion."

Turned out he wasn't kidding. On April Fool's Day, 1865, a week before Lee surrendered, he rode to Sylvania, his fine plantation house near Marianna. He went upstairs. He put the barrel of a shotgun in his mouth, and pulled the trigger.

Still, a win is a win. Some of the young people couldn't see why the governor would do such a thing when Natural Bridge had been a success, when Tallahassee had been saved, and by all these brave boys who could go help General Lee real soon, right after the party.

It was April 9, 1865. Florida was still, as Susan Bradford called it, "a sovereign power." Susan's cousin Bettie played "Une Pluie du Perle" on the grand piano. Another girl recited from *The Lay of the Last Minstrel,* the part about the "heart hath ne'er within him burned, / As home his footsteps he hath turned." The girls sang "Dixie." The cadets looked at the girls. Luther Tucker was there: who knows which girl he was smiling at? A quartet started "The Southern Marseillaise." And just then a man came rushing in with a telegram. He jumped up on the stage and finally, in a shaking voice, read it. The telegram was dated April 8, the day before: "General Lee surrendered the army of Northern Virginia today, at Appomattox."

For a long minute, like the long minute just after the secession vote in the same place four years ago, there was silence, the silence of utter and unfathomable change. Then people started to cry, even the cadets, even the Babies. Luther thought again it was like something in a play, only not one where the good knights captured the kingdom, not *Henry V,* not St. Crispin's Day and Agincourt this time. He just wanted to go home.

When the Confederacy went belly-up, Jefferson Davis's cabinet, hangers-on, and courtiers ran south as fast as they could. Florida became, as ever, the place where reality might be denied, time pushed back, piper-paying avoided, at least for a little while. They figured that if they could just get to Tampa Bay or the Keys they'd be okay. If they could just make it to some thick, wild, empty place on the Gulf near the Steinhatchee River where, more than a hundred years later, marijuana smugglers would land small planes or skiffs on the quiet, they could arrange for passage to Canada or the West Indies or Europe or South America, away from charges of treason and the hangman's noose. They could go into romantic exile like Bonnie Prince Charlie. Some of them thought they'd go way, way down south, maybe build a new Confederate slave empire in Brazil or Argentina.

Most got caught before they ever saw a Florida palm tree. The Federals sent one of the famously combustible General Sherman's aides to Key West to keep an eye out for fugitives and organize patrols from the western reefs to Cape Sable to the Atlantic. Jefferson Davis and

Stephen Mallory, his Floridian secretary of the Navy, were arrested in Georgia. Davis's papers, and what was optimistically referred to as the "Confederate Treasure," had been sent to Cotton Wood, David Levy Yulee's plantation. When the "treasure" was discovered, it was nothing but Confederate dollars, worthless as Jefferson Davis's signature.

Some other cabinet officials got snagged in Key West. A few got clean away. Confederate Secretary of State Judah P. Benjamin, a cultivated Louisianan lawyer, hid out on Major Robert Gamble's sugar plantation south of Tampa. When the coast looked (literally) clear, he pretended to be a Frenchman, hired a boat, and made it to Marathon Key. There he took ship for Nassau and then for England. In London he reinvented himself as a barrister, the first, last, and only Confederate Queen's Counsel. He owed it all to Florida and the two thousand miles of coastline that still make the place impossible to police.

In Florida, January 19, Robert E. Lee's birthday, is a legal holiday.

Jefferson Davis's birthday on June 3 and Confederate Memorial Day on April 26 are legal holidays. Most people don't get time off work, though sometimes Lee's birthday and Martin Luther King, Jr.'s, birthday coincide. There they are, the two most revered Southerners of all time (leaving out Elvis), bound together on a winter Monday while most of the descendants of the people whose lives they shaped commemorate the momentous shifts they wrought in American history by going to the mall. But that's not everybody. Some of us, mostly natives, but sometimes immigrants from other parts of the South, start acting like initiates of some weird Dixie Freemasonry. We talk to one another in half-proud, half-ashamed code. We show off Great-Great-Granddaddy's sword—ironically, of course. We refuse to throw out our grandparents' picture of Robert E. Lee (all white people had one), even if we don't give it wall space anymore.

There's a lady in Tallahassee who owns a holy talisman of the white South. It's known as "the soap." Robert E. Lee, in full dress uniform, of course, handed his sword over to a muddy-shirted and allegedly drunk Ulysses S. Grant at Appomattox. Lee put his name to the surrender, signing away the dreams of the Bradfords and the Tuckers and the Browards and the Gilberts and maybe even Richard Roberts, everybody who believed in the Sir Walter Scott–land South, where all the (white) girls were angels, all the (white) men were Galahads, and all the darkies happy as they could be with their banjos and cotton sacks. Then he went into another room to wash his hands. His aides took the bar of soap he used and cut it into pieces. They divided it among themselves like the Roman soldiers with Christ's garments. The Florida heirs of the soap keep their piece in a silver box like a reliquary, like something that would hold the finger bone of a saint or a splinter of the True Cross.

A little more than a hundred years after that war, one of my cousins, Luther Tucker's great-great-grandson, went to a civil war in Southeast Asia. He came back more or less in one piece. One spring day the Sons of Confederate Veterans pinned a medal on him at Natural Bridge. Maybe Ho Chi Minh versus Ngo Dinh Diem wasn't exactly Grant versus Lee, at least to the Tuckers and the Robertses. But you take the war you're given.

My great-aunt Vivienne arranged for my cousin's medal, just as she enrolled me in the Children of the Confederacy, unbeknownst to me, when I was eleven. I didn't find out till I was eighteen. She also arm-twisted the Winnie Davis Chapter of the United Daughters of the Confederacy into awarding me a scholarship when I started college. I got $250 and a certificate. I took the money; I bought what I thought were subversive books with it: *The World the Slaveholders Made, The Burden of Southern History, Soul on Ice*.

Aunt Vivienne would say she was just proud that I wasn't a hippie. She would say *hippie* the way other people said *Communist,* with a curled lip in a half-whispered voice. My cousin who went to Vietnam and now had a Confederate medal wasn't a hippie, either. There were some hippies in the family, though, wearers of homemade tie-dye and embroidered jeans, owners of black light posters, McGovern voters.

North Florida was dangerously full of hippies, over in Gainesville and in Tallahassee, too. They were all over the campuses with their love beads and their long hair and their free love. In eastern Leon County, a bunch of them had bought up old plantation land, land that had once belonged to Thomas Jefferson's great-grandsons. They called it the Miccosukee Land Co-op. Aunt Vivienne imagined them out there, "smoking mary-wanna," she said, "with little nekkid children running around."

She and the other ladies of the Winnie Davis Chapter of the UDC were firm in the conviction that being a hippie and being a true son or daughter of the South were antithetical. When some of the hippies would come out for the reenactment at Natural Bridge, Aunt Vivienne would avert her eyes and hope the hippies would be the first to die in battle.

Every year she'd say to Papa, her older brother, as they watched the Confederates win one more time, "Lest we forget, Lee." And he'd say, "All right, Vivienne, all right."

Lest We Forget is what it says on the monument at Natural Bridge.

The road to Natural Bridge is now punctuated with houses and mobile homes and satellite dishes and real estate signs—the St. Joe Company, Florida's largest private landowner, is looking to develop southern Leon County as a spare bedroom community to their master bedroom community on the old Southwood plantation land. Property used to be cheap down here. It isn't the beach and it isn't town. It floods. The soil is silver-gray, mostly sand. People would park a trailer on a half-acre lot, figuring one day to build a real house. But then they never quite get that kind of money. So they replace the Plexiglas with stained glass and put an above-ground pool out the back. They erect swooping iron fences with curlicued tops and lamps and put porticoes with Ionic columns on the front of their double-wides. They fly American flags and Confederate battle flags. These days there are poster board and Magic Marker signs tacked to tree trunks or propped in yards that say "Bomb Iraq" and "Saddam Can Kiss My American Ass." There are mildewed limp yellow ribbons wrapped around skinny oaks and pines: It's the rainy season.

The paved road ends at the battlefield. The dirt road carries on through a landscape of sinkholes, slash pines, and rust-colored water, with the occasional stand of hardwoods on a little hill. It dead-ends not far from the Wacissa River on land that once belonged to Prince Murat. On a fine day people come down here to fish, coolers full of iced tea and Bud Lite, bags full of Deep Woods Off! and sunblock. You can see the Confederate breastwork, swells of earth turfed over, on the west side of the river. The Union troops were on the east side. You can see why they couldn't cross: The natural bridge itself isn't paved over but a slender earth path between two pieces of the St. Marks. It's no wider than a sidewalk. The ones who tried were shot.

The monument is taller than a house, a cloud-colored shaft of marble with a stone battle flag draped on top and a stone eagle perched on the battle flag. There's a pair of crossed rifles and the dates "1861" and "1865" and "In Loving Memory" like a grave marker. On one side it reads, "These brave men and boys who, in the hour of Sudden Danger, rushed from home, desk and field" to save "their Capital from the Invaders." On another side is carved the old state seal, the one designed by someone who'd never been to Florida. It has a Native American woman wearing the headdress of a Plains Indian chief, scattering unidentified flowers on a beach with mountains in the background. *Mountains,* people said, shaking their heads. *Florida mountains*.

5

Tales of the Reconstruction

ON JANUARY 1, 1866, Miss Susan Bradford of Pine Hill Plantation woke up in an empty house. It was cold. It was quiet. There were no clattering breakfast sounds, no sounds of dusting or sweeping or discreet feet moving about on polished floors. Nothing. She lay there on Grandmother Branch's Irish linen sheets, meticulously patched and ironed by Lulu, wearing a nightdress embroidered and laundered (and also patched) by old Aunt Morea, listening to the silence. Then she got up.

Downstairs, her mother and father sat in the foodless, fireless dining room. Their breathing made little clouds in the chill air. The servants had left in the night. "All our people gone? All?" said Susan.

"It was a clean sweep," said her father. He was thinking of leaving Florida, going to Brazil. The emperor Pedro II was keen to have *los Confederados* with their expertise in growing cotton. Thousands had already gone, with their miniature portraits of Robert E. Lee, locks of their dead children's hair, folded battle flags. There were still plantations in Brazil. And slaves.

The Bradfords didn't know how to do anything. There had always been a black hand on the bucket handle, on the skillet handle, on the button, on the plow. They could barely dress themselves: all those collar tabs, all those laces and ties and hooks. Who would clean the house, get the breakfast, drive the carriage, work the fields, chop the wood? "Not a servant, not one," Susan kept saying. "And we unused to work. Unused to work."

Mrs. Bradford, so sickly she usually had to be carried from room to room like a baby, thought she might be able to mix up a batch of muffins if somebody could figure out how to bake them. Dr. Bradford thought he could make coffee: He had often seen it done. Susan remembered how to make a bed, so that was good, but she didn't know how to build a fire or milk a cow. But then, she said, "Neither can anyone else in the house."

That night she scrawled in her diary:

> *I am tired—tired tonight, will all the days of the year be like this one? What are we going to do without the negroes? Or will we have to do these manifold duties for ourselves? Or can we hire white servants as they do at the North? I wonder where the negroes have gone, and why did they not tell us they were going? Life is a puzzle sometimes.*

The ex-slaves knew that Moses had whipped Pharaoh. They knew they were free. In April 1865 Union General McCook read the Emancipation Proclamation from the porch of a grand house in the middle of Tallahassee, not far from the May Oak where the May Queens of Florida once sat in state. He was sarcastic. A reiteration of postbellum realpolitik was in order "for the information of those who seem to be ignorant of the fact, that the President of the United States, on the first day of January, 1863, issued a proclamation changing the status of persons held as slaves."

Over in Fernandina and Jacksonville, black people had been free for years, what with the Union Army running the place out of some off-to-Virginia Confederate's mansion and earnest ladies from the North operating Negro schools and Negro orphanages. But in the Red Hills, black people stuck around on the plantations. The only jobs were the jobs from the old times: working in the fields, looking after white folks. There was no economy. There was no money, not real money. There were bills issued by the State of Florida or the Florida's Atlantic and Gulf Railroad Company during the war. They had engravings of pale, overripe women in see-through dresses lounging on cotton bales while slaves dragged picking sacks. They were pretty good to light your stove with.

A week after Appomattox Dr. Edward Bradford went out to his plantation yard and said: "My people, I have sent for you to tell you that you are *my* people no longer. We are no longer master and slave, but we can still be friends."

For a while they mostly stayed, though Appomattox had, according to Susan, ruined them. Emeline the cook refused to rustle up dinner, sassing the white folks: "Take dat basket back ter your mother an' tell her if she want any dinner she kin cook it herself."

Uppityness had broken out like measles. When Martha Bradford, Susan's older sister, married Patrick Houstoun of Lakeland Plantation, the rumor went around that the ex-slaves planned to force their way into the big house and, said Susan, aghast, "mingle with the guests on terms of equality." Some nice Union soldiers (as opposed to the mean ones who went around telling the Negroes that they were entitled to take whatever they wanted from their old masters since, after all, their labor had paid for it) stopped the rabble from disrupting the ceremony.

Another night twenty black teenagers came waltzing up the Pine Hill road, singing to the tune of "John Brown's Body":

We'll hang Jeff Davis on a sour apple tree,
We'll hang Jeff Davis on a sour apple tree,
We'll hang Jeff Davis on a sour apple tree,
As we go marching on!

Susan was sensitive about Jefferson Davis. Not long ago at one of her Uncle Arvah's Goodwood parties a "Yankee man" had taunted her with a *Harper's Weekly* cartoon showing the fallen president getting busted by the Feds while wearing women's clothes. Davis was pretty convincing: petticoats, hoops, shawl, and all. Only the big boots gave him away. Susan got so mad she cried. Now, hearing these young black kids insulting the President of the Confederate States of America, a planter and a *gentleman,* in her own front yard, Susan lost her temper. She grabbed the brand-new carriage whip, whale bone with a lash made of braided silk, ran out into the yard, and starting laying it about right and left. The kids screamed and ran away, vowing to tell on her to the Union soldiers.

Some Pine Hill people left soon after Appomattox. Lulu went because Susan's mother, Miss Patsey, forbade her to visit the alcohol-sodden and prostitute-festooned carnival that was the Union camp up the road in Centerville. Susan lamented the loss of her "dear black mammy." As Lulu left Pine Hill she shook her fist at Susan's mother: "I'll miss you—the Lord knows I'll miss you—but you'll miss me too—you see if you don't."

Susan sighed. "I do not think Mother realizes they are free."

Maybe that's why Frances tried to kill Miss Patsey—Frances, Susan's birthday present from Miss Patsey's father, Frances, whom Susan had taught to read, Frances, to whom Susan taught the Ten Commandments, Frances, who taunted Susan about John Brown's raid. One morning just before dawn, Frances stood over Miss Patsey as she lay sleeping and poured chloroform all over her pillow.

None of the Pine Hill Bradfords seemed to realize why the servants chose New Year's Day to disappear. But New Year's could be the worst day of the year for slaves. Aunt Morea or Dinah or Lulu could have explained it. In Susan's descriptions of prelapsarian New Year's entertainments in the Pine Hill parlor, there's always "the richest of plum cakes, beautifully ornamented," and wine punch to which the gents "helped themselves liberally." Susan (who thought that alcohol made men act like animals and, despite her father's offer of good champagne, refused to serve anything but water at her wedding reception) mentions some of the men getting plastered by midafternoon. But she leaves out one of the other things they often did on New Year's. While the white ladies gossiped about who got engaged over Christmas and whose baby was due when, some of the white gentlemen got together in the gun room or the plantation office and cut deals: who wanted to buy a field hand, never mind that he had a wife; or who wanted a couple of children, light-skinned, raised in the Big House so they'd be good for the dining room, never mind that they had a mother. Often slave traders would ride a circuit of plantations in December: the cotton crop would be in and the owners would know that they needed to buy some more hands or sell somebody to make up a loss. Frances could have told how it felt to be sent away from your home, your family, and given to someone else like a puppy, Ten Commandments or no Ten Commandments.

So on December 31, 1865, the Pine Hill servants washed up the New Year's Eve wineglasses, put the lid back on the flour barrel, locked the silver cupboard, and walked out into the dark North Florida woods.

The world was upside down. Florida belonged to no country. The Red Hills gentry may have been surrounded by food, unlike during the War when whatever there was often got sent away to the troops or taken by Union soldiers or cost too much—a bag of sugar could go for the price of a small house—but they weren't sure what to do with it. There was corn and cattle, cream and pork, chicken and strawberries and oranges. The Bradfords lived on boiled eggs and batter bread. That's all Susan knew how to make. A neighbor lady sent them milk every day, even though Pine Hill had lots of cows. Susan just couldn't stand to get near them: "You see I am so terribly afraid of Bossy. She looks like a dreadful monster to me."

The Guernseys weren't the only dreadful monsters. There were the soldiers, camped just outside Pine Hill, marching on the streets of

Tallahassee, showing up at parties at Goodwood in the same chandeliered ballroom where the belles and the boys used to toast General Lee. Susan's uncle Arvah Hopkins, a storekeeper before he became a planter, a man who understood maintaining friendly relations with your best customers (or at least the only ones with some cash), was pleased to entertain the Union officers. The Bradfords swiftly got the point that they were no longer monarchs of all they surveyed; as far as the United States government was concerned, they had no rights; they were enemy combatants.

Susan tells how one day her mother was sitting in her white-curtained, white-counterpaned, white-cushioned bedroom, reading her Bible, when "into this pure and peaceful atmosphere walked Peggy, unkempt, unwashed, dirty and disgusting beyond description."

Peggy said, "I is jis' kum fur a visit, Miss Patsey. De ladies what kums here sets in dese cheers an' I is jis' as good as dey is."

Martha Branch Bradford didn't see it that way. She had two of the other servants kick Peggy out. Peggy hightailed it to "dem Yankees" and said she'd ben insulted by the white folks. The next thing the Bradfords knew, a Union soldier arrived with a note from Lieutenant Zachendorf, commanding the Centerville camp, threatening to arrest Mrs. Bradford if she didn't apologize.

As if this weren't enough, Lieutenant Zachendorf went around trying to create some sort of second Haitian Revolution ("The terrors of San Domingo rise before our eyes," said Susan), exhorting the ex-slaves not to take any crap from their ex-masters. They might, on the other hand, take a few silver candlesticks or mules:

"You made it," said the lieutenant. "It is all yours."

Susan recounts a story about how Union soldiers in Georgia, searching for Jeff Davis, smashed open the door of a fine old house, menaced the old ladies cowering upstairs, beat up an old man, burned all the antique furniture, and, just for the hell of it, shot the family cat and the family dog.

Occupation

Semmes decides we should break into his house so we can keep drinking. The senators renting it for the 2003 legislative session don't arrive till tomorrow. Happy Hour at Andrew's has been over since 7:30. We left, not wanting to pay full price for over-iced Maker's Mark or corky California chardonnay. Happy Hour at Andrew's hasn't been all that scintillating since the 2000 vote recount anyway. So Matt, Clare, and Monica the Hungarian architect go off to the ABC Liquor while Semmes, me, Anna-Kate the ex-mermaid, and Semmes's old King Charles spaniel Ruby sneak around back.

We don't really break in, of course. Semmes has a key. He owns the place, spent years restoring it, turning it into a *Southern Living* magazine dream of an old house with new stuff: gleaming German dishwasher, ice maker, air conditioner, serious water pressure to go with the restored claw-foot bathtubs, and heirloom candlewick bedspreads on Sealy posturepedic mattresses. The South Florida politicos love it. It's a real "antebellum home" in Florida's capital city.

Semmes's great-great-great-grandfather—or rather a black man named George Proctor—built the place in the 1840s. George Proctor was free, an in-demand artist who built houses for the white people who could afford him: Judge Randall, the cotton princes of the Chaires family, the banker "Money" Williams, who was so rich people said there was a nickel embedded in every brick of his house.

George Proctor's father, Antonio, had been born in Jamaica. He saw the Battle of Quebec in 1759, body servant to an English officer. He was at the Battle of Lexington, too. Antonio Proctor spoke English, Spanish, and Creek and worked as an interpreter in the Seminole Wars treaty negotiations. He bought his freedom, or was given it, nobody knows for sure. His children were born free, too, but their freedom was precarious, made ever more fragile by Toussaint L'Ouverture, Denmark Vesey, and Nat Turner. George Proctor had a wife but she was a slave. He worked to try and buy her from her master.

Matt, Clare, and Monica get back with three bottles of Hungarian red (Monica insisted), a bottle of Spanish champagne, some Diet

Coke, and a fifth of bourbon. Soon we're sitting in the parlor, drinking out of the senators' nice glasses: Anna-Kate the ex-mermaid says she can't taste anything in plastic. It's a high, wide room, the color of marzipan, with generous windows and brocade sofas. In 1865 Semmes's ancestors sat here silently, probably dressed all in black, while Union General McCook read the Emancipation Proclamation two doors down.

Semmes tells a story about how they used to store the May Queen's throne in his basement. He tells another story, this one probably nonsense, about how the Union general's officers stabled horses in the cellar. "Manure everywhere. They never cleaned it up," he says, "but at least they didn't burn the place down."

It sounds like those stories of Vikings who used Irish convents as brothels before they burned them down. Desecration. We all shake our heads. "Yankees," says Semmes.

"Yankees, Jesus," says Clare.

"Damn Yankees," says Monica. In her Countess Dracula accent, "Damn Yankees" sounds like some lost tribe of the upper Amazon.

Monica is from Szombathely.

Clare is Norwegian Irish from Hawaii. She came here to go to school at FSU's Creative Writing Program. She writes novels about the South Pacific. Matt, her husband, was a child of the midwestern diaspora, his parents riding down U.S. 441 from Ohio, looking for low taxes and year-round golf. He played running back for the Fighting Colonels of Plantation High School. Plantation, Florida, is a few miles inland from Fort Lauderdale.

Semmes was brought up on old silver and smart real estate deals. Anna-Kate was a Kappa at the University of Florida and worked summers at Weeki Wachee Springs. She wore a shiny blue tail and a spangled brassiere. She swam two shows a day, underwater, lip-synching to the Mermaid Anthem:

We're not like other women,
Living lives that are a bore.
Don't have to clean an oven.

And we never will grow old.
We've got the world by the tail!
We've got the world by the tail!

"I can't believe y'all keep using the Y-word," says Anna-Kate. There used to be a lot of people from New Jersey and New York and the Midwest at the mermaid shows. They liked having their picture taken with Anna-Kate, as she sat on a bench by the spring, slowly waving her fin.

We started on this anti-Yankee rant back at the bar when the governor and some of his henchpersons sauntered by, the men in Friday-casual guayaberas, the women in South Beach–colored linen shifts, laughing and cell-phoning on their way to the Mansion or maybe to Jasmine to eat grouper sashimi for dinner. And the security: Instead of one guy with the curly flesh-tone cord coming out of his ear, three wired-up, canine-jawed dudes wearing we-just-want-to-ask-a-few-questions-ma'am suits. Clare took a big swallow of her half-price cabernet and hissed, "Jeb Bush is a carpetbagger."

We considered the point. For all their postured pork-rind eating, mannered Texas twanging, and cowboy-boot wearing, there's no doubt that the *Social Register*–Kennebunkport–Greenwich–Andover–Yalie Bushes are Yankees in the strictest sense: New Englanders. Jeb came to Florida because George W. got dibs on Texas. Besides, Jeb was married to a Mexican, and that had to be good for the South Florida Latino vote, even though most of them are Cuban and Cubans think Mexicans are illegals who mow the lawns, pick the tomatoes, and, if they slip their leashes, turn into crypto-socialist union organizers.

Jeb and Columba Bush did just fine in Miami. She shopped for lightweight Chanel suits and ate lunch. He made a lot of money out of the proposition that an unbuilt-upon beach, an old hardwood hammock, a patch of scrub would all look better decorated with condos and "town homes." He wasn't above using his old man's name in business deals selling water pumps to Nigeria. When he decided to run for office, he took to calling himself Jeb! with an exclamation point.

Jeb! lost his run at the governorship in 1994, beaten by the Democrat Lawton Chiles. Chiles, a slow-talking relic of Ur-Florida, wore Sears work pants and campaigned on foot from Pensacola to Key West. He was given to piney-woods aphorisms like "the old He-Coon walks before dawn."

Chiles's bon mots, uttered as if prophecy, sent the blazered College Republicans of the Bush camp into a frenzy of Internet searches and "How to Talk Southern"-reference-book hunting. ("Christ, Tad, what's a 'he-coon'?" "Fuck if I know, Courtney.")

But Chiles couldn't be governor forever. Four years later Jeb!, now reinvented as a nice guy via photo ops with cute African American children or mom-and-pop sugar cane farmers, had won the election. Chiles couldn't live forever, either. He keeled over from a heart attack in the last few days of his term in 1998. He was riding his Exercycle in the Mansion's gym. The biggest Presbyterian church in town couldn't hold all the people who wanted to come to his funeral. Jeb! and Columba showed up, looking expensive. They got to go to the front of the line. A lady way back in the throng, giving the play-by-play to her friend via cell phone, said, "There's that *Columbia* Bush. She ain't no bigger'n a little *dawg*."

Now Jeb! Bush isn't just any carpetbagger, he's the brother of the president of the United States. And as his curly-corded security dudes like to say, "a target." *Don't you know there's a war on?*

On September 11, 2001, the Capitol in Tallahassee was evacuated. The governor declared a state of emergency. Then things calmed down a bit. There were no more attacks. There were also no more tourists. No more money. The governor traveled the country explaining that Florida's state of emergency was nothing for them to worry about and didn't they *need* a little fun and sun after the recent national trauma? Besides, Disney'll cut you a deal! Hotels on the Gold Coast, hotels on the Emerald Coast, hell, fish shacks on the Nature Coast were offering discounts out the wazoo!

If you tried to visit the center of government in Tallahassee, however, you might encounter the majesty of the state in heightened alert mode. I saw a woman, a church-lady type, marched off by cops when she tried to get into the Capitol one time. She passed the metal detector and purse searches just fine, but she had a sealed manila envelope she didn't want to open. *Verboten!* The cop said, "Don't you know there's a war on?"

War—except the 1861–1865 thing—has generally been good to Florida. World War II brought 172 military installations and a new occupying force: hundreds of thousands of soldiers at Camp Blanding and Eglin Air Force Base and the Jacksonville Naval Air Station and MacDill Air Force Base. The state was swimming in money. Soldiers rehearsed their Normandy invasion techniques in Carrabelle and frogmen learned to blow up enemy subs at Fort Pierce. Florida was a temporary home to hundreds of German POWs, too. Even though U-boats had attacked American ships off the Atlantic coast of Florida, the state treated the Germans very nicely, so nicely that when some of them, put to work in the kitchens at MacDill, complained about having to peel potatoes in company with *Negroes,* American officers sympathized entirely and worked out a different duty roster. The fight against fascism was *over there,* after all.

Other POWs picked oranges in Winter Haven and Dade City and cut cane in Clewiston. Maybe they didn't mind working alongside Latin Americans and what respectable people called "poor white trash." In 1945 Governor Millard Caldwell instructed the sheriffs of the state, who often ran counties like their own personal palatinates, to eradicate the deadly sin of sloth in the State of Florida. In other words, round up the no 'counts in the juke joints and put them in Big Sugar or Big Citrus labor camps. Florida operated a system of neo-slavery (respectable people called it "good honest labor"), and business was good, so good that Florida cotton topped 20 cents a pound for the first time since the 1860s.

Florida is still profitably warred up. MacDill Air Force Base is the central command base for our various Middle East wars: the one in Afghanistan, the one in Iraq, the one on Terror, and on who knows what other countries we may have invaded by now. In 2003 at Eglin, a huge military installation in the western Panhandle, they practiced bombing Iraq back to the Stone Age with a "Massive Ordnance Air Burst" (as the military guys called it) of 21,000 pounds, dropped from a C-130 transport plane somewhere over the pristine wilderness of the air force base—a lot of Eglin is wildlife preserve. Pretty much everywhere you go in Florida, or everywhere a member of the Bush family goes at least, there's some military installation suitable for election-year backdrops. All those flags you can see. All those sharpshooters you can't see.

Anna-Kate tells us she heard they're doing a patriotic show at Weeki Wachee. Three mermaids in red, white, and blue tails perform underwater maneuvers (the best is the wheel, where they hang on to each other's tails and rotate while waving miniature versions of Old Glory) as Lee Greenwood sings, "And I'm proud to be an American, where at least I know I'm free!"

Anna-Kate hung up her shiny tail a long time ago. Lately she's been standing in designated "free speech zones" to protest George W. Bush's frequent descents on Florida. Usually they put the "free speech zones" where the president will never see them. She and Clare and Matt have been demonstrating to save the state library in Tallahassee, the treasure house of Florida, where we keep the sixteenth-century polychrome map of St. Augustine from the time when Sir Francis Drake raided the city, the diary of the man who double-crossed Chief Osceola, the letters exchanged between Governor LeRoy Collins and the Reverend C. K. Steele during the bus boycott, bills of sale for Jefferson County slaves, plans for art deco hotels in Miami, and Jacques le Moyne de Morgue's *Narrative* from 1591 with the pictures of the long-nailed, panther-tailed Timucua chief. Jeb Bush wants to shut it down; this is a tough budget year. Closing the archive will save a good $4 million or so. Matt's sign said, "STOP! Book Thief!" Clare's said, "Hey Jeb, Read a Good Book on Florida History Lately?"

The governor is spending $11 million on a new campaign called, "Just Read, Florida!" Clare says, "Just read *what*?"

Impotent rage, sarcasm, irony: We have all the hopeless, dainty rhetorical tools of the defeated. Here we are, a bunch of Gore voters, nattering nabobs of negativism, enemies of ordinary decent Americans, sitting around on rosewood sofas in a house built when Queen Victoria was still wasp-waisted and pretty, when Fizeau first measured the speed of light, when Poe was trying to work out his attraction to dead women—here we are drinking and cursing Yankees, complaining about the loud men in $1,000 suits on their cell phones in restaurants we consider our own, the million-dollar houses going up on beaches we used to think only we knew about, our powerlessness in the face of a reconstructed Florida that exists for tourists, developers, and the military-industrial complex. Not lovers of the *ancien régime* like us, old guardians of the old ways.

Bourbon and Diet Coke have turned us into Susan Bradford.

Aunt Harriet's Mansion

After the Civil War, a cabal of high-toned Northerners concocted a plan to de-Southernize Florida. The Unionist God had loosed the fateful lightning of his terrible swift sword. They would save Florida's slaveholding soul by colonizing it with progressive New Englanders. They would Yankeefy the place. Import so many right-thinking settlers that between them, the Yankees and the ex-slaves could outvote anybody. Take over. Burn the Big House down.

There were Reconstruction grandees, such as Harrison Reed from Massachusetts, who became governor in 1868, and his future wife, Chloe Merrick, from New York. She volunteered in the National Freedman's Relief Association and ended up in Fernandina, where she started an integrated orphanage in the home of an absent Confederate officer. Then there was the Reverend John Swaim from New Jersey, the master theorist of Florida as a tourist destination for New Englanders who'd get so sweet on the place they'd relocate, become a colony of abolitionists deep in Dixie. He promoted cheap Duval County land to Northerners like a chamber of commerce pro.

Their Florida project got a public relations boost when an antislavery megastar decided to relocate. It was none other than Susan Bradford's nemesis, the architect of the planter caste's destruction, the woman Matthew Arnold insultingly described as "middle-class" (the slaveholding patricians loved that), the best-selling, world-famous author of *Uncle Tom's Cabin,* Mrs. Harriet Beecher Stowe herself.

She started a Florida tradition of celebrity semi-residency that continued with Thomas Edison, Meyer Lansky, various Kennedys, Jack Kerouac, Gianni Versace, and Michael Jackson. Those reforming Yankees doing their damnedest to lure the tough-minded and clean-living children of the Puritans down to this decadent remnant of the plantation South were thrilled. It would be in all the Northern papers. Real estate could go nowhere but up.

In 1865 Stowe sent her son ahead to rent a plantation just south of Jacksonville. It was called Laurel Grove. Frederick Stowe had been wounded at Gettysburg and still suffered crippling headaches. He was also an alcoholic. His mother thought growing cotton (with hired labor, of course) would be therapeutic. And even though a plague of army worms decimated the crop, costing her about ten grand, Stowe still thought Florida was such a good idea that she soon descended on Laurel Grove herself, bringing trunks of English china and French chairs and Persian rugs. She also brought her brother, the Reverend Charles Beecher. He needed to make himself scarce after scandalizing his Massachusetts congregation by expressing his belief that souls had multiple existences. His church tried him for heresy. He got off, but *still.*

You can see why the Yankee progressives thought Florida was the place to start with the wholesale moral, spiritual, and economic reform of the South. Georgia, the Carolinas, Mississippi, Alabama, Louisiana had people in every corner, people implicated in the plantation power structure. Florida seemed to them as wide open as the steppes—with more trees, of course. It had nearly 60,000 square miles of land (admittedly 6,000 square miles were underwater most of the year) and a population of less than 188,000. To the Beechers and the Stowes and the Reeds and the Swaims, Florida was a blank page to be written on in a firm, Calvinist copperplate hand. The first attempt to recover humankind's old Eden, or else to build the New Jerusalem—the Pilgrims never could decide whether they preferred the prelapsarian or the postapocalyptic—had not come to pass in New England. Maybe it would in Florida. The sin of slavery had been paid for in blood. Now it was time to build a just society.

Of course it didn't work. Never was going to work. No matter how much the likes of the Bradfords and the Browards lamented that the sky had fallen, the world was upside down and the old order overthrown, the structures and patterns of antebellum Florida were mostly intact down there under the rubble. The Reconstruction was a bump in the road. Sure, some Rebel malefactors, Senators Mallory and Yulee, Governor Allison, were locked up in Georgia; and the Andrew Johnson administration had Samuel Mudd, the doctor who had set the broken leg of John Wilkes Booth, incarcerated on the Dry Tortugas. But for every clear-eyed young seminarian or Connecticut schoolmarm who landed at Jacksonville or St. Augustine, toting a Bible and a copy of *Harper's,* there were ten monumentally pissed-off ex–Confederate soldiers, some deserters, some paroled regulars, returning to the ruins of the home place or holing up in those nearly empty tracts the Reconstruction grandees had such hopes for. Taylor County, Lafayette County, the unimproved interior lands, with their pine forests, swamps, and miles of unwatched Gulf coastline, also harbored Union deserters avoiding the disapproval of their superior officers. No matter whose side you'd been on in the Late Unpleasantness, the enemy was now the government (carpetbagger, Bourbon, who cares?) and the Negroes. The Law was best avoided, and freed slaves—economic competition—had to be kept in their place.

Florida's Reconstruction government, led first by Harrison Reed, campaigned on a Beecherish agenda of moral improvement, public education, fiscal probity, and expanded suffrage. Indeed, Charles Beecher himself was, for a while, a member of Reed's administration. Every time anybody black thought about voting, however, somebody white would start shooting. Night riders of the Ku Klux Klan or the Young Men's Democratic Club terrorized ex-slaves. John Dickison, a former Confederate officer who billed himself the Swamp Fox of Florida, would lead vigilante cavalry charges through groups of black men trying to get to a ballot box.

No wonder Reed couldn't deliver on black cabinet members or public education or civil rights protections. He even had to battle his own Republican Party. Lieutenant Governor William Gleason connived with the legislature to impeach Reed for the usual undefined "high crimes and misdemeanors"—which really meant that the state had no money and people were mad about it, plus Gleason was U.S. Senator Thomas Osborn's boy, and Osborn thought that Reed was a mite too bleeding heart over ex-slaves and such. Reed resisted, posting guards around the capitol, locking out Gleason and his gang. Gleason took to signing official papers as "governor" from a nearby hotel room. Finally, an exasperated State Supreme Court ruled that the impeachment wasn't lawful; Gleason hadn't been a citizen of Florida for three years prior to his election, so he wasn't even eligible for state office.

Reed didn't do much to renew Florida, what with Republicans undermining him, the Democratic press sniping at him, and the old planter class playing him like a two-penny harmonica. But he did create the cabinet position of Commissioner of Immigration, who was supposed to write pamphlets and newspaper articles to lure Yankees down. It worked: The state's population grew by forty thousand in three years. The problem was, though, that most of the new people weren't Massachusetts Transcendentalists with lifetime subscriptions to *The Liberator,* determined to drag the Old South out of its retrograde ways through creative farming and progressive education. They were often tourists out for fun, land speculators out for a quick buck, and people with TB figuring the warm air would stave off death for a few more years. Even when what the Beechers and their kind would consider promising young men and women came down to grow lemons or cucumbers, something happened to them, something transforming. It had happened to Charles Beecher and Harriet Beecher Stowe, too. Rather than leading Florida on the paths of righteousness, Florida seduced them.

They went on excursions to Silver Springs, with its translucent waters throwing colors around, said the Reverend Swaim, like "flashes of the Aurora Borealis." They had picnics under the half-burned columns of some once-grand Waverley Hall or Rose Hill. They went to hospital benefit balls (those consumptives flocking south needed somewhere to die) at the Villa Alexandria, where they ate ice cream, waltzed under palm trees, and marveled at the indoor plumbing—the only properly flushing commodes south of Charleston. Harrison Reed's very rich sister had built the villa on the site of a plantation house, an Italianate fantasy with windows by Tiffany, ninety-five kinds of roses in the garden, and $50,000 worth of mahogany in the dining room alone.

In 1867 Harriet Beecher Stowe bought an orange grove at Mandarin on the St. Johns, six miles south of the Villa Alexandria. It was to be her winter home and a nice little moneymaker, too. Stowe amused herself by writing sensuous pieces for Northern magazines and newspapers, at once trying to lure people to the warm, orange-scented "reverie" that is Florida, while deploring the way new settlements on the St. Johns "succeed in destroying all Nature's beauty, and give you only leafless, girdled trees, blackened stumps, and naked white sand, in return."

She recommended pleasure boat trips on the moss-canopied Oklawaha, while raging about the tourists' need to shoot at gators, herons, ospreys, anhingas, deer, anything that moved. She became a tourist destination herself. People would come to Mandarin to catch a glimpse of the writer whom Abraham Lincoln had supposedly greeted with, "So this is the little lady who made the great war." The Stowes started charging admission: 25 cents.

Stowe soon found it hard to concentrate on making the revolution in Florida. She was lulled by its "soothing and sedative climate." Being rich and white, she found neo-plantation life quite comfortable: all that gorgeous land and all those charming servants so available and so cheap. Many of the Northern reformers and entrepreneurs, heirs of William Lloyd Garrison and John Brown, began to buy into the romantic Old South myth of happy, hardworking darkies. As long as there were some Normal Schools and plenty of AME churches, well, wasn't that an improvement? It wasn't *slavery*. Stowe disapproved of the way that black folk often found themselves back in the cotton or tobacco fields, picking for wages that weren't a whole lot different from what they were getting before 1865. Then again, as she said, "The Negro is the natural laborer of tropical regions. He is immensely strong; he thrives and flourishes physically under a temperature that exposes a white man to disease and death."

So that's all right.

The Reverend Charles Beecher wasn't as rich or as famous as his sister—nobody'd pay a quarter to look at *him.* He couldn't afford an expensive place near Mandarin, where the right-on Yankees, along with their more cupiditous colleagues, had driven up East Florida property prices. So in 1869 he bought a house in the Wakulla County village of Newport, where Luther Tucker and the Baby Corps had stared across the St. Marks River at New England white boys and Southern black boys, waiting to try and kill each other.

Newport, by the late 1860s, was almost deserted. The railroad had gone, which suited Charles Beecher just fine. He wanted quiet. He was trying to get over the deaths of three children within a year—his son killed out west fighting Indians; his two daughters drowned in a boating accident. For him, Florida wasn't a project, it was an opiate.

Beecher believed that the souls of the dead came back to earth for purification. Maybe he thought he met a number of them among the orange trees of his little farm, maybe he even met his own children. It's a shame the Reverend Charles died before the founding of the afterlife-obsessed community of Cassadaga, Florida. He is, in a sense, its spiritual father.

In 1893 a clutch of clairvoyants, faith healers, and mediums from New York converged north of Orlando. They said there was a powerful lot of psychic juice in this one spot in Volusia County. They lived in a tent city for a while, ministering to seekers after occult knowledge and communications from the Beyond. Then they got a clue about Cassadaga's tourist potential and built a hotel. You can still buy Tarot readings, palm readings, have your astrological chart done, your numerology enumerated. You can be taken through your past lives. One of my great-aunts would go there to talk to her ancestors from the Other Side. Ghosts are a speciality at Cassadaga. But, as Papa knows, ghosts enjoy the rest of Florida, too. I like to think that if the Reverend

Charles Beecher met spirits in Wakulla County, some of them were my kinfolks.

Hard Labor Creek

The war came. The men went. The cotton went. The slaves went. The children kept coming: four playing in the yard, one crawling, one in the cradle, one in the graveyard, and one inside her.

It was hard for Roxanne Bradford Gilbert to remember what it was like to not be pregnant, to be able to lace herself tight again, to wear her shell pink silk, refashioned from a young girl's wedding dress to a matron's party dress. Not that there were any parties. And no sense in wearing silk to hoe beans or go draw water from Hard Labor Creek. So mostly she wore a skirt with the waistband let wide as a wash pot, a calico blouse, and a pair of old brogues on her swollen feet. It didn't seem to matter to John Wesley. He still wanted her, Lord only knows why. Every time he was home from the war, even if it was for one day in a year, they made a new baby.

Mary Etta, named for Roxanne's sister, and Amanda, named for Roxanne's aunt, were working their way through *Cathcart's Literary Reader* when the War came. Charles Porter, named after the Reverend Porter Everett who married her and John Wesley, and John, named for his daddy, were wearing britches by then, about to start school. Laurens, the one she lost, the one named after the place in Georgia where she had been born, came a year before the Secession Convention. He didn't live even four months, taken by the fever. The next year, when it became pretty clear that there would be fighting, she had Lorena Blanche. Then, not long before the Battle of Second Manassas, she had Thomas. Rebecca Roxanne, called Roxy, arrived just after Chickamauga. And Alfred Chandley, born two weeks after they got the news about Appomattox.

Washington County was full of people who weren't Confederates and weren't Unionists, just trying to sit the war out until they could go back to raising a little crop and fishing. There were these invisible people, too, deserters from both sides, renegades, runaways. Slaves disappeared off the farms, two or three a week. It was said they went and hid out in Harry's Bay, a damp tangle of hardwoods, bogs, and vines on the eastern side of Orange Hill. Harry had escaped years ago from the Everett plantation to hide in the wilderness. He preferred the lightless woods full of moccasins, panther, buzzards, and bear to chopping cotton. Harry was still in there, too. He'd come out at night, stealing from barns and smokehouses and orchards to feed his growing colony of refugees. He was like a ghost. Maybe, by 1864, he was a ghost.

Sometimes it was hard to know who was on what side during the war. Sometimes people switched sides, Rebels then Yankees, back to Rebels again. Then they might be for some country as yet unfounded, one of their very own. Sometimes it was hard to know what side John Wesley Gilbert was on. In 1861, after getting in the cotton, he took a field hand and went off with the Confederates, telling Jamaica and Caesar to look after Miss Roxy and the young 'uns or he'd know the reason why. When he came back in early 1862, he said he'd been in Virginia. Then he'd go again, and Roxanne heard he was down on the Gulf coast now. He and the field hand were making salt west of St. Andrews. They'd carry big sugar kettles to the beaches and boil seawater down to nothing, then spread the salt on oak planks to dry. George Washington Gilbert told it around the county that his brother John Wesley was making salt for Confederate blockade runners. George Washington had just sent a son off to the 3rd Florida Regiment.

Still, there were rumors that John Wesley was selling salt to Rebs, Yanks, anyone who could pay. Roxanne and Jamaica made their own salt—there was none to buy, even if you had $500—by scooping up the earth of the smokehouse floor, cooking it down, sieving it, and drying the salt that had dripped from the meat over the years. It made all the food taste of clay. Roxanne said now they're just like the white trash dirt-eaters in the sand hills.

In 1864 the Federals under Brigadier General Alexander Asboth decided to hit the rich nearby planter town of Marianna, home of Governor John Milton, HQ for Confederate forces in West Florida. Asboth was a Hungarian exile who had fought with Lajos Kossuth in 1848 in the insurrection against the Hapsburgs. Liberating the slaves of the South was a continuation of the revolution, another blow to the high and mighty, the princes and princesses who owned the land. Also, Asboth was bored and ambitious and wanted to get Ulysses S. Grant to notice him. So in September he marched his seven hundred men up from Fort Walton to Open Pond and Eucheeanna and Cerro Gordo, sweeping north, taking a few Confederate prisoners along the way.

In Marianna, volunteers calling themselves "Cradle to Grave," pimple-faced teenage boys and old men who remembered Andy Jackson, hid behind the oaks and azaleas that grew in front of the fancy slave-built houses on West Lafayette Street. When Asboth marched in, Cradle to Grave let loose a blast of crossfire from either side of the road. They were outnumbered, though, and trapped. They tried to surrender but the Federals ignored the attempt, maybe because the Cradle to Grave commander wasn't wearing a Confederate uniform or any kind of uniform—uniforms were in short supply in 1864. Some of those who frantically tried to make it clear to Asboth, who'd been wounded himself, that they wanted to give up were beaten to death by his troops.

Despite what the Daughters of the Confederacy–sponsored historical marker in front St. Luke's says, the Federals actually won. Only poor old Asboth, freaked out by the sight of twelve-year-olds leveling muskets at him, thought they were about to lose, that Confederate reinforcements were just around the bend. So he lit out toward the coast at midnight on September 28. On the way he passed near enough Orange Hill that Caesar and Charles Porter led the last mule and the last cow to Take In Swamp on the edge of Hard Labor Creek while Roxanne took a pistol, Jamaica took Baby Roxy, Mary Etta held Thomas, and Amanda, John and Blanche hung on to their mother's skirts as they hid in the woods up by the Indian mound, waiting to be raped, pillaged, tortured, and killed by Asboth's soldiers.

Only they weren't raped, pillaged, tortured, and killed. The house wasn't burned down or looted. The barn was still standing. Asboth wasn't the problem, anyway. The problem was this bunch of irregulars called the 1st Florida Cavalry: local Unionists (there were a lot of them lurking in the hamlets and bogs of West Florida), mercenaries, deserters from the Confederate Army, deserters from the Federal Army. There were women dressed as men. There were men dressed as women (the better to get close to a farm where there was only a woman—maybe a woman with a pistol—at home). A lot of them were local. They saw themselves as pro-Union (sort of) Robin Hoods, stealing from the rich white people who got the South into this stupid war to start with.

One night Roxanne heard a noise. One of the Russ boys was sneaking up onto the porch. She'd been to school with his sister. She heard that he'd become a first lieutenant of Company K, 6th Florida Infantry. Then she heard that he deserted. A lot of them deserted: they had no food and no shoes and hadn't been paid for six months. The Russ boy joined the 1st Florida and stopped wearing anybody's uniform. And now there he was, meaning to rob John Wesley Gilbert's house. Six months' pregnant, she leveled John Wesley Gilbert's second-best shotgun at him. Neither of them said a word. He melted back into the blue dark toward Hard Labor Creek.

A few months after the war was over, the 1st Florida disbanded. Some of them, trying to go back to the farm, back to the family, were shot on the road at night or beaten to death in a midnight field or hanged in some lonely stand of trees. The county didn't forget.

The war stopped. The men came back, the ones not dead in Virginia or Georgia or still in somebody's jail for deserting or fighting on the wrong side or still hiding out in the swamps. John Wesley Gilbert came back, limping from what he said was a bullet in his leg, meaner than ever. The cotton got planted, but too much under the sign of Sagittarius, which the old men said was too late. The slaves were free, more or less. Somebody said something about forty acres and a mule, but nobody in Washington County, white or black, believed that.

The war stopped. The Reconstruction began. But that was over there in Tallahassee and farther east and farther south, where the Northerners were arriving to fix their bad lungs or buy land for hotels or railroads or orange groves. Nothing in Washington County got reconstructed, not so's you'd notice.

John Wesley was still full of plans. As long as you had land, you weren't powerless. You could make something of it. John Wesley's acres were full of hardwoods and yellow pines he never got around to clearing for crops. He started looking to buy more forest land and land up on Hard Labor Creek, toward the Davis place. There was talk that Old Man Davis might sell his sawmill. If John Wesley could just get in a few decent crops and make some money, he'd ride up to where Hard Labor's waters were impounded, making a millrace deep and fast enough to keep pushing that wheel no matter who was running things in Tallahassee or Washington, and see what Davis would take for it. If he lived. If the young 'uns didn't bankrupt him. If Roxanne didn't take the second-best shotgun to him.

Mary Etta and Amanda were married and living beyond Holmes Creek. Charles and John were farming nearby. New children came: Uriah in 1867, Zet in 1869—his real name was Zete Rehonzia Leonidas—Henry in 1871, Margaret Viola in 1875, Leslie in 1878. Roxanne lay in the bed longer and longer after each one, her hair now thinning, her face the color of hominy, her hands so thin her wedding ring kept falling off. Old Jamaica tended to her, bringing her cane syrup biscuits and shooing away the children. Jamaica and Caesar had stayed after slavery went. Nobody talked about it, or asked why, they just stayed in their cabin and kept up their vegetable garden—collards, sweet potatoes, pole beans, sweet corn. Caesar worked alongside John Wesley and Thomas in the cotton fields and kept the two hired boys in line. Nobody knows if Jamaica and Caesar ever got paid cash money. Sometimes Jamaica brought greens and potatoes and onions from her gardens up to the house to cook for Roxanne.

In 1878 Roxanne had her last baby. In 1878 John Wesley died. The county turned out at Bradford Church for his burying: Everetts, Rooks, Gainers, Tharps, Sapps, Davises, Roches, Roulhacs. He was, they all said, a hell of a fellow. Roxanne sat there listening to the preacher read some Psalms and tell John Wesley's life: planter, trustee of the schools at Davis Mills and Econfina, justice of the peace. Jamaica stood in the back of the church holding Leslie Winfred, who was colicky and cried all the time. Caesar was out digging John Wesley's grave.

They said John Wesley died from wounds he got during the Civil

War, though that was over thirteen years ago. Roxanne thought he died because he could finally see that the big ideas weren't ever coming true. There would never be a mansion with a name out of a poem, there would never be three hundred slaves, Bohemian glass, silk dresses for his daughters. His sons would never go to academies in New England. He couldn't even find the money to buy Davis's Mill.

Semmes just got through telling the story about how his great-great-grandmother on his mother's side saved her house from the Yankees, who wanted to burn it, by sitting in a rocking chair in the parlor and refusing to move. The Yankee captain was a gent: he wasn't fixing to lay violent hands on a lady, and he wasn't going to burn a house with her in it.

This is one of those archetypal stories of the Confederate South, right up there with the loyal mammy who refuses to let herself be freed and the silver buried in the orchard so the Federals wouldn't steal it.

When Semmes pauses, I tell them about seeing John Wesley Gilbert and Roxanne Bradford's graves for the first time.

It's Easter, 2002. Howard Gilbert, John Wesley and Roxanne's great-grandson, is taking my mother, Betty Gilbert Roberts—John Wesley's great-granddaughter—my brother, Bradford, and me to the place on Orange Hill. John Wesley and Roxanne's children, grandchildren, great-grandchildren, nieces, nephews, all the other Gilbert and Bradford kin lie in friendly little Methodist and Baptist churchyards with granite monuments carved with scrolls and curlicues, Bible verses, and droop-necked angels, at Oakie Ridge and Bradford Church and Orange Hill. Someone remembers them there: In the spring they get an Easter lily; in the fall it's a chrysanthemum; at Christmastime it's a poinsettia.

John Wesley and Roxanne have their own secret place among the oaks and the hickories, the gums and the bays and the nettles. We are not far off the blacktop where Orange Hill Road and Pioneer Road meet. But there are no cars. This, my mother says, is the wilderness.

Howard has led us through grapevines and scrub saplings onto a patch of ground where the shadows are green under oaks wide as a truck tire, oaks with scalloped leaves like the Druid oaks in England. You can see that this used to be a cultivated square of grass, set off from the woods. My brother Bradford says, pointing to a line in the turf, "Here's where the fence would have been. It was probably wooden and rotted pretty quick."

There are some broken pieces of stone with smooth, shaped edges. It might be marble, maybe fragments of a headstone. The stone is green, as well. No one has brought flowers to these graves for a hundred years.

"He's in the ground here somewhere. So's Roxanne," says Howard, "but I wouldn't want to bet you five dollars exactly where. Aunt Bankie said there was two slaves in here, too."

Roxanne died in 1890. Nobody knows when Caesar and Jamaica died. No one bothered to write that down.

Roxanne and John Wesley's third daughter, Lorena Blanche, became the keeper of the stories. She lived with her mother until her mother died, at the age of fifty-five. Aunt Bankie, born during the secession crisis, come of age the year the Federals withdrew their troops, saw the railroad arrive, lived through the great freezes of the 1890s, the Spanish American War, the Great War, the Great Depression, the New Deal, the eve of Germany's invasion of Poland. She never surrendered. She was never reconstructed.

Mourning doves call farther up Orange Hill. My mother used to ride her pony up the hill, picking blueberries from his back, eating handfuls of them till palms and fingers were indelibly purple and had to be scrubbed back white with Octagon soap. Howard teases her: "Betty Jean, I'll bet you can't call that pony's name."

After a pause my mother says, a little haughtily, "Tony. Tony the pony."

She always claims she doesn't remember anything, but she does. She remembers Aunt Bankie—she thought Aunt Bankie was a witch, this old woman with wiry wild hair wearing a black silk dress so worn you could see the individual threads, this old woman who talked about dead people all the time, her mother, Roxanne, and her father, John

Wesley, her sisters, Mary Etta, Amanda, Margaret Viola, her brothers, Alfred, John, and Leslie. One time Mama's mother dressed her up in a white puffy-sleeved frock and brought her to visit her great-aunt. Mama was sat down on a horsehair chair and given a plate of pound cake. She was scared to eat it, thought it might be hexed.

Howard's wife, Suzanne, wears a piece of Aunt Bankie's buried gold on a chain around her neck. Howard was a commercial jet pilot for Eastern Airlines, when there was an Eastern Airlines. They lived in Miami and Atlanta and Dahlonega and other places. But the only place Howard ever wanted to live was Orange Hill, on the land John Wesley Gilbert farmed 150 years ago. "I was looking over my shoulder when I left this place," he says.

He dreamed of coming home, talked about it, planned it.

Suzanne said, over my dead body. When they were first married, she watched her mother-in-law and other Gilbert ladies dipping snuff as they sat on the front porch swapping recipes for pickled watermelon rind. Howard was inclined to join them, to be, as he said, "sociable."

"I told him, I'll never kiss you again as long as I live," said Suzanne. "Howard's mama could spit as far as from here to that rock."

But Suzanne also says, "I wouldn't live anywhere else in the world now."

Howard and Suzanne have a son named John Wesley.

My brother picks up a little piece of stone, an oak leaf, a wild rosebud to press. We walk down toward Hard Labor Creek, swollen with the March rains and brown as a dried tobacco leaf. There's the sound of a car on the blacktop and we're in the twenty-first-century again.

"Jesus, it's so Faulkner," says Clare.

Monica passes around the bourbon.

Semmes looks a little appalled at the snuff. He's what Howard would call "high class." Monica asks if you could also smoke the snuff.

Anna-Kate asks if we knew that Susan Bradford had lived not far from where we're sitting. She had married Nicholas Eppes, the boy from L'Eau Noir Plantation she called "My Soldier in Gray" in 1866. They were poor—or what Susan considered poor. But, as she says over and over, they were happy for thirty-eight years. He was the Leon County School Superintendent. Then, one September evening in 1904, Nicholas Eppes was driving home alone from Tallahassee when somebody came out of the trees by the road and shot him. The scared horse pulling the buggy bolted for home. When the buggy arrived at Pine Hill, Nicholas Eppes was inside, dead.

Three young black men, Isom Edwards, George Caldwell, and Nelson Larken, were arrested. Terrified whites said they were members of the Before Day Club, an underground Negro outfit dedicated to overthrowing white rule in Florida and Georgia. Susan Bradford Eppes always believed that a cabal of corrupt state officials, including my cousin Napoleon Broward, hired Isom Edwards to kill her husband because he wouldn't go along with a public land sale swindle. Isom Edwards said he shot Nicholas Eppes because he owed him twenty cents.

When Susan moved to town, she dismantled the Pine Hill staircase and took it with her. She stored it in her garage. It was as if she were waiting for some restoration of the world of her girlhood, some second coming of the Old South. As if the picnics at the Mound of Dreams and balls at Casa Bianca would go on again. As if the great houses would be remade and some later Bradford would rebuild that staircase in a resurrected Pine Hill. As if Nat Turner and Harriet Beecher Stowe and John Brown never existed. As if the Lost Cause weren't well and truly lost and Florida was still her Florida.

"Those people were so full of shit," says Matt.

Semmes, me, Matt, Clare, Monica the Hungarian architect, and Anna-Kate the ex-mermaid sit looking out the big parlor windows. Ruby's asleep at Semmes's feet. The moon is rising over the May Oak's stump. We are still fussing about the Yankees. And drinking. Suddenly there's un-Aprilish suggestion of cold air. The ghost of Susan Bradford walks into the parlor, sits delicately down on a lyre-back chair, crosses her legs like a movie star, and smiles.

PART II

6

The Pleasure Dome

IN FLORIDA, KUDZU AND POISON IVY will cover your yard in a day; condos and strip malls will appear overnight. Otherwise, things are pretty slow, especially in state government. Maybe it's the heat. Florida took forty-nine years to ratify the Nineteenth Amendment. Florida took twenty years to pass (and then repeal) a bottle bill. We're still working on integration. And voting rights. The only time the State of Florida moves at speed is if 1. there's a lot of money involved; 2. there are a lot of votes involved; or 3. both.

"Terri's Law," for instance. It took Governor Jeb Bush twenty-four hours to frog-march a bill through the legislature forcing this poor South Florida woman, thirteen years in a persistent vegetative state, to keep on living. Terri Schiavo's husband wants her feeding tubes removed so she can die quietly. Her parents want her kept alive on the off chance she will wake up one day; they accuse their son-in-law of wanting Terri out of the way so he can marry his girlfriend. The right-to-lifers and "traditional values" holy rollers are on the parents' side (the Lord has a *plan* for your coma!). Everybody else (and the law) is on Michael Schiavo's side.

When Jeb Bush did the political calculus, he chose to flout the judges who had ruled for Michael Schiavo (they're probably all liberal activists anyway) and stroke his most reliable supporters, Evangelicals. Florida is home to thousands of those Wal-Mart churches, super-size churches with four- or five-figure congregations, firm in their belief that it's okay to execute teenagers, the mad, and the developmentally disabled when they transgress, but everybody else has to carry on till God wants them dead. The governor will need these people if he wants to run for president in 2008. The Speaker of the House, Johnnie Byrd, agreed. He was already working on his 2004 U.S. Senate race and this was free media exposure. The rest of the legislators reckoned they could use some impassioned, tearful, Jesus-bedecked sound bites for future campaign videos. They, too, voted for sticking the feeding tubes back in the woman. Using the pixie-dust power of branding, they called it "Terri's Law." That sounds so much better than "Unconstitutional Invasion of Privacy Legislation to Appease the Christian Right."

The only other time anything this big moved this fast in the capitol was when a billionaire wanted to dump his certifiably insane wife so he could marry his well-bred piece of North Carolina poontang. In Florida, the political is personal. But more about that later.

There had always been two Floridas, silk hat and wool hat, white shoe and no shoes. The old gentry went around saying the plantation died in 1865, but it didn't. The New South's New Florida just found a new way to exploit the land. And a new set of masters. After the social, economic, and psychic wreckage of the Civil War, Florida was about broke. So Florida sold itself. Buy enough land, buy enough legislators, and they'd name a town, or even a county, after you.

In 1881 Governor William Bloxham, an ex–Confederate soldier, scion of a Leon County planter family and Great White Hope of the Bourbon Restoration, came into office facing huge debts from antebellum bonds and annoyed creditors wanting to know when the state was going to make good on the notes. Impressed with the strange (yet possibly shrewd) desire of rich Yankees to own Florida real estate, he convinced the Internal Improvement Fund to sell 4 million acres downstate to a man from Philadelphia. The man's name was Hamilton Disston. He was heir to a company that manufactured tools. During the Civil War, he wanted to do his duty to the Union and fight against slavery, so he kept trying to join the Federal Army. His father kept buying him discharges so he could keep working at the family firm. When Disston Senior finally upped and died, Disston Junior cut loose and headed south. He'd conquered the world of saws. He wanted him some Florida.

The land was supposed to be swampy and blank as a mud puddle. Disston was supposed to drain it. Florida was going to be the new South of France, sporting its own versions of Antibes and St.-Tropez with beachfront promenades where cavaliers in white linen and ladies twirling Battenburg lace parasols would stroll, marveling at summer in January. Maybe a New World Tuscany, with long-windowed villas shining in the sun, surrounded by voluptuous lemon groves and supplied with the latest in indoor plumbing.

Some of the land the state sold Disston wasn't really underwater. Some of it was prairie or piney woods or scrub. It wasn't all empty, either. Way down around Lake Okeechobee and the Caloosahatchee River and the Kissimmee basin—where, ninety years later, a corporation that made its fortune from a cartoon mouse would build a cheesy version of Mad King Ludwig's Bavarian *schloss* and make you pay forty bucks to get in—actual people lived, skinny white people, most of them, with skinny long-horned cows, descendants of the long-suffering beasts the Spanish brought with them 350 years before. These Crackers weren't too thrilled about having the place they'd homesteaded yanked out from under them for the knock-down price of 25 cents an acre. They'd been there since the last Seminole War and the land, too poor for cotton, too wet (or too dry) for much else, didn't look like anybody else even wanted it. The state tried to smooth things over, offering to sell the Crackers their own farms for only a dollar an acre.

Disston tried; he tried hard. His crews dredged a deep channel in the Caloosahatchee and dynamited limestone falls to make canals connecting lakes called Lettuce, Hicpochee, Bonnet, and Flirt. Lake Flirt dried up and later on, as a state engineer said, you could find "a bodacious collection of old fossil bones of dinosaurs and all them old timey critters and mammoth's teeth as big as a cow man's hat."

There were reports of dogtrot-dwelling Crackers using dino vertebrae for doorstops.

Disston, a big contributor to the Republican Party, took President Chester Arthur for a steamboat ride up the (also dredged) Kissimmee River to talk about planting sugar cane, do a little fishing, and stare at the picturesque Crackers, their porches littered with prehistoric femurs, and the Seminoles, dressed in bright patchwork and rickrack.

The steamboat ran aground. Disston's Florida empire ran aground, too. Some in the legislature said Disston had only reclaimed fifty thousand acres. Disston said he'd drained 2 million acres at a cost of $250,000, thank you very much. But the Depression of 1893 hit him hard. Banks called in his loans. The Disston Land Company went bankrupt. In 1896 Disston sat in the bathtub at his Philadelphia mansion and blew his brains out.

While Disston was fooling with the middle of Florida, Henry Plant and Henry Flagler were conquering the edges. Plant took the Gulf; Flagler took the Atlantic. They ran railroads down the coasts and plopped hotels down along the way like pieces on a Monopoly board. Plant was from Connecticut. He'd had business interests in the South before the Civil War; one of his companies collected the tariff for the Confederacy. Plant himself spent the war in Europe. During Reconstruction, he bought up bankrupt train lines in the South and created more. You could take a Plant train right up to the front door of a Plant hotel, and a Plant hotel might look like anything—a chateau, a wedding cake, or, in Tampa, like somebody's tipsy idea of a Moorish palace crossed with a Russian Orthodox brothel.

Flagler was from Ohio, more or less. At least, that's where he spent his business-formative years, selling molasses and brandy for a while, refusing to join up in the Civil War (he said he had other priorities in the 1860s), then getting together with John Rockefeller to create Standard Oil. He made barrels of money and lived in a gingerbread mansion on Euclid Street, the Millionaire's Row of Cleveland, Ohio. He had a pied à terre in Manhattan. He voted Republican because the Republicans were obviously the party of millionaires.

Flagler's wife, Mary, had severe bronchial complaints and was a near invalid. In 1876 her doctors said Flagler should take her to Florida for her health. That medical professionals figured a bug-infested, malarial, storm-prone peninsula far, far away was good for sick people is a testament both to the powerful idea of *heat* and the relentless marketing of Florida to frostbitten Yankees with weak chests. People actually called Florida "the national sanatorium." The Flaglers headed south, taking a train from New York to Savannah, then a steamboat to Jacksonville and another steamboat and a rackety wagon to St. Augustine.

It was godawful: The hotels were lousy (literally); most of the other guests were in the last stages of tuberculosis. Florida's rivers were fat with fish, the woods thick with game, the fields plump with tomatoes and carrots and lettuce, but, except for desserts, which were made with boxcars of sugar, vats of cream, crates of chocolate, and acres of eggs, the food in St. Augustine and Jacksonville hotels came out of cans. Flagler complained to the chef. He complained to the manager. He complained to God. After a couple of weeks of living on tinned ham and meringues à la Chantilly, he flounced back to New York. He was perfectly happy for his wife and children to remain in nasty, primitive (yet balmy) Florida, but he had deals to make. Mary, however, refused to stay without him and left, too. Her doctors, horrified, said she needed to avoid northern winters. But she wouldn't go back to Florida without Henry, and Henry wouldn't leave Standard Oil (all that money!). He bought her a Fifth Avenue palace and hired a green-eyed former actress called Ida Alice Shourds as a companion.

The air on Fifth Avenue may have been rarified, but it was not temperate. Mary Flagler died in 1881. Maybe Henry Flagler felt guilty;

maybe he didn't. At any rate, he took to going out to smart restaurants with Mary's ex-companion, Alice. People noticed she had a new wardrobe and big new jewels. People said they'd been carrying on since long before his wife was buried. Henry Flagler and Alice Shourds got married in 1883.

Meanwhile, Flagler had been reading in the papers about the Disston land deal in Florida. Unlike Alice, who required inducements encased in Tiffany boxes before she'd put out, the state was practically giving itself away. He decided he'd try St. Augustine again. And this time, two years later, the place was much improved. Flagler declared the San Marco Hotel "one of the most comfortable and best kept hotels in the world and filled, too, not with consumptives, but with that class of society one meets at the great watering places of Europe."

It struck him that Florida had prodigious business potential; you just had to give rich tourists the right things—fancy places to stay, fancy food, obsequious service, luxurious travel, gorgeous vistas—to spend money on. The mildewy sheets and watery Spam of 1876 were now just a bad memory. Flagler, on a delayed honeymoon with Alice in St. Johns county, fell hard for the place. He'd create Xanadu out of the wet, mosquito-worried, gator-harried, cheap vastness of Florida. It would be more fun than oil refineries. In fact, he liked Florida so much, he thought he'd buy it.

These days St. Augustine is grimly quaint, Colonial Williamsburg with girls in mantillas instead of mop caps. You can stroll the Spanish Quarter and the Castillo de San Marcos. You can light a candle in the Cathedral-Basilica in the Plaza de la Constitución and sashay around the Zorayda Castle. And when the ruffles and velvet and doublets get too much, you can head for the alligator farm south on A1A that used to raise gators for their hides and ostriches, too. Now the ostriches are gone and the alligators are safe, fat, happy, and mostly immobile—you suspect they're fake, or maybe dead.

You can take in the World Golf Village and Hall of Fame, which pretends to be a museum dedicated to the thrilling sport of golf but is actually an interactive informercial for a vast housing development where you can buy a pastel cottage close enough to the fairway that you have to fear for your windows. You can see Marineland, an underwater movie studio founded by Cornelius Vanderbilt Whitney and Count Ilya Tolstoy. You can drink of the Fountain of Youth—if you like the taste of sulfur.

In Flagler's day, rich people did like the taste of sulfur: It was supposed to cure what ailed you. Flagler, a details man, made sure that his first St. Augustine hotel offered water with and without brimstone. Flagler was also au fait with local history, even if it was wrong. St. Augustine billed itself as "the oldest city in America," which was more or less true, but the tourist attractions of the Oldest House, the Oldest School, the Oldest Store, and the Old Jail were not quite as advertised. Never mind: This was all about show. Flagler had seen a pageant depicting—quite incorrectly—the landing of Juan Ponce de León at St. Augustine on Easter Sunday. So when he built a pleasure dome for his generation of Vanderbilts and Whitneys and counts and countesses, he called it the Ponce de Leon. It was made of cast concrete, the sand-based material of Florida's future that would make roads and bridges to bring the entire North down south, and coquina, the soft lime rock larded with the remains of the ancient sea creatures of Florida's past. It had 540 rooms and covered four and a half acres. It looked like a demented version of the Alhambra.

The Ponce de Leon was a wonder of the new Florida, sporting windows by Louis Comfort Tiffany, a "tropical" courtyard lined with palms, and a band playing the hot numbers of the day. Everything had to be the best. The dining room served croquettes of shrimp and pommes Parisienne and broiled golden plover on toast. Rooms cost $40 to $75 a night at a time when teachers made $6 a week and laborers maybe 75 cents a day—unless they were Florida teachers or Florida laborers, and then they made even less. But no one from Florida stayed in the Ponce de Leon.

After his first triumph, Flagler built more hotels in St. Augustine, with swimming pools and steam baths and masseuses. He paid to pave old colonial roads and ruled city government like a Hapsburg prince, forcing them to abandon a planned streetcar line because it might compete with a transportation system he thought he might construct, making them put water and sewer systems in areas he wanted to develop, lying about land use with impunity (he implied he was going to create a park in one part of the city when in fact he planned yet another hotel), terrorizing them with the power of his money.

When he'd bought everything there was to buy in St. Augustine, he headed south, buying up railroad lines and the rights to railroad lines. For every mile of track he put down, the state gave him eight thousand acres of land. He got a charter to extend the railroad still farther from the then terminus at Daytona all the way to the bottom of the state at the mouth of the Miami River. Even that wasn't far enough. He figured there had to be a way to lay track across the sea itself, all the way to Key West, to the end of America.

Flagler leased convicts to do the work. You could get a man for 40 cents a day, maybe less if you rented a whole lot of bodies. The convicts were mostly black; nobody much cared if a few were worked to death in the name of progress. It was like the old plantation, only without that warm family feeling Susan Bradford liked to brag about. This suited Flagler: He got his transportation network built fast and cheap. This suited the state. Progressive politics were *so* 1870s. Unreconstructed white governors like the Confederate war hero Edward Perry or the Duval planter Francis Fleming were back in charge. A virtual return to the social system pre-1865 accorded with their sense of order, in which white masters—even if they were white masters from the North—ruled.

Here is the railroad Flagler made: from Jacksonville to St. Augustine to Ormond Beach to Daytona to New Smyrna, then past the point in the Atlantic where Juan Ponce de León really first saw the land of flowers, to Rockledge, and down the Indian River, a hundred-mile Atlantic lagoon, past Jupiter and Juno to Lake Worth, then down to the eerie water and grasslands of the Everglades.

And here are the cities Flagler made: Dania, Delray Beach, Perrine, Homestead, Fort Lauderdale, Miami, West Palm Beach, Palm Beach. Fort Lauderdale was a Tequesta settlement for three thousand years, then a Seminole outpost, then a fort named after Major William Lauderdale. Flagler and his trains made it possible for Fort Lauderdale to come into its own as the land of Spring Break, where the boys were, where the girls first went wild. Miami wasn't even called Miami in the 1890s; it was Fort Dallas, after the military encampment built there during the Second Seminole War. Until Flagler started hurling his millions at it, the place was a ticky-tack village inhabited by misanthropes, cane cutters, wreckers, Caribbean refugees, a few Seminoles, and some Yankee second-chancers. Cleveland was far more glamorous.

But Cleveland was cold. Sometimes even Florida—at least the upper two-thirds of it—got cold. So, during the freeze of 1895, which ruined the citrus and vegetable crop and sent the paying guests at the Ponce de Leon scuttling home to where there was heating or at least the coal to make a damn fire, Julia Tuttle, an Ohio widow woman and small-time hustler, decided to market the ass-end of the state to Mister Megabucks Flagler. Where she lived was *warm*. She wrapped a bunch of orange blossoms in a damp square of cotton, boxed them up, and sent them up to him.

Flagler got the point. In fact, he'd had the point for some time; his agents told him that the soil south of the Miami River would grow anything you stuck in it, there were coconut palms and banana trees and a wide bay with first-rate boat-traffic potential. But those creamy little flowers and their glossy, unfrostbitten, Christmas green leaves impressed him. Their sweet-sharp scent smelled like money. And that Mrs. Tuttle owned land right where he might want to lay track.

Flagler headed south by boat and mule and finally turfed up on the porch at Julia Tuttle's house at Fort Dallas. According to the story, he gazed at the pillow-soft sand and the sea the color of Persian turquoises. Sweating like a hog (it really *was* warm), he swept off his damp Panama hat and said, "Madam, I am Henry Flagler and these must be the shores of paradise."

They cut a contract soon after: a good chunk of her property, the right to lay pipe and put telegraph poles across it, and a right-of-way to the water's edge. He brought the railroad down. He built a hotel. By 1896 the town had been incorporated. The locals chorused that they wanted to call it "Flagler" after the demiurge who uttered the *"Fiat!"* (or at least coughed up the cash) that allowed it to come into being. He declined. Flagler found that a low business profile was usually more profitable. Besides, he thought the poetical old Calusa name "Miami" would draw more paying customers.

In February 1897, on the shores of paradise, the citrus trees were in bloom, the young vegetables were tender in the fields, and pine saplings were pushing up through the earth. Then the temperature dropped. And dropped. Thermometers read fourteen degrees. This time Miami was iced.

Never mind, Flagler had plenty of money to lend to bankrupt farmers and tree growers. The tourists would soon forget the sight of brown grass and cold-burned gardenias. After all, it was fourteen degrees in Ohio every day for four months.

Anyway, for Flagler, Miami was a sort of redheaded stepchild, necessary but not beloved. His favorite, his magnum opus, his Garden of Earthly Delights, his Babylon, was up the line a ways. In the late 1880s he had sailed his yacht from St. Augustine down the Atlantic coast to escape his wife. Sometimes Alice sparkled like the diamonds he gave her, but she was moody, sometimes downright spooky. She pitched temper tantrums. She was increasingly obsessed with the spirit world. Maybe a new project would perk her up. Maybe a new project would get him out of the house.

From the deck he spied a slim barrier island of pale topaz sand with stands of big-haired palms. It had been "settled" (using the word loosely) during the Civil War by one Charles Lang, a Georgia boy trying to dodge the Confederate draft. The place was so remote that Lang didn't hear about Appomattox until 1867. When he was told there was no longer a danger that he'd be press-ganged into fighting for Marse Robert and the Southern Way of Life, he decamped, maybe back to Georgia, and other white people took over his palmetto cabin and his oleander garden. They called the place "Hypoluxo," claiming that was an Indian name that meant something like "water all around, no get out." Flagler preferred Palm Beach: it was easier to spell.

Flagler bought land on the ocean side and the lake side and some in the middle. For the island's little scrap pile of residents, it was Christmas. Before Flagler single-handedly quintupled (or more) their property values, the biggest thing that had happened to them was in 1878, when the *Providencia,* out of Barcelona, threading her way through the Caribbean to Havana, ran aground, and broke up, festooning the beach with its cargo of twenty thousand coconuts and one hundred cases of wine. With Flagler and his checkbook, they had it made, they thought, they were in the big time, they thought, until they saw the private train loads of the really rich, robber barons and baronesses with midwestern or Swiss finishing-school accents, swanning into the green velvet and gilt salons of the Royal Poinciana with maids and valets and personal physicians and Havana cigars and trunkloads of dresses from Poiret and Paquin. Hotel regulations said that "no native of Florida" was allowed inside.

Palm Beach has its own rules. Drinking, gambling, and fucking people you weren't married to were all illegal in the rest of Florida but quite *comme il faut* at the Royal Poinciana or The Breakers, Flagler's other swanky joint on the ocean, and the only one you can still pay to sleep in. Even a little transvestitism was all right as long as the man in the dress was a mogul. At the 1898 Washington Birthday Ball, Flagler wore a Watteauesque gown in the colors of the Florida East Coast Railway with a palm leaf corsage. Brother moguls appeared in hooped hand-embroidered lace and white fishnet sewn with alligator teeth. One well-known judge came costumed as Marie Antoinette.

Florida Luxe

Henry James stayed at The Breakers in February 1905. He was on a rare trip to the U.S. to see if his native land was as ghastly as he remembered. It was. He called Palm Beach "Vanity Fair in full blast."

Flagler's resorts were, however, very comfortable, like a really nice padded cell in which the guests, denizens of what James called "hotel-civilization," lumbered around soporifically "beguiled and caged." The fruit of Palm Beach—"the admirable pale-skinned orange and the huge sun-warmed grape-fruit, plucked from the low bough where it fairly bumps your cheek for solicitation"—was good. The gardens of Palm Beach were good, if overstuffed with "extravagant plants" and bougainvillea that would, if you turned your back on it, smother a whole house in a night. The houses were impressive, if vulgar, with their imitation antique vases and sarcophagi conjuring up Lake Como on Lake Worth. The ingenues were decorative rich girls "as perfectly in their element as goldfish in a crystal jar."

There are still grand villas in Palm Beach—20,000-square-foot beach shacks full of Aubussons, Gobelins, ormolu, humidors, cellars provisioned with ancient Armagnacs and crates of 1961 Lafite Rothschild. There are gardens of Sun King splendor, with hothouses for the orchids and the French radishes. There are still heiresses: Pulitzers, Hiltons, Kennedys. It's still Vanity Fair in full blast. In fact, *Vanity Fair,* the magazine, recently featured a glossy story with glossy pictures of young Palm Beach women called Bettina and Celerie and Tantivy, all of whom do strangely, still, resemble goldfish. Or dessert. There's Pauline Pitt, looking a bit like nougat, blond and white-draped, "with her dachshund Maxie," in front of a portrait of her great-grandmother Mrs. Charles Alexander Munn, a creamy lady wearing a dress that seems to be made of almond paste. There's Ivanka Trump, a syllabub of a girl, blond and white-draped, lounging at Mar-a-Lago. The caption says, breathlessly, that her boudoir was created by a set designer for the Metropolitan Opera with "a rug attributed to the young Walt Disney."

Palm Beach is the best-preserved place in Florida. Not the Fakahatchee Strand with its otherwordly orchids and its numinous greenness, nor Gadsden County with its antebellum houses and antebellum social attitudes, nor Carrabelle, where the people still eke out a living as hunter-gatherers of oysters and mullet—none of these are as untouched by modernity as Palm Beach. Air-conditioning, limos, Botox, and high-speed Internet access aside, Palm Beach is just as Henry Flagler left it a hundred years ago. You can't say that about anywhere else in the state.

In Palm Beach, the high WASPs belong to the Everglades Club and the Jews belong to the Palm Beach Country Club. In Palm Beach, Batista's Cuba lives: the Fanjul family, whose Big Daddy Alfonso was a pal of the dictator, presides over an empire of U.S. government–subsidized sugar, 180,000 acres merrily polluting what's left of the Everglades. In Palm Beach, ladies have nothing to do but stand beside a royal palm, looking out at the Atlantic, and get photographed and captioned, "Kentucky Fried Chicken widow Alyne Massey at her home on South Ocean Boulevard."

It's like one of those snow globes; not a cheap plastic one obviously, but one made of, say, Baccarat crystal. Instead of faux snow, there are tiny flakes of gold leaf to impersonate the sun-licked sand of the beaches. It can be shaken up temporarily—one very rich person kills another very rich person, or one very rich person dumps another very rich person for yet *another* very rich person, or a member of the British royal family starts hanging around—but it always settles back down into shiny quietude.

Palm Beach is like Camelot: It's not allowed to rain till after sundown lest the tanned, tucked ladies in Prada or hibiscus-hued retro Lilly Pulitzers darting like hummingbirds in and out of Van Cleef and Arpels or Ralph Lauren muss their artful golden hair. No one wears polyester. No one is poor. No one is fat. No one is black—except the servants. Until 1946 guests at Flagler's hotels were conveyed in what one visitor called "an Ethiopian-propelled wheel chair," or rickshaws, "Afromobiles" pulled by uniformed black men. Until the early 1970s, black people weren't even allowed on the streets of Palm Beach after dark unless they were employed by some Palm Beach white person. They had to carry permits.

Flagler banished all hint of the dirt of work, all the machinery of Xanadu, not behind a curtain but on the other side of Lake Worth. He bought several hundred mainland acres in 1893 to house his laborers, who had to row across to their jobs every morning. At first, the men working on the Royal Poinciana and The Breakers lived in a tent town on the island. But the robber barons and baronesses paying premium prices to loll about the pleasure dome didn't want to see sweaty, smelly lower-class people. *Natives of Florida.* So Flagler created for his fellahin a zone of their own. On Palm Beach, they called their camp either the Sticks—as in far from the good parts—or the Styx—as in the river that started in Arcadia and ended up in the Underworld. Flagler named their new town West Palm Beach. A lot of the workers still called it Styx. The name literally means "Abomination."

Flagler owned most of what could be owned: land, cities, hotels, railways, boats, oil, women, men. He owned the utility companies that served his cities, the water, and the electricity. He owned, or secretly controlled, the newspapers in his realm: the Miami *Metropolis,* the *Miami Herald,* the Jacksonville *Times-Union,* the St. Augustine *Record,* the Palm Beach *Daily News.* They reported on his parties, described his wife's jewels, cheered his deals, and sang his praises like the angels in heaven glorifying God. He owned politicians, local and state, who were beholden to him for bringing settlers and revenue and votes. All it took to separate Palm Beach from Dade County or stop the building of a wharf or a fish camp or a road or a rival hotel was a word, maybe a little note, from him. He was the Roi Soleil of the Sunshine State—*L'état, c'est* Flagler.

The New Revolutionary

Alice Flagler was crazy in love with the tsar. Not her husband, not the one who actually ruled Florida, the other one: the one in Russia. And he was crazy in love with her: the Ouija board said so.

It didn't matter that Nicholas II had gone and married some German princess. It didn't matter that she had never met him. She had her portrait painted in miniature and set in diamonds at Tiffany's. She mailed it to him, handsome Nicky. Nothing could keep them apart. The tsar would have Henry murdered. Or maybe Alice would kill him herself; she was still deciding.

Florida may have been the national sanatorium, but Henry Flagler saw that the Palm Beach air wasn't softening Alice's potentially homocidal Russophilia. Therefore, he thought he'd rather not allow her within a thousand miles of him. In late 1895 Alice moved into a more particular sanatorium: Henry had her committed in Pleasantville, New York. He told them to keep her away from scissors.

Insanity was no grounds for divorce. Adultery, now, that was grounds for divorce. Except Henry was the one screwing around. He kept a few chippies in fine style in New York, even gave one of them $400,000 in Standard Oil stock. He'd taken up with his niece's best friend, too,

Mary Lily Kenan, a North Carolina postdeb with a secret taste for bourbon and laudanum. Mary Lily and the niece would travel down to Palm Beach on the *Alicia,* the private rail car Henry had originally fitted out and named for Alice. They'd stay in one of his beachfront cottages. The niece provided cover. She became conveniently deaf and blind when Uncle Henry padded into Mary Lily's room in the night.

The Kenan family took a dim view of Mary Lily's sleeping with Flagler, who was old enough to be her father—indeed, in some parts of Florida, old enough to be her grandfather. It wasn't the immorality they minded so much, though they were as respectable as deacons; it was the economic uncertainty. Mary Lily was thirty, technically an old maid. Her chances of marrying someone else weren't good since (as the Yankee scandal sheets made clear), she wasn't exactly undamaged goods. Her brother William Kenan, who had designed the electrical systems for Flagler's Florida hotels, hinted that the great man needed to do something about his marital situation: Alice, having tried to cut one of her doctor's hands off, was clearly mad as a March hare. Or he should at least provide for Mary Lily's financial future, now that he'd ruined her reputation.

In 1899 Henry gave Mary Lily an "engagement" present, a necklace of Oriental pearls, big as grapes, with a 12-carat diamond clasp; a house in Palm Beach; and a million dollars in Standard Oil stock. Now all he had to do was figure out a way to change the law.

However, a lunatic wife was still a wife, with rights, in New York. Flagler's legal residence was New York. So he changed his legal residence to Florida. Lunatic wives had the same rights in Florida as New York, but Flagler didn't own any New York railroads or any New York newspapers or any New York legislators. By the time the 1901 session convened in Tallahassee, a bill had been filed declaring, as if butter wouldn't melt in its mouth, that "incurable insanity in either husband or wife shall be a ground for the dissolution of, and divorce from, the bonds of matrimony upon the application of the other party to the marriage" in the State of Florida. That was April 9. By April 19 both the House of Representatives and the Senate had passed the bill. On April 25 Governor William Sherman Jennings signed it into law.

From inkwell to statute, it took sixteen days. Sixteen days flat. That's probably the 1901 time (no computers, no fax, no cell phones, no Blackberries) equivalent of a day, which was how long it took to get "Terri's Law" approved.

In 2004 the Florida governor and legislature were trying to appeal to their core constituents; in 1901 the Florida governor and legislature looked to *their* core constituent, the Lord of the Tropics. Henry Flagler got his bill passed the old-fashioned way, through intimidation and the generous application of cash. He already controlled the money at newspapers in Jacksonville and Miami and points in between, so they more or less had to endorse the "innovative" ideas of Florida's "number-one citizen." But there was also the $20,000 to the Florida Agricultural College. Just coincidentally, one of its trustees, editor of the *Ocala Banner,* wrote that divorcing a woman who was nutty as a fruitcake seemed perfectly reasonable to him.

Fifteen thousand dollars went to ex-Governor Francis Fleming and $14,500 to Representative George Raney of Tallahassee, for "legal assistance." Then there was the $106,942 in "expenses incurred": Flaglerspeak for bribes. Nobody is sure how many legislators Flagler purchased wholesale, but the vote on what everybody except those in state government called "the Flagler Divorce Bill" wasn't even close. Three months later Flagler ditched Alice legally, giving her a couple of million in properties and stocks—not that she knew it, what with her being confined in her cushy loony bin still planning his demise.

There was a little dust-up in May 1901 when Flagler, seventy-one years old, was named as a corespondent in a Syracuse, New York, divorce. While romancing Mary Lily, Flagler had also bought a house for one Helen Long Foote and taken her sailing on his yacht. Her husband was unimpressed. Flagler probably threw money at the case to make it go away. Evidently, Mary Lily forgave him (her regular dose of laudanum might have helped) and on August 24 married him, wearing white silk, orange blossoms, and a straight face.

The brand-new representative from Duval County, Napoleon Broward, voted for the Flagler Divorce Bill. He swore he never took a bribe. But then he would, wouldn't he?

Napoleon Bonaparte Broward was a piece of work, an operator, a smart political cookie from a long line of smart political cookies, starting with his great-grandfather François Brouard and coming on down to the Tuckers and the Robertses. Napoleon was the first of us to figure out the power of being a class traitor, or at least pretending to be a class traitor, a play populist but a real progressive. He was surely the inspiration for the high-bullshit style of his younger cousins' careers in elected office: Senator Luther Tucker strutting around like the cock of the walk spouting Snopesisms, his son Donald, the Speaker of the House, playing country boy for all he was worth, and Justice B. K. Roberts coming over all backwoodsy and baccy-chawy when it suited him. These guys were smart, educated: sub rosa sophisticates who knew all about power but had sense enough to hide it.

Still, Napoleon took the cake. He was a Democratic romantic with a vision of Florida as a place where the wilderness is conquered not for the benefit of the tycoons but the working man, a state where the poor had a shot at dignity and a decent life, a light (an electric light, of course) shining in the economic and social darkness of the Deep South. He was a revolutionary, too, like his great-grandfather François, like his namesake the emperor, the kind of revolutionary who believed in *égalité* as long as some men—the special ones, the talented and the strong—were more *égal* than others. He wanted to overthrow the Bourbons and Yankee industrialists who had reinvented the plantation, called it "progress," and ran a railroad down the middle of it. He wanted to overthrow the Spanish in Cuba. The *insurrectos* of 1895 seemed as mythic as the *citoyens* at the dawn of the French Revolution or the patriots of 1776. Besides, Cuba was in Florida's sphere of influence; hell, Cuba was almost part of Florida, just like a long time ago Florida was more or less a part of Cuba. At the very least, it should be Americans, not Spaniards, running the place.

Broward had a lot of Cuban friends in Jacksonville, particularly a cigar manufacturer called J. A. Huau, head of the scheming expats who called themselves the *junta.* The *junta* were like today's Cuban American National Foundation or Brothers to the Rescue, the guys who go out to the Everglades on weekends and practice invading Varadero

Beach shouting *"Cuba Libre!"* No matter where they live, no matter how rich they get, the only thing that matters is what's going on in Havana. The *junta* figured Napoleon Broward could be useful; the man had a boat, the fastest tug in the South. So they cut a deal with him in 1896 to smuggle war supplies and fighters from Florida to Cuba. Which, though it was breaking U.S. neutrality laws, he did: 3,000 Winchesters, 500 Remingtons, a couple of rapid-fire cannon, 500 pounds of sulfur, 500 pounds of dynamite, and assorted Cuban exile generals and colonels with their dreams of gold epaulettes and high poetic notions and insistence on ignoring suspicions that *los norte Americanos* might have a dog in this fight.

Napoleon Broward was one wily tug captain. He would lie about where *The Three Friends* was headed; he would have her repainted and renamed: one time she became *The Ox* to get past U.S. and Spanish patrols. Everybody knew what he was up to, though: He made sure it was in the newspapers. In July 1896, after a successful gun run, the citizens of Jacksonville threw him a parade. Just a year and a half later somebody blew up the *Maine* in Havana Harbor, pushing the United States into the Spanish-American War. The Spanish almost certainly didn't do it (they knew it would bring war). The Americans denied they did it. But then, they would, wouldn't they?

Napoleon Broward, gun runner, smuggler, imperial adventurer, neo-pirate, was obviously a natural for politics. As a state legislator he may have voted to let Henry Flagler divorce his dreaming mad tsarina of a wife, but Broward had a larger agenda, and it did not include helping out the big boys (he was, after all, a rebel). First, he supported Jennings, the liberal candidate for governor, over W. H. Milton and Dannitte Mays, sons of old planter families. Then, when Jennings announced for Congress, he decided he'd go for governor himself.

Broward ran as the anti-railroad, anti-corporation, anti-Bourbon Democrat. He ran as the plain-speaking ex-sheriff of Duval County, a self-made man, a man's man. He ran on his Robin Hood–Swamp Fox–Scarlet Pimpernel persona as the captain of *The Three Friends*. Before the 1903 campaign, even Whigs in Florida didn't bang on and on about their humble origins and tough childhoods and lack of book learning. Most candidates for high office wanted to impress on you that they were white men of cultivation, property, and connections. Broward convinced the plain folk of Florida (the plain white folk, of course—since the institution of poll taxes and "literacy tests," there *was* no black vote) he was one of them, just a good country boy trying to stand up to the plutocrats. He created Cracker chic.

Cracker chic is a form an inverse snobbery still infesting Florida politics. It has little to do with real Crackers, who raised gaunt cattle on sandy land that was, said the artist Frederic Remington in 1895, "truly not a country for a high-spirited race or moral giants."

Senator (and before that, governor) Bob Graham might be a Harvard man, son of a Miami millionaire, but his campaign song proclaimed him a "Graham Cracker," and his campaign gimmick was to spend a day or two each month performing some *regular guy* job: garbage man, bricklayer, grocery-bagger. He even did a stint as a Christmas elf. Governor Lawton Chiles came from the landed classes, a University of Florida old-line fraternity boy, member of Blue Key, yet he got elected by droppin' his *g*'s and gettin' on the road in a pair of work boots and billin' hisself as "Walkin' Lawton." Governor Jeb Bush comes from some of the bluest blood and oldest Yankee money in the country but never seems to want to talk about prepping at Phillips Andover and summering in the compound at Kennebunkport. He's found it far more profitable to wear guayaberas and eat Golden Flake potato chips (as advertised on TV by FSU Coach Bobby Bowden) and drop *y'all* into his conversation whenever possible.

Napoleon Broward published a pamphlet promoting himself during the primary campaign and papered the state with it from the Blackwater River down to Flagler's Atlantis. As the resurgent Unreconstructeds liked to say, since Florida Republicans were now no more use than tits on a mule, whoever won the Democratic primary was as good as elected.

Broward's *Autobiographical Sketch* worked on the minds of Florida voters as powerfully as Bill Clinton's *Man from Hope* video or Jimmy Carter's *Why Not the Best?* It was a masterpiece of obfuscation and selective memory. It was fairly economical with the truth. In other words, it was a kick-ass piece of spin. He didn't tell about the old days on his family's old plantation when Marcellini, "an old Spanish Negro," played Viennese waltzes on his fiddle, or the summer cottage at White Springs, or the fields of fat cotton planted by the slaves his daddy, Napoleon Bonaparte Broward Senior, owned, or the sixteen thousand acres on the upper St. Johns given by decree of the king of Spain to his granddaddy John Broward, who was also the first senator from Duval County after statehood. He didn't tell about the lands on the river now named after his family, granted to his great-granddaddy by the Spanish colonial governor.

No, Broward made himself sound like Oliver Twist crossed with Huck Finn with a pinch of Abe Lincoln thrown in. He practically claimed to have been born in a log cabin he built himself. He told affecting tales of being orphaned at twelve and how he and his brother Montcalm, two young boys, had to fend for themselves in the woods, growing food and making a little money logging and fishing and living off "hominy, peeled sweet potatoes, and a piece of pork all boiled together in the same pot."

The *Autobiographical Sketch* drove Napoleon Broward's aunts Margaret and Florida crazy, what with it making the family sound like white trash who'd never seen an indoor privy and wouldn't know what to do with a finger bowl or an oyster fork to save their lives. The *Autobiographical Sketch* also drove Robert Davis crazy. He was Napoleon Broward's primary opponent, a Bourbon hanger-on, the preferred candidate of the big money boys, the big hotel and railroad boys: chief among them, Henry Morrison Flagler. In his stump speeches, Davis would argue that the *Autobiographical Sketch* proved that Broward was unqualified for high office, pointing to the story about how Napoleon and Montcalm let a cow get through a broken fence and eat their sugar cane, or the one about how they planted four sacks of potatoes but only yielded a one-sack crop. "Why," said Davis, "when I was a farmer's lad, I planted four sacks of potatoes and they produced twenty. See how much smarter I was?"

With the help of Flagler's newspapers, Davis ridiculed Broward's plan to drain the Everglades. Broward, in turn, campaigned outside the cities—especially Flagler's or Plant's cities—staying in the little towns and rural areas where the chandeliers and champagne of the Royal Poinciana or the Ponce de Leon were just rumors, as fantastical as a fairy tale. In May 1904 Davis and Broward appeared on the same stage at a sort of Democratic unity rally in Jacksonville, at which the usual dissing of Republicans and promises of beer on election night took place.

Broward, not usually known as a natty dresser, sauntered up in a linen suit the color of new butter and proceeded to lambaste Davis for his alliance with "land pirates and purchased newspapers." Then he sat down with a little mysterious smile on his face. When Davis got up to make his speech, he didn't get three words in before there came from the Laura Street dock a hell of a noise. It was Broward's boat, *The Three Friends,* blowing its whistle for all it was worth, drowning out Davis's speech. Davis finally had to give up and sit down.

Okay, this wasn't sportsmanlike, but in Broward's mind, neither were the railroads and their lavish use of influence on Davis's behalf. Mud was slung. Pro-Davis factions accused Broward of being a Catholic. The paper in Pensacola said he was an Apache Indian. The paper in Tallahassee asserted with the greatest of confidence that Broward *dyed his moustache every day*.

In the primary, he lost St. Johns County and Dade and Hillsborough, the city/money/railroad fiefdoms. He lost his home county of Duval. But he won overall by 714 votes. In the general election, he took 80 percent of the vote.

His good-old-boy marketing strategy worked. The high-toned, pissed-off Mrs. Dannitte Mays was heard to sniff, "Anybody can get to be governor of Florida these days, even a jack rabbit. All you have to do is wag your ears and you are chosen."

Lizzie and Lease and the Emperor of the Glades

Mary Elizabeth Tucker's first mistake was called Morgan Spears. He was ten years older than she was, a big talker, a petticoat-chaser. She had two babies with him, a girl, born in 1890 when she was barely eighteen, and a boy who died. By 1895 she had divorced Morgan Spears, or thought she had.

Her second mistake—that's what some of them said—was Valarious Lafayette Roberts. He was three years younger, a little redheaded banty rooster man, a charmer. He went by "Lease." They got married on October 20, 1895. They got married again on December 10—the divorce hadn't quite been final. For more than a month, Mary Elizabeth Tucker, a good Methodist girl from a founding family of Wakulla County, was an adulteress and a bigamist.

So what with the divorce and the bigamy and the living in sin and the two weddings (tongues wagged in churches from Smith Creek to Vause Branch all the way down to Carrabelle) and the first young 'un, Harriet Jane (named for her grandmothers Harriet Vause and Jane Broward), and the next one, John Richard (named for Lizzie's great-uncle John Broward and Lease's father Richard Roberts), and then Edgar Lafayette, my grandfather, named for his daddy, Lizzie didn't see her cousin Napoleon Bonaparte Broward inaugurated governor in January 1905. She may have never even met him, though her father, Luther, kept in touch with his Duval County cousins, at least until just after the Civil War. They were doubly kin: Luther Tucker's mother was a Broward; Napoleon Broward's grandmother was a Tucker. Exogamy wasn't a priority in Old Florida.

The Browards lost their large fortune and large plantations, and the Tuckers, though they still owned most of old Rufus's land, were slipping from what passed for middle-class gentility in the swamp to the tough life of subsistence farming. The Tuckers tried to hang on to some scraps of that former status: Luther Tucker taught his ten children at home when there was no money for a teacher at the school. Florida was full of money, it just wasn't in Wakulla or Leon or Gadsden or Franklin Counties. It wasn't in the cotton fields or the tobacco barns. It was on the railroad lines or in the big hotels or in the cities; the money was in places where there were white beaches and clear water or phosphate in the green rivers. The two Floridas grew still farther apart: the silk-hat sunshine Florida of Tiffany glass and Worth gowns on Worth Avenue, and the wool-hat shadow Florida of dogtrot cabins and collard patches. My family belonged to the Florida of the shaded creeks and the deep woods.

Lease Roberts was a Napoleon Broward man. It wasn't just because the governor was his wife's cousin (he never expected to waltz at Tallahassee balls or smoke Cuban cigars with the old aristocrats of the Red Hills), and it wasn't just because Broward said he was for the plain man, the common man (Robertses might be Crackers but they never thought of themselves as ordinary), he was a Broward man because Napoleon Broward didn't sit on his linen-upholstered backside doing nothing. Henry Flagler and that bunch just signed checks with their soft manicured hands; Napoleon Broward's hands knew North Florida dirt and engine oil and soot and pine tar. It said so in his autobiography.

Broward's people had operated a sawmill. Lease started logging at fifteen, when his father died. He had eight oxen, named Big Red, Little Red, Rat, Pet, Jack, Lewis, Brood, and Bright. They'd drag pines through the palmetto scrub, then float them down the Sopchoppy or the Ochlockonee to the Apalachicola Lumber Company. I have a photograph of Lease and the oxen in the longleaf forest. He wears a shirt with its sleeves rolled up as he drives them. Big Red and Brood lead the team, their faces ancient as a cave painting. Way in the back you see the log cart, with wheels more than six feet high. They're moving a tree a grown man couldn't hug his arms around. Lease's belt buckle gleams like he polished it regularly. His hat is set at a jaunty angle on his head. He looks like he owns this forest, owns this Florida.

Like Napoleon Broward, Lease was a boat captain. *The Belle of the Bend* wasn't a slick patrol-buster with concealed holds and a rapid-fire Hotchkiss gun mounted on its bow like *The Three Friends,* but it was a tidy craft, gasoline powered and suitable for hauling people and timber and oil and suchlike from Apalachicola up to Smith Creek or St. Marks or Chattahoochee. When he gave the *Belle* her name, he was thinking, he said, of Lizzie.

Lizzie was thinking of the babies, who came about every other year, ten of them. Lease was around only on the weekends, which was quite enough. The children knew to behave themselves, to keep quiet—quiet and out of the way. They stayed in the yard as much as possible when Daddy was home. His own grandchildren agree Lease was a mean son of a bitch. It was probably the drink. He'd fly off into screaming rages. He'd hit the children, he'd hit Lizzie. Sometimes he'd take a knife to her dresses (she didn't have many) or smash up the dishes. Then sometimes he'd be as happy as the Fourth of July.

At night, after he'd cooled off and before he'd gone to the corn liquor, he'd tell things he heard from passengers on the *Belle,* about doings in South Florida, about a hotel in Tampa that looked like a castle, about train cars done up in damask and velvet like a Calhoun Street parlor; about women swimming in the sea wearing scandalous costumes of thin wool and stockings rolled just above their knees or women down in Palm Beach who smoked cigarettes like men and argued politics; about that Henry Flagler and the marble palace called Whitehall, bigger than the biggest plantation house you ever saw, built for the wife he married after he got rid of the doollally one; and old Napoleon Broward, who was going to show those railroad boys who was boss in Florida. He'd already showed the Spanish down in Cuba. Now he aimed to shake things up at home. He aimed to be the new emperor of Florida, an emperor with big ideas. He was going to drain the Everglades, open up 5 million acres to the small farmer, 5 million acres of the most fertile land, they said, outside the valley of the River Nile.

Lizzie read the Bible: *I will lift up mine eyes unto the hills, from whence cometh my help.*

Napoleon Bonaparte Broward was going to change the world. Or, at least, Florida. Even though he'd voted for it, he did away with the Flagler divorce bill—which had outlived its usefulness—had it repealed with a maximum of righteous table-whacking and rococo speeches from legislators about the sanctity of marriage. Just because a person is deranged is no reason to fool with the inviolability of wedlock.

And just because people were poor didn't mean they shouldn't get decent book learning. There would be schools all over the state. Teachers would get paid a living wage. Children would stop being worked like slaves for almost no money. Fish, oysters, game, and forests would be conserved. He'd break the power of the railroad barons by building roads and encouraging the use of automobiles (that would show that old goat Flagler). He'd regulate textbooks and judges and businesses.

There would be three colleges: one for white boys (the old Seminary East of the Suwannee at Lake City), one for white girls (formerly the Seminary West of the Suwannee, home of Luther Tucker's Baby Corps), and one for Negroes at the normal school in Tallahassee, at least until he could get the United States Congress to, as he put it in his 1907 address to the legislature, "purchase territory, either domestic or foreign," and "organize a government for them of the Negro race, to protect them from foreign invasion; to prevent white people from living among them on the territory; and to prevent Negroes from migrating back to the United States."

It's not like Broward had to worry about the black vote. Since 1877 there *was* no black vote. If a black man tried to exercise the franchise, he'd be subject to a crippling poll tax or a citizenship "examination" in which he could be asked to recite, word perfect, the Eighth Amendment to the U.S. Constitution or asked how many windows there were at the White House. There was always the threat of uppityness: Some Floridians had never gotten over those interfering Northern do-gooders with their Negro schools and social programs. Still, advocating getting rid of the built-in cheap, statutorily subservient workforce and shipping them off to Liberia or Utah or somewhere was an eccentric position for a son of the old plantation to embrace. The Bourbons weren't impressed: They still had cotton and tobacco to harvest. The Yankee developers weren't impressed: They sold Florida as the Old South without any of that uncomfortable *Uncle Tom's Cabin* stuff, happy darkies in white coats serving rum punch on the terrace, breakfast cooked by Aunt Jemima herself (or one of her close kin), and postcards of pickaninnies up a palm tree with the caption "Gator Bait."

Just because Broward was a revolutionary didn't mean he couldn't be a white supremacist. He surely didn't expect the U.S. government to round up black folk (who were, according to that dadblame Constitution, now citizens) and park them somewhere off in a corner, but the idea was a good little vote-grabber, a gesture toward his loyal constituents, who were suspicious of any whiff of "nigger-loving." Lease Roberts, whose people had never owned slaves and who regarded Negroes as an economic and social nuisance, no matter Lizzie's fleeting childhood memories of those loving, long-gone, old-time Negroes on what was left of her daddy's farm, approved.

But the really big idea was taming that "pestilence-ridden swamp," the 'Glades. John Broward had the same notion when he was a state senator in the 1840s: Suck the water out of those vast acres to get at the impossibly fecund muck underneath. Nobody cared back then. Christian white folks weren't about to go live down there in that wet, snakey, alligator-infested Indian territory. It did not look like good cotton land. But now Florida was more farms and cattle range than plantations. Farmers demanded terra firma. Floods in 1903 destroyed crops in badly drained South Florida fields. Then-governor Jennings cut a deal with Teddy Roosevelt to turn over almost 3 million acres of the federally held Everglades to the state.

This suited Broward. The lumber lords, the railroad lords, big farmers and little farmers, and steamboat companies all wanted a piece of the 'Glades. Broward would see that they got it, or at least *think* they might get it. He wanted to blow a hole in the bedrock, let all the water out that way. He wanted to dig a canal into the St. Lucie River and other canals in the Kissimmee and Caloosahatchee. He'd create a spider-leg canal system down there connecting the Gulf of Mexico with the St. Johns and the Atlantic, running ships through Lake Okeechobee. Florida had too much water. He, Napoleon Bonaparte Broward, would solve that problem. The water used to rule, now men with dredging machines and dynamite would rule. There would be dry land for thousands of small farmers down there on that sable-colored, molasses-sweet soil, thousands of small farmers who would ever after be Broward voters, propelling him beyond the governorship of Florida to a senate seat and maybe even the White House itself. It could happen. It could.

"Water will run downhill!" Broward declared, by way of a slogan. Everybody nodded sagely. Water would do whatever he said.

What really happened was this: Dredging began in 1906, digging up the New River, blasting through limestone and hacking through forest. To keep the dredgers running, the state had to sell off big chunks of land, not to the Cracker homesteaders, the Lease Robertses, of Broward's speechifying, but to speculators and con artists and liars who then subdivided it into lots and dangled them before shivering Yankees. Genuine Florida real estate! Would grow anything—oranges, sugar cane, tomatoes, roses! Would be worth a fortune, as soon as those canals were dug and those roads built and those towns populated. But it would still be Paradise, Paradise you could buy with a dollar down and a dollar a week. Never mind that most of it was still, despite Broward's best efforts, under water.

Papa Roberts would tell that his father had a notion to move south for a while, leave the branched-over, shaded skies of North Florida for the big yellow-green emptiness of South Florida. He could get rich down there, down where they said the dirt was like chocolate cake. Lizzie kept quiet: She didn't want to leave her parents and her brothers and sisters and cousins, or the pine-and-cypress cabin Lease had built for her on Red Lake. This was her home and her children's home, not the palm-treed flat places down there where the leaves never changed color and it never got cold enough to slaughter a hog. Lease would have his big ideas, too, then he'd calm down: There would be another run on the *Belle,* or he'd take Big Red, Little Red, Rat, Pet, Jack, Lewis, Brood, and Bright out to log another part of the forest to pay for this year's winter clothes. Lease often forgot ideas as soon as he had them.

Highway 1 starts west of François Brouard's Spanish land grant and passes through John Broward's erstwhile acres, not too far from the Broward River. It runs through Duval County and crosses the St. Johns near where Napoleon Broward docked *The Three Friends* and through St. Augustine, within throwing distance of Henry Flagler's Alhambras and Alcazars, and on down south, paralleling the line of his railroad through West Palm Beach, looking enviously across Lake

Worth at Palm Beach like the chambermaid at a Budget Inn watching a *Town and Country* cover girl try on tiaras.

I drove up to The Breakers, only to be stopped by the guard at the gatehouse. I thought he was going to deny me admittance on the grounds that I was a native of Florida and so prohibited by the Founder. But he just looked pityingly at my rented Alero and told me it was valet parking *only,* $20. If you spend $20 in one of the restaurants, parking is free.

I sat in the Tapestry Bar, dim and woody as the library of a great English house, drinking a single glass of Veuve Clicquot, which cost, appropriately, $20. The Breakers is a compendium of Jamesian high style: Roman loggias curtained in heavy silk, gilt French salons, Venetian chandeliers garlanded with pink glass flowers. The place gazes out over the waves like a princess in exile longing for Europe. It's still as cool as lemon sorbet and as gilded as the Winter Palace. The Atlantic is still the color of Burmese sapphires. But Henry Flagler's ghost—surely he haunts the sybaritic spa—must have been outraged: a *native of Florida* sucking down champagne in his exclusive establishment.

Not that The Breakers is so exclusive anymore. The guests are mostly convention-going dermatologists or cable TV execs who come to eat five-course banquets in the Gold Room and play at being posh. The committed rich, old money or nouveau, the aging rock 'n' rollers, the adding machine or floor wax heiresses, the real estate rajahs, the advantageously divorced—they don't stay at The Breakers these days. They have their own walled haciendas and *hôtels particuliers*.

This is the Florida Flagler built, the Florida of shell-colored castles and cold champagne and smiling waiters and no unpleasantness, where the water is always blue and the golf courses smooth as a supermodel's thigh. Still farther down Highway 1, the rest of Flagler's coastal kingdom: Fort Lauderdale, Miami, Miami Beach, and all the way to the for-once literal end of the road at Duval Street in Key West. We got rid of the water a hundred years ago. Now, with all these people moving to Florida, we want it back.

Just as now, in Flagler's day the Florida of the advertising agency took precedence over the Florida of the earth: Flagler's imagineers came in and cut up the hammocks, tore out the native vegetation, drove away the turtles and the panthers, and reshaped the rivers and wetlands. The banana trees and the guavas were nice enough, but they had to go to make room for the streets of the new Miami. They left the palms and they left the orchids (they had the right look, what you'd find in the Hesperides or Elysium as illustrated by Maxfield Parrish), but then planted other trees and flowers, from Australia or Japan, or that made Florida look somehow more like Florida—Disneyfication before Disney—more like Umbria or Andalusia or Persia or some other province of the mind.

The money clings to the edges, looks out to sea.

The funny thing is, Palm Beach is bracketed by elemental forces even Flagler couldn't buy off. Three miles out in the Atlantic, there's the Gulf Stream, seventy fathoms deep nearest to shore, stronger than all the engines of all of Flagler's trains. Farther out in the blue-gray waters, there's the incubator of storms that periodically knock over the airy palaces and the spun-sugar towers. In 1906 and 1926 and 1928 hurricanes came and did their best to drown the pleasure domes, though, as usual, they mostly flattened the flimsy huts of the poor who rolled the lawns of the estates or harvested the crops over in the moody regions of Okeechobee.

A couple of dozen miles west from Flagler's ice-cream village lie the 'Glades themselves: water, grass, sky, muck, cane. This is the Florida that Napoleon Broward built, or tried to, his engineers trying to cage or kill the giant lake, the largest in America after the Great Lakes themselves, to make a political empire, to make the water run downhill. All he really did was make Florida safe for U.S. Sugar, which now runs the great plantations with their squared-off canals and field after field of the bayonet-leaved plant from which you get the most important drug in the world.

In Palm Beach, at the end of the pretty street called Cocoanut Row, sits the Everglades Club, built by the heir to the Singer Sewing Machine millions, a Moorish fantasy of a country club that looked ancient even before it opened. Addison Mizner, who didn't have anything better to do, made the workmen install roof tiles crooked and fire shotguns at the wood beams so they'd look medievally wormy. The Everglades Club is supposed to be the first "Mediterranean Revival" building in Florida, the fantasy that started the fantasy boom of the 1920s that let Coral Gables pretend it was Granada and Miami pretend it was Seville. Nothing native to the Everglades has ever entered the Everglades Club.

Lease and Lizzie Roberts never saw the Everglades, much less the Everglades Club. They wouldn't have been allowed in there. They never went south of Apalachicola. The phosphate mines, the orange groves, and the confetti-scatter of lakes in Central Florida, the ocean of hot chartreuse-colored cane around Okeechobee and the bromeliad tangle of Big Cypress and Fakahatchee, places their children would see, places their grandchildren would put houses and roads on, were just postcard pictures or mellifluous names to them. They stayed in their Florida, in the deep green shadows.

I have this other photograph; it's of the family in about 1901, when Napoleon Broward had first got into the legislature. Lizzie wears a high-necked black silk dress—her best, no doubt, even though it's clearly not new—and has done her hair in an approximation of a Gibson Girl pouf. Lease wears a coat and tie that's not quite as tight as it ought to be. He has sloping shoulders: You can see he's small, with an unconvincing mustache. Five-year-old Harriet Jane wears a white pinafore with a set of beads and a bow in her hair. John is in the middle of the frame, his round face framed by a ruffled baby smock. His little fist is closed on a rope and at the other end of the rope is a broad-faced dog, a dog with a look of utter resignation on his kind, ugly, muttly face.

In 1908 Napoleon Broward, his support still strong (despite the unrealized dream of Everglades muck making all the Crackers rich), his mustache just silvered by age, decided he'd become Florida's next U.S. senator. The senior incumbent had just died of typhoid fever, and the Marianna aristocrat Broward appointed to fill out the term wouldn't, he figured, want to exert himself for a real campaign. The newspapers were rude: "Like another Minerva, springing in full armor from the forehead of Jupiter, Broward sprang into the senatorial arena clothed almost in ethereal glory as one specially anointed."

He lost in a primary runoff to a man almost as progressive as he, just less, as some of the editorialists put it, "colorful." So he hung around for a couple of years, calling himself again "Captain Broward," as if to remind everybody of his *Three Friends* exploits, until Florida's other Senate seat opened up in 1910. He won the first primary by a whisker, the second by a set of whiskers, and was on his way to Washington when, in the fall, he developed severe gallstone problems and a high fever. He was dead before he could make another campaign speech. My grandfather told how his grandfather Luther wrote a letter to Annie Douglass Broward and her daughters to convey the sympathy of all the Tuckers. And he told how Lease went on a three-day 'shine binge to express his own sorrow.

In March 1913 Henry Flagler was kicking around in Whitehall, his and Mary Lily's Palm Beach monster of a marble *palais*. He'd had a few setbacks: the 1906 hurricane that killed 200 workers trying to ram his railroad all the way down to Key West. And before that, the 1903 fire that destroyed The Breakers. The place was made of heart pine, oily as Beluga caviar. It was bound to burn.

Mary Lily was in the house somewhere, maybe in the salon, which was taken splinter by gold-leafed splinter from a French chateau and reassembled, or maybe in the great hall modeled on St. Peter's in Rome or in her lacy boudoir, doing a little well-deserved opium. Henry was alone downstairs when, it seems, he needed to use the gents. Now, the lavatory in Whitehall was no ordinary *pissoir* but a symphony of porcelain and alabaster. It also had these pneumatic doors that would close automatically. Henry didn't get out of the way of the urinal door in time and it whacked him in the back, sending him sprawling. The servants found him unconscious with a broken hip. It took him nine weeks to die. He was eighty-two.

Up in New York, his death didn't register with Alice. She was still plotting, still speaking to the spirits, though, evidently, not Henry. When she died in 1930, she was still about to marry the tsar. No one had the heart to tell her about the Russian Revolution or that Nicholas II had been shot to death in a cellar.

7

Bradford Gilbert Sees the World

ON THE WALL HE'D HUNG two girlie calendars, one for 1947 and one for 1948. I think they came from the feed company or maybe the tractor place in Marianna. They were twenty years out of date, but that wasn't the point: 1947 was a champagne blonde in a black silk evening dress with a giant pink hibiscus, stamen distended, on the skirt; 1948 wore poison green velvet slit up to *here*. On her finger a long-tailed macaw bright as Christmas tree lights sat and stretched out his wings. Nineteen forty-eight had red hair. I wanted to be her. When I said that to my grandfather he laughed and said, "Well, Captain. We'll see what we can do."

Summers at the farm in Washington County, I would hang around in his office, even though it was hot as a box in there. The house had air-conditioning, growling window units that kept the place at about 60 degrees Fahrenheit. Grandmama could leave a bowl of tapioca pudding on the kitchen table and it would stay cold for half a day. The office was separate from the house in what had once been a barn, a big, pine-paneled room. There was a gun cabinet, which I wasn't allowed to touch, and a fishing cabinet, which I was, stacked with rolls of line, round cardboard boxes of corks and sinkers and hooks in every manufactured size and then some, weird feathered lures and fake worms made out of some gooey translucent substance in psychedelic purples, pinks, and blues. I would steal them and hide them in my underwear drawer.

There was a cherry bench and an oak table made from wood off the Hard Labor Creek land and planed at the mill. There were stacks of *National Geographics* in the corner, along with some magazine that always had either a big buck or a wild-eyed fish on the cover. There was a framed photograph of my mother taken for the newspapers when she got engaged, her face and shoulders the color of cream, her hair almost black, her lipstick such a deep ruby it looked almost black, too. There was a picture of Granddaddy and Commander Rollo standing by the camphor tree. Granddaddy wore a summer straw hat and a stern expression. Commander Rollo wore a brass chain collar and an even sterner expression. Commander Rollo was a prize polled Hereford bull. His hair was the same color as Miss 1948's.

In the corner by the door squatted the safe. It was black as pencil lead, big as the biggest console TV you could get in 1969, with a silver ball and bar in the middle of its nine-inch-thick door. Inside Granddaddy kept the treasures: the deeds to the land, the silver dollars, the few gold pieces saved from Aunt Bankie's Orange Hill hoard. Granddaddy's journal was in there, too, and the postcards and the photographs. He'd written the journal in 1918 and 1919, from the time he left the fort in Georgia, as he put it, "entrained for an unknown destination, riding in Pullman cars," to after the Armistice, when, even though the fighting had stopped, his engineering corps kept on building camps and hospitals next to the ruins of castles and cathedrals for those who wouldn't be going home anytime soon. He was nineteen when he joined up and turned twenty demobbed—had his birthday on a tear in Monte Carlo. I never thought it was funny that he kept the journal in the safe. The journal was valuable. It showed that Bradford

Gilbert had been somewhere. He'd been to places way older than the farm and the mill, to where he couldn't understand what they said in church or even know what he was eating, places where there was blood mixed in the soil and graveyards big as whole counties. He knew that millions of boys had died. He saw and smelled death all over the green fields of Brittany and Normandy and on the Langres Plateau.

He was a Gilbert, raised on Aunt Bankie's tough-it-out-son stories of the War Between the States, and so wasn't going to get all het up, even about world war. He wrote at the top of the journal: "My Trip to France."

I never got tired of reading it, even though I had to do it on the bench in the office, which was harder and more upright than the pews in the First Presbyterian Church in Chipley: The journal did not leave the confines of the office. He'd work on accounts with his prehistoric adding machine, and I'd sit there reading in the humid quiet, the sound of crickets singing in the grass and the *dup-dup-dup* of the fan trying, and failing, to do something about July. Granddaddy's teenage prose is stripped down, creatively spelled, telegraphic, slangy. He doesn't go in much for feelings.

> *Sunday, Sept. 8, 1918: Passed thru South Carolina and North Carolina to-day, met Red Cross canteen at Sumpter and Florence; they gave us cigarettes, candy, apples, and cool fresh water which was indeed a treat as we had been drinking the water which I know had been in the tanks for at least three weeks.*

He'd couldn't decide what he wanted to do with his life. Down in South Florida, they were making big hotels and railroads and getting rich off phosphate mining. But he didn't want to live with Yankees. And best he could tell, Florida was a mess. That white-trash preaching lawyer Sidney Catts had got himself elected governor, scaring people about how whisky, Roman Catholics, and "niggers" were tàking over the state. He went around saying that the only friends the common man had were Jesus Christ, Sears Roebuck, and Sidney J. Catts.

Bradford Gilbert reckoned Florida could handle moonshine, Negroes, and the pope without him. So he went off to the army *on purpose,* as his father said, disgusted. He'd wanted to go earlier, even before 1917 when the U.S. got in, go fight with the Canadians or the British, those boys. They were almost as good as Southern boys. But then he would have had to lie about his age, and his mother, a big Baptist, said he'd go to hell if he did that.

He was so bored. Running the lumber company with his brothers, running the turpentine still, overseeing the hands at his father's sawmill out there on Hard Labor Creek: What kind of life was that for a young man whose great-great-grandfather Moses Gilbert had fought in the American Revolution and whose grandfather John Wesley Gilbert had got wounded in the Civil War? A young man who had read whole books about the Crusades and the Wars of the Roses and thought Teddy Roosevelt was the greatest fellow since Richard the Lionheart?

> *Monday, Sept. 9, 1918: Passed thru Richmond about ten thirty, crossed the James river, passed thru beautiful Virginia country, went thru Washington, saw the national Capital and the Washington Monument from a distance. We saw men from the Q.M. Corps who were ready for overseas service; we were all impressed by the caps.*

His father, Zet Gilbert, had bought the mill in the early 1890s, before Bradford was even born. He'd bought the old Carter place and the Slay Field up above the mill. He planted corn and cotton. He bought piece after piece of property, cutting the timber but keeping the land, expanding his holdings. He built a farmhouse, two barns, a church. He built a school. He built cabins for the hands, who were mostly black, in the piney woods. He built a commissary up past the house, a long, low building with barrels of flour and sugar, hoop cheese, candy, salt pork, hominy, dried peas, cane syrup. Zet Gilbert didn't pay much in wages—none of the turpentine lords did—but he fed his people, everybody gave him that, and he didn't work them to death.

In 1890 he'd married Mary Broadwater, who'd come from South Georgia to teach in the school. By 1910 they had three sons, Fred,

Homer, and Bradford, and a mess of girls. Zet owned more land than his father ever had. He ran his farm and his lumber business and his turpentine business sitting on the front porch overlooking the millstream. Soon it was on the map of Florida: Gilbert's Mill.

In April 1917, just a few days after America declared war against the German Empire, the Florida Naval Militia was called up. Boys were going to Georgia and Key West to enlist. Fred was eligible for the draft. Zet Gilbert wasn't impressed. He didn't hold with foreign entanglements. On the other hand, the shipyards in Tampa and Jacksonville were going to need a lot of lumber. A lot of lumber.

Wednesday, Sept. 11, 1918: At Camp Mill, near Jamaica, New York. Had inspection all day, checking clothes. I think that we will get some new clothes soon. Some of the boys went to the Big City and had wonderful tales to tell about it.

Thursday, Sept. 12, 1918: Turned in all unserviceable clothes and drew some of the overseas equipment. There were no matches in cloth and about half of the mens clothing fits.

Friday, Sept. 13, 1918: Same old thing: drawing and turning in. I don't think we will ever get a complete outfit that fits.

Bradford Gilbert had been named for his grandmother Roxanne Bradford. She'd dreamed of seeing London and Paris and Rome as described in the Orange Hill Academy history lessons but was pretty much stuck in Washington County, Florida, her whole life. Bradford had one of her schoolbooks: She'd sketched the Coliseum on the flyleaf. At least he thought it was the Coliseum. But he got lucky: He was a boy and there was a war. A war was how farm boys who weren't rich got to travel. A war was how farm boys could get away from their older brothers and their mamas and their daddies and all the expectations and duties and assumptions and go see how other people live. And meet girls someplace other than church.

Roxanne died in 1890, nine years before he was born. But her daughter Blanche, Aunt Bankie, had the stories. She lived up on Orange Hill in a little house ringed with oaks and a bottle tree heavy with blue Milk of Magnesia bottles out back—bottle trees catch evil spirits. She told about the Bradford family coming from Yorkshire, England, almost three hundred years ago. She told about her mother's pink wedding dress. She told about her father's red-gold hair. She told about hiding from the Yankees in the woods with the shotgun. She told about the house John Wesley built that never had a chance to get old, what with it burning down so soon. She told about ghosts—haints—in the swamps. Bradford Gilbert didn't say much but he listened. His mother said he was "different" from the other young 'uns.

Saturday, Sept. 14, 1918: At last we have drawn all of our equipment and most of the boys have been fitted so that they can pass muster. We were not given liberty but most of us took it and wandered off to the Big City that we had heard so much about.

My grandfather was probably the first Gilbert ever to go junketing around New York City, even if he wasn't the first Bradford. His rich cousins in Leon County went to cooking school and finishing school and bought books and furniture and clothes in New York before the War and even after the War, when Susan Bradford kept writing about how they had no slaves and no investments and no cash: nothing but land. There are different ways to be poor.

No Gilbert since Sir Humphrey, Walter Raleigh's half brother who helped bankroll the colonization of Virginia in 1578 and to whom some of the family claimed kin, had the money or the desire to do anything but go ever farther south, where things got ever cheaper and easier. But there he was, Bradford Gilbert, who knew how to get rosin out of a pine and knew which tree would make the best roof trusses and knew how to scare the weevils off cotton; there was Bradford Gilbert, who had not been given liberty but who took it anyway in his sharp-cut gray-green tunic and his cap set at an angle on his head that said what the hell, striding in riding boots around Manhattan, taking in the tall buildings and the smart shops and automobiles and electric lights as if he saw things like this every damn day of his life.

He walked down Wall Street to look at the banks and Fifth Avenue to look at the mansions. With "some of the boys," he took tea in one of the hotels (he didn't say which) with palm trees in pots in the lobby. He thought this was extremely funny. Palm trees grown like his mother's African violets because they couldn't stand the cold. The boys ate food at a restaurant where the fellow barely talked English and went on to some kind of club. Bradford Gilbert said that even if you admitted you were going Over There to build bridges, not kill the Hun, the girls were still nice. They liked the uniform. The uniform that finally fit.

Monday, Sept. 16, 1918: Well, we are off but where to, no one knows. From Cunard Pier No. 5 we embarked on the SS. Balmoral Castle. There are thirteen ships in our convoy, not including three destroyers, one battleship and one torpedo boat, arranged in battle front, and believe me it will take some submarine to get us.

Wednesday, Sept. 18, 1918: In conversation with one of the crew I learned that this boat was formerly a mail boat in South African waters, and this is her second trip across the Atlantic. We will not land until about the 30th, the trip taking from 12 to 14 days. The ships travel in a zigzag course to ward off submarines. From 1st Cl. sergeants down, the men are quartered in what we call the Cootie Hole, on the third and fourth troop decks, sleeping in hammocks, or rather dozing, as someone falls out every five minutes and wakes us all up.

He'd never had a room to himself in his life, not really. At Gilbert's Mill, he slept in a room with Homer. Fred used to be in there, too, but he'd got married. The closest Bradford got was a little attic where he stayed when he went to town to see his mother and his little sisters Vardelle, Charlsie, Inez, Rilla, and Lucille. They mostly didn't live at the farm anymore, except in the summers. Bradford liked being in the town house, up high, away from the chaos of lace and hat trimming and white stockings and ribbons and *McGuffey's Readers* and embroidery hoops and chocolate boxes and giggles, noisy as a whole city of girls.

In 1900 Mary Gilbert was agitating for the children to go to school in Chipley. There was no school out at Orange Hill anymore, and the school at Gilbert's Mill was just for little young 'uns. She wasn't about to tolerate living among a brood of ignorant wild Gilberts. She had come from cultivated (if poor) folk, with antimacassars and atlases and framed engravings of *The Tournament at Ashby-de-la-Zouche* and *Prince Charles Stuart Escapes to Skye* on the walls. Those children needed to be in town so they could learn to identify the principal capitals of Europe, read the poetry of Henry Wadsworth Longfellow, and wear properly tied sashes to tea parties. Those children needed to be in town so they could learn to wear shoes.

So Zet had his head sawyer put aside the best planks of yellow pine—heart pine—until there was enough. He had the men carry it on mule carts into Chipley to where he owned a lot on South Sixth, the second most fashionable street in town. By 1901 Mary had a high, pointy, gabled house, surrounded by a porch. There was a stable, where Zet could put his buggy when he commuted in on weekends, and space for a cow.

By the time Bradford was through with school, his mama and daddy didn't much like each other anymore. Zet tried. He sent wagonloads of the best farm produce to 515 South Sixth, gave Mary and the girls an allowance, bought a piano. Mary tried. She lived at the mill in the summer, grew calla lilies and runner beans and sang in the choir at the Oakie Ridge church. Zet told the boys he was tired of nobody saying thank you, at the very least. Mary told the girls she was tired of having to pretend she enjoyed farm living. The story at Orange Hill and up and down the creek was that Zet took to visiting a woman who lived up on his Slay Field property. Her two children had no daddy. She had dyed yellow hair and a painted mouth that was always smiling.

Thursday, Sept. 19, 1918: Had a good day to-day, no excitement, water calm.

Friday, Sept. 20, 1918: Nothing happened to-day. We have 101 Nurses on aboard, but they can't look at an enlisted man. All we can do is sing to them and watch them promenade the top deck with the xxxxx officers.

The Gulf of Mexico was one thing, warm and gently greeny-turquoise like a dragonfly. He'd seen it plenty of times, even been out in a boat on St. Andrews Bay. The North Atlantic, now: That was another thing. It was as drab as a jay and cold as a slab of marble. Big, too; the biggest thing in the world. Sometimes there were waves as tall as a barn. Taller, from down in the cootie hole. And full of Germans trying to kill you.

Saturday, Sept. 21, 1918: It is getting foggy and everybody is getting blue. The Y.M.C.A. men have introduced some athletics on board to-day. In the midst of one of the prize fights, the boat behind us nearly rammed us, and believe me there was some excitement then. The fog keeps getting heavier and heavier.

Sunday, Sept. 22, 1918: Had church this morning and some of the Nurses sang for us. The sea is getting rough.

Monday, Sept. 23, 1918: No change, same old routine, lifeboat drill and same old fog. Same old rough sea.

He didn't write about how lousy it usually was, not really. He would later tell my brother and me, briefly, that there were men so ill they never got out of their hammocks except to crawl to the side of the deck or men with the runs so bad they could barely walk.

He almost never told about going to the Marne. The rotting bodies stacked up like corded wood, stinking even in the sharp October air.

Wednesday, Sept. 25, 1918: Half the men on board are seasick and they are all holding on to the rail to keep themselves from going over. One cure for seasickness, offered by a sailor, was raw oysters with sugar. Another said salt pork and sea water. How much sicker it made us to think of it.

Friday, Sept. 27, 1918: Some weather now, water washing over the decks. Torpedo boats reached us this morning. Some of us on guard saw them just over the horizon, signalling with their lights.

One of the boys was buried to-day, poor fellow. We expect to see land tomorrow.

Sometimes Granddaddy would bring out the annotated postcards. The French in the First World War were keen on before-and-after photos, as in here's the Place de l'Hôtel-de-Ville in Château-Thierry before bombardment and here it is after bombardment, *bonnes* in brogues and aprons carrying market baskets in front of almost-tidy piles of shattered stone. Granddaddy developed his own West Florida Franglais: "A front vue before the town hall was repaired—note the gen de arme."

He did some work in Soissons, in Champagne, and bought a postcard of the Église Saint-Waast. He wrote on the back, "Cathedral once, now a mass of rocks. Shot up for four years." He spent a couple of weeks in Château-Thierry, a little town on the Marne. The French had blown up most of the bridges across the river, trying to stop the Germans. Then the Germans came and blew up the rest of the bridges, trying to hem in the French. In the summer of 1918, the 3rd U.S. Division arrived and fought for most of June and July, finally forcing the Germans to retreat. In one postcard of la Place du Champ-de-Mars ("vue prise en 1914"), my grandfather drew a huge, zeppelin-looking arrow over a mansard roof pointing at a window. On the back he wrote, "The hotell in which we stayed."

He was sociologically inclined: A picture of the Hôtel de Ville before it was blasted says: "Notice how the French have their food stands in the street." He sampled the local wine (his connoisseurship was limited to "sweet," "not sweet," tastes like "cat wet"). He was interested in rubble. A card of the Rue du Pont in Château-Thierry, the bones of seventeenth- and eighteenth-century buildings standing naked under a silver sky, says, "Notice how the brick is pulled back to open up the street."

I wasn't interested in sociology or problems in postwar reconstruction. I was interested in castles and casinos and countesses and all the other fascinating things that I understood Europe had in spades and Florida lacked almost entirely (at the time I didn't know that Palm Beach was draped in countesses) and made him tell about the châteaux he saw. And he did see a lot of them, up and down the rocky rivers of Brittany, not the airy, impossibly vertical things I knew from Disney's desexed version of *Sleeping Beauty* or Cair Paravel, the castle of the kings and queens of Narnia, but heavy, squat, dour strongholds with fat round towers or large and symmetrical houses of the Enlightenment with gracious windows and chandeliers glittering like my mother's engagement ring in the sun.

Once, somewhere near Kerhoun in the Breton countryside, he had been repairing a bridge: he was only nineteen and a grunt private in Company C, Engineering Corps. This butler or footman from the *manoir* up the hill must have mistaken him for an officer and came by to say that the *famille* wished him to come for a drink and a little *déjeuner*. They didn't have much, *je regrette,* just some eggs from the farm and perhaps a chicken.

The house was really a small fortification, with a square tower at one end and walls thick as the oldest magnolia growing on Orange Hill. There was an old lady, a girl of twenty-one or twenty-two, and a boy who was about eleven. There had been a son, the girl's husband, but he was dead. They all wore black. The girl's hair was black, too, and she'd cut it short.

She spoke pretty good English. So did the boy. The old lady, who had pearls hanging down to her knees, did not. And he had not yet learned the basic but useful French that got him smokes and coffee and dates with the Clothildes and Yvonnes he'd meet in Paris or Brest. But he could smile and nod and say "Merci," which came out as "mercy."

They gave him sherry or brandy or something, he wasn't sure, but it was about as fierce as the corn liquor from down in the sand hills. And they gave him an omelette and most of the roast chicken. They ate almost nothing. The dining room was freezing cold. It had a tapestry with lions. The food was served on thin plates with tiny flowers. Some of the plates were chipped.

The chicken was good, he said, the best he'd ever had. His own mother couldn't make chicken so good, and they raised chickens at home. He told them about Gilbert's Mill and the farm and Orange Hill. They wanted to know the name of the part of America that was his. "I'm from Florida," he said.

The girl told the old lady. "La Floride," she said. "Florida."

The old lady said she had been to Florida, in 1905, and ridden Monsieur Flagler's train down to Palm Beach. She smiled and gestured with her fine hands, so pale they were almost blue. The girl translated. "She wants to know if you have been to The Breakers Hotel. In Palm Beach. In Florida. It's a nice place, she says, if a little ostentatious."

My grandfather laughed. He said no. He explained that he'd not been more than sixty miles away from his family's place in West Florida until he'd left for the war. The Breakers was for rich folks. The Gilberts weren't rich.

"But you have land," said the girl.

They had coffee in another room, with golden-framed mirrors and portraits of women who all looked like Marie Antoinette. The coffee was as black as the old lady's silk dress, and bitter.

"He was going to take me there," said the girl, "my husband. After the war, he said. On the *France*. And we would go to New York and to St. Augustine and to Palm Beach. These places I have read about, with the fantastic birds and the lemon trees. Like Provence. Or Spain. But then he was at Verdun."

"Florida," said the boy. He wanted to know if it was always warm there, and if the sea was like bathwater and if the crocodiles were as big as plow horses. And if it was true that there were storms so strong they could rip the roof of a house and tear up the palm trees by the roots.

Grandmère did not tell him anything interesting about her trip, just who she met at balls and what they wore.

My grandfather said that the crocodiles were alligators and they were very large and could kill a man or a deer in a few minutes. And that there were snakes whose poison could paralyze you. And that some of the palm trees were thirty feet high and no bigger around than your arm. And that roses and peaches and the best blackberries you ever had grew on Orange Hill. But that sometimes, in the winter, it snowed, snowed in Florida.

"Snow," said the boy, not buying it for a second. "In your Florida?"

The girl translated. *"Impossible,"* said the old lady. "M. Flagler would not allow it."

Other People's Palm Trees

I left Florida for Britain in 1980. The British left Britain for Florida about the same time. Sir Freddie Laker and all these package tour companies had made trips to Miami and Disney fashionable and cheap. I had a scholarship to Oxford.

The British, who lived within spitting distance of Romanesque cathedrals and gardens laid out and ministered to for three hundred years and pubs that were established businesses when Henry VIII was dumping his fourth wife, wanted to eat over-mustarded hot dogs in the shadow of Cinderella's Castle or drink an overcooled Bass Ale in some fake pub in Orlando. I, who lived within spitting distance of beaches with sand like confectioner's sugar, I, who lived in a temperature-controlled house, wanted to be where it was more often dark than not and more often cold than not, in a sixteenth-century college where the nearest bathroom was across the quadrangle and the only source of heat needed a match to get going.

They all said it: "You're from Florida? You don't have a tan."

I didn't have a tan. I sat on discount flights to London from Orlando or Miami, looking at the British tourists. They didn't have tans, either. They had third-degree burns. Their skin was the color of boiled tomatoes.

They'd been to Disney World or Coconut Grove or Cape Canaveral or Busch Gardens. They carried mouse ears or Burdines ("the Florida Store") shopping bags. They wore T-shirts printed with rockets or flamingoes. When they got back home to Surbiton or Hartlepool or Manchester, they could lord it over their pale and shivering peers. They could wear their redness like a prize ribbon: Look at me; I've been in the sun; I've been to Florida.

My grandfather Bradford Gilbert died in 1980, just before I left the country. He didn't know I was going. He didn't know much. He had severe dementia. We had to cover all the mirrors in the house because he kept complaining that there was some old man hiding in there. We had to fence the place and keep the gates shut because he kept running off and getting retrieved by the Highway Patrol. He was trying to go home to Gilbert's Mill.

His father, Zet, died in 1947, also suffering from dementia. Zet had hit his head in some tangle of wagon and mule out at the farm. He was never right after that. He would light out down the road going God knows where. Bradford would chase his father in the car and, when he caught him, growl, "Get in here, old man." They finally had to put him in the state mental hospital in Chattahoochee.

When I was fifteen, Granddaddy helped pay for my first trip abroad. "Traveling is good for young 'uns," he said. "See other people's palm trees."

There were six Tallahassee kids, sent off by our parents to Get Culture: the daughter of the doctor who delivered me, the daughter of the doctor who delivered my brother, the son of the man who paid for Florida State to have a hot-shit football team, assorted sons and daughters of lawyers and professors. There were also two chaperones, Episcopalian widows with perfectly done hair and a lot of experience in quelling *haute-bourgeois* teenage malfeasance.

We were enrolled in a history and art summer school in Aberdeen, where our chaperones herded us through Scottish museums and took us on tours to Glamis Castle. Then we went on a supposedly educational cruise through the eastern Mediterranean on a Greek-registered tug called the *Hermes*. We put in at Istanbul, Rhodes, Dubrovnik, and

Venice. We rode the train down to Rome, where we were marched around a lot of ruins and churches. The Palatine Hill and St. Peter's Basilica and the Vatican Library all looked just like they did in Granddaddy's *Ricordo di Roma* from 1919, with its picture of the she-wolf and the tiny figures of Romulus and Remus underneath her on the cover, and the bold declaration (as if nothing had changed in two thousand years) SPQR. The accordioned postcards in the *Ricordo* also showed the Villa Borghese festooned with ladies in clingy diaphanous dresses and an interior view of the Coliseum, where a bunch of limp-looking Christians in togas were fixing to get eaten by a large, bored lion. We saw nothing so thrilling, even in the Catacombs.

Still, my tour of the Old World and Granddaddy's had a lot in common: I drank French wine, I drank Macedonian brandy, I drank Dutch beer. I smoked British cigarettes. I made a foreign friend, an Aberdonian Presbyterian minister's son who wore black, played rugby, and quoted Led Zeppelin lyrics like poetry. I didn't see a war, unless you count the Greek versus Turk gunfire we could hear from Cyprus when we sailed past Kyrenia, but I did have a few battles to fight, all the Tallahassee girls did, with libidinous Italian guys and this waiter from Piraeus on the *Hermes* who had a bet with his buddies about how many American chicks he could make between Samos and Antalya.

> *Sunday, Sept. 29, 1918: Last night we anchored at the mouth of the Firth of Clyde. At daybreak we sailed up the river Clyde and were all enchanted with the beauty of the place. Passed some of the largest shipbuilding plants in the world. Saw ruins of old castles and green hills with sheep grazing on them. Landed in Glasgow at ten o'clock this morning at the Princess Mary Pier. Loaded onto dinky little cars with sidedoors and tiny compartments. Passed thru Scotland and were impressed with the healthy look of the women and children of that country, rosy cheeks and fat faces. Passed through Birmingham, England and was given hot coffee by the English canteen workers.*

On October 5 I arrived in Oxford on the train, one of those old trains still common in 1980, with the skinny corridor on one side, and the compartment with ferocious sliding doors and high-backed facing seats made of fabric so scratchy you could scrub the floor with it, on the other. My two suitcases and the footlocker my father took to the Naval Academy somehow made it into a taxi, which somehow got past the barrier at Radcliffe Square and dumped me and my stuff in front of Brasenose College.

Brasenose has a huge set of seventeenth-century wooden gates, which are only fully opened for a visit from the sovereign or an especially important funeral. Instead, there's a little Alice-in-Wonderland door, made for a time when people never got taller than five foot two. As I dragged the footlocker through the door, I could see window boxes full of white geraniums and grass that looked like green mink. Except for the scraping of luggage on stone, it was silent.

Michaelmas term hadn't started yet. They always sent the Marshall scholars over early to get "acclimated." Acclimated meant going to a couple of parties at the Foreign Office, where we stood around in vast rooms hung with paintings of Hanoverian monarchs and prime ministers called Pitt the Younger and Earl Grey, drinking good claret and eating smoked salmon in aspic. Then they gave us a train ticket and a check. When I arrived I was wearing a gray tweed suit and pearls and a Burberry raincoat. I thought this was what you wore in England. It was what people wore in movies set in England.

"What the hell do you want, then?" said the porter, a bookcase-size ex–London cop. I said could he tell me where I belonged, please.

"Where the hell you from, then?" he said.

"Florida," I said.

"Florida," he said. "I've been. Didn't like it. Minnie Mouse." And laughed while he found the key to my room. "Sodding Minnie Mouse. Miami Beach was all right, though. Lot of swimming pools. Lot of skin." He glared at me as he dug out a key that looked like it would open the nastiest, dankest dungeon in the Tower of London. "You don't look like you're from Florida."

Tuesday, Sept. 31, 1918: Arrived in Winchester, England yesterday about 2 am. It was cold and raining and we foot slogged up winding hills and block pavements to camp. We were told that it was three miles but we were all satisfied that it must have been six. We were given breakfast and assigned to barracks.

We are confined to this dismal camp but again some of us fellow slipped off and went to Winchester where we saw a handsome cathedral and old ruins. The city is nearly in darkness to avoid air raids.

It took me about three weeks to lose the tweed and the pearls. I clad myself in the Morticia black Oxford belles wore so as to appear serious and semi-tragic and as thin as possible. I never lost my accent, though. I just figured out how to use it.

Everybody at Oxford had a gimmick, a persona. You could be the throwback to *Brideshead Revisited,* toting a teddy bear and a bottle of Veuve Clicquot; you could be the titled Trotskyite whose daddy might own a stately home but who was nonetheless fomenting the Revolution that would bring down the System; you could be the working-class hero who claimed you'd rather be at the polytechnic except it would break your old mum's heart; you could be the jolly hockey sticks type who got up at 5 A.M. to jog on the tow path and always threw up on the quad after the Boat Club Dinner.

Most of the Americans, Marshall scholars, Rhodes scholars, and the rich and despised "Daddy scholars," didn't get that if you failed to create your own character, it would be created for you out of stereotypes, television, and a bad haircut, and before you knew it you were tagged as a library-haunting, flat-voweled future secretary of agriculture or an insinuating creep who goes to parties at Rhodes House to schmooze potential references for Harvard Business School.

Before I got the hang of self-fashioning, I got teased a lot about Florida, about Miami. People asked me if I water-skied every day, if I knew a lot of whingeing Cubans, if my family used a palm for a Christmas tree. People asked why I didn't have a tan. (Oxford students got their tans in Tuscany or Provence, not Fort Lauderdale.) I finally developed this persona that oscillated between Scarlett O'Hara and Ellie Mae Clampett. That was okay. The British figured I lived with my bourbon-sozzled relations in a falling-down plantation house hung with smoky Sully portraits of slaveholding ancestors and ate fresh-killed meat off antique Limoges before sinking gently into Tennessee Williams madness. My fellow Americans figured I lived with my bourbon-sozzled kin in a double-wide with space for the cows and the chickens and the shotguns and ate fresh-killed meat off paper plates before scratching off to town in pickup trucks to commit unspeakable acts of racism and brutality.

At the senior dean's sherry party, this Yale girl, also a Marshall scholar, said to me—and I'm pretty sure she was trying to be nice—"I think it's so wonderful that someone like you could get a Marshall."

Thursday, October 3, 1918: Left Winchester at six-thirty. Never got to see London. Never got to see Oxford and all the colleges. It was a twenty-five mile ride to Southampton. Stayed at the docks all day with corned beef, jam and bread to eat. Loaded on ship at four-thirty and set sail across the Channel for France. The weather was rougher than it had been on the Atlantic.

When I went abroad at fifteen, I sent my grandfather a postcard every day, especially from the places that he'd been: Paris, Venice, Milan, Rome. His favorite postcard, though, was of some place he'd never been: the Palm House at Kew Gardens. It made him laugh. "All them royal palms and cabbage palms and coconut palms all living there in that cold country in a big old greenhouse while it snows outside." I told him that when you walked inside, the air was as humid as Chipley in August.

Friday, October 4, 1918: Arrived in Le Havre at two o'clock. Foot-slogged three miles to a barbed wire camp which was nearly like a prison. Loaded on boxcars, marked "Hommes 40, Chevaux 8" which translated means Men 40, Horses 8. We had practically no room to turn around, much less sleep.

Sunday, October 8, 1918: Will we ever get thru travelling? Passed thru Le Mans and LaVal. Passed through Morlaix this A.M. A very attractive-

looking city built in a valley. Arrived in Brest about noon. Foot slogged out to pontanezen barracks with packs and rifles to base section No. 5. And a Hell of a section it is. From what we can hear, we are to build a large receiving camp in this mud hole.

I went to Paris by myself in early December 1985. I had split up with my English boyfriend. I was writing a dissertation on white womanhood in the novels of William Faulkner. I had four days before the plane left (London to Miami, Miami to Orlando, Orlando to Tallahassee), so I took the ferry to Calais (sat in the bar drinking Coke, terrified of getting seasick), then the train to the Gare du Nord. It was raining.

The Eiffel Tower is 985 feet high, 300 feet broad at base. This tower holds 800 people at once.

By December 1918 my grandfather had an English box camera he used to take pictures of all the sights. He was a dedicated tourist: the Arc de Triomphe, Notre Dame, the Opéra, the Madeleine, Les Invalides.

The box that now holds the ashes of Napoleon the First. Note the flags he captured in his time.

He carried a booklet from the American YMCA he bought in Hatchette's on the Boulevard Saint-Germain called "The Story of Paris" and another, a glossy, fat, illustrated "Day at Versailles," which cost three francs. He had pictures of cafés in Montmartre and sagging mansions in the Marais and one of the Champs-Élysées full of boxy black cars that look like buggies stripped of their horses menacing each other all over the road. Maybe these were the taxis the French took to the front in 1914.

He liked Versailles best. He went three times and probably would have gone more except in January 1919 they started the peace negotiations there, and he decided it was time to head south. Still, he just couldn't get over the bigness and the fanciness of the palace and the gardens and the lakes and the statues. He took notes on what he called "Queen Antoinette's private bedroom" and "Queen Antoinette's farm." *The queen liked to play like she was a farmer. She raised sheep and cattle, I believe. She wore a shepherdess dress and carried a crook.* He was interested in the height and the width and construction of everything. He took a ride on the great Ferris wheel La Grande Roue and reported, *it is 318 feet in diameter and each compartment carries 16 people.* He thought in terms of building—and repairing. *This country is beautiful and in sad shape. It needs lumber.* On the back of his photo of the Fountain of Neptune, he wrote: *The Fountains flow only once a year on May 1st from 4 pm until 5 pm.*

I took my grandfather's "Day at Versailles" with me. I walked around the Fountain of Neptune, which still wasn't flowing. Maybe it broke again or else the weather was too cold. There were patches of dirty ice on the grand promenades and the sky was a cross between sepia and silver. I walked through the Orangerie, which was bare of trees. My grandfather's picture from 1918 shows them in white buckets, placed in perfect rows around a pool.

> *When it gets to freezing they set the trees back under the subways. None of them are as big as Aunt Bankie's old tree on Orange Hill. But they say that some of them are 200 years old. 200 years old and yet bearing fruit.*

His favorite place at Versailles was the Fountain of Apollo, a great broad pool of water with the god in his Phoebus phase, driving a chariot pulled by a bunch of wild-maned, fiery-eyed horses (even made of lead you can see they're hot), taking off like an airplane for the heavens. *Notice the way that the god Apollo's chariot rises out the water toward the royal palace.* He took several photographs of it with the English box camera. *It is well known that Louis XIV had the Sun for his emblem and that poets and courtiers compared their master to Apollo. It's supposed to be that he's the sun rising out of the sea over France.*

On the back of the guidebook, for some reason, he scribbled in pencil: "Oranges. Orange Hill. Summer."

Wednesday, October 9, 1918: Began works on Hospital Barracks in Brest. It rained all day and we never see the sun. The mud is knee deep.

Thursday, October 10, 1918: It did not rain to-day. We were issued warm clothes, rubber boots, rain hats, coats, etc. Also Bull Durham and chewing tobacco.

There's the photograph of the girl in the white feathery dress, white stockings, white shoes, white hat so big you can't really see her face. We don't know which *petite amie* she is: Suzanne from the eighteenth arondissement or Yvonne from the Maison Wirix (*Modes, Chapellerie*) in Brest. There's one of these two children in woolly coats and boots standing in front of a backdrop painted like a Fragonard garden and marked "Beata 7 yrs, Catherine 8 yrs, 1919." There are loads of "the fellows," sitting in dainty ballroom chairs wearing uniforms and boots, leaning on a stand with a rubber plant, standing in front of blown-out buildings, Florida boys with names like Scruggs and Sapp, Roche and Roulhac.

The best one is of the two brothers from Jacksonville my grandfather called "those Jew boys," probably the first Jews he ever met. Their family owned a department store. They went off to war with dinner jackets and a gramophone. They got big boxes from home: smoked salmon, raisins, dates, and some kind of lemon cake, which they shared. Even in the mud, under a leaky pup tent, they'd crank that gramophone up and show dance moves to the country boys. My grandfather didn't own a dinner jacket, but he was eager to learn how to dance. French girls all knew how to dance.

November 11, 1918: We quit work on the barracks, which we were building at nearly ten per day, when we heard the Armistice was signed. All the boys went to the wineshops to celebrate. We were a drunk and happy bunch.

My grandfather told me that the Jew Boys had a little Armistice party of their own, with contraband bourbon mixed up with other things in a drink they called a cocktail (your Bordeaux and your Burgundies and your Beaujolais were all very well, but you just couldn't beat the nectar of Kentucky) and cheese straws their mother's cook had made and sent all the way from Jacksonville, all busted up but still good. Granddaddy remembers them playing a song with some title like "Louisa from St. Louie" (he never was sure about that) over and over as they toasted President Wilson, Marshal Foch, George V, and "les demoiselles de la belle France" over and over again. He remembers drinking a bunch of those cocktails. He remembers singing "La Marseillaise," which Yvonne, from the hat shop, had taught him.

The next day he and the Jew Boys from Jacksonville were detailed to go up in a barrage balloon over Brest harbor. Just because there was an armistice didn't mean there wouldn't be any Hun submarines. They floated in a high-blue Breton sky over where the Bay of Biscay, the English Channel, and the North Atlantic all slap together, cold as hell and hungover, too. But still, Granddaddy remembered, it was so beautiful. Then, back on the ground, they returned to the bar.

We weren't given liberty but took it anyway and went to the wineshop. We were seeking to drown our homesickness with French Liquor.

On Sunday afternoons at Brasenose I used to climb up onto the library roof to look at the view. You had to have an after-hours key to the library, which was built by Nicholas Hawksmoor in the seventeenth century and couldn't decide if it wanted to be neoclassical or neogothic. You had to know just where the secret stair and the secret ladder to the trapdoor were. It was masonic knowledge handed down generation to generation in Brasenose. But you could get up there and see all the colleges gleaming golden-stoned and many-gated like the New Jerusalem. Farther out were the ocher hills and the villages of Iffley and Osney Island and church spires everywhere. Then, about 4 P.M., it would get dark and you could watch the stars come out in a violet sky over the towers of All Souls. I had to get off the roof before 8 P.M. Sunday night was *Miami Vice* night in the Middle Common Room. Some people went to College Prayers and sang "My soul doth magnify the Lord." I watched *Miami Vice.* The British and Canadian and German and Australian and American graduate students all loved it. I loved it, even though, living in Margaret Thatcher's Britain, my official position was that I was never homesick for Ronald Reagan's America. *Miami Vice* was less a cop show than a sabbath ritual. It presented a Florida of perfect—if decadent—pastels, a Florida of moral confusion, historical displacement, bad women, bad men, demon rum, demon blow. Watching it was a penance and an absolution, all at once. One of the two romantic detectives, Crockett and Tubbs, would fall in love. Then he would have no choice but to shoot his amour because she would always, always, turn out to be a Colombian drug dealer.

I had spent more time sleeping on the floor of the Miami airport (it was real easy to miss the last flight to Tallahassee, and I didn't have money for a hotel) than I had riding in a convertible down Collins Avenue or drinking mimosas at the Biltmore. But Miami was the most visible manifestation of Florida. There would never be a TV show called *Tallahassee Vice.* I mean, we *have* vice (it's the state capital), and crime, and murder and drug-dealing. In the 1820s Ralph Waldo Emerson said that Tallahassee was an immoral place. I'm not sure how he knew. Anyway, Tallahassee has too much rain. Too few mean streets. No pastels, unless you count the hoopskirts on the Springtime Belles.

Miami Vice marketed an anti-Disney, weary, grown-up Florida to the world. It didn't matter if a lot of it was filmed in California. It didn't matter that Crockett was too small ever to have played quarterback for the University of Florida and that it'd be pretty hard to keep an alligator as a pet, even in Miami. It didn't matter that Tubbs didn't look comfortable wearing that earring. It didn't matter that they never showed the miles and miles and miles of boring 'burbs and trailer parks and traffic jams and retirement condos and strip malls that were the real Miami. Tourists in Oxford didn't ride the bus out to the car plant at Cowley or the projects at Blackbird Leys, either.

Miami Vice was my private assertion of participation in Florida, even more than the Monday edition of the *International Herald Tribune,* which I would snatch out of the hands of aspiring economists even as they read the financial pages just so I could see if FSU had won or lost Saturday's ball game. Hearing the recitation of Florida streets, Florida food, Florida history, Florida geography, Florida insects, Florida hurricanes, Florida felonies—I wasn't homesick, swear to God, Oxford was almost as much home as Tallahassee, but even then I knew I'd go back. I would complain about Florida—the retrograde politics, the provinciality, the heat, the bugs—and I would live there. I would die there. Most people who live in Florida are just lightly perched on its sands; I'm dug in like an old, old cypress. Whether I like it or not.

December 22, 1918: We have not been paid for November as yet and hope to get it next week. We are at least going to get as good a dinner as we had on Thanksgiving Day, barbequed pig, potatoes, pie and cake. The dope is that we will leave for the States by the 15th of January and let us hope so for the whole bunch is disgusted with this rain and mud.

After the Christmas carol service in Brasenose Chapel (I was going to Paris the next day), they showed what was, I guess, the season finale of *Miami Vice.* It was pretty much like the others: slow-motion techno-sound-tracked convertible rides under night palms. Some South American drug lord was trying to mess with South Florida. As usual, Crockett killed him and then had an existential crisis in the middle of Ocean Drive with a sunset in lava-lamp colors as backdrop. As usual, Tubbs talked him out of it.

December 24, 1918: Some of the Christmas boxes have been delivered and we are still in hopes of receiving ours. It has rained all day and we are staying in our barracks in hopes that the rain will let up. What we do tomorrow, I can't say.

Bradford Gilbert, Given Liberty

The Hôtel de l'Hermitage, Monte Carlo, sure knew how to treat a doughboy, a Yankee, even a doughboy who wasn't a doughboy but an engineer, even a Yankee who came from the Deep South.

My grandfather turned twenty on February 25, 1919, in Monaco.

He was on furlough with some of the fellows from the 106th Engineering Corps. They'd headed south. Heard there were sights to see, good weather, girls in bathing costumes, cocktails, casinos. The rich brothers, the Jew Boys with the dinner jackets and the gramophone, went down to Monte Carlo on the chemin de fer. Granddaddy rode a motorcycle he'd won in a bet with a Scotsman and took in the French Riviera while he was at it. He almost quit writing in his journal—a fellow got too busy moving around to write much—though he still scribbled instructive notes on his postcards. He wrote letters to his mother, Mary, too, short letters, postmarked Cannes, Antibes, and Nice. She wrote back to the poste restante, longer letters telling him that Fred and Elia had a baby, Fred, Jr. The turpentine business was bringing in good money. Inez could play four songs on the piano. And thanks for the pictures of Paris, especially King Louis's palace, but his daddy needed him at the mill so could he come on back home soon? The letters never seemed to quite catch up with him.

Later he forgot the names of most of the places he went through as he made his way south, but he could call up images of lavender fields and one-street villages that smelled like bread baking, and, always, broken stone, roofless houses, burned churches. He remembered Suzanne Demulder from the Rue Clignancourt in Paris. She had tobacco-brown hair and tobacco-brown eyes. She took him home to Sunday lunch (he called it dinner) with her parents, who asked him questions in French. He was only up to *"Moi, je suis né en Florida, aux États-Unis"* and *"Voudriez vous un café, Mademoiselle?"*

He remembered Yvonne (but not her last name) in Brest, who wrote him letters on blank invoices from her hat shop. She would say, "You are happy in your good U.S.A., aren't you? On your beautiful farm in beautiful Florida. Here at Brest there is very few American. I guess they are glad for they have had enough France." She would apologize for her English: "I have not a very good style. It is not same to write French." And she would say, "I miss to see you, my friend."

I found this one card in a box of his. I guess he forgot to give it to his pal. On the front it says, "Souvenir de Chaille-les-Marais" and has tiny pictures of the church, the Hôtel de Ville, a street. On the back it says: "Dear George—I love you with all my heart. Do not forget me. Write to me soon. Pauline."

Yvonne said she would like to live in Florida. She said she would like to live on a farm. He didn't think she meant it, Yvonne in her voile-swathed straw hats and high-heeled kid shoes. He said he sent her a last present in 1920, a Florida souvenir silk scarf in a pattern of orange blossoms. He couldn't remember if she ever wrote back.

So maybe he toasted Suzanne and Yvonne at Ciro's in Monte Carlo, where he celebrated his birthday with the first champagne he'd ever drunk in his life with the Jew Boys from Jacksonville and some of the other fellows. They ate oysters, which were smaller than the ones he'd had on trips to the Gulf, but tasty in their way. Then they went to the casino and lost a little money. The next day they went to the Monaco Oceanographical Museum, which my grandfather liked better than the champagne and the oysters and probably the girls because it contained the real wonders of the world: a white bear (*Ursus maritimus*), stuffed Weddell seals, an entire Siberian larch tree found frozen in the ice in Wijde Bay off Spitzbergen, a bathysphere, a taxidermified giant crab of Japan in, said the guidebook, "a curious defensive attitude."

There were skeletons of whales harpooned by the prince of Monaco: a European fin whale, a killer whale, a sperm whale. There were jars of exotic squids, including the one named after the prince, *Lepidoteuthis grimaldi*. There were pictures of His Serene Highness, in spotless sailing whites and a yachting cap, spearing a pilgrim shark. In the central hall, as if it were the rarest of the rare, was the skeleton of a manatee. My grandfather was most taken by this. He underlined it in the guidebook and wrote: *I have seen this creature in the Chipola in summer. This creature is friendly and curious and prefers to be warm.* He liked to say how seeing a manatee, albeit a dead manatee (the prince killed it in the tropics), made him almost feel like going home. *Almost.*

Instead, he headed to Italy and took weirdly angled photographs of the Piazzo San Marco in Venice and bought his mother a pair of embroidered black gloves. Then he turned his motorcycle south. He wanted to see Rome. He wanted to see Naples and Mount Vesuvius. He wanted to see everything. He thought—secretly—that he might never go back. He scribbled on a postcard of Capri: *Notice that their palm trees, while different, are as handsom as our palm trees.*

Of course, he did go back. There were crops that needed harvesting and pines that needed tapping. He helped his father plant corn in what Zet called the "doodle hole," a dry sinkhole where the soil was particularly rich. He looked after the turpentine still. He went for walks up Orange Hill to the Indian mound and thought how old the world was, after all.

Still, he always had the stories to tell, first to his little sisters, open-mouthed, hypnotized by descriptions of princes and whales and castles and gladiators and volcanoes, later to my mother and then my brother and me or whoever came by to talk about something that bunch over in the legislature were up to or some article in the *National Geographic*. I don't know if he told the stories to my grandmother. He didn't meet her until 1922, in Ohio. She didn't approve of Suzanne and Yvonne and champagne and gambling and harpooning and gallivanting all over the world. And she was German.

8

Moonshine

DRUNK ON YANKEE MONEY, borrowed money, and funny money, Florida in the early 1920s careened about, tripping over its own satin dance slippers. Florida was the endless party, the bottomless cocktail.

There you are in New Jersey, New York, Ohio, Michigan. You are cold. But you can jump in your Model T, your Regal, your Aurora, or your Empire. You can drive down to St. Petersburg, pitch a tent in a tourist camp, sit in the warm air smoking a Hav-A-Tampa and coddling a pink gin. Or there you are in New Jersey, New York, Ohio, Michigan. You read in the paper about lots for sale, 25 feet by 40 feet, genuine Florida real estate, complete with genuine Florida sun and genuine Florida sand. Fifteen bucks down and you'll never shovel snow again. The fellow that's selling it says you'll walk out your front door and there will be the Atlantic Ocean, laid out in front of you like a fancy dinner. The fellow that's taking your fifteen dollars quotes Acts 8:26, when an angel of the Lord says: "Rise and go toward the south."

God meant for Americans to be rich. God meant for them to have a second home in Florida. God meant for them to do Florida like he did the undifferentiated matter floating around in the original Chaos—*make something of it*. So Carl Fisher, millionaire inventor of the automobile headlight, took a 1,600-acre mangrove jungle of a key in Biscayne Bay, dredged and filled and cut and shaped until it was 2,800 acres of tropical treasure. He called it Miami Beach. George Merrick took the pine wilderness near the Coconut Grove Congregational Church where his father, Solomon, had been pastor, designed boulevards lined with royal palms and royal poincianas, designed canals that looked like they wanted to be in Venice, designed houses that looked like they wanted to be in Capri, designed fountains that looked like they wanted to be in Monte Carlo, and called it Coral Gables. Let there be light, let there be suntans, let there be a firmament in the midst of the waters, let there be a rise in property values, let there be tourists, let there be the *Biltmore Hotel*.

The *Miami Herald* was so fat with ads selling acreage, everything from beachfront to swamp to scrub, you needed both hands to pick it up. One edition of the *Miami News* in 1925 had 22 sections and 504 pages. In Miami alone there were 25,000 likely lads, fast-talkers in two-tone shoes who'd ditched their jobs in Cleveland or Birmingham or Baltimore or Jersey City to buy and sell Florida. Everybody called them "Binder Boys": 10 percent down on a lot held it for thirty days. But before the rest of the money came due, they'd sell the binder at a profit to speculators, who'd in turn sell it to other speculators and before you knew it, that lot cost five times the starting price, and profits, at least paper profits, shot up like weeds after a good rain.

Charles Ponzi, an Italian con man who gave his name to an elaborate method of thievery still popular with white-collar felons today, couldn't resist Florida. He was free on bond in 1921 (the feds were prosecuting him for bilking investors in a foreign currency plot), so, naturally, he headed for Florida. Lurking in Jacksonville, he concocted a plan to sell cheap lots in Columbia County for ever-vaster profits. Unlike most Florida fraudsters, he got busted fast. The last the state heard of him, he was a fugitive, and his wife was appealing to Benito Mussolini for help.

Finally, inevitably, predictably, the clock struck midnight. The local banks crashed, the land bubble burst, the swindlers skedaddled to Cuba or Bermuda or Brazil. The *Prinz Valdemar* capsized in Miami harbor, blocking it, keeping ships and freight from getting in or getting out. The *Prinz Valdemar* was undergoing a refit to become a floating cabaret; some saw it as a sign.

There were other portents that happy days were not here again. The Breakers burned to the ground in 1925—the hotel dance band, evacuated to the beach, played "There'll Be a Hot Time in the Old Town Tonight." The hurricane of 1926 killed four hundred and left fifty thousand homeless. People called it "the Big One" until the hurricane of 1928, which killed two thousand. There were so many dead around Lake Okeechobee, Bahamian cane cutters and tomato pickers, they had to be stacked on funeral pyres. There were so many dead that for years farmers found skeletons in the fields.

In 1928 Florida was $600 million in debt—and the whole state budget was only $29 million. The newspapers up north said Florida was finished, over, gone. Grown men cried. You could start praying; or you could start drinking.

It was a good time to be a bootlegger—or a bootlegger's lawyer.

Al Capone moved to Miami Beach in 1928, tired of the cops messing with his speakeasies and his whorehouses, tired of those murderous Chicago winters. Florida property was pretty cheap, what with the bottom falling out of the market in 1926. He bought a house on Palm Island, fourteen rooms, quarters for the servants, built in the fantasy-Spanish style for brewer Clarence Busch. Mae Capone spent a fortune remodeling and redecorating. She filled the house with Italian brocades and French gilt mirrors and included personalized touches like reinforced concrete walls and heavy wooden doors. Just in case. But Capone thought he'd go respectable. He and the missus would buy their way into Miami society, give seven-course dinners, go to charity balls. He told everybody—whether they asked or not—that he was a dealer in secondhand furniture.

Miamians loudly claimed to be shocked! shocked! that a person mixed up in gambling, prostitution, and illicit booze would have the brass-faced gall to move to their wholesome family-values community. Evidently the cathouses on the edge of town and the gambling that went on at Joe Smoot's Miami Jockey Club (later Hialeah Race Track) didn't count. The rum-running that had been going on since, oh, the seventeenth century, moving from Grand Bahama and Nassau and Havana to Gun Cay, where Blackbeard used to hide out, up and down the Gulf and Atlantic coasts, wasn't defined as smuggling but vigorous participation in the free market.

Sotto voce, Miamians liked to flirt with Public Enemy Number One—gangsters are always more exciting than real estate developers (unless the real estate developer is also a gangster, which sometimes happens in Florida). Capone laid on a lavish banquet and got sixty of Miami's most prominent citizens to show up. One of them even toasted him as "the new businessman of the community." Capone plied Roddy Burdine, of the Burdines department store family, with champagne and a $1,000 "charitable contribution." In return, Burdine, who counted as "Old Miami" (which meant someone who remembered when Collins Avenue was a mangrove jungle), tried to get Capone admitted to his country club. The board pitched a fit and made Burdine give the check back.

Further indignities followed. The *Miami News* editorialized endlessly on "Scarface," exhorting him to, for God sake, go back up north or something. The city sued him on the grounds that his Palm Island mansion harbored racketeers, wiseguys, and fugitives from justice. The governor demanded his arrest, citing the damage to Miami's reputation. The American Legion hatched a plan to place the state under martial law, just so Capone could be stripped of his constitutional rights. Unloved but rich, Capone carried on throwing cash all over town and, in his spare time, planning the Chicago Valentine's Day Massacre. He had to take a little vacation from Florida in 1929 when he got nailed on a concealed weapons charge, but his absence didn't quell the bolita-betting, race-wagering, extralegal alcohol, facilitated sexual impropriety, and sanctioned fraud that was beginning to make Miami a magnet for scofflaws everywhere.

Capone, hurt, said, "Public service is my motto." Capone, resigned, said, "Ninety percent of the people drink and gamble. I've tried to serve them decent liquor and square games. But I'm not appreciated."

As the members of the Everglades Club would be the first to assert, Palm Beach attracted a better class of criminal. Joseph Kennedy, bootlegger to the northeastern elite, brought his wife, Rose, and his expanding brood of proto-politicians down from Boston to schmooze with the WASP elite. Kennedy also liked to use the Royal Poinciana as a place of assignation. In 1928 the object of his lascivious attentions was the black-haired, black-eyed Marquise de la Falaise, better known to her swooning public as the movie star Gloria Swanson. He offered her nice but obviously dim French husband, Henri, a job in Paris and promised to "look after" Swanson while Henri was away.

It turns out he not only wanted to sleep with her, he wanted to go into business with her. She gave him power of attorney. Kennedy took a few hundred thousand of his bootlegging money and commissioned Erich von Stroheim to write and direct a film for Swanson. She's this sweet, innocent convent girl, see, who gets seduced by a libertine prince and ends up living in her aunt's brothel somewhere in Africa. The movie was later released as *Queen Kelly,* but at the time its working title was "The Swamp."

Von Stroheim, nicknamed "the Hun," would charge champagne and caviar to Kennedy's account in order to loosen up his starlets and get them to take off all their clothes for orgy scenes. These scenes would never make the final cut, but they were still fun to film. Kennedy, for his part, would charge Cadillacs, rewards for favored screenwriters, to Swanson's account—her *personal* account. She found out, and one night at dinner says, hey, Joe, what the fuck is going on? And he walks out in a huff, severing their financial ties, severing their emotional ties. He never even called to say he was sorry. Later she found out that the presents Joe Kennedy had given her, the diamonds, the sables, the barrel-size bouquets of perfumed orchids, had also been charged to her personal account.

What with Joe Kennedy and Al Capone and the notorious Ashley Gang and the freelancers running a million gallons of liquor from Nassau or making poteen and white lightning in the cypress hammocks and piney woods and scrub country, it's no wonder that Fiorello LaGuardia said that Florida had more "Prohibition lawbreakers" than New York. In the desiccation of Prohibition America, Florida was drenched, swimming, wet as a frog. One impressed British tourist said it was "the wettest country I have ever known."

In Florida you're never more than sixty miles from the sublime sea. In the 1920s you were never more than six miles from sub rosa booze: bathtub gin, corn liquor, scotch whisky, Jamaican rum, Cuban rum. When it comes to states of matter, Florida has always been liquid, ever balanced between the solid and the gaseous, with almost as much rain in a year as England, with springs and rivers and lakes and marshes and sinks and bogs and swamps and all that invisible water underground. *Aqua* to *aqua vitae, eau* to *eau de vie*.

Sea distance from the Bahamas to Jupiter Inlet was only fifty miles. While the Law filled the town coffers by operating a speed trap on the Dixie Highway, especially stopping cars with Yankee plates on their way to Miami, the citizens contributed to the local economy by fetching hooch from the West Indies. The Ashleys, a covey of Cracker brothers who'd been living in the 'Glades, plus a tall, mean woman called Laura Upthegrove, started in the bank-robbing trade. The boys, John (the good-looking one), Ed, and Frank, would stroll into the bank. The story is they were so scary all they had to do was *say* "Ashley" and tellers would open their drawers without a peep. Laura, who was John Ashley's paramour, drove the getaway car.

But the Ashleys swiftly figured out that smuggling liquor was a lot more lucrative. Times were hard, and there wasn't, after all, that much money in small-town banks. Sometimes, to maximize their profits and lower their overhead, the Ashleys didn't bother importing their own alcohol but just pirated it from other rum runners before they hit the

Florida coast. Laura Upthegrove would wait on the beach in the moonlight with her .38, supervising the unloading. In case supply lines got clogged, the Ashleys also operated three huge stills in Palm Beach County (got to keep the customers happy). They made gobs of cash. Then one day Ed and Frank Ashley sailed to Bimini with $18,000 in cash to stock up on merchandise, ran into a storm, and were never seen again. Soon after, in 1924, their brother John Ashley was executed by cops after he surrendered at Sebastian Inlet. Laura Upthegrove was so distraught that she drank a whole bottle of Lysol and died.

Money Trees

To a nation gone bug-eyed reading Hearst newspaper stories about rum runners in the Keys and Romanian princesses at The Breakers, Al Capone buying a stuffed alligator on Flagler Street or Gloria Swanson wearing Chanel and South Sea pearls to stroll on the shores of Lake Worth, Florida meant exposed skin and illicit liquor, nightclubs with hot jazz and rouged lips, a Lotusland where you could lounge under palm trees green as crème de menthe, bask in golden champagne sunlight, and swim in the blue Curaçao-colored waters of the Atlantic. Florida, despite the hurricanes and the screwy economy, still looked like nothing but fun.

There was baseball in the dead of winter with the Hectors and the Achilleses of the majors tossing balls like kids under warm Florida skies. In Sarasota, the circus was in town—the circus was *always* in town. John Ringling, the circus impresario, stored his lion tamers (and his lions), his trapeze artists, his fire-eaters, bearded ladies, two-headed boys, and dancing midgets there. In Miami Beach, Carl Fisher hired long-legged girls to hang around his "Roman Baths," helping to sell lots, wearing the kind of bathing suits that got preachers all over the nation to thumping the pulpit in outrage. Fisher also brought in a couple of elephants, which he named Carl and Rosie after himself and his wife. Rosie took a shit on the pristine sands of the beach, a gesture that, in retrospect, seems prophetic.

In the other Florida, the Florida that hadn't gone bust because it had never boomed, small-time moonshiners were making a living with whatever they could brew from corn and springwater. One 'shiner in Duval County retailed his jugs out of the back of a truck, hidden under sacks of sweet potatoes and pecans. He sold the sweet potatoes and pecans, too—all fine Florida agricultural products.

In the almost-empty counties of Levy, Dixie, Lafayette, Taylor, Liberty, Franklin, and Wakulla, 'shining supplemented oystering, mullet fishing, farming, and logging. North of the orange groves and west of the Suwannee, this Florida wasn't Florida at all to the shivering millions of the North. Who'd want yellow pine woods and tobacco barns, palmetto hammocks and Primitive Baptist churches, so far from Worth Avenue, the Tamiami Trail, and the Royal Palm Hotel? This wasn't the beach, it was just the South.

Some people, though, reckoned backwater Florida could, after all, turn a profit. Property taxes were low. In 1924 the state amended its constitution to outlaw income tax. Even better, the constitution also prohibited inheritance taxes. If you had it, Florida would let you keep it. So Alfred duPont, of the more money than Croesus duPonts, cast an eye on Florida and saw potential.

He had fond memories of the St. Johns country, his mother having been one of those rich ladies in poor health who'd visit the state for its palliative air. Florida certainly looked better than Delaware—Delaware was run by a cabal of his megabucks cousins with whom Alfred did not get along. One of them, Pierre duPont, had become Delaware state tax commissioner and was hell-bent on tightening up collections to benefit state education, his pet project. Alfred hadn't, it seems, paid income tax for five or six years, though he certainly had an income. A large income. Alfred packed up his young wife, Jessie Ball duPont, her business-savvy little brother, Edward Ball, and a few bank accounts, and moved south.

The duPonts had made their fortune in black powder. They supplied ammo for the Union Army in the Civil War. Jessie and Edward Ball, children of one of Robert E. Lee's officers, may have been raised in genteel poverty but came from a First Family of Virginia: George Washington's mother was a Ball. It's appropriate that they would all end up in Florida, the old Confederate state now running on new Yankee money. Despite their Vanderbiltian wealth, Alfred and Jessie duPont weren't Miami Beach nightclubbing material, nor were they Palm Beach Mar-a-Lago costume-ball types. They were progressives, do-gooders, reformers. They looked at the benighted condition of rural Florida and envisioned a new social order with good hygiene, wholesome food, and opportunity. They built an Italo-Iberian-Moorish manor by the St. Johns River south of Jacksonville on land left over from a real estate deal that failed when the mirage that was the "Florida miracle" vanished. Ed Ball, who had an eye for a foreclosure sale, bought the place for his sister and brother-in-law. Cheap. Then he commenced to buying other things for Alfred: repossessed property, banks that had imploded, the wreckage of other people's investments.

Unlike his schoolteacher sister and philanthropist brother-in-law, Ed Ball was not a bleeding heart. Any new social order should have him at the top of it, him with lots of money. He was obsessed with taxes, unions, communism, and uppity Negroes. He admired J. Edgar Hoover and may have been an FBI informant. He liked to win. Florida was easy pickings; the place was full of posthurricane, post-railway-strike, post-financial-collapse, post-Boom bargains. Everybody, including the state government, was in hock up to the sweaty hatbands of their Panamas.

By 1928 almost 10 million acres had been seized for nonpayment of taxes. The state couldn't pay on its bond debt. There were bankruptcies and suicides and general desperation. Leaving out the plutocrats who descended on Florida only to party, the people doing okay were the moonshiners and duPont. Even before the stock market crash in 1929, Ball acquired failed banks in Lakeland and Bartow (heart of the phosphate industry), Orlando and Daytona, St. Petersburg and Miami. And land, too: ten thousand acres here, ten thousand acres there, pretty soon you were talking about real property. It finally added up to one million acres. The size of Delaware. *One million.* The company still owns almost all of it.

Thanks to Ball, duPont had promising land covered in promising timber from which you could harvest turpentine, cellulose, lumber, and paper. The country consumed something like 8 million cords of pulpwood per year. The thing was, there were hardly any roads to the duPont land: not decent, civilized, commerce-friendly roads anyway. The 1923 official road map of Florida showed no paved roads in Walton, Bay, Franklin, and Calhoun Counties, and just a couple in Wakulla County. A state subsidy or two was in order. In 1926 duPont—which means Ball; he was the business end of the business—spent $45,000 on "political expenses," lobbying legislators, an art form halfway between threats and bribery. He'd invite senators and committee chairmen over to this big house in Tallahassee, a place he called, almost with a straight face, the "Highwayman's Hideout," and, with the best in fried shrimp and bootleg liquor, greased the wheels of the mule cart of state. He'd point out that Florida needed long-term investment in industries that didn't live and die on the whims of hurricanes, cold snaps, and bubble-headed tourists. What was good for Ball and duPont was good for the people of Florida.

Ball also went into business with a Liberty County pulpwood dealer named G. P. Wood to harvest and deliver duPont timber to a paper mill in Panama City. Mr. Wood the pulpwood dealer also happened to be a member of the Florida House of Representatives and eventually became Speaker. He was happy to be helpful. Florida spent more money on highways than anything else; North Florida got more roads than anyone could believe, roads into the parts of Wakulla and Franklin and Liberty and Calhoun where there were only bears, bobcats, wild hogs, and timber belonging to the duPont pulp company, which would eventually be named St. Joe after the little Gulf coast town where Ed Ball built his own mill in 1936. In the 1960s Gloria Jahoda, author of *The Other Florida,* was amazed to see all these big, sleek, wide blacktops down in the swamp, leading nowhere. "I reckon Mister Ed Ball must of wanted a road there, is all," people would tell her.

Ed Ball's been dead for more than twenty years but the state's still giving St. Joe roads. And airports. And tax breaks. And love, lots of love. St. Joe's out of the pulp and paper business and into the development business. Now they cut trees for "new urban" pastel retro housing developments that have strange capital letters in the middles of their names: SouthWood, SummerCamp, WaterColor. St. Joe works like God (money and a million acres are all it takes to achieve apotheosis in Florida), moving water, moving land, moving highways. It plans to shove US 98, the old coast road along the Gulf, back a bit inland. It'll give the company more beachfront property. St. Joe wants a "Gulf Coast Parkway" through what's left of the piney woods so the Navigator and Escalade-driving swells from Atlanta or Dallas who'll come to live at their "river camps" and golf "communities" never have to get stuck on Highway 20 behind some Cracker's old raggedy-ass dragging-tailpipe truck.

Taxpayers will be forking out for most of this, we, the citizens who voted for the governors and the legislators because of the TV ads we saw telling us how great they all are, TV ads largely funded by the campaign contributions from the feudal lords of sugar, subdivisions, phosphate, theme parks (*We just moved here—that Jeb Bush, he looks like a nice man*). We get what *they* paid for.

This ain't new. Florida's always been passed around like a roofied-up girl at a fraternity party. From the Spanish to the British to the Americans, Florida's been used for whatever profit you could fresh squeeze out of her. In the 1960s, what Carl Hiaasen calls "Team Rodent" acquired forty-three square miles of Central Florida using spies and proxies who smiled like gators and never whispered the blue-chip name of Walt Disney. Didn't want property prices to get *silly,* now, did they? Using the same grinning all-American line of just-trust-us crap, the Mighty Mouse wanted Florida lawmakers to accord it powers more appropriate to a sovereign state than an amusement park. High on the smell of millions in profits from the millions of tourists Disney promised, the state rolled over on its back, smiled, and said, *Anything you want, baby*.

It's not just the teeth-grinding tackiness. Hiaasen says: "Suddenly there were no limits. Merely by showing up, Disney had dignified blind greed in a state pioneered by undignified greedheads. Everything the company touched turned to gold so everyone in Florida craved to touch or be touched by Disney. The gates opened, and in galloped fresh hordes. The cattle ranches, orange groves, and cypress stands of old Orlando rapidly gave way to an excreble panorama of suburban blight."

Disney World is close to being an extraconstitutional entity, a business palatinate within a soi-disant democracy. It can't declare war—at least, I don't think it can—and doesn't maintain a standing army, unless you count the legions of abominably perky Mormon missionary types it employs, but Disney can run its own utilities, establish its own building codes, hire its own building inspectors and fire departments. Disney can build schools and lay out cemeteries. Disney has its own cops in blue uniforms with badges, only they call themselves "hosts" and "hostesses."

In 1991 Disney found out that one of its employees was spying on the girls who worked at Cinderella's Castle, masturbating as he watched them change costumes and videotaping them. According to Carl Hiaasen's *Team Rodent,* Disney security "investigated" this for three solid months without telling the young women that a Peeping Tom pervert was eyeballing every hook, button, and strap, choking the chicken while he was at it.

Not content with colonizing the dreams of children everywhere, Disney is colonizing all of Central Florida. Disney is so powerful that Florida's bullet train (if it's ever built) will stop at Disney's own Lake Buena Vista instead of Orlando. Team Rodent has built itself a model village, Celebration, a beige masterpiece of ersatzery with front porches and flags and hairsprayed grass. Disney may, if it chooses, build its own international airport, levy its own taxes, and build a nuclear power plant. Just imagine it: Mouse meltdown.

The duPont-Ball interests benefited from Florida's sweetheart deals with Hamilton Disston and Henry Flagler, and, in turn, duPont-Ball paved the way for Disney's ever-so-special relationship with state government. After all, everybody wants to have his picture made with Mickey and Minnie, kiss Cinderella, sing along to "It's a Small World After All." And it *is* a small world, after all: In one of those corporate "coincidences" that makes Florida seem so cozy at the top, the man who ran Disney's real estate business, selling "homes" (never "houses"—only foreigners have "houses," Americans have "homes") now runs St.

Joe and means to propagate his tastefully pale, clapboarded, covenanted new towns all over a part of Florida proud of its peeling paint, its gaudy awnings, its lawn flamingoes, its Chevy Impalas defiantly up on blocks in the weed-knotted front yard right next to the inflatable wading pool.

Modern Florida likes to pretend that it's a twenty-first-century, information-economied, high-tech "marketplace" that runs on a computer chip or three and a slew of cell phones. But that, as Ed Ball would have said, is a load of bull. Land is still power; land is still money. Scarlett O'Hara's old daddy called it right: "Land is the only thing in the world that amounts to anything."

The Wakulla Volcano

Malcolm and Edgar Lafayette Roberts, intermittent schoolboys, full-time farm and logging hands, decided to make their own still in 1918. They had a spot by a little spring down toward Langston Branch. They had an old sugar-boiling kettle. They had a wooden barrel top for a lid. They had a big water bucket Brother John had found up at Great-Granddaddy Smith's place. They had a stash of baling wire. They bought a broken-off copper coil from one of the Spears boys. He charged them 2 cents and wouldn't say where he got it. One Sunday afternoon when Mama had gone over to Sister Harriet's to see the new baby, they took a little sugar and a little yeast and a little malt and a little meal from the kitchen.

They'd seen plenty of stills: The country from Vause Branch to Morrison Hammock, from Smith Creek to Sopchoppy, from Red Lake to Whitehead Lake, was full of them. They'd heard all the stories put about to scare people away. There were ghosts: the ghosts of dead Indians, of dead Spaniards, dead Civil War soldiers, dead babies. There were monsters: the giant gator (forty foot long if he's an inch and terrible as Beelzebub) that lived in Hitchcock Lake; the hoodoo doctor with his necklace of black cat bones and witch spells scratched in the sand; and the bears—Edgar Lafayette (known to his brothers and sisters as "Lee" and his grandchildren as Papa) had seen with his own eyes a bear as big as any one of his daddy's oxen, eyes red as raw meat, chained to the front porch of the house where those strange old boys were living, three brothers who never wore anything but overalls without shirts, winter or summer, and never said anything to anybody. Word was they had three stills back in the hammock, and they'd turn that bear loose on anyone who came calling.

Fiercest of all: the volcano. Way down in the deep forest maybe around Wakulla Springs, maybe as far east as the Wacissa River, there was this volcano. It wasn't a mountain volcano like the ones in the pictures of Aetna or Krakatoa. This was a *swamp* volcano, a volcano special to Florida. A fellow from *Lippincott's Magazine* came down in 1882 and wrote a whole article about it. He called it "the Wakulla Volcano."

Not that he saw it up close; few people had seen it up close. Mostly you saw a line of smoke going straight up like a portico column, sometimes white as a cowbird, sometimes black as a crow. At night the thing would glow a kind of gray green. Some days you could look out the south windows of the Capitol and there it was, twenty, maybe twenty-five miles away. In the 1850s Princess Murat used to invite her salon guests to take their glasses of Madeira out onto the veranda at Bellevue and look at the ashy spray through opera glasses. The princess would remind everyone that, of course, the late prince had been brought up in the shadow of Vesuvius when he was crown prince of Naples.

Cabeza de Vaca had seen the smoke rising from it in 1529 when he was crashing around directionless in a bog. Jane Broward and Rufus Tucker had seen the strange, silvery eruption from a boat on the Wakulla River in 1844. Richard Roberts told Ellen Smith he'd been real close to it, near Tiger Creek, and that was over in Liberty County. Granddaddy Tucker would tell the young 'uns that he knew where it was but reckoned it wasn't his place to pander to the curious and the vulgar.

Like everything else in Wakulla County (rivers, borders, stills, houses, husbands), the volcano moved around.

The volcano had its uses. Somebody spread the rumor that the volcano would kill you with a swamp disease if you got too close. The old-time colored people said it was Satan stirring his tar kiln. White preachers would point out the door in the general direction of the swamp and say that the fiery pit of hell (which might be right out there just off the Newport Road) awaited evildoers, lawbreakers, and drunkards.

Despite the threat of eternal damnation for taking liquor, there was, as everybody said, a *power* of it around. Papa and Uncle Malcolm reckoned the county put out enough corn juice to float the *Belle of the Bend,* enough white lightning to light up every speakeasy in Miami. Not that the produce of Wakulla County made it that far south. There were plenty of buyers right there in Tallahassee, lawyers and senators and doctors and farmers and such. They said the governor *hisself* liked to take a snort of the 100-proof, though never in front of the ladies.

In Wakulla County, the women didn't drink. The men drank. And sometimes the animals. Free-range hogs would get high on the fermented mash they found rooting around stills in the swamp and sometimes drown in the slough. Papa liked to tell about the bears. They'd get in the mash, too, or sometimes knock over the kettle and lick up the liquor. Sometimes in the deep woods you'd come upon bears staggering around, Papa said, "like they'd just left the saloon. They'd be muttering and grunting like they was talking to themselves and not paying nobody no nevermind."

A drunk bear was easy to shoot. But there were women in Wakulla County who'd demand to know if that bear her husband or son brought home to be dressed had been drinking and refuse to cook him if the bear had indeed taken spirits, on the grounds that alcohol was a sin and an abomination whether in man or beast.

The men drank. Papa and Uncle Malcolm's father, Valarious Lafayette "Lease" Roberts, would come on home from running the *Belle* up and down the river and once the sun went down commence to hitting the jug. The women didn't drink; the women went to church.

Papa's mother, Lizzie Tucker Roberts, was a foot soldier in the Cold Water Army. If there'd been a locatable saloon in the county, she might well have helped the Carry Nationals smash it up. As it was, she just killed his and his little brother Malcolm's still. She walked out there one afternoon and took a hatchet to it. The boys hid behind a gum tree and watched. She chopped it up good, wrecking Papa and Uncle Malcolm's career prospects as big-time 'shiners wearing diamond stickpins and driving Model Ts. The mash never even had a chance to ferment. Then she walked back to the house, hung up the hatchet, and started stewing a mess of squirrel for supper. She never mentioned the still. Neither did they.

Papa carried on having this furtive relationship with hooch. In 1922 he married a preacher's daughter from a long line of preachers, and not just preachers, Scots, Presbyterians so heavy-duty they couldn't stay Presbyterian (the church had become decadent, in their opinion) but had to take refuge in becoming denominational freelancers or even Baptists, and so, wouldn't you know it, Frances Susanna Arigdhe McKenzie was anti-booze, too.

Granny—people other than her grandchildren called her "R.E.," which was as close as they could get to pronouncing her Gaelic name—did not hold with drinking or swearing and took rather a dim view of dancing. She would threaten my cousin Ray with a toothbrush and a bar of Dial soap for saying "darn"—and he'd been in Vietnam. Every year at my mother's Christmas Eve party, Granny would police Papa. We had two punch bowls, one spiked, one not. We'd conspire with Papa to appear to dip his out of the unspiked bowl, pull a switcheroo, and give him the good stuff. My mother would make the punch with vodka so Granny couldn't smell it on Papa's breath.

Papa knew this moonshine song; he said he heard it down in Sopchoppy:

A drop will make a rabbit whip a bulldog;
A taste will make a rat whip a wild hog;
Make a mice bite off a tomcat's tail;
Make a tadpole raise the mud with a whale.

In a triumph of aspiration over experience, Florida in the early twentieth century would insist that its presiding genius was "Prosperity" or "Progress," maybe "Pride." In Wakulla County, the presiding genius was Alcohol. For us, Robertses and Tuckers, Vauses and Revells, Langstons and McKenzies, interbreeding since the 1840s to the point that everybody in the county was some kin to everybody else even if sometimes nobody could tell exactly how, alcohol was everything from a curse to a career opportunity.

For years the highly flammable mix of Roberts drinking, Roberts rage, and Roberts firearms meant that life in the swamp was not merely hard, it was potentially lethal. Lease would haul out Richard Roberts' Civil War musket if the boys sassed him. Or even if they didn't. The boys, in turn, would self-medicate with the local brew and chase each other in the woods brandishing shotguns. Papa liked to say he was lucky his daddy and his brothers had bad aim.

Drinking and fighting didn't seem to impair Lease Roberts' long tenure in elected office as a Wakulla County commissioner. Drinking and fighting didn't stop Lizzie and Lease's nephew Luther Tucker from getting elected to the state senate. Alcohol lubricated the wheels of his political career; alcohol also ran it off the road and into the ditch.

There's a story that used to be told in certain roadhouses and in the Silver Slipper Restaurant about Luther Tucker and a call girl. Seems the senator took a fifth of home brew and drove to the Floridan Hotel downtown. He got him a room and dialed a certain number. In Tallahassee in the 1950s you couldn't order a pizza over the phone but you could get a whore. When the prostitute showed up, the story goes, it was one of his kinfolk.

The Tuckers and the Robertses (most of them), including me, do not believe this. Several distinguished journalists and members of the Florida Bar nevertheless keep telling the story. There's no denying the drunk-driving and assault charges, however. According to Luther Tucker it was all a "political frame-up."

One day in 1962, the senator thought he'd eat lunch at Garcia's, a Spanish café in Tallahassee popular with lawyers and businessmen. He had a broken foot and was on crutches, having had a run-in with a Wild Turkey or something. This did not stop him from picking a fight in the parking lot. One W. H. Wilson, a building contractor, had finished his arroz con pollo and was on his way out. Senator Luther Tucker was on his way in. He claimed Wilson had recently called him "an SOB," so the senator, six foot four and at least two hundred pounds, crutches or no crutches, hobbled up, hauled off, and decked Wilson. Old Mr. Garcia looked up from his frijoles negros and called the police. The *St. Petersburg Times* account says that Officer Horace Barineau arrived to find the senator ready to confess:

> "I assaulted his battery with my left," said Tucker. "Let me at him and I'll assault him with my right."
>
> "Will you please shut up?" said Barineau. "You're under arrest."
>
> "Boy, I'm Luther Tucker, senator from the Fifth District," Tucker said, glaring at Barineau, "and I am going into Garcia's to get me some bean soup."

Tucker later told the judge that all he was doing was "defending my American heritage."

In 1966 Senator Luther Tucker smashed up his big, black Cadillac on the Crawfordville Highway. He was killed. Some said there was a jug of 'shine on the seat beside him.

Other kin turned to the practice of law. Papa's niece Evelyn, daughter of his brother Luther Roberts, became what some of the kinfolk called "a she-judge," the first in Wakulla County. Bonny Kaslo Roberts made it to an even higher bench, profiting from liquor more creatively than his cousins. After all, what a bootlegger really needed was a good lawyer.

He always billed himself as B. K. Roberts. His mother was a Wakulla County Morrison, descended from a Scotsman who fought in the Revolutionary War. She thought "Bonny" was a nice name, Scottish as in good-looking, Southern as in the "Bonnie Blue," the Confederacy's first flag. He thought it was a bit girly.

He was ambitious, studying on getting himself out of Wakulla County. He was smart, the whole county said so; while the other boys were making practice stills or catching gophers, he was building a radio in the barn. He qualified to be a schoolteacher at thirteen. At sixteen he went to the University of Florida. He was poor, and he was from the swamp; he didn't have the right accent or the right clothes or the right daddy. He cleaned up in the college cafeteria to pay for his board. He worked construction. He plowed. He lived in an attic when he had rent money. When he didn't, he lived in a pup tent out near the football practice field. One day a delegation of upperclassmen came to call at the pup tent to suggest that, since the University of Florida was a gentleman's school, perhaps he belonged somewhere else. He was embarrassing them.

By the age of thirty he had his revenge. He owned downtown property in Tallahassee. He owned beach property on the Gulf of Mexico. He owned a Lincoln dealership. He was a lawyer, a rich, well-connected lawyer, graduated from the University of Florida College of Law at twenty-one, a prodigy, a dime-novel hero. B.K. didn't fool with a lot of Clarence Darrow nonsense fighting the uphill battle for the social justice, standing up for the downtrodden: Florida's rode-hard-and-put-up-wet Crackers or always-cheated sharecroppers or always-oppressed black folks. His first customers were moonshiners. During the Depression, they were about the only ones with any money.

Some of B.K.'s clients were kin; many weren't. But he provided excellent service and mostly won cases ("Your honor, gentlemen of the jury, my client is a Christian man who takes nothing stronger than grape juice at communion and wouldn't dream of flouting the Constitution of the United States by producing illegal alcohol.") 'Shiner versus revenuer cases weren't only a good living, they were good public relations: Nobody liked revenuers; nobody, except the ladies of Wakulla County, liked Prohibition.

At the age of forty-two, B.K. was appointed to the State Supreme Court, transforming himself from poor white trash to white-shoed legal aristocrat in only a few years, becoming *plus royaliste que le roi,* grander by far than the snotty old-line Kappa Alphas and SAEs at Florida who had snubbed him. Not only had he made a tidy fortune defending the God-given right to sell a little ruckus juice now and then, he'd been talent-spotted even before he took the bar. His uncle the sheriff of Wakulla County had introduced him to Mister Edward Ball of the duPont Company in 1928. Ball liked this young fellow. He smelled ambitious. B.K. liked Ball: *He* smelled like money.

Soon a lot of North Florida, thanks to Ball and B.K., would smell like paper mills. Alfred duPont died in 1935, leaving his millions in a trust for the crippled children of Delaware. Sort of. Ed Ball was really in control of the money, crippled children or no crippled children. In between white lightning cases, B.K. took care of real estate closings for Ball as he took over more and more of the state. Ball had been buying up still more huge tracts of land, 66,000 acres in the piney, underpopulated counties of Franklin, Bay, and Walton, and 13,000 acres on ten miles of Gulf coast. North Floridians could not for the life of them figure out what anybody'd want with all that sand: You couldn't grow a damn thing in it.

People at the St. Joe company would tell you that Ed Ball got up every morning and asked, "Who do we fight today?" If there was a clear answer, he'd call B. K. Roberts, who was happy to take care of problems from women to governors, liberals to legislators.

In 1943 B.K. handled Ball's ugly, mud-slinging divorce from Ruth Price Ball. Ten years before she had, poor woman, signed his prenuptial agreement laying out nineteen rules and requirements. She had to keep her figure. She had to dress to his taste. She had to refrain from criticizing him in public. Other men must not be charming to her. Not that he was around much to enforce the contract. She charged him with emotional neglect. He charged her with concealing her inability to bear him a Ball princeling. The case went as far as the Florida Supreme Court.

Ruth got $250,000 and a house. It was a good deal—for Ball. B.K. had saved him from forking out maybe a million to a woman who couldn't even breed.

A few years later B.K. handled an even more threatening crisis in Ball's life: the possibility of a tax that would actually cost him money. Ball and others of his ilk had terrorized the Florida legislature when, in 1935, lawmakers had flirted with repealing the state's prohibition on an income tax. Ball had successfully staved off attempts to raise property taxes or institute an inheritance tax as well as other shifty schemes by which the socialist Roosevelt administration and its Florida stooges—including Senator Claude "Red" Pepper—meant to soak the virtuous rich. In 1949, just as B.K. was named to the state supreme court by his pal Governor Fuller Warren, the legislature decided that maybe a sales tax was the way to go. What could be fairer? You only have to pay if you actually up and *buy* something. Ball supported it. His lawyer, Justice B. K. Roberts, always accommodating, helped draft the sales tax bill in his own study. The judge might one day have to rule on its constitutionality, but surely he could still be perfectly impartial.

B.K.'s client was on a roll: He'd got shed of the nagging wife; he could eat at the Silver Slipper (steaks and snapper and lemon meringue pie!) every night if he felt like it; he'd laid in cases and cases of Kentucky Tavern bourbon (though the county was dry); he was living the bachelor life at Southwood, his plantation house near Tallahassee. It was haunted—one time a guest woke up with a radio cord wrapped around his neck—but Ball didn't hold with the supernatural. He'd pour a big glass (or three) of Kentucky Tavern and offer the toast, "Confusion to the enemy."

Here is how powerful Ed Ball was: Though Port St. Joe, where his paper mill was located, lay on the western side of the Apalachicola River and thus in the Central time zone, he preferred that the town run on Eastern Standard time so as to be in sync with company headquarters in Jacksonville. It still does.

And here is how powerful Ed Ball was. He decided to get rid of Senator Claude Pepper. Relations between Ball and Pepper, a big-time New Dealer who had been praised in the *Daily Worker,* started off cordial. Pepper, too, thought roads were a good thing for poor, rural areas. This didn't last long. A 1946 entry in Pepper's diary says: "The sinister and dangerous character of Ball's domination of the state of Florida becomes more distinct as one sees it more closely." Ball called Pepper a "buzzard." When Pepper was up for reelection in 1950, his opponent's Ball-fueled campaign charged Pepper with being a "nigger-loving" comrade of Uncle Joe Stalin who consorted with "thespians" and let himself be photographed with Paul Robeson. Pepper lost the primary to the "duPont lawyer" George Smathers. B. K. Roberts had practiced with Pepper when they were starting out. Still, he was Ball's lawyer. B.K. disappeared gently into a noncommital mist, leaving only his smile behind, just like the Cheshire Cat.

Ball built a pretend hacienda at Wakulla Springs in 1937. It had painted cypress beams, marble and tile floors cool as the spring waters themselves, and a fireplace big enough to roast a hundred-year-old alligator without folding him up. It also had a vault to keep his liquor in. Ball would have house parties for politicians he wanted to buy, businessmen he wanted to schmooze, and ambassadors and minor royalty he wanted to impress. B. K. Roberts was often invited to stay at the Lodge. E. L. Roberts—Papa—was not. But Papa was often in the neighborhood, hunting on Ball's land, fishing in the Wakulla River.

Inside the Lodge, drinking bourbon and eating fried oysters, Ed Ball would tell his guests about how Ponce de León came to that very place to die, and he'd pull out the bloodstained arrow. "This is the fountain of youth," he say. And he'd tell about the Wakulla Volcano, smoldering out there in the darkness somewhere, smelling of hellfire and brimstone. Sometimes the guests would stand on the terrace above the springs, scrutinizing the sky, hoping to see a smoky tower off to the east in the violet twilight sky. Ed Ball would laugh over his glass of Kentucky Tavern and say softly to himself, "Confusion to the enemy."

In August 1886 there was an earthquake in North Florida. Windows broke, horses bolted, pictures fell off parlor walls. After that, the volcano smoke disappeared though the country people saw it whenever they needed to.

In the fields and the turpentine camps and the logging camps and at the hog killings and juke joints, even in Mister Ed Ball's kitchen at the Lodge, the sawyers and the pickers and the farmers and the cooks would crack a new jug of Panther's Breath, ruckus juice, white lightning, and commence to singing:

Make a fyce bite off a elephant's snout;
Make a poodle dog put a tiger to his rout;
Make a toad spit in a blacksnake's face;
Make a Hardshell preacher call for Grace.

Fire

Tarzan the Ape Man moved to Wakulla County. The Creature from the Black Lagoon came over later, he and his girlfriend. But in 1940 it was old Tarzan, wearing his leopard-skin loincloth, pummeling his swimmer's chest, hollering his jungle holler, swinging from a vine right there on the Wakulla River.

Milton Roberts heard they were making a Tarzan movie over at the springs. There were fellows in Cadillacs and Packards and big lights and cameras and girls to light your cigarettes. Over at Mister Ed Ball's place there were Cuban cigars. And fried chicken every day, that's what he heard. There was Johnny Weissmuller, smiling a big-dog smile and signing autographs. Johnny Weissmuller was tall and tanned and muscled and rich. Milton Roberts was small and pale and poor.

He'd never seen a Tarzan movie. He knew about them: Some of the Tucker cousins had been to the picture show in Tallahassee. He had a couple of beat-up Edgar Rice Burroughs novels a teacher had given him, and he'd like to have watched the Ape Man wrassling a bobcat or one of those real big gators that lived around the river and catching a grapevine back to his tree house where Jane was waiting. Still, it didn't occur to him to sneak over there to look at movie stars. Some of the kids said they might go, hitch a ride partway and walk through the woods. But he had chores, sawing wood, hoeing the beans and peas. He had school. His daddy was always harping on school, getting an education, getting somewhere. There was no good living in breaking your back logging or farming or putting out fires. The good living was in your brain. And his brain, as his daddy said, was "mighty fine."

Milton Roberts was Lee and Frances Roberts' second son, skinny, green-eyed, redheaded. His cousins called him "Tiny." He was my father. He was named for his great-great uncle Milton Tucker, who was named for the English poet who made an epic of the sin of Adam and Eve. Uncle Milton was the seminary cadet who'd wormed his way onto the train heading for the Battle of Natural Bridge, the one who was killed and set to burn on a raft in San Carlos Bay.

They'd all been downwardly mobile since Appomattox. The Tucker lands had been divided. So had the Vause property. The Robertses never had much to start with. Luther Tucker could recite Latin poetry; some of his grandchildren could barely read English. The Depression didn't help. When my father was born in 1930, in Sanborn, Florida, there were already two children, Wendell and Thelma Leola. By 1937 there were three more: Gladys LaJuana, named after their cousin whose daddy was the lighthouse keeper at Crooked River; Maria Elizabeth, named after Uncle Milton Tucker's only daughter, who in turn had been named for one of her Broward aunts; and Marlan Glenn, named after no one in particular that we know of, but it sounded distinguished, like a movie star. There had been another, Ouida Jean, born in 1932. She had water on the brain. Thelma remembers that her head was so big and her body so small that they had to carry her around on a pillow. She lived less than a year. Their house had no running water, no electricity, no glass in the windows, no screens, either. In the winter, the dipper froze in the ice bucket. The place was rickety as toothpicks. When Thelma played jump rope on the porch, the house shook so hard they thought it might fall down.

They were poor as possums, the lot of them, but they had fancy names to live up to, which I guess was the idea. The Browards had gone in for French Imperial and Romantic Revolutionary with their Napoleons and Josephines, Washingtons, Pulaskis, and Osceolas. The Tuckers followed suit, with Benjamin Franklins and Robert E. Lees and Andrew Jacksons, while the Robertses went for sub-Roman grandeur: Theophilus, Valarious. As for the McKenzies: My father's mother's people had probably been in straitened circumstances since before the Battle of Culloden. My great-great-great-great-grandfather Daniel McKenzie lost an eye fighting with Francis Marion, the Swamp Fox, in 1778. He was illiterate. His will shows that he was able to leave his four children only $1.25 each. Even in 1815 that was a pretty sad little bit of money.

Still, their names were opulent, biblical Susannas and Samuels, Shadrachs and Pharaohs and lyrical Amarinthas and Almiras and Julianas. Many of them had not two but three or four names. Granny was probably named after Colonel Francis Marion, her great-great-great-grandmother Susanna Lawhon, and some ancestor from the moonscape islands of the Outer Hebrides where they sang the psalms in Gaelic. The psalms sounded like the rise and fall of the waves of the sea. My father and his brothers and sisters with their grand names and their grand ancestry figured to get out of the swamp one day, just like some of the other Tuckers and Robertses had commenced to doing. Not that it was fixing to be easy. The poverty was always right there, circling overhead like a buzzard waiting for a wounded deer to die. A bad crop, a sick child, a little while with no work—catastrophe.

As much as Hell and the Holy Spirit, fire, water, and snakes were the realities of my father's childhood in the 1930s. His mother kept the yard grassless, sweeping it smooth as a dance floor with gooseberry brush brooms to keep the rattlers and the moccasins away from the house. One afternoon his brother Wendell and his sister Thelma got trapped by a giant rattler stretched all the way across the road, watching them with its angry eyes. Granny finally came looking for them. She sized up the situation, disappeared, and came back, this time with the hoe, and hacked the monster's head off in the afternoon sun.

When I was six or seven, my father showed me the snakebite kit in the glove compartment of the car. It was Mercurochrome, a tourniquet, a bandage, and a razor blade. The idea was that you cut above the bite, apply the tourniquet, suck the poison out (and spit) to keep it from reaching the heart and brain, then finish the job with the Mercurochrome and the bandage. It turns out this wouldn't save anyone, since a rattler or a coral snake or a cottonmouth's venom is full of antigens, and what you die of is anaphylactic shock. But that wasn't received wisdom and Daddy, being raised in the swamp, followed the methods he was taught as a boy. Nobody doubted that if Satan came to Sanborn, he'd take the form of a cottonmouth.

Sometimes fierce storms came up through the Gulf and spawned tornadoes and floods. People talked about the 1894 hurricane. The highest high winds bypassed Wakulla County, but they got tornadoes and thunderstorms and rain, nail-hard, stinging rain that turned roads into streams and fields into lakes. The county's average elevation is seven feet above sea level. Even without a storm, warm-weather rains would make the creeks and sloughs and rivers and branches rise. You'd wake up in the morning and water that looked like milky coffee would be lapping at the front porch. The water brought disease; the water brought more snakes.

When it wasn't floods, it was fire. Cabins, barns, everything was made of pine and cypress, good fuel wood when it was dry. Things were always burning. Somebody would be careless with a kerosene lamp or a wood stove, and barns would go up faster than you could think about it. Lightning would strike an old tree and flames would run through the pines like mercury. The fire would blaze for miles, blaze for days.

The great event of Papa's childhood occurred on July 7, 1913, when everything his family had burned to nothing. Papa's mother, Lizzie Tucker Roberts, was cleaning the living daylights out of the place, spring cleaning, though it was summer. It was easier to do when Lease was off somewhere. She scoured the floorboards with sand, she wiped the windows down with ammonia, she aired the ticking. She swept all the trash into the fireplace and set it alight.

It was a dry, dry summer for once. The dirt and stick chimney caught fire so fast, and the fire leapt up onto the roof so fast, Lizzie barely had time to grab the youngest children, Malcolm, who was four, and Vivienne, who was only two, and run outside. She was eight and a half months' pregnant with Franklin Theodore, as well. John, Lee, and Luther kept running to the hand pump and hauling buckets of water, which they threw on the house. But the water just hissed up into steam and the ashes shot high above the live oaks like this was the Wakulla Volcano itself. The house went up like a parcel of brittle old love letters, the flames growing hotter and redder, red as yaupon berries, red as lung blood.

Finally they just gave up and watched. On the front porch, the thrust of the heat pushed a rocking chair back and forth. It rocked as if there were someone unseen sitting there, one of the ghosts from the little graveyard out back, old Richard Roberts himself, maybe, waiting patiently and relaxed for the rest of the world to burn. The chair rocked and rocked until the boards finally collapsed around it, black as the deeps of Tate's Hell swamp.

In the late 1930s, Papa got hired by the Forest Service to spot fires from the tower at Sanborn. When he saw a fire, he'd go put it out. Before that he worked construction on the bridge over Ochlockonee Bay. His shirt would be stiff with salt and his milky skin blistered sausage pink. Working for the Forest Service, he'd show up at home completely covered in soot from hat to shoes, everything except for his eyes. But soot and shade beat salt and sunburn. After World War II, Papa would get the best job he'd ever have, driving a bus for Tamiami Trailways. But the fire tower was pretty good. It paid $63 a week.

Milton liked to climb the towers, the one at Sanborn and the next one his father went to, at Otter Camp, even though he coughed a lot when he got to the top. Above the treetops, sky and forest made up the whole world, the one blue as the deepest part of Wakulla Springs, yet near enough to touch; the other green as a lizard and impossibly remote, even though you knew that's where you really lived. Some days he felt like the sun was a magic lantern. You could see boats in St. George Sound and seabirds flying above Dog Island. Straight south from there, across the Gulf, across the Tropic of Cancer, was the Canal de Yucatán, which washed into the Caribbean Sea, which splashed against the top of South America where the Amazon was, and the Andes, and Tierra del Fuego. Straight north—and over a ways east—was the Atlantic Ocean with Africa to the right and Europe up a ways east: the Congo, Mount Kilimanjaro, the Nile, the diamond mines, King Solomon's Mines, Paris, London, Rome. He memorized the atlas at school, though it had been printed before the Great War and so still had an Austro-Hungarian Empire and a united Ireland and German principalities with hyphenated names full of *h*'s and *z*'s. He read the encyclopedia, too. He was going to get to all these places because he was going to go to the Naval Academy at Annapolis. That was only in Maryland. Maryland was, compared to the Pyramids, just up the road.

All the Roberts young 'uns would go up the towers to look at the universe, though they were pretending to help watch for fires. Maria Elizabeth—she was "Betty" to the family—attempted her first solo ascent at the age of three. Papa had to stay up there day and night looking for the rise of dark gray smoke, slow as a hawk ascending, or the flash of vermilion that meant that somewhere the precious wood of the Apalachicola country was burning.

Unless it was raining. If it was raining, and not too hard, he'd come down and work in the vegetable patch or go get a croker sack of oysters to roast. Saturday nights they'd make a washpot of pilau (which was pronounced "per-lo") rice, and the aunts and cousins would come around from Sopchoppy and Arran and Carrabelle and Vause Branch and Smith Creek. Papa would play the harmonica and sing "I'm Walking Down That Lonesome Road" and "Johnnie Reb Fill Up the Bowl" and a ballad none of them could recall the name of about a girl in Scotland who died waiting for her man to come back from the wars—what war, they couldn't say.

When they said "the War," it was always capitalized and it always meant the Civil War. So they'd tell stories, too, about the Tuckers fighting at Natural Bridge and Virginia and the Vauses at Murfreesboro and Kennesaw Mountain and the McKenzies at Charleston and Richard Roberts at Petersburg. And they'd tell the story of the volcano and ghost stories and fishing stories and always fire stories.

My father and his favorite cousin, Mary Joan Roberts, Uncle Malcolm and Aunt Alma's daughter, liked to hear about the hammer that had been made from a star. Great-Great-Granddaddy Ephraim Vause, whose mama was part French, part English, and part Creek, had come down to Arran from Carolina. He was plowing in the field one day when the blade hit something that rang like a bell. It was stone. Not limestone, either, but something dark and hard and shiny as tar. Ephraim Vause picked it up, knocked the dirt off it, and reckoned it might make a good hammer head. He showed it to Preacher one time, and Preacher—who was a man of some erudition—said it was a piece of a comet that had come down from heaven. Great-Grandmother Harriet Jerusha Vause Tucker used it to crack pecans.

Milton knew what it really was—a meteorite, maybe a Perseid or Leonid, crashed down through the hot gauze of the atmosphere and landed in the county, which not so many million years ago was part of the sea. It was a treasure, cold as space now, but better than any piece of gold Tarzan ever found in darkest Africa or Wakulla Springs.

9

Sunshine

THE BOY HAD ACCOMPLISHMENTS. She could play the piano, sing, crochet. She could arrange flowers, make a pound cake, gut a fish. She could recite a poem in Latin, answer the first ten questions in the *Westminster Shorter Catechism,* shoot a pistol. She could milk a cow, waltz, split an arrow at two hundred feet. She could ride a horse, run a tractor, and drive a car—fast. Her daddy put one of the Buicks in a pasture at his farm, a pasture without Herefords in it, and made her practice shifting and braking until, as he put it, she was unlikely to kill anyone on the public highway.

The Boy looked good in high heels, too: that was important in 1952.

"Boy" was what Bradford Gilbert called his daughter. She was an only child.

Now the Boy had met a boy. He was related to a Supreme Court justice and a senator and a governor but his father was a bus driver for Tamiami Trailways and his mother worked in Mendelson's department store. His name was Milton Roberts. He was going to design bridges to vault across the rivers and lakes and sloughs and swamps and damp low-lying places all over Florida. She was pretty sure that her daddy would like him.

Betty Gilbert set off for Florida State University in 1949, majoring in Getting Off the Farm. She started out in Physiology, but Dr. Kitty Hoffman's chemistry course just about killed her. Dr. Kitty Hoffman was a relic of FSU's pre-post-war, pre–GI Bill, pre-man-invaded self, the Florida State College for Women, created by Governor Napoleon Bonaparte Broward in 1905 out of the old West Florida Seminary with the stated mission of creating, for the State of Florida, the *femina perfecta*. That perfect woman would be white (colored girls went to Florida A&M), and she would find deep meaning in the recitation of *hydrogen, helium, lithium, beryllium, boron, carbon,* at least until she got married to one of the not-so-perfect men from the University of Florida.

Then there was cutting up cadavers in the attic of the Williams Building. It wasn't just the gross horror of death: Betty Gilbert had seen hogs slaughtered and could kill, drain, scald, pluck, gut, and cut up (not to mention fry) a chicken herself. It was the heat. It was the severed arms and legs you'd have to take a scalpel to at the top of a building that was already creepy, with turrets and gables and dim staircases to nowhere. It was the tendons and veins and muscle and gristle, and the smell of raw meat just starting to go bad. She switched to PE.

Physical Education was great. You got to be outside. You got to wear shorts. The dean of women had decreed that shorts in public for non-sporting purposes were Unladylike and Would Not Be Tolerated.

Betty Gilbert, my mother, still insists on wearing shorts unless it's below freezing outside. She was a jock—a graceful jock. She was good at soccer and hockey and swimming and golf. She was good at dance and took classes from an aquiline-profiled, bohemian, scarf-favoring professor who had studied with Martha Graham. She was a good archer. There's a picture of her in full Diana the Huntress mode, almost-black hair blowing back, about to let an arrow fly. You can see the muscles tensed in her arms and her long slim legs, the concentration on her face. She wears a smart short-sleeved shirt in a checkerboard pattern, tucked into her very white, rather tight, belted short shorts. She wears lipstick and a little smile.

The problem with PE was basketball. Coach Grace Fox, another of the *femina perfecta* sisterhood who welcomed men to campus in 1947 with the enthusiasm of Poles greeting Germans in 1939, wanted a women's basketball team. Betty Gilbert was lousy at basketball. Couldn't pass, couldn't jump, couldn't shoot. Old Lady Fox suggested Recreation.

So my mother majored in Recreation, where you did a little of all the sports, as well as music and art. In the summers she worked for the City of Tallahassee at Levy Park, showing children how to play softball and Chinese checkers, teaching them how to make pot holders and papier-mâché animals. One day she was hanging up the tetherballs, and there was this guy. He had screaming orange hair. He was kind of little, and his skin looked like skimmed milk.

He was staying with his mother and daddy at their house on Tenth Avenue, near the south end of the park. This was the best house the Robertses had ever lived in, thanks to paychecks from Mendelson's and Trailways, in a white folks' neighborhood of white wooden bungalows on the edge of the black folks' neighborhood. It had once, a long time ago, been the French folks' neighborhood, back when some of the Norman peasants la Fayette brought over decided to stick around in Tallahassee even after the whole olive-, silkworm-, and lime-growing social experiment went bust.

There were no French people left in Frenchtown. There was, instead, a subtle line that everyone understood. Levy Park was for white children. Black children played in their yards or in the rutted, red mud street. A few of the white families in the Levy Park neighborhood had colored maids or laundresses or yardmen who lived so close they could cut through a lot or two and be at their employer's back door in about a minute. But most of the people around where the Robertses lived were not the sort to have domestic help.

Sister Thelma was married now. Sometimes Milton watched her two little kids, Sheila and Ray, on the Levy Park swings. She was working as a secretary at the Public Welfare Department, over on Gaines Street by the jail. Brother Wendell was married, too, with a baby, taking courses in geology at FSU and working as a bookkeeper at a sand company. Milton had gotten a degree in civil engineering from the University of Florida. He'd been student body president at Leon High School. He'd been voted "Friendliest." He'd graduated at sixteen, a mathematical genius without being a nerd, a real teacher's pet, everybody's pet.

Wendell had won an appointment to the Naval Academy in 1944 but had turned it down. He said he was in love. He refused to sign a pledge that he wouldn't get married during his four years at the academy.

Milton was disgusted: "He's no brother of mine if he's stupid enough to throw his life away over a *girl*."

Milton decided he would get into Annapolis. He aced all the written exams. He passed six physicals with six doctors. Got his picture made in his sailor suit, hat and all. Then the seventh doctor discovered that his spleen wasn't doing its job. It wasn't producing the red erythrocytes that send oxygen through the body. It wasn't properly storing iron. It wasn't helping run his immune system. His blood was messed up.

The Robertses were plagued with injuries and ill health and congenital horrors. Lots of them were, to some degree, manic depressive. Maria Elizabeth had convulsions. Thelma got bad eye strain from staring into a microscope to remove mosquito stomachs—this was when she was still in high school and working in the Malarial Research Department at Florida State College for Women. Granny had migraines. Wendell eventually committed suicide. Marlan Glenn fell off a second-story porch and cracked open his forehead. When Papa was working as a fireman in Tallahassee, he wrecked his back and had to make repeated trips to St. Luke's Hospital in Jacksonville for operations that helped in inverse proportion to what they cost. He couldn't straighten up. He planted his garden crawling on his hands and knees.

Milton was sick the most. He had ulcers. He couldn't eat regular food but lived off poached eggs and toast. He was in and out of the hospital. Sometimes he had to have a complete transfusion, shipping the bad blood out, importing the good stuff into his body. Betty Gilbert, with her long golden legs, her graceful arms, a bat in one hand, a catcher's mitt on the other, and that whistle she wore on a lanyard around her neck—she must have looked like some kind of Amazon, tall and strong and blooming like the crimson amaryllis lilies his daddy grew. He asked her out to a baseball game.

And then to a football game. They drove down to Gainesville on weekends when the Gators played at home. At Homecoming, she wore a corsage with orange and blue ribbons and learned to sing: *We are the boys of Old Florida, F-L-O-R-I-D-A.*

They went to football games and basketball games at Florida State. They went to football and basketball games at Florida A&M, where they sat in a roped-off segregated section for white people. They ate dinner at the Silver Slipper or out on Lake Talquin at the Talquin Inn. They went to dances. Betty bought a poison green evening dress from the Vogue on Monroe Street. It had a velvet halter top and a net skirt. She wore it with silver kid slippers. They were flat, so she wouldn't tower over him.

In the spring they went to more baseball games and on double dates with Milton's best friends, Charlotte Allen and Ernest Williams. Charlotte had been secretary of the student body of Leon High School when he was president and a maid of honor on the 1947 May Court. Ernest had been on FSU's first men's basketball team in 1948. Ernest could pass, jump, *and* shoot. He could play baseball, too, and pitched three seasons with the semipro Tallahassee Capitals.

Milton's mother and daddy said to carry this girl home so they could lay eyes on her, so he did. She admired Milton's mother's dinner: ham, fried chicken and pork chops, mashed potatoes, sweet potatoes, black-eyed peas, field peas, fried okra, biscuits, gravy, coconut cake, peach pie, and tea so sweet it was like a slap upside the head. She admired Milton's daddy's flowers: dahlias, marigolds, gladioli, amaryllis. She tried to be smaller, but she was the tallest person in the room. She may have been the tallest girl they'd ever seen.

In September 1954 Betty had a job with the City of Tallahassee;

Milton had a job with the state road department. They got married, married in a big way at the First Presbyterian Church of Chipley, Florida, with the Reverend MacDuffie in full Covenanter thump, bridesmaids in old gold carrying bouquets of bronze mums and groomsmen in summer dinner jackets, and large, loud organ music and solos by the best soprano in three counties and silver forks and lots of almond extract in the cake. The wedding presents (Towle Old Master sterling, Royal Doulton "Tiara" bone china, Russell Wright for every day, saucer champagnes, several toasters, a Baccarat jardiniere, several more toasters, several iced tea pitchers, and a two-tone hot-pink polka dot ruffled Fenton glass vase that would have terrorized any flower that got put in it) were laid out in the dining room in Chipley. Teas and luncheons were given and duly reported in the newspapers from Chipley to Tallahassee (there weren't very many newspapers between Chipley and Tallahassee) with descriptions of the floral centerpieces (sweetheart roses, Michaelmas daisies, ivy), the food (sherbert punch and cheese straws and petit fours with crystallized violets on top), and what my mother wore (a powder blue georgette afternoon dress with a matching hat accented by a spray of velveteen pansies, a cream linen sheath with chestnut brown gloves). My father was referred to only once in each of these articles, the excuse for the party.

The wedding was written up, too, my mother's tulle, taffeta, and lace, her mandarin collar and forty self-covered buttons, her Juliet cap and silk illusion. She carried a complicated bouquet with gardenias and chrysanthemums and an orchid that must have been the Big Bertha of its primeval rain forest.

This time the Boy didn't try to not be tall. This time the Boy wore duchesse satin shoes in diamond white with four-inch heels.

Chipley Tigers

My mother was born in 1931 in a bed made from black walnut cut at Gilbert's Mill. It had a curving headboard with a yellow rose painted on it. Her mother would sit me, age four or five or six, on that bed to get me ready for church, which was no joke, since I hated petticoats, I hated starch, I hated gloves, I hated hats, I hated sashes, I hated having my hair combed, and Sunday involved all those things at once. Church started at eleven. Grandmama would start working on me at nine. Sometimes she resorted to bribery: If I would submit to the blue voile dress and the black patent leather shoes, I could open the trunk and look at her wedding veil, now yellow as old newspaper, and the bandeau of flowers, dipped in wax, she had worn to hold it in place in 1924. Sometimes I'd break the deal; I'd go ahead and pitch a temper fit anyway, jumping on the bed, rolling on the bed, beating my fists on the pillows she had plumped and fluffed so carefully when she made the bed.

"Your mama was born in that bed," Aunt Rilla would say, if she got wind of my transgressions. Aunt Rilla Gilbert was my grandfather's sister, and smelled of mothballs.

"Your mama was born in that bed," Cousin Regina would say, not scolding, though, just telling. Cousin Regina was there while my mother was being born, or almost. She was only seven, so they made her go play outside. It was late August. Regina was Aunt Lucille's daughter. She married a soldier from up north named Tommy. Still, she liked to come to Chipley for long visits. My mother first met Tommy in 1944 when he was on leave, standing out behind Big Mama's carriage house, smoking. "Big Mama" was Mary Broadwater Gilbert, my grandfather's mother. My mother was twelve or thirteen, with skinny legs and a slightly grubby satin ribbon in her hair. "What's your name, Chipley Tiger?" he said.

"Betty Jean Gilbert," she said. "Give me a cigarette."

The Chipley High School mascot was a tiger, a snarling, prowling, gold-and-blue-striped tiger. Why a tiger, no one seems to know, since there weren't a lot of tigers in Florida except down where the Ringling Brothers Circus wintered. Bobcat, sure, even panther. But not tigers.

My mother's mother stayed in that bed for a long time after my mother was born. She was very sick, probably with puerperal fever; we don't know for sure. That was female trouble. You didn't ask and didn't tell about anything like that in a decent Presbyterian household. All that was said was that there would be no more children.

My mother's mother, Selma Henrietta Georg Gilbert, hadn't started out Presbyterian, nor had she started out to marry a farmer from Florida and live where she had to battle slugs and cutworm and aphids and black spot on her roses day in and day out. She was raised Lutheran, a German-speaking child of German parents who had emigrated from Hesse and ended up in Garrett County, Maryland, after the Civil War. Selma was the eldest of eight children, living in Accident, Maryland. She was a big girl, sturdy, with olive skin and dark hair, unlike her sisters Elsie and Ada, who had butter blond hair and china blue eyes. By the time she was seventeen, both her parents were dead and she was the head of the household. So she worked. She worked in dairies and on farms. She cooked and cleaned, slowly moving farther west. My grandfather met her in Akron, Ohio. She was a parlor maid in the mansion of some tire-manufacturing millionaires.

After the Great War (almost a year after), Bradford Gilbert finally went home to the farm. It was like he'd never been to France, never seen the aftermath of the Marne, never gone up in a balloon, never seen the Vatican or the Coliseum, never drunk champagne in Monte Carlo. He went back to overseeing the hands at the turpentine still. He drew up contracts for naval stores. He helped with the corn patch. He despaired at the boll weevil. The most fun thing he got to do was to blast the whistle at the sawmill: starting time, lunchtime, break time, suppertime, quitting time. In a couple of years he was bored out of his head again and there wasn't a decent war to be found anywhere. So he reckoned he'd travel north, work on the B&O Railroad.

Chipley was founded in 1882, itself a mushroomed-up creation of the railroad. The Gilberts would say, snippily, that they had a *mule* older than Chipley. They had, however, hoped that the Louisville and Nashville, the L&N, would run through Washington County at the bottom of Orange Hill. This would have been helpful in moving Gilbert cotton and Gilbert lumber and Gilbert turpentine. However, Colonel William Dudley Chipley, a Georgian who'd been wounded at the Battle of Shiloh and a vice president of the L&N, decided to run the line to the north, where there was, my grandfather used to say, "zero minus nothing." The settlement had track before it had anything else, then an empty boxcar acting as a station/post office, then somebody opened up a liquor store. The town of Chipley was born.

The Baltimore and Ohio must have paid well; Bradford could afford to indulge his post-Paris dandyism. We have photographs from the early 1920s with him in textured silk ties and waistcoats that would have made his daddy hoot, boater hats, silver watch fobs, and sharp suits with the trousers cut so narrow he looks like a South London mod circa 1962.

My grandfather was a good-looking fellow and he knew it. What we don't know—my mother says she never knew—is how the outgoing, smooth, been-to-France Bradford Gilbert met the shy and awkward Selma Georg, who spent most of her days in a black dress with a starched and ruffled apron and a starched and ruffled cap, moving discreetly with a feather duster around the tire millionaire's rosewood and brocade-stuffed rooms.

By early spring 1924, he had given her a diamond engagement ring and a string of pearls. He had also bought a Model T. He took Selma and her sister Ada for spins in the country. There's a picture of the three of them standing by the side of the car: Bradford wears a light summer suit with the jacket unbuttoned; Ada's stockings are shiny silk; Selma's hat is broad-brimmed, skittish, and her dress has a wide lace collar. Both she and Ada hold huge bouquets of delphiniums, stocks, and larkspur—I can just see my grandfather sidling into some swank Akron florist and ordering flowers for his best girl and her sister. Selma has her arm firmly around Bradford's waist. She is also, just as firmly, wearing her spectacles.

My grandmother always wore her spectacles, even when she was having a glamorous flapper portrait, with long beads and a long scarf and bare arms, taken just after her engagement. She wore those spectacles for her wedding. There she is, in a low-waisted, ankle-length beaded silk dress, white silk shoes, her long veil curled like a train at her feet, the pearls he gave her around her neck, and these round-lensed, black-rimmed glasses. I'd whip my glasses off and hide them behind my back if I saw a camera. At an Oxford commem ball in 1981 I clung to my boyfriend's arm, smiling like a jackass at everybody because I couldn't actually tell who anybody was. I'd stashed my glasses in the pocket of my moiré Laura Ashley ball dress (all Laura Ashley clothes, even evening clothes, had pockets), too vain to risk being seen seeing. I asked Grandmama once why she didn't take her specs off for her wedding photos. "I wanted to watch what was going on," she said.

The Gilberts wanted Bradford home. Again. Zet offered to buy him a chicken farm, halfway between the mill and Chipley, set him up in business. Maybe he'd quit this gallivanting now he was married. Imagine Selma and Bradford arriving in West Florida in that Model T, her meeting the Gilberts, all those Gilberts, two brothers, six sisters, seven nieces and nephews, Big Mama Mary, Daddy Zet, the lot of them spread out now over five or six houses and three towns. Imagine them looking at her, with those glasses and lace collars and hats that had come from Akron's best department stores, bought with the last of the parlor-maiding wages, and her Lutheran prayer book (in German) and her German accent (didn't Bradford go off to war to fight the Germans?) and her shy ways. Imagine her coming to this place where palm trees and orange trees grew and the people all spoke like their mouths were full of cane syrup and acres of cotton like beaten egg whites and the smell of turpentine and colored women to do white people's cooking and washing and colored men to work in the fields. And no Lutheran church. No Lutherans.

Selma put her foot down about the chicken farm, though. She had been raised in the boondocks with no running water, not even gaslight, and the outhouse a cold, rainy thirty-yard walk away. She'd lived in the city, in a big nice house that was warm when it needed to be and comfortable—even if she was only the help. She didn't want to live in the boondocks anymore; she wanted to live in town. With electricity. And indoor plumbing. So Bradford bought land at the edge of Chipley, a quarter of a mile from Big Mama's house of girls, ten miles from Orange Hill, where John Wesley Gilbert aimed to become a cotton prince and Roxanne Bradford drew pictures of classical ruins in her schoolbooks. Pastureland stretched behind; downtown Chipley, such as it was—a railroad track running bang through the middle of it, the high school, the post office, a Piggly Wiggly, a hardware store, a drug store, the Alford Brothers' Naval Stores, the Methodist church, the Baptist church, and the Presbyterian church—lay half a mile in front. There was a little hollow to the north where black people, mostly descendants of the slaves of a French Huguenot planter, lived.

Bradford built her a bungalow, with a porch and electric light and an actual flushing commode. In her own house, with her own feather duster, she would sing a little: *"Ein feste Burg ist unser Gott, Ein gute Wehr und Waffen,"* and "Blue skies, nothing but blue skies, from now on."

The Jazz Age came to West Florida in 1924 and lasted until the boom's gaudy balloon went splat in 1926. It was a short party. But then the Gilberts weren't dealing in intoxicating beachfront property and high-kicking speculation. They stuck to wood, turpentine, poultry. Everybody in the world needed a house and something to paint it with and a chicken or a turkey to eat.

The Gilbert boys settled down to serious farming and lumbering. Bradford missed running around the world, though: One day in 1925 he took a photo with the English box camera and wrote on the back, *This is what they call a Blimp. It was going over our house and I snapped it.* Still, he stayed put in Washington County. His brother Homer, Homer's wife, Mary Isabel (called Maybelle), and their baby, Hubert, were living next door to Big Mama in Chipley. Fred and his wife, Elia, and their children, Fred Jr., Ellen, and Katherine were in Cottondale, where the cotton gin was, the cotton gin that was about to become the peanut mill and produce Gilbert Select Seed Peanuts.

The girls, except for Ella Ruth, who'd got married in 1919, and Charlsie, who operated the telephone exchange switchboard out of her front room, shortened their skirts, bobbed their hair, and scandalized their daddy. They stayed away from the farm as much as possible. Town boys—boys from towns as far away as Marianna, even Panama City—would drive over to take them out. The boys didn't even bother to come and ring the doorbell, they'd just honk the horn and out of the big pointy house at 515 Sixth would fly a muster of young women with strawberry blond hair and high complexions in buckled shoes and muslin dresses and swooping hats.

One morning Maybelle heard somebody vomiting behind the cow

shed. It was Lucille, the prettiest of the Gilbert girls. It happened again the next morning, and the next. Maybelle figured she knew what was up and told Homer. Soon it was pretty obvious. Homer and Zet disappeared in the car for days on end, driving, it was whispered, as far as Panama City looking for "the man responsible." His name was never spoken, even if they knew what it was.

Regina Gilbert was born in Big Mama's house in 1924. People didn't ask questions. The Gilberts didn't volunteer answers. Eventually Lucille lucked out. She got charming letters from a young Philadelphia man called Thomas McCue, who worked for the duPont companies. He'd found "Lucille Gilbert, Chipley, Florida" on a slip of paper in a box of cigars he'd bought and thought he'd try a letter. She responded. He came down to visit.

What happened was that there was this other Lucille Gilbert, a distant cousin, who worked in the cigar factory in Quincy. West Florida cigar factories were not like the ones in Tampa, where the *lector* read from Cervantes or *The Conditions of the Working Classes in England,* and the *trabajeros* would discuss the plight of the masses later over strong coffee. West Florida cigar factories were full of Baptists wholly uninterested in fomenting the Revolution, though keen on advantageous marriages. These were fancy cigars they were rolling, expensive ones, so the girls would put their names in the boxes hoping that a rich man would write to them and maybe fall in love with them and take them away from West Florida and the cigar factory. Thomas McCue wrote to Lucille Gilbert, Chipley, Florida, and the mailman, who knew the Gilbert girls, knew they lived on Sixth, duly delivered it to the wrong one. Or the right one, depending on your point of view.

Another Day in Paradise

The past smelled like pears. The sheets on the bed I slept in (my mother's bed) were dried next to the pear tree in the ferocious blast of summer. All around the laundry, pears were ripening, falling into the grass and rotting. You didn't dare walk out there barefoot: Bees and wasps love rotten pears and bored into the pear flesh, getting drunk off that sweetness. But the sheets absorbed pear scent like cologne. I'd lie there with my nose in one of Grandmama's pillowcases, edged with crocheted lace and fiercely ironed, wondering why everything and everybody in Chipley seemed so old.

There's something about these West Florida towns that puts you in a heat haze of slow motion and quiet, as if the rest of the state is racing around, paving itself, wiring itself, covering itself in concrete, dizzying itself with images and noise and charging admission to boot, while Chipley and Marianna and Cottondale and Bonifay and Chattahootchee and Graceville and Vernon and Alford nod off in the afternoon sun. I would read my mother's books: *A Girl of the Limberlost, Anne of Avonlea,* and *The Password to Larkspur Lane*. I would have tea parties with her miniature Blue Willow dishes: me and a baby chick I'd sneak in the house from one of the incubators. I would have to be careful my grandmother didn't catch the chick doing its little chick business on her polished floor—mostly I'd encourage it to shit on my bare foot. That was easy to clean.

My mother's room, robin's egg blue, flouncy-curtained, was just as she left it when she went to college. The pine desk had her blotter, "Betty Jean Gilbert" written over and over in curly letters, and a pair of bookends made of varnished cypress knees with the feather end of an arrow sticking out of one and the point end out of the other to make it look like somebody'd shot through *Webster's Dictionary, Bartlett's Familiar Quotations,* and the 1947 Chipley High School yearbook. Tacked to the wall above the desk was a blue and gold Chipley Tigers pennant and a gold pom-pom on a stick. In the desk drawers were some of her engraved visiting cards, "Miss Betty Jean Gilbert," a pink feather fan mounted on ivory sticks, a golden *C* made of wool with a yellow-eyed blue tiger prowling across it. A football player boyfriend had given her his varsity letter. It was a courtship ritual, a pledge of devotion.

This was before she met my father.

My mother's boyfriends, some of them in the military, sent her stuff: silver bracelets from Siam, a porcelain box from occupied Japan, 78s from Japan: There was one I'd play over and over on my grandparent's 1930s radio-Victrola, "Tokyo Boogie Woogie." It was a dance record, sung in Japanese by a woman with a high, trilling voice. The best things they sent, though, were postcards from Bangkok and Okinawa and Honolulu and Pensacola and Paris and Miami and Key West. Like her father, Bradford Gilbert, my mother collected postcards. I'm pretty sure it was the pictures she liked, not what the guys wrote, which was always about the weather and the food. Most were blank anyway; unlike my grandfather, she didn't believe in annotation. And mixed in with the ones from far-flung places, lots of Florida postcards. There was "Greetings from Miami Beach" with a huge curved deco hotel, sugar pink, squatting on silver sand next to a bright sapphire ocean. There was "Southern Belles at Cypress Gardens" with a couple of girls in daffodil hoopskirts and matching parasols posing on peridot green grass framed with flowers in nylon blues and lavenders. There was "Another Day in Paradise." Sky and sea merge in a streaky fit of violent red, orange, and purple bands with the silhouette of a lone sabal palm in the foreground.

Did other places have these? "Another Day in Ohio"? Maybe each state had its own illustrated versions of the Tupperware Museum and the Gatorama. I couldn't imagine they'd be as high-colored as ours. Just saying the names: Tarpon Springs Chimp Farm and Sponge Docks, Sunken Gardens, Six Gun Territory. Just calling up the images: water-skiing pyramids of "Aquamaids" and Seminole chiefs wrestling snarling alligators and miniature golf courses full of dinosaurs and glass-bottomed boats and pink stone bell towers in the middle of nowhere that played "Nearer My God to Thee."

I could see why my mother hoarded the postcards. The palm trees and bougainvillea gardens and parrots and monkeys and ski shows and flamingos were as exotic in West Florida as they were in Ohio. Nobody came to take snapshots of Chipley and Marianna, Cottondale and Bonifay, Chattahoochee and Graceville. There were no postcards of the peanut mill or the cotton gin or the turpentine still or the First Presbyterian Church. The nearest thing to a tourist attraction around here was Florida Caverns, a series of limestone caves in Jackson County where you could see stalactites and stalagmites and bats. It was nice enough if you liked rocks, but it was no Cypress Gardens.

I know a lady who used to work at Cypress Gardens, down in Winter Haven. Her job was to wear a ruffled flamenco dress—short in front and long in back—and lean against a cypress tree, preferably with a knee showing, so that GIs could come and look at her. This was during World War II, back when proprietors Dick and Julie Pope still thought they were running a botanical garden (eight thousand varieties of plants!) on the swampy shores of Lake Eloise, back before they got the electric boat rides and the ski ballets going.

Soon Cypress Gardens was the greatest tourist attraction in Florida. Everybody went there, snowbirds and natives alike. Where else could you see a four-high pyramid of tanned girls in Janzten two-pieces being pulled behind a speedboat going forty miles an hour while waving miniature Confederate battle flags?

A couple of years after they were married, my mother and father took Granny Roberts to Cypress Gardens. The ski performance was not a success. Granny didn't care for those hussies in skimpy bathing suits jumping around on skis. She liked the flowers, though. She liked the Florida-shaped swimming pool. It had been built for Esther Williams's movie *Easy to Love*. She liked the Belles. The Belles were not hussies. They didn't jump around. They just sat on dainty benches or on the licked-clean, silky grass, their skirts spread out in a perfect circle.

I went to Cypress Gardens in 1999 and got to talking to a couple of the Belles, Melissa and Britni. Melissa's crinoline was iceberg lettuce green and Britni's toothpaste blue. They were juniors in high school. They liked working as Southern Belles: it beat squirting special sauce on Big Macs or waitressing at the IHOP. "We just kind of wave at the tourists when they go by," said Melissa, "and they take our picture."

"Sometimes it gets really hot in the hoop," said Britni. "Some of the benches have little air conditioners under them to cool you off when you sit there."

"Oh my God, Britni," said Melissa. "Remember when that girl fainted that time because it was so hot?"

"I heard it was two girls," said Britni.

I suddenly had a vision of Cypress Gardens' lawns covered with collapsed Southern Belles like blown azalea blossoms, a couple of them near the giant teddy bear topiary, a couple of them near the chrysanthemum-covered rabbit. I headed over to the waterfront seats where the show was already going on. A Chris-Craft roared across Lake Eloise with five women standing on the shoulders of five men on skis while Jefferson Starship chirped loudly over the speakers, "We Built This City on Rock 'n' Roll."

I was disappointed that they didn't do the number where the dog drives the speedboat.

Cypress Gardens is closed at the moment, another victim of Team Rodent up the road in Orlando. People had a fit when they heard. A passel of Southern Belles, past and present, went up to the capitol to lobby the governor. They wore their hoops. The state, knowing that disappointing white girls in crinolines is always bad PR, caved in, allocating money to save part of the place as a "cultural treasure" for the future. Cypress Gardens was, after all, Florida's first theme park.

"So, Betty, how's college?" said one of Mama's postcards, this one of the Fountain of Youth in St. Augustine. It was signed "Davis." "Storms all the time, not such good fishing xxx C," said one with a picture of the Royal Palm avenue in Palm Beach. Another has a hand-tinted morning sky, roses and corals and aquamarines, with a quiet blue bay on one side, mossy green cypress trees on the other, and, in the middle, a road, starting out wide and tapering off to the vanishing point. The caption says "Sunrise Over One of Florida's Modern Highways." On the back is written, in my father's small, perfectly legible hand, in pencil (probably mechanical pencil): "When are you coming Back?"

The Flower Refrigerator

My great-aunt Rilla Gilbert, Granddaddy's sister, was the fanciest florist in Chipley, Florida. She did the weddings and the funerals for all the best Presbyterians and Methodists and even a certain class of Baptist. She didn't trade much with Episcopalians. Their church was over in Marianna, the one that the Yankees burned in 1864. They had their own florist.

Aunt Rilla had glassed in the front porch of the house in town her father, Zet Gilbert, had built, turning it into her FTD showroom, complete with sample easel sprays in artificial lilies, photos of altars festooned with garlands of cabbage roses and baby's breath, and coffin blankets of maidenhair fern and carnations dyed mint green. The rest of the house was choking in rolls of ribbon, cords of Styrofoam, acres of oasis, cases of green tape, bundles of wire, boxes of fake parrots and toucans with real feathers and clip-on feet, bags of fake holly berries and snowflakes and red, gold, and silver Christmas balls, plus all the embroidery, tatting, quilting, crocheting, and cutwork Big Mama had almost finished when she died in 1956.

On one side of the front room Aunt Rilla had built a refrigerator big as a boxcar with a picture window. On the window there was a little gold-painted picture of Mercury in winged flight, carrying a dozen gilt roses to some lucky lady. From the street you could see the buckets of tiger lilies and arum lilies, gladioli and delphiniums, tulips and peonies on the refrigerator shelves, rich colors jammed up in there any old way. And sometimes you could see me, a short-legged child sitting there between the Queen Elizabeth and Étoile de Holland roses, sitting there where I shouldn't be at all, scaring the customers.

My grandmother took me over to Aunt Rilla's every Wednesday afternoon. I didn't like Aunt Rilla much. She always asked me what I had learned in Vacation Bible School that week and did I accept Jesus as my Lord and Savior? Aunt Rilla had been an old maid for a long time, and even when she married Uncle Allie, a parchment-colored man who never did anything but watch *The Fort Rucker Report* on TV, she still—according to my grandfather—acted like one. She wouldn't let me go into Big Mama's violet-smelling room upstairs and only rarely would she let me look at her best hat, a Schiaparelli crusader cloche that had come from Paris by way of Daffin's in Marianna.

She and Grandmama would sit eating orange cake watching her assistant, always known as "the Girl," work on an easel wreath for somebody's funeral. Aunt Rilla would criticize the Girl for putting a carnation next to a chrysanthemum. I was told to go play outside. Instead, I'd sneak into the flower refrigerator and sit there in the cold pink scent of blooms that never had to go out in the West Florida sun.

I'd sit in there thinking about the swimming pool in Tallahassee, how they shut it because colored children wanted to swim there. I wondered if something would come off the colored children and get in the water, if that was the big deal about all of this. I thought about Daddy sitting in his chair in the family room, drinking ice water, saying to Mama that all this with the Negroes would die down. Mostly he said "Negroes." Mama said "colored people." When he forgot and said "niggers" she would hush him. We didn't use that word.

When John F. Kennedy was shot, I didn't understand what was happening, except that the man who was always smiling and waving on television was gone. I confused him with my father anyway: They both had red hair and freckles and wore suits and ties. I confused Jacqueline Kennedy with my mother: They both had dark hair and wore hats and gloves. My mother's clothes were modeled partly on hers, but made from Vogue patterns. I also confused Mama with Princess Margaret, whose picture was often on the cover of magazines.

The day they buried the president, my father came home for lunch. Dorothy the maid was ironing in the family room. I was sitting on the floor with a bunch of my stuffed animals, who were organizing their own kingdom. My mother made tuna salad. "The thing about Kennedy," Daddy said. "He loved the niggers too much."

My mother gave him the look. "The Negroes," said Daddy.

Daddy hadn't voted for Kennedy. Kennedy was a Catholic. They wanted the pope to rule the world. "That's what killed him," said Daddy. "You can't serve two masters." Dorothy turned a pillowcase over, sprinkled it with water, and kept on ironing. It made a loud hiss.

In the flower refrigerator I'd imagine Aunt Rilla's and Grandmama's conversation. It would be about whoever had just died. It would be about my father. It would be about my mother. It would be about me. About the terrible red hair I'd got from my daddy. About the terrible temper I'd got from him, too. About the way I fidgeted in church and traced "SHUT UP" with my finger on the velvet nap of the pew cushions whenever the preacher went on too long. About the way I refused to play with my distant cousin Angela Nichols, who also had red hair, but who never got dirty.

I'd sit in the flower refrigerator and think about Daddy. He had died the year before, in 1967. He was in the hospital in Jacksonville for three months. My mother sat there every day. She wouldn't let me or my brother go to the funeral, but she and my uncle Wendell took us to see his grave afterward. There were flowers in pots and vases, flowers in the shapes of circles and crosses and fans, flowers stacked three deep, big as room. There were lots of yellow roses. Daddy had liked yellow. I tried to remember what he looked like. I got a picture of John F. Kennedy in my head.

So I'd sit there ignoring the Chipley people walking down Sixth who'd catch sight of my face among the leaves and say, "There's Betty Jean Gilbert's poor little child." And I'd think how wherever Daddy was, it would be yellow with sunlight but, unlike most of Florida, cool and clean-smelling like the flower refrigerator, and quiet, and impervious to July, and lonely in the best kind of way, waiting for the Presbyterians and Methodists and Baptists to get married and die.

10

Deepest South

MY MOTHER WAS BROUGHT UP in a dreaming Florida silence, not discussing sex or religion or politics or race—especially not race—or anything else tricky except the condition of the animals, the condition of the tractors, the condition of the land. She didn't know about the lynchings—Bill Young in 1901, Claude Neal in 1934, and lots of others in between—until she got married and overheard her father telling my father about them. She was "Boy," but she wasn't a man.

Bradford Gilbert may have been a wild internationalist in his youth, but by the time he was in his forties, he was like most white men of the landowning class in Florida: that is, he believed that the Lord had ordained perfectly sensible roles for gentlemen, ladies, children, animals, and Negroes. He disapproved of Claude Pepper because he was always "standing up for white trash who don't deserve it" and going "soft" on Negroes. He disapproved of Eleanor Roosevelt, inviting colored women to tea at the White House. He disapproved of Franklin Roosevelt because the New Deal was "a socialistic monstrosity."

Which was easy for him to say, since the Depression didn't really hit him hard. The Gilbert wealth (if that's the right word for it) wasn't based on cash to start with. The Gilberts, in the traditional Southern manner, had land. Therefore, they had food: beef, poultry, vegetables. It was like there was a high garden wall around Washington County, keeping out the news that Florida was going to hell in a handbasket—not that the word "hell" was spoken in the Gilbert household except in a biblical context.

Florida had trouble: money trouble, climate trouble, race trouble, bug trouble. The Mediterranean fruit fly had been discovered in an Orlando grapefruit grove in 1929, bringing on years of embargoes and quarantines and burned groves and bankruptcies, but the orange tree and the lemon behind Big Mama's house, and Aunt Bankie's citrus trees, bore sweet, fat fruit. In 1933 an out-of-work bricklayer called Giuseppe Zangara tried to assassinate FDR in Miami. The president was making a speech at Bayfront Park when the shooting started. Roosevelt had come south to cheer everybody up, even though banks were collapsing like damp cardboard (the Bank of Chipley went in 1931) and people went around grimly chanting:

Lawyers are red,
Business is blue;
If you were a banker
You'd be white-headed, too.

On Labor Day, 1935, a mean bastard of a hurricane hit the Keys, destroying Henry Flagler's railroad and killing several hundred veterans of World War I, members of the "Bonus Army" that had marched on Washington to protest massive unemployment. The ex-soldiers had been put to work in Civilian Conservation Corps camps on Windley Key and Lower Matecumbe.

Throughout the Depression, Florida drew jobless, homeless people who figured that if you were going to be destitute, you might as well be destitute and warm. They'd congregate in tents or salvaged tin "Hoovervilles." The state government had the vapors, throwing up roadblocks and posting patrolmen at the borders with Alabama and Georgia to keep "hoboes" out. In June 1937 the whole state, the whole country, perked up when Amelia Earhart took off from Miami in a Lockheed Pegasus to fly all the way around the world. In July 1937 Amelia Earhart disappeared somewhere over the Pacific.

Claude Neal had been lynched up in Greenwood for the usual reasons: He was accused of messing with a white girl. Not quite dead, so the story goes, he was cut down, brought to the Jackson County seat, and hanged in front of the courthouse so more people got to join in the fun. Souvenir hunters cut his fingers off. They cut off his penis and testicles, too. Somebody took a photograph, which eventually became a postcard you could buy. On it was printed, proudly: "Marianna, Florida."

Bill Young was a turpentine hand, almost certainly working for Zet Gilbert. The report in the *Chipley Banner* says: "Last Friday evening, Miss Barrow, the 14 year old daughter of Mr. Cull Barrow, was criminally assaulted by a negro brute."

A mob of white men caught him running toward Cottondale—who knows if there was a Gilbert among them?—down the Orange Hill Road. They lashed him to a tree and shot him repeatedly. A coroner's jury found that he had died of "heart failure."

The Klan marched through Chipley in their regalia, white, green, and red, Dragons, Wizards, Cyclops, Spooks, hands raised in their own Dixiefied version of the fascist salute. The townspeople looked at them, then around at one another, trying to see who wasn't there watching and therefore might be under one of those pointy hoods.

My grandfather didn't hold with the Klan: If you knew how to treat Negroes, you didn't need bedsheets and burning crosses. My grandmother refused to have a cook, but there was Maggie, who did the laundry, everything from soaking my mother's angora cardigans in the porcelain tub to boiling my grandmother's linens in a black witch-cauldron out by the washhouse. Later, when Granddaddy was in the fish-bait business, there was Frankie, who picked worms and fed the crickets and helped with heavy cleaning, and Frankie's son Booster, who did odd jobs, and various men who cut the grass and trimmed the hedges or looked after the peach trees and the catawba trees while my grandfather marched around his acres wearing a pith helmet like the owner of a tea plantation in India.

My mother says she didn't think about this stuff, she just got on with living the way everyone else did. She went to school, she did chores—milking, feeding chickens, weeding—she went to church, she went fishing, she went out to the mill or the turpentine still with her father, who let her take anything she wanted (oranges, candy, cheese) from the farm commissary. She put on gloves and dotted swiss to call on First Presbyterian ladies with her mother. She rode Tony the pony, or Dolly, the Gilbert workhorse, around Orange Hill. She and Suzanne Alford and Mary Jean Retherford rolled rabbit tobacco in tissue paper and smoked, or sometimes cadged an actual cigarette from somebody's older brother. She played with her Shirley Temple doll and her kittens. When she was in high school, she wore bedsheets, but not to promote the Purity of the White Race. The Chipley High School Latin Club had a toga party at the Green Lantern, a roadhouse over in Cottondale. They had that "race" music on the jukebox in the Green Lantern. You could get booze there, too.

New Negroes

In 1955 the ex-governor had to swear that my father was a white man. Daddy wanted to buy some land in northern Leon County, out the old cotton road to Bainbridge, Georgia. It had been part of Major Butler's plantation, then it became the Florida Pecan Endowment Corporation, and when that was being broken up, the covenant said that the land could never be sold to a Person of African Descent. Millard Caldwell, who'd been governor right after World War II, and who lived at Harwood, the plantation house across the road, certified that Milton Roberts was a known white man from a long line of white men.

The Southern Way of Life was under attack in Florida. You'd have thought Nat Turner, John Brown, and William Tecumseh Sherman themselves were about to drive down the Old Dixie Highway in a fleet of rented Cadillacs to reinvade the state.

Harry Truman had gone and integrated the army, giving the Negroes *ideas*. The National Association for the Advancement of Colored People had reared up and stirred up the contented, hymn-singing colored folks, got them to imagining that they had the right to eat lunch and go to movies and, worst of all, vote. Harry T. Moore, an NAACP organizer, had got more than 50 percent of blacks in Brevard County registered by 1950. Even though he was *from* Brevard County, whites denounced him as an "outside agitator." Somebody bombed his house on Christmas Day, 1951. The blast killed him and his wife.

White women weren't safe. White children weren't safe. The Florida Bar wasn't safe; in 1956 the U.S. Supreme Court upped and ordered that the University of Florida admit Virgil Hawkins, a black man who'd been trying to get into the state's only decent law school since the 1940s. Two years earlier the U.S. Supreme Court had ruled that segregated schools were unconstitutional. Southern states, including Florida, pitched a fit, then began inventing ways to subvert, circumvent, and refuse to comply with the radical notion that educational opportunity should be color-blind. The Florida Supreme Court resorted to what it almost certainly did not think of as its version of a Mahatma Gandhi–Martin Luther King–Henry David Thoreau act of civil disobedience, but nonetheless sat down on the ruling like mules on an uphill road and refused to budge. The state offered Virgil Hawkins money to go to law school out of state, one of those *colored* law schools, far, far from Florida. That didn't work. Then, in a shining example of the crystalline ratiocination and prudent use of money that has made Florida government renowned around the world, the state thought it would save the University of Florida from race-mixing and create its own colored law school at Florida A&M.

Justice B. K. Roberts had written a majority opinion barring Hawkins's admission on the grounds that (I paraphrase somewhat) states have a right to do pretty much anything they want, say, secede from the Union; and if you go letting a Negro man, even a nice Negro man, into the University of Florida (which is, after all, a gentleman's school), chaos will ensue. The Klan will burn crosses on the lawns of fraternity houses. Interracial dating will break out. Mongrelization of the white race will occur. Racial anarchy will destroy Christian Civilization.

Some people are not, after all, UF material.

Chief Justice Glenn Terrell wrote a concurring opinion citing Divine Providence (this is *not* a paraphrase): "when God created man, he allotted each race to his own continent according to color, Europe to the white man, Asia to the yellow man, Africa to the black man, and America to the red man, but we are now advised that God's plan was in error and must be reversed despite the fact that gregariousness has been the law of the various species of the animal kingdom."

Nobody pointed out to the chief justice that God must have screwed up because the white man now had *two* continents to lord it over, three if you count Australia. The red man only had bits and pieces of land out west, some in the more inaccessible regions of Canada, and a few alligator-wrestling parks in the damper regions of South Florida. Never mind: Justice Terrell knew what he meant. Most Florida white people knew what he meant.

Observers of the Florida court over the years could tell you this is by no means the most outlandish stuff they've come up with. Indeed, one time during B. K. Roberts' tenure as chief justice he had a fellow justice hauled to the Oxner Clinic in New Orleans to discover if the fellow justice were, clinically speaking, crazy as a cut snake. Justice Boyd (who did appear mentally unmoored to many) went around for years afterward bragging that he was the only member of the high court ever to be declared legally sane.

In 1955, the same year Daddy was declared white, two truckloads of Negro children appeared at a park in Tallahassee. The park was whites only, of course. There were no parks for black kids. The next year a couple of girls from FAMU sat down in front of a couple of white people on a Tallahassee city bus. The students got arrested. A cross was burned on the lawn where they lived.

Inspired by Rosa Parks in Montgomery and the two FAMU students, the Tallahassee Bus Boycott began. The Tallahassee White Citizens Council, the Klan for middle-class people, asked Governor Collins to declare a state of emergency: the main emergency being that maids and yardmen now had to be picked up by their employers. One white citizen asked, "Since when has it become a sin to be a white American?"

The Barbarians, the Outside Agitators, were at the gate. They were picking the lock, too. LeRoy Collins, who'd been elected governor in 1954, privately thought that segregation was a bad idea whose time had gone. Nonetheless, he still felt the political need to defend it: "We will not surrender in our battle to protect our state's customs and traditions."

Until his second term, anyway.

Florida's "customs and traditions" included land sold only to "known" white people; segregated seats at the Florida Theatre; fountains dispensing chilled water for white people and tepid water for black people—separate and seriously unequal. The black maid (all maids in those days were black) could eat with the white children she cared for but never the white woman she worked for. When I was a kid, home from school in the summertime, it was my job to make the yardman's lunch: a ham sandwich, some coleslaw, a piece of chocolate pound cake, iced tea. I'd assemble it, put it on a TV table, and take it out to where he ate it under our carport. You didn't have a black man in the house, not unless he was toting a sofa or some major appliance and there was a white man to supervise. Our yardman, whose name was Roosevelt, had his own plate, glass, knife, fork, and spoon. Dorothy, the maid, washed them separate from ours, and put them in a separate place on a shelf in the kitchen.

There were store boycotts and lunch counter sit-ins and shocking displays of interracial fraternization, like when writers from FSU's student newspaper, the *Flambeau,* sat down to eat, *in public,* with colored students from FAMU. It was the end of the world as the white suburbs knew it.

Even the governor turned. At his second inaugural in 1957, LeRoy Collins stood on the steps of the Capitol where the cannons were fired to mark secession, declaring that Florida could not defy the U.S.

Supreme Court any longer. Customs and traditions be damned. White people would have to "face up to the fact that the Negro does not now have equal opportunities." Then he quoted from a hymn by James Russell Lowell, a *Yankee abolitionist:*

Once to every man and nation
Comes the moment to decide,
In the strife of truth with falsehood,
For the Good or Evil side.

What *ailed* the Negroes of Florida? white people asked. *What did they want?* And had LeRoy Collins *lost his damn mind*?

Whites were annoyed—and scared: They thought they had this thing settled. Okay, no more slavery, that's fine. We'll take care of the economics by getting them to cook the food and scrub the floor and diaper the children and cut the grass and pick the fruit and pick the tobacco and cut the cane and lay the roadbeds and dig the ditches, and we'll even pay them. We'll let them have their schools (and give their young 'uns our old textbooks when we're through with them) and their colleges; we'll let some of them be doctors and lawyers so white folks don't have to take care of them. We'll hire them to play music at the country club and we'll go watch them play basketball and football (that Coach Jake Gaither over at FAMU got some boys that can *run like jackrabbits*). All they have to do is say "Yes, sir" and "No, ma'am" and get off the sidewalk and ride in the back of the bus. That's not much to ask considering we let them have their own beach over on Amelia Island, owned by their own Afro-American Life Insurance Company. *Their own beach*. They call it American Beach.

It was these *new Negroes,* the white people said, sighing deeply for the *old-time Negroes* of old times not forgotten. Susan Bradford Eppes titled one of her books *The Negro of the Old South*. In it she laments the passing of the Mammy Lulus and Uncle Neds of yesteryear. Susan Bradford Eppes was still hanging on to her Confederate money in the 1940s.

In an appropriate collision of the old Florida elite and the new (and two prime exhibits from my kudzu tangle of a family tree), B. K. Roberts used pay lawyerly calls on Susan Bradford Eppes. One time while they were visiting she pulled out this box full of thousands of dollars' worth (in a manner of speaking), of CSA notes and bonds, signed by half of Jeff Davis's cabinet. B.K., loyal Dixiecrat and accomplished social climber that he was, wanted a hundred-dollar bill to display in his office. He asked her how much. She looked at him like he'd lost his mind. She wanted $100 for it: $100 USA. "My husband told me before he died that if I sold any of our Confederate paper for less than par this would be a serious insult to the Confederacy."

So B.K. paid $100 for a near-worthless scrap of paper. When Ed Ball saw the thing hanging in his office, he, too, wanted some of Old Lady Eppes's CSA relics. B.K. knew how to treat an aristocratic, if poor, client. He explained that Ball would have to pay face value; otherwise he'd be insulting the Confederacy. Ball said he'd never dream of insulting the Confederacy and coughed up $3,000 for a bond. Susan hauled out a few more boxes of Confederate paper and found no lack of white people eager to demonstrate their refusal to insult the Confederacy by paying hundreds, thousands, for money and bonds that were now about as good as notes drawn on the First National Bank of Mars. Somebody estimated that by the time she was through selling the yellowed relics of the Old South, she'd made enough to buy back all the old Bradford and Eppes lands.

New South

Since the late 1960s, official Florida has pretended, pretended *hard,* that it's not part of the South, that it belongs to, say, some mythic golf course nation stretching from Fort Lauderdale to San Diego, gerrymandered to take in only the condos and resorts in between, populated by old people in pink pants armed with nine-irons. Maybe Florida is really the northernmost of the Greater Antilles, Margaritaville, a wholly owned subsidiary of the Cuban National Foundation; or maybe it's the sixth borough of New York, a cast-adrift county of New Jersey, anything but part of the trailer-dwelling, baccy-chawing, semi-literate, dentally challenged, possum-eating, cousin-diddling, race-baiting South. Sure, Florida's population is more diverse than that of other states from the Old Confederacy (if you make Georgia leave out Atlanta and Louisiana leave out New Orleans and Texas leave out all those Mexicans and Vietnamese); it can be hard to get grits in Fort Lauderdale, and "y'all" is not heard in most parts of Orlando.

But Florida, for all its attempts to cash in its Confederate bonds and secede to join the sunstroke latitudes of California, or declare itself a tropical branch of the Midwest, behaves more like Mississippi than Santa Monica or Minnesota. Florida ranks near the bottom, sometimes worse than Mississippi, in spending on education. The taxes are regressive, structured to protect Big Sugar, Big Citrus, Big Phosphate, Big Tomatoes, and, of course, Big Condos (*still longing for the old plantation . . .*). If the Florida legislature got its way, there'd be prayer in public schools (Jesus loves you), no abortion (even if your daddy raped you), no flag-burning, no gun control, no Darwin, no commies, no feminists, no faggots (well, put a fence around South Beach and call it a zoo), and an American flag, a big one, in every yard.

In late 2000 Florida was suffering from a case of Dixie dropsy. Somebody decided the Highway Patrol ought to set up one of them there *routine* roadblocks. On election day. In an area of Leon County where (*I be dog!*) mostly African Americans lived. Elsewhere, preachers, teachers, and members of the PTA got turned away from the polls because they were felons. Or, rather, because Secretary of State Katherine Harris, the cabinet officer in charge of elections, ordered elections supervisors to purge from their rolls nearly 58,000 heinous criminal types and not allow them to vote. Except the list, for which Florida taxpayers had paid four million bucks and change to a company splendidly named Database Technologies (Jeb Bush is big on public-private partnerships especially if the private partners—or their fellow travelers—contribute to the Republican Party), was grossly wrong.

The supervisor of elections of Madison County found herself on the list, branded a felon. Busted! She was pretty upset, being a respectable character who'd probably never had so much as a speeding ticket in her life. She was even white. Most on the list were black.

You have to wonder if the producers of the purge list subcontracted the work out to the clairvoyants at Cassadaga. Many of the people denied the franchise discovered that they would become criminals in the future. A guy named Thomas Cooper found that he'd be convicted of a felony on January 30, 2007. Others were convicted in 2005, 2006, 2020. Some of the wage slaves, the nonpolitical workers, in the Department of Elections discovered this unfortunate attempt at prescience and said hey, y'all, this is kind of messed up, huh? The bosses told them to blank out the dates that seemed a trifle unlikely. Wouldn't want to upset county elections officials: They're simple folk.

One day during the 2000 imbroglio a BBC TV news crew was interviewing my cousin Clayton Roberts up on the eighteenth floor of Reuben's Erection. He and the reporter, an American named Greg Palast, were lolling on the sofa outside his office. Clay was director of the Division of Elections, the young lawyer forced to, with a straight face, refer to Katherine Harris as "the constitutionally independent officer elected by the people of Florida as the chief election officer of the state" while trying to explain the state's election statutes to her in words of one syllable or less. But when the BBC reporter started asking about the purge list for the voter rolls, Clay pulled off his mike, demanded that the cameras be shut down, and retreated into his office, slamming the door. State troopers "escorted" the journalists out of the building.

They showed the film on British television, and one of my London friends, who always had trouble telling the difference between the Democrats and the Republicans in America anyway, phoned to ask if I were related to Clay Roberts. Then one of my cousins, one of my Democratic cousins, called up to see if I'd heard that Clay Roberts had run like a palmetto bug when you cut on the kitchen light the minute somebody had asked a question about disenfranchised voters or something. "My Lord," she said. "And Clayton graduated from West Point." She added, "We might as well bring the damn poll tax back."

All the while urban white Floridians, their eyes tightly shut, their fists clinched at their sides, kept repeating their healing mantra: *We are not Mississippi! We are not Alabama! This is not the South! It's not! It's not! We are not Mississippi! We are not Alabama! This is not the South! It's not! It's not!*

In the interior of the state, though, in the swamps and the scrub and the rangeland, in the little towns—Chiefland, Lakeland, Palatka, Pahokee, Bartow, Bristol, Moorehaven, Micanopy—crosses are sometimes still burned in the yards of black families who move to the wrong place, Confederate battle flag bumper stickers are stuck to Honda Accords, not just Ford pickups. There are protests when the school board wants to rename Robert E. Lee or Jefferson Davis High School, protests when Orange Avenue becomes Martin Luther King, Jr., Boulevard.

While working for the *St. Petersburg Times,* I ran into a nest of angry self-proclaimed Southern white men in Tampa. I had written a piece about the League of the South, a group of neo-Confederates that used to be called the Southern League until Minor League Baseball offered to sue them. A delegation wanted to talk with me about my "misleading" depiction of their movement, so I met them for meat and three (fried chicken, your choice of beans, sweet 'taters, black-eyed peas, squash, greens) at a neo-Southern diner. The league wants the South to re-secede (what with it working so well in 1861), and they're not kidding. Their new nation will be all about "Christian culture." Men will be men and women will be ladies. They will adopt British spelling (Webster of dictionary fame was a Yankee). They like moonlight; they like magnolias. Their website is www.dixienet.org.

They wanted to explain to me that they are *not bigots*. My column had implied that the league's stated dim view of interracial relationships was not exactly progressive. They wanted me to understand that people of all colors are welcome in their new Southern Republic as long as they talk nice about Stonewall Jackson. They wanted me to understand that I didn't understand.

"But," I said, "I do understand."

Their head guy, who had a beard that Lee himself would not have scorned, quoted Faulkner: "You don't understand. You have to be born here."

"*Y'all,*" I said, "I *was* born here."

Then we got into an ancestor competition. ("My great-granddaddy was at Shiloh!" "Well, *my* great-great-granddaddy was at Gettysburg!") He had six known Confederate army ancestors. I whipped his ass with nine. "And," I said, "I was a *Child* of the Confederacy!"

My mother and father, children of the Confederacy, descended from a slew of gray-coated delusionists, built a house on land that had been worked for 120 years by people descended from a slew of black-skinned laborers—realists by necessity. Once our fields would have been dappled with the dirty white of cotton bolls; now they were planted in chevrons of pecan trees. There was a slave cemetery back in the woods there and a little, nearly paintless, colored church on the corner. It had a tin roof and a bell. On Sundays and Wednesdays you could hear them singing up a storm: "Couldn't Hear Nobody Pray" and "Precious Lord."

The land was high, or what counts for high in Florida, maybe 150 feet above sea level. This was important, since there was a 4,000-acre lake nearby and a river with a habit of rising fast in the fall and the spring and smashing the wooden bridge over it like a bird's nest. Daddy had studied the one-hundred-year flood plan for the county. He concluded that the day our house ended up underwater was the day Florida can just hang it up; maybe next thing you see will be that Lamb with the seven horns and the seven eyes and a road sign pointing to the New Jerusalem.

For a young married couple just starting out, the house was nice, what Granny Roberts called "faincy." The brick, made from the clay of the Red Hills of North Florida and South Georgia, looked like my aunts' and uncles' hair, ranging from Aunt LaJuana's rosy tangerine to Uncle Wendell's dark auburn. There were big windows that cranked out for a breeze. There were two bathrooms and built-in bookcases. There were ninety-two brushed stainless steel handles on the kitchen cabinets, a brushed chrome stove, and a brushed chrome double oven. The closets and the drawers were all made of pine with mysterious formations (ghosts, unicorns, rockets) appearing in its grain. The floors were made of quarter-sawed red oak, which you can't get anymore for any money. Bradford Gilbert chose the wood himself: It had to be just so for the Boy's house. Those floors were varnished to the color of tupelo honey and slick as an otter's coat. My brother and I could grab one of the cats, turn him on his back, and slide him all the way down the hall so fast he couldn't get on his feet before the bathroom tile slowed him down.

There were two new cars under the carport, a new washer in the utility room, rows of new ties in my father's closet, and new shoes in snakeskin, suede, peau de soie, and calf in my mother's shoe drawer. The cupboards were full of new Revere Ware pots and pans and new Pyrex bowls and new dishes. The counters were covered with new appliances: percolators, mixers, toasters. There was almost no furniture: a kitchen table, beds, and a sofa made of cushions propped on a hollow-core door that had been given six legs. Furniture would come later. The old hadn't been entirely banished: There was a rocking chair that had belonged to Roxanne Bradford, with curving arms and a lyre-shaped back, the chair, Bradford Gilbert said, that had helped send four generations of young 'uns to sleep.

One afternoon after a heavy rain—the bulldozers had leveled the top of the hill before the foundation for the house was built—my mother went out and picked up arrowheads and hatchet heads and spear heads, lying exposed and miraculously unbroken in the carnelian-colored clay. She rinsed the relics of five thousand years with the hose and put them in a bucket.

My father was building bridges. My mother joined the Garden Club, Azalea Circle. He charmed everybody at the Road Department. People said maybe he should think about running for office someday. Daddy had kinfolk in the state Senate, on the court, in the Florida Bar. Mama came from landowning people in West Florida. She was shy, but her manners were perfect. She could tell good silver from silver plate at a glance. She could tell real engraving from fake just by running her hand down an invitation. She could also play softball, but didn't have much of a chance to show off her batting.

On Saturday afternoons Daddy put on a slate gray or biscuit-colored suit and tie, and Mama put on stockings, high heels, a hat, a linen or poodle-cloth Chanel knockoff, gloves, and lipstick. Off they went to the ball game at Doak Campbell Stadium. Daddy had converted from being a University of Florida Gator fan to being an FSU Seminoles fan, which was sort of like a high-church Episcopalian embracing Sufi Islam.

Football games were social events, another place to meet the bright young white people who were, like them, going to own and run Florida. On Sundays they put on similar outfits (football and church were more or less sartorially synonymous), wiped down my brother and me, dressed us up, and drove to the Presbyterian church, where we'd get a sermon on how Bad Things Are.

Then we'd go home in a hurry so Daddy could watch *The Bill Peterson Show* on television. Bill Peterson was the football coach for the FSU Seminoles. He did a recap of each game. Daddy would wait for dinner to be ready and wonder, sometimes out loud, how soon it would be before "a ni—I mean, *colored* boy," would want to play ball at FSU or the University of Florida.

Rosewood

There is a secret history. For the longest time, only black Floridians knew it. They whispered cautionary tales, warned about the terrible things they were capable of, the white people, the Crackers, even the new people who never had a granddaddy in the War but who took a shine to Florida's Jim Crow and expected to be treated like Miss Scarlett or Mister Rhett.

Among themselves they told of the lynchings, the riots, the massacres. On election day in 1920, in Ocoee, a black orange grove owner named Mose Norman had the temerity to show up at the polls to try and cast his ballot. Two whites were killed in a shootout, a friend of Norman's called July Perry was tied to the back of a car, dragged, and finally hanged from a telephone pole. Whites trashed the Negro section of town, burning thirty houses and two churches. Thirty-five Negroes died. The violence spread to Orlando, Winter Garden, Apopka. Zora Neale Hurston wrote an extensive account of the Ocoee riots for the WPA guide to Florida. It got edited down to a paragraph when the book was published.

Even more secret, hidden, or ignored, for years, was the Rosewood Massacre. Every detail of it is disputed by somebody, even whether we should call it a "massacre." The only certainty is that people died.

On a hard-frost day in January 1923, a white woman may or may not have been attacked by a black convict who'd run off from the county road gang. He may or may not have hidden somewhere in the cedar-milling village of Rosewood. Model Ts full of white men with Winchesters and shotguns and pistols and kerosene, some Klan, some just Levy County freelancers out for a bit of recreational violence, roared over. They heard that the Negroes had an arsenal at the Carrier house. They heard that local law enforcement—peace officers of the state—had no problem with this particular lynch mob. White women must be protected.

The vigilantes rolled up in the bright moonlight and shot Sarah Carrier in the head, right in front of her children. Her son Sylvester unloaded his pump-handled shotgun and got a white man, a onetime "quarters boss" for the mill, in the face. He got another white man, too, before they filled his body with bullets. The rest of the children, their mother's blood crimsoning on their nightgowns, escaped into the woods.

The white men kept moving, shooting a widow named Lexie Gordon as she crawled out of her burning house. She'd sent her daughters into the swamp when she heard gunfire, but she was laid up sick with typhoid fever and too weak to follow. They made an old man dig his own grave, then they shot him, too. They burned the whole place, the churches and the houses and the school. Meanwhile, everybody left alive was smuggled out, sent to kinfolk or friends in Gainesville or the little town of Lacoochee to the south. Rosewood was a blackened ruin, smelling of blood. The public story insisted that homicidal and rapacious Negroes had got what they deserved.

There are parts of Rosewood victims' bodies, trophies, kept in jars around Levy County—that's the story. Ears, hands, fingers, toes, testicles, penises. Nobody will talk about it. A teacher from Chiefland, up the road from Rosewood, told Michael D'Orso, who wrote a book on Rosewood, that he had seen a man's thumb at a gas station in Bronson. Sometimes people in Bronson or Chiefland or Yankeetown or Cedar Key would whip out a pocket watch and claim that it had belonged to Sam Carter, another black man murdered in Rosewood. They say that Sam Carter faced down the white mob in the dark Florida woods. He underlined the pointlessness of what they were doing just before they blew his head off. "You can kill me," he said, "but you can't eat me."

White people in Levy County still won't talk about this. Or if they do, they claim it never happened. Rosewood itself is gone. White people in trailers live where black people once lived in houses. But like all secrets, repressed in their terribleness, Rosewood returned. In the early 1980s a reporter from the *St. Petersburg Times* started following up rumors, and the story started emerging. Survivors started telling. A black state representative and a Cuban state representative, aided by a lawyer whose daddy had doctored some of the kin of Rosewood survivors in Lacoochee, filed a bill to compensate the victims and their children for loss of life and loss of property.

The Rosewood compensation legislation was fought out in the early 1990s, but to hear some Florida politicians you'd think it was the 1890s. White people had been lured to their deaths. Or everyone was *awfully* sorry, but you know that was way back then and things were different, and if you start paying people for the nasty doings of a bunch of racists, well, that opens the can of worms over slavery reparations and paying the Indians for their land and pretty soon the whole country will be bankrupt because everybody's had a tough time, you know? One state senator, a white Democrat, whined, "How long do we have to pay for the sins of our forefathers?"

Governor Lawton Chiles, also a white Democrat, signed the bill. It didn't pass by much. The Rosewood families didn't get much, either. Not the millions and millions Levy County white people said they were getting. A handful of survivors of the massacre received

$150,000. Others got a few thousand, sometimes a few hundred. At the same time the people of Rosewood were getting slaughtered, Susan Bradford Eppes was working on the manuscript of her book, *The Negro of the Old South:*

> *The white people and the Negroes of the Old South were so intimately associated that it is impossible to tell the story of the one without a large mixture of the other. In these days, when it is quite the fashion to rail against 'The Free Negroes,' we, of the Old South, to whom many of them are still dear, take but little part in this. . . . Ungrateful would we be if we put a ban on the entire race because some have proved themselves unworthy.*

Susan made as much or more off her Confederate money as most of the Rosewood families made off the State of Florida.

11

As Large as Life and Twice as Natural

THE RUSSIANS WERE FIXING to kill us. They were aiming missiles right at us, us in Florida, us in Leon County, us in Tallahassee, us at 3323 Old Bainbridge Road. They were fixing to shoot the missiles from Cuba clean across the Florida Straits, and then the Americans would shoot missiles back, and pretty soon, boom! mushroom cloud, radioactive fallout, everything in the incandescent oranges and scarlets and magentas of one of those postcards you can buy at every roadside citrus stand: "Florida Sunset."

The Russians were fixing to wreak atomic havoc on us, so my mother sent the maid home. She stacked up the lawn chairs and put them in the utility room. She took the hanging plants, ferns and impatiens, down from the limbs of the pecan trees. She moved my tricycle and my red wagon from the carport into the kitchen. Then she filled the washing machine and all the bathtubs with water.

President Kennedy got on the TV and said that the USSR stashed the Bomb in Cuba. My father was off in Central Florida doing something with bridges, scribbling formulas for even-better prestressed concrete on the backs of envelopes. He called my mother to say he'd be back soon and to make sure she kept the .38 cleaned and loaded.

Daddy hated Communists. He was pretty sure Nikita Khrushchev, Martin Luther King, Earl Warren, Eleanor Roosevelt, and John F. Kennedy were in league to destroy the Southern Way of Life. Kennedy might have been a Democrat, but he was also a Yankee and a Catholic and the son of a bootlegger.

My brother Bradford was a year old. I was four. We had no opinion on the Soviet Union. Our biggest terror was that the gravity-defying Wicked Witch of the West in *The Wizard of Oz* would land on us, laughing horribly. We weren't exactly in a position to help with the geopolitical crisis at hand. Anyway, my mother didn't need a disquisition on how Adam Smith was right and Karl Marx was wrong, she needed batteries and extra baby food, Starkist tuna, Campbell's condensed soup, candles, dog food, cat food, and canned English peas. She need more masking tape.

My mother says sure she was scared, everybody was scared, but you did what you could. Daddy didn't tell her it was damn near the end of the world. She found that out later. Like most Floridians, she treated the Cuban Missile Crisis as if it were a Category 5 storm about to bust loose in the Gulf. Hurricanes were the only kind of cataclysmic disaster they really understood. Hurricane Donna had launched 175-mile-per-hour winds at us only two years before in 1960. Donna did $144 million worth of property damage. She whacked the citrus crop. She killed a dozen people. Even in North Florida, old oaks tumped over and the tin roofs of houses went flying like bats in Donna's spin-off tornadoes. The sky stayed an angry hot gray for three days.

I think I remember the Cuban Missile Crisis, but I could be getting it mixed up with one of the early '60s monster storms that knocked out power for days on end, or one of the rocket launches from Cape Canaveral, or even the assassination of JFK—anything that preempted broadcast of *The Bugs Bunny Show* on Saturday morning. I know I remember my mother applying long strips of masking tape in a star pattern to the picture windows so that if a tree limb or an airborne Radio Flyer or a Soviet MRBM hit, the glass wouldn't shatter all over the floor.

The End of the World isn't a particularly far-fetched idea in Florida. Never was. There were always hurricanes and floods and plagues of mosquitoes and plagues of boll weevils. When Robert E. Lee surrendered to Ulysses S. Grant, Susan Bradford and all her parlor-sitting, joust-attending, white-missy kind wrote in their diaries that it was the end of the world. When Henry Flagler got a divorce from his crazy wife in 1901, Free Will Baptist ministers pummeled the pulpit and proclaimed the end of the world. When Jim Morrison undid the front of his leather britches at Miami's Dinner Key Auditorium in 1969 and rode the snake (or was it just his shirttail?) in front of a sweating and irascible crowd of Doors fans, guardians of public morality predicted the end of the world. When Miss Myrtice McCaskill of Perry ran for a seat in the Florida House of Representatives in 1922; when students at Florida A&M sat down at the lunch counter in the Tallahassee Woolworth's and ordered coffee; when students at FSU elected a man Homecoming Queen (his nom de guerre was "Billy Dahling"; his campaign slogan was "Why not a real queen?"); when Fidel Castro (son of a sugar plantation owner, for God's sake) led the revolution against Batista, one of the fraternity of bastards the U.S. government was pleased to call their own, and a good-size segment of the Cuban population relocated to Florida, well, a good-size segment of Florida population thought, okay, that's it, apocalypse now, end times, Pale Horse and Wormwood time. The local newspaper, the *Tallahassee Democrat,* ran an ad once a week that demanded, in boldface: "WHY DO THE HEATHEN RAGE?"

Something about Florida attracts eschatological thinking. Maybe it's the sense that the place rose—barely—out of a testy sea and is headed back there. Maybe it's the rockets. Even before the Cuban Missile Crisis, the rose-gold glare of ignited solid fuel haunted the dreams of Floridians. The army started launching modified V-2s from Cape Canaveral in 1950, courtesy of Wernher von Braun. Dr. von Braun's handiwork during the Blitz had got the attention of the U.S. government. They'd wanted to use White Sands in New Mexico, except a rocket that could actually go somewhere might hit something, say, Los Angeles. Then they thought Baja, but the Mexican government took a dim view. So they ended up with a popover-shaped piece of land in Brevard County, Florida, between the Banana River and Mosquito Lagoon.

Juan Ponce de León had anchored his ships off Cape Canaveral in 1513. There was nothing there but sky, water, wildflowers, sand, and reeds. The place hadn't changed much in 440 years. The army had to haul their V-2 over pig tracks to get to the shore and pour a concrete slab for it to take off from. Mission Control was a tar-paper shack. Once a Polaris missile lurched off course and headed for a trailer park. They blew the missile up before it could decimate anybody, but some pieces came crashing down anyway onto the odd single-wide, and other pieces exploded, igniting the scrub, which made a lot of rattlesnakes homeless and angry. The rattlers headed for the blitzed trailer park. It took days and whole boxes of ammo to get rid of them all.

As rocket science goes, Cape Canaveral was pretty laid-back. You had to drive miles to find a bar or a decent steak, still the sea breeze was nice and warm. But in 1957 the space program got a fire lit under it; the USSR launched *Sputnik*. There was a Commie eye in the sky and the Americans were caught napping. Congress, the president, and the Pentagon brass went red in the face, foamed at the mouth, and wanted to know what the hell those boys were doing down there on the beach and what the hell was that Nazi scientist doing all day. They quickly created the National Aeronautics and Space Administration and threw money at it. Cape Canaveral got in gear. They sent up a satellite of their own in 1958. They sent two monkeys three hundred miles into space. In 1961 the Soviets made them crazy again by launching a human, Yuri Gagarin, who orbited the earth in 108 minutes. A month later Alan Shepard went up from the Cape and came down again. Okay, he didn't orbit, but an American had now been in space, so there, and we were going to the moon. The president said so.

From Florida to the firmament of the stars, paradise to Heaven: Preachers preached sermons on it; college professors raised philosophical issues about it; the rest of us watched it on television, rocket after rocket hauling its big pointy self through the thick Florida air, groaning through gravity till it looked like the tail end of a blowtorch flame moving through a gray sky (we had a black-and-white TV). Some people didn't believe it—figured it was a government hoax. If it was, it was a moneymaker for Florida. The filigree of barrier islands and protuberances and strip-malled towns on the Atlantic from Titusville to Eau Gallie, where the Banana River and the Indian River converge, is now called, for touristic purposes, the Space Coast.

One of Florida's current senators, Democrat Bill Nelson, has been in space. He flew on Columbia in 1985, the last shuttle mission before Challenger blew up. He likes to say things look different from space. He likes to say that from space you can see how we're dirtying up the planet, especially Florida.

Bill Nelson's opponent in the 2000 senate race was Bill McCollum, one of those stiff-haired, tight-fannied, sex-is-sin House Republicans who had wanted *so bad* to impeach Bill Clinton. His campaign put out a bumper sticker: "Save Florida, Send Bill Nelson Back to Space."

I never wanted to be in space, I just wanted to look at it. My brother and I would climb onto the flat roof of our carport with binoculars, having calculated the position of various planets using the handy-dandy mathematical formula in the back of *The Field Guide to the Stars and Planets,* and check out Jupiter and Saturn and Mars. Sometimes we'd look at the moon, but we weren't, unlike NASA, all that interested in the moon. Too close. We were into seeing how many Pleiades we could count (six? seven? nine?) with the naked eye and checking out the orangeness of Antares and the blueness of Vega. This was in the days when nights were still dark, unpolluted by the dirty apricot of suburban streetlights, and you could see the Milky Way, arching over across our fields like a sequinned sash.

Provisioned with Tang (made for actual astronauts!) and Chips Ahoy, saturated in Off! and armed with star maps and a piece of red cellophane to put over the flashlight, we'd scan the sky over our backyard. Lightning bugs yellow-green as the star Capella formed and reformed their own constellations below us. Above us wheeled millions of years.

Florida is older than the Pleiades. Five hundred million years ago there were mountains—volcanoes, real ones, not like the Wakulla Volcano—now buried thirteen thousand feet under Sebring Racetrack and the Avon Park Bombing Range and Lake Istokpoga and Lake June in Winter. Four hundred million years ago Florida was part of Africa, until the continents smacked into each other and glued Florida to south Georgia. After that, the peninsula winks in and out of sight for 50 million years like a variable star. First Florida is an island south of North America, then it's underwater, then there's an ice age and it appears again as the ocean level drops, then it's inundated when the glaciers melt. Florida is made of bits of the eroded Ur-Appalachians and fossilized shellfish, billions and trillions of oysters and scallops and periwinkles and crabs and shrimp like a vast and lavish seafood buffet, piled over millennia one on top of the other, the delicacies of antique oceans transformed into limestone bedrock maybe four miles thick. The land emerged at the end of the late Pleistocene like a manatee coming up to breathe.

Now the sea is rising again. In a couple of hundred years Miami and Tampa, Palm Beach and Pensacola could be drowned like Atlantis or Lyonesse where, when the waves are calm, you can hear the sounds of underwater church bells—or, since this is Florida, maybe car alarms.

Dreaming of Djinnee

Blue sky land, that was Florida. In the 1960s everybody thought beach; everybody thought Barbara Eden. *I Dream of Jeannie* was a TV show about an astronaut living on the Space Coast: Cocoa, I think it was. His capsule had come down out of orbit on this island where he found this bottle. In the bottle was a genie, a gorgeous, long-eyelashed, blond-headed *Playboy* centerfold of a genie in a pink chiffon harem outfit. He called her "Jeannie." She called him "Master."

The astronaut brought the genie back to Florida to live with him.

She took to the palm trees and the sand, said they reminded her of home, back in Arabia. She complicated his life. As if space weren't complicated enough.

Everybody thought NASA; everybody thought rockets. Florida started out with airplanes, though. The state had three airlines by the 1920s. In the 1930s blimps bumped clouds over South Florida. Miami staged "All-American Air Races."

Anybody could be a pilot. Florida had flight schools all over the place; Florida even had an establishment calling itself an "aeronautical university." When it turned out that twelve of the nineteen September 11 hijackers lived in Florida, hanging out on the transient, interstate-anchored, anonymous, strip-malled, shadeless coasts, paying cash for flying lessons in which they showed a strange lack of interest in learning how to land, nobody was surprised. They *would* live in Florida: the place with the space on the ground and above it, the place where the hedonistic sensibility crashes into the apocalyptic mind-set like tectonic plates back in the Precambrian day.

Waleed al-Shehri graduated from Embry-Riddle in Daytona Beach with a B.A. in aeronautical sciences. Mohamed Atta, the one the newspapers call "the ringleader," and his cousin Marwan al-Shehhi brushed up on their piloting skills at an Opa Locka air school and at Huffman Aviation, Inc., in Venice, Florida. The sign over the gate says "Learn to Fly Here!"

Mohaid al-Shehri and Saeed al-Ghamdi enrolled at FlightSafety International in Vero Beach. They and their co-conspirators lived in Hollywood and Vero and Coral Springs and Boynton Beach and Delray Beach, coastal or golf course towns made up by developers in the twentieth century—Coral Springs dates from 1972—with no past, no history, only a relentless, cement-block present.

Maybe the palm trees and the sand reminded them of home, back in Arabia.

They were no more native than most Floridians. They were no more permanent than most Floridians. They may have been homocidal jihadists, but they became Floridians. They lived along I-95, once the bed of the ancient Pamlico Sea, now a vast conurbation stretching from Miami to West Palm, an endlessly repeating combination of McDonald's, Motel 6, Pizza Hut, Publix, and Wal-Mart, the DNA of modern Florida. They embraced the temporary, the ersatz, the unapologetically plastic, the unthinkingly paradoxical. Most of them didn't actually go up in airplanes; most of them did their "flying" on simulators. They didn't wear the robes of pilgrims and follow the strictest interpretations of the Prophet's words: one drove a fuck-me red Mitsubishi Eclipse, one was a Florida Marlins fan, several liked to play Grand Theft Auto. Mohamed Atta liked to drink vodka. He ran up a $50 tab on the well brand at Shuckums Oyster Bar one night. He and his cousin and another guy hung out in a Palm Beach County titty bar doing shooters and watching girls shake their immodest and unveiled flesh, thinking, no doubt, about all those virgins they were going to score in Paradise. They left behind a pitiful tip and a copy of the Koran.

Less than a month later, after the towers in New York fell, the catastrophic conspiracy grew larger. There was anthrax in Boca Raton, one turn of the highway helix south of Delray Beach, anthrax in the offices of American Media Inc., publishers of the *National Enquirer,* the *Weekly World News,* the *Sun,* and the *Star*. A photo editor for one of the tabloids died of anthrax poisoning. It came out that two of the hijackers had subscriptions to the *Sun* and a couple of other tabloids. They had reported that Mohamed Atta's western girlfriend, at the time hiding out in Lebanon, claimed that, on the "manhood" front, he was "underdeveloped" and so was terminally sensitive.

Presumably the situation would be corrected in Paradise, or else his allotment of virgins wouldn't mind. Presumably the anthrax was the hijackers' revenge from Beyond Death, which became a check-out-line headline in itself. Alien babies, the current whereabouts of Elvis, and the obvious fact that Camilla Parker-Bowles had murdered Princess Diana with a voodoo curse disappeared for a little while from tabloid covers, replaced by the sort of connection-making respectable Ivy-educated Washingtonians or Manhattanites do when they've had a couple of glasses of pinot gris: *George W. was **in** Florida when the twin towers fell. He acted like he wasn't even surprised, just kept reading a book to* *those kids. The military took him off to some bunker in Nebraska like they knew something. And what about the 2000 vote recount? Did Bush steal the state? Was the Carlyle Group involved? Were the Saudis involved? Were the Illuminati involved? Did we really land on the moon in 1969?*

At the Bimini Motel Apartments on Ocean Drive in Hollywood, Florida, a critical mass of the guests read the *Weekly World News,* the *Sun,* the *Star*. The rooms don't cost much—you can get a whole month for $650, and that's for two people. Waleed al-Shehri and another hijacker stayed there, sharing a room, paying for an extra bed, a roll-away. Joanne Solic, the manager, says they were nice, quiet, polite guys. When they left she said, "Are you going back to Saudi Arabia?"

"No," they said. "We're going up north."

Tourism Day

Once a year Senator Dempsey Barron would walk into the chamber carrying a mermaid. He enjoyed that. I don't know if the mermaid enjoyed it. She was smiling, certainly, as the green stretch satin of her tail and the silver spangles of her mermaid brassiere shimmered in the fluorescent lights, and smiling as she wrapped her tanned arms around the senator's neck. Somebody had to carry her. It's not like she could walk.

Dempsey Barron would tote her around letting the other senators get a good look at her as she tossed her long, dark (sometimes it was golden or red) hair, waved her tail, and said, "Hey!"And then he'd hand her back to the guy from the Weeki Wachee Springs, City of Mermaids, and the guy would carry her off to sit on a bench under an oak tree outside the Capitol and get her picture made with various legislators, lobbyists, and anyone else who showed up for Tourism Day.

I'd be in the press gallery taking notes ("green stretch satin"). I worked for a small newspaper most legislators called "radical." Some graduate students had summer jobs: Since Oxford's Easter vacation coincided almost exactly with the Florida legislative session, I got a spring job, writing columns for the *Florida Flambeau* and sometimes United Press International. I needed to earn plane fare.

Opening day would be in early April (but never April 1: even legislators had more sense than that), a fit of pomp and preemptive campaigning. The House of Representatives is jammed with more flower arrangements than a Baptist funeral. The governor sashays in, elbow-grabbing and hand-crushing down the aisle, dodging the potted azaleas, the "gourmet" baskets and the Girl Scout cookies lobbyists present to lawmakers (Florida government runs on sugar), acknowledging the yelps of insincere appreciation from the members, many of whom live to thwart him, then delivers the "state of the state" speech.

Back when Democrats—most of whom were just as Jesus-drunk and power-mad as the Republicans are now—were in charge, Governor Bob Graham told us to "grasp the nettle" of change. Governor Lawton Chiles held up a three-legged stool to illustrate to the Republicans, many of whom had evidently never read the Constitution, that our government has *three* branches, not two. Saw a leg off and the stool won't sit right.

These days Governor Jeb Bush just informs us that, thanks to him, Florida is pluperfect Heaven (*the state is building on average thirty new golf courses a year!*) and can be improved only by one more corporate tax cut. And maybe some judges who won't behave like they did in 2000, stirring up all that trouble: Bush recently appointed Cuban dictator Fulgéncio Batista's grandson to the State Supreme Court.

I didn't write much about particular bills unless they were spectacularly idiotic. Senator Donnell Childers, D-TrailerWorld, once thought legislation ought to be passed to stop AIDS-infected children slobbering on other children at school. Representative Luis Morse, R-CubaLibre, concocted a plan to legalize betting on pigeon racing. I liked to watch the goofy rituals, the overwrought alpha-male tussles and chest-thumping, that made Florida government in the 1980s as much fun as the court of the Borgias. I got a whole column out of the Legislative Trail Ride, when a senator from outside Orlando squealed like a scalded rabbit because he got horseshit on his new boots. At the press corps skits in 1986, Bob Graham, wearing a standard-issue white South American dictator uniform (gold brain, red sash, dubious medals), drew a sword and declared himself Governor for Life.

We could have done worse—what am I saying? we *did* do worse.

I took comfort from what little continuity Florida government offered. Sessions got stupider, but the World's Largest Key Lime Pie (approximately one quarter acre) remained the same. Every year people from Key West would come up, declare Tallahassee the Conch Republic for a day, and give everybody a piece of pie. They browned the meringue with an industrial blowtorch.

This was the best job I ever had.

My column was called "Das Kapital." Go on, laugh: *We* all did. I got well known in a small way, or at least, this person called D. K. Roberts got well known in a small way, famous in two, possibly three, rural North Florida counties. Some readers thought I was a black man, a "militant," one letter snarled; some thought I was a fictional character; some got me mixed up with B. K. Roberts, an ignominy that, whatever dubious decisions the justice made over his career, he surely did not deserve. I got a lot of hate mail: I was a communist, a socialist, a feminist. I should go back to Cuba/Russia/Nicaguara where I belonged. I was a traitor to my race, to my class, to my state. All because I put it in the paper when the chairman of the Higher Education Committee declared, "We got to make sure them kids is learning!" and revealed that the "fresh Florida" seafood hors d'oeuvres at the Florida Homebuilders Association party not only had been frozen, they were *still* frozen and may have come from Texas.

On Tourism Day all kinds of fantastic beasts showed up: drugged alligators; long-tailed macaws perched on the shoulder of the pirate José Gaspar; a young bored-looking lion from the Ringling Bros. Circus; pick-wielding dwarves; pocket-watch-checking rabbits; talking dogs; talking crickets; sometimes an infestation of talking mice with falsetto voices and Michael Jackson gloves from Disney.

Senator Dempsey Barron would greet them all. He enjoyed the way the mermaids and the peanut queens and cotton princesses made eyes at him. Over at Clyde's, haunt of lawmakers, the lobbyists who wanted to buy the lawmakers drinks, and the big-haired young women who had drinks bought for them by both lobbyists and lawmakers, and who never seemed to feel the springtime cold despite those skimpy outfits, they all said Dempsey had been *carrying on* with his aide. Barron was the porkchopper's porkchopper, the West Florida Machiavel who ran the Senate—and thus the state—for decades. He was Senator Luther Tucker's idol. He was a legend—as he'd be the first to tell you.

Dempsey Barron liked to dress up as a cowboy. He had his official portrait as Senate president painted with him in a bolo tie and line-dance dress shirt, sitting on the back of a palomino. Senator Jack Gordon, Bob Dylan to Barron's George Jones, liked to dress up as a banker, which is what he was. Gordon came from Miami Beach, a place Barron barely considered part of Florida, what with the Cubans and the Jews and the rich liberals. Gordon was a Jew and a rich liberal. He quoted Wordsworth in floor debates. He suggested that since people came to Florida from so many countries, all road signs should be in ten languages. He was a strict adherent to the Pritikin diet. He would use words like "mastication" just to savor the look of shock on the faces of dimmer bulbs, such as Senator Donnell Childers and Senator Javier Souto, who would tell anybody who'd listen (and plenty who wouldn't) that he had been "one of the founders of the Bay of Pigs invasion."

One time in the 1970s, Barron and Gordon got together and floated legislation to decriminalize marijuana. Barron the populist reckoned the government had no business fooling with what you were smoking—or drinking or fucking, for that matter, as long as it wasn't livestock (he owned a ranch). Gordon the intellectual figured there was little defensible difference between a good bowl of ganja and a good bottle of Châteauneuf du Pape. As the funk philosopher George Clinton (now a resident of Jefferson County, Florida) says: *Free your mind and your ass will follow.*

Barron's and Gordon's realms bracketed Florida, which, by the 1960s had embraced conscious unreality from coast to coast to coast. Barron's district contained Panama City Beach, home of, among other things, Petticoat Junction, a theme park named after a TV show, and Tombstone Territory, another theme park named after a TV show. Ads for Tombstone Territory said, "Ride the Iron Horse to Tombstone Territory—next to Goofy Golf."

At Petticoat Junction, the people who built it forgot that the show was about a Southern widow woman, her three busting-out-all-over daughters, Billie Jo, Bobbie Jo, and Betty Jo (a blonde, a brunette, and a redhead), and their nubile adventures running the Shady Rest Hotel in Hooterville. The Florida version featured a train obviously intended for the midgets of the Old West, plus a ghost town. No actual petticoats were in evidence. This was a *family* fantasy realm. So was Tombstone Territory, with its nonalcoholic saloons and general stores made of gen-u-wine Florida cypress, sunburned totem poles, and giant statues of longhorn cattle and pained-looking Plains Indians propped on the side of U.S. 98.

Senator Barron also represented a sizable population of ghosts, fairies, dragons, sea gods, dinosaurs, witches, and Icee Bears, all of whom occupied the stretch of tarted-up Gulf beach between Fort Walton and Panama City known as the Miracle Strip. The sand looked like 10X confectioner's sugar and the water was blue as a peacock's belly, but you couldn't see it for the amusement parks, miniature golf courses, roller coasters, volcanoes, castles, caves, jungles, shell shops, reptile farms, and theme restaurants: The Sir Loin Steakhouse was hard to miss—it had this enormous armored knight outside. The knight was advertised as "the largest known statue in Florida."

You could subject yourself to three different haunted houses. You could putt through the legs of a triceratops, under the Sphinx of Egypt, around Neptune's tail, and sink your ball into the pouch of a six-foot kangaroo. You could visit the pit vipers at the Snake-A-Torium, watching them watch you from what you thought was a safe distance, little knowing that, according to Tim Hollis's magisterial catalog of tourist traps *Dixie Before Disney,* the owner had trapped a lot of those water moccasins right next door behind the Stuckey's.

Senator Gordon's constituency didn't technically cover Seaquarium, Lion Country Safari, Monkey Jungle, and Parrot Jungle, all those dancing porpoises, overheated cheetahs, macaws, chimpanzees, lemurs, jai alai players, and the gator-wrestling remnants of the Seminole Nation who had been holed up in the 'Glades since the federals wrecked Billy Bowlegs's banana trees. District 35 was more condos, gated communities, and golf courses than exotic species—unless you count retirees from Yankeeland. But Gordon belonged to South Florida, and South Florida was a great tangle of fakery, too, desperate to turn itself into Kenya, Brazil, Madagascar, Tahiti, Hawaii, Kentucky, the Pyrenees, or prerevolution Santiago de Cuba. There was money to be made in a place with modern American plumbing and *National Geographic* critters.

When I started hanging around the state capitol, taking notes on politicians, some of them, amazed to meet a person who was actually born in Florida, told me that I was exotic. That's wrong. Fan dancers, pearl divers, kudzu, and the Africanized bee are exotic. I'm just an endangered species.

One time I went to interview Representative Michael Friedman of Surfside (a name property developers affixed to the northern end of Collins Avenue in Miami Beach), and he acted like I was the Oldest Living Confederate Widow or something. "You're a *native*?" he said, looking like he didn't believe me. "Your family's been here *how long*? *In Wakulla County?*"

He was too polite to ask if we were all kinfolk-screwing, Dixie-singing, automatic-weapon-toting creationists.

Friedman, who looked like Emilio Zapata collided with Frank Zappa, was from another planet as far as I was concerned. He was a New Yorker who'd been in Dade County since the age of three and still spoke Manhattan, a guy who thought he might become a rabbi until he figured out that the prayer he learned in Hebrew said, as he put it, "'Thank God I'm a man,' and I go wait a minute—there's an issue here," a guy who sponsored bills to protect migrant workers, consumers, and children. Needless to say he had no political future in Florida.

Actually, that's not quite true: He could have had Jack Gordon's Senate seat when Gordon retired, but by that time he'd decided that Florida government was a rank slough of venal morons who cared no more for the people than they did for a roadkill armadillo. Friedman went back to teaching.

Friedman and Gordon and some ACLU lawyers and a few of the less prissy journalists (opinion people, radio people) used to flout the strict separation between Them and Us and ride out to the Roberts house during the session to eat grouper. Senator Gordon would scrape off the sauce. We'd sit around and argue about just how stupid Dukakis looked riding in that tank and why did McGovern lose *really* and do you think that Dempsey Barron has everybody's office bugged, or is it just that God tells him everything?

Now Friedman had met my mother and so was disabused of the notion that we were inbred white trash (but too polite to ask if there was a plantation house and a mammy hidden somewhere on the premises). He did show, however, an inordinate interest in our relative aboriginality. This was the mid-1980s, when you could buy a fake license plate with the orange silhouette of the state and a big green NATIVE emblazoned across it. You could also buy one with the orange silhouette of the state and a big green WHO CARES? Friedman wanted to know if it was strange that Florida was now in the hands of rootless, oddly accented people who were almost wholly without Confederate ancestors. He wanted to know if, when my brother and I were kids, we had felt different or weird or something, being eighth-generation Floridians.

But as for who was in charge of Florida, well, as best we could tell, that was still *us*. At least half the last twenty years' worth of Speakers of the House had been rural types, North Floridians like James Harold Thompson from down the road in Quincy, or Bo Johnson from outside Pensacola, or my cousin Donald Tucker from outside Tallahassee, one of the first Speakers to serve two terms, or T. K. Wetherell from Daytona Beach. Johnson, known to the press gallery as Cat Head for his strange comb-over, ended up serving time for tax evasion. T.K. became president of Florida State University, where he'd played football, and Donald ended up lobbying. Same thing in the Senate, where a disproportionate number of presidents came from the top half of the state, which makes no sense, what with all the people being in South Florida. Dempsey Barron used to smile like an old lizard when some reporter would ask him why that was exactly.

As for being conscious of flouting the statistics that say the Robertses and the Gilberts and the Browards and the Tuckers and the Bradfords should have been good, mobile Americans instead of sluggish northern European types who landed with a thump in a British colony, hung around long enough to make a few bucks, then hauled themselves down to Florida, a Spanish colony, and subsequently refused to budge—no, we knew a lot of people like us.

We craved the other Florida, though; we wanted to see performing porpoises and cockatoos and alligator wrestling and stay in motels called the Palmaire or the Mermaid Manor or the Banyan Beach (which had no banyan tree and no beach) with their sulfury-tasting water and roaring window units and swimming pool fenced with chain-link and circumscribed by a list of rules (NO splashing, NO diving, NO alcohol, NO food, NO two-pieces, NO dogs) two signboards long.

I told Friedman, "We liked the jungles."

"The jungles," he said.

"Parrot Jungle," I said. "Monkey Jungle, Jungle Gardens, Sunken Gardens." We'd get in the Chevy station wagon and head south, searching for strange animals and pointless buildings and a bright blue swimming pool where, if the light is just right, you could see the chlorine fumes dancing in the sun.

We had our pictures made with parrots perched on our heads and shoulders and arms at Parrot Jungle and looked at the gibbons and macaques at Monkey Jungle. Monkey Jungle is not to be confused with Noell's Chimp Farm in Tarpon Springs, where you should take the sign "Caution: Dung Throwers" seriously. The ad for Monkey Jungle said: "Where the humans are caged and the monkeys run free!" You stood there in a sort of wire walkway while the simians would do gratifyingly simian things, like swing from trees. Sometimes, in the 1960s, the chimps would be wearing silver space suits. The time my brother and I saw them, they were wearing Beatles wigs.

In the 1990s Monkey Jungle got in trouble with Jane Goodall over King the Gorilla. She said he was unhappy. Certainly in the news photos of him he looked unhappy. She wanted him moved to the zoo in

Atlanta where they had a decent-size gorilla habitat. Monkey Jungle said that King was *not* unhappy. He was just of a serious turn of mind.

We rode up the elevator at Citrus Tower in Clermont to look out at the orange groves, row after perfect row of dark green circles like buttons on a card. We rode the elevator down again. This was before Disney opened. Expectations were low. We walked up the hill to the Bok Tower at Lake Wales, which is made of lacy pink stone and looks like part of a lost tropical cathedral. We found, to our disgust, that you're not allowed to climb to the top. It's not that kind of tower: It's a carillon and plays Bach cantatas and Negro spirituals and Christmas carols at you, all of which sound kind of alike, but pretty, very pretty. And there's a good view: You can see the Florida's Natural orange juice plant down on U.S. 27 and the phosphate slime ponds all the way over toward Bartow.

Friedman always sounded like he had spent more time in the Museum of Natural History in New York than he had with the parrots and monkeys and Goofy Golf dinosaurs of Florida tourist traps. "I can't believe they made chimpanzees wear wigs," he said. "And space suits."

Friedman was big on animals. He'd stand up on the House floor inveighing against cockfighting and vivisection of live frogs in high school biology classes, even if he knew the bill was DOA.

"There was a show at Weeki Wachee where the mermaid wore a space suit," I said. "I think it was after the moon landing, but I'm not real sure. She didn't have on a tail but she did have silver flippers. They played the Strauss thing from *2001—Also Sprach Zarathustra.*"

Friedman said he could not, for the life of him, imagine why anyone would live anywhere except Florida.

I told Friedman that if he got bored with the session he should ride down toward Perry and see if Reptileland was still in business. "They had gators and snakes and a dancing chicken. They had a giraffe."

Friedman shook his head. I remembered that the reason the chicken would dance was that you put in a quarter and the floor of her cage got electrified.

"A giraffe does not need to be living in Perry," said Friedman.

You could smell Perry before you could see it. Procter & Gamble ran a cellulose plant there and dumped waste into the Fenholloway River. Perry was mean; Perry was Klan. When my father was a teenager, and his school, Leon County High, would go down there for the football game against Taylor County High, the teachers would tell them to *be real careful*—and these were white kids.

Reptileland was a long low building by the side of the road. The rattlers and the cottonmouths and the chicken were inside. The giraffe lived at one end of the sandy parking lot in a room-size pen. I could see Friedman was writing a bill in his head. So I told him they also had a cigarette-smoking monkey. I don't remember if you had to pay the monkey to smoke, or what. I don't remember what his brand was, either. But one night some guys from what would become North Florida's premier garage band, the Slut Boys, got liquored up and decided they'd drive down there and liberate the monkey. The monkey was a fellow creature. The monkey was a fellow smoker.

Peacocks on the Roof, Iguanas in the Toolshed

Here's what the sign at the Goofy Golf said: "This is the MAGIC WORLD, where the ages of time abide in a garden of serenity with perpetual peace and harmony."

I'm ten hours' drive south-southeast from the Goofy Golf, but it doesn't matter. I'm still in Florida. I have a table to myself at the Versailles, drinking a tiny cup of thick, sweet Cuban coffee. The Versailles is a bakery, a restaurant, a hangout, with gilt and mirrors and chandeliers defiantly hanging from its too-low ceilings. Except for getting bigger and bigger to accommodate more and more homesick Cubans and now Salvadorans and Guatemalans and, God help us, Nicaraguans who come looking for empanadas and flan, the Versailles doesn't change. Certainly not as much as the rest of Calle Ocho has changed since all those Cubans came over after the revolution, all those wronged *hidalgos* who owned all those *Gone with the Wind*–ish plantations where they were nice to their workers, and look what it got them: nothing but that *hijo de puta* Marxist and exile in the land of Mickey Mouse and *los hermanos* Bush. Calle Ocho is gentrifying. There are art galleries with expressionist paintings of roosters and sculpture made from gourds. There's a boutique where all the clothes—wedding dresses, suits, prom gowns—are made from guayaberas.

Calle Ocho is Southwest 8th Street in Miami. *Hablamos espanol*. It's nearly the tail end of the Tamiami Trail. Go west and, eventually, past the mini-malls and the scorched-earth subdivisions, you finally hit the wet, warm emptiness of the Everglades. The road runs through the River of Grass.

I always feel foreign in Miami. Not because of the language thing (it's a *Miami Vice* myth that all you hear is Spanish; there's Creole and Portuguese and Quechua and various Englishes ranging from Newcastle to New Jersey to New Orleans) but because the place looks so completely unlike my Florida, with its hot plastic greens and pinks, its curves and its glass, its nervy noisiness and its terrible brightness. When I walk on the beach I know I'm probably the only native; I know I'm the palest person there. And I'm overdressed: I feel like Jane Broward or Roxanne Bradford might—where's my parasol? I was raised in the shade.

I'm thinking about one of those spinach empanadas. They're better at the Versailles than most places on Calle Ocho. I'm thinking about Friedman, too. I lost touch with him after he left the legislature. He's out there in the city somewhere, teaching some kid about the redistribution of wealth or the dignity of animals.

I'm thinking about my mother and father. They lived in Coral Gables in the late 1950s. My father spent his days inspecting concrete plants, drawing bridges, staring hard at the shoulders of roads running through places that had been empty since the Spanish deposited their germs and sailed back to Cádiz. My mother spent her days cooking wonderful new-bride dinners he was mostly too sick to eat and going places he wasn't very interested in: Burdines to shop, or the café at the Eden Roc (he didn't mind going to the aquarium and the Hialeah racetrack). Her favorite place was Vizcaya, tractor millionaire James Deering's art-stuffed palazzo on Biscayne Bay, which the county recreation department had turned into a museum. She figured it might be as close as she ever got to Italy.

My mother was fascinated by color, shape, and beauty: flamingoes landing on a lake like a pink cloud, Christmas red royal poincianas in bloom, the elegant one-footed balance of the marble Venus at Vizcaya, the chemical pastels of terrazzo floors and tables in diners. My father was fascinated by sand, stress, petroleum, steel, gravity, gravel, tar, concrete: the physics of making a road, the mathematics of making a bridge. Raised where earth would revert to water with no notice, he liked the idea of imposing something on the landscape of Florida that would damned well stay there. That's one reason he went to work for the State Road Department, figuring out how to put cars in places where cars were not meant to go.

Daddy disliked strangers, he disliked crowds, he disliked tourists, he disliked Yankees, and he spent his short but successful career making it easier for Florida to become full of strangers, some of whom were tourists, some of whom intended to live here, and most of whom were Yankees.

He had nothing to do with the Tamiami—Tampa to Miami—Trail. It opened to traffic in 1928, two years before he was born, but he read everything he could about this engineering marvel, this triumph of white man over matter. On April 4, 1923, ten cars and twenty-five men, two of whom were Seminole guides, left Fort Myers and set off across the vastness of the 'Glades to Miami. It took three weeks. They kept getting lost. Three of the cars had to be abandoned. The trail was surveyed chest-deep in muck and water. The big drillers were brought in, and a lot of nitroglycerine, too. They contrived the roadbed by first dynamiting the lime rock underneath, then piling it up. Explosives killed a lot of the workers; snakebite got others, and drowning and malaria. But what the hey? So you lose a few Negroes, Spics, Crackers, and Indians. It was *progress*.

The Tamiami Trail cost $13 million. It was mostly straight as a rifle barrel. People could go from the Gulf to the Atlantic. Stuff could go from the Atlantic to the Gulf. Driving got even better when Alligator Alley, now I-75, was built. Floridians were no longer thwarted by that alien world of gray-green wet vastness with its rapacious mosquitoes, rattlers, moccasins, gators, big cats. The 'Glades were girdled. Money would be made. So the natural flow of the marsh's complex waters has been interrupted. So there lay the muscled, honey-colored bodies of Florida panthers by the side of the road, hit by another Lincoln Navigator, another Mack truck, another Jeep Cherokee. So: The animals lost; we won. It's progress.

It's not like South Florida was hostile to animals *qua* animals. The place has always been full of animals, famous animals, and not just the parrots and the monkeys in their miniature jungles. Gentle Ben, for example. Flipper. Producer Ivan Tors pulled Flipper off the back row of the Marineland porpoise chorus and made her a star, just because she could smile and dance on her tail at the same time.

Flipper's real name was Mitzi. Pilgrims visit her grave on Grassy Key.

Tors's Florida studios also made *Daktari,* a TV series that felt kind of bad about colonialism in Africa, but not bad enough to let the nice black guy get next to the white vet's daughter. The black guy didn't get a spin-off show, but Clarence the Cross-Eyed Lion did. You'd never know that Tors's Dark Continent was within half an hour's drive of where Jackie Gleason would ooze into his own show with "How sweet it is!" and the June Taylor Dancers would make kaleidoscope patterns on the stage floor with their legs.

Poor Clarence. He was probably dying in that humidity. Looking at these TV programs, you'd think South Florida was some kind of prelapsarian peaceable kingdom where if you get into trouble, a smiling porpoise, a kindly chimp,or a friendly bear would save you.

What you do in Miami is what you do in Madrid: sit in cafés, sit in bars, sit in restaurants. I abandon the Versailles, which has hit Disney World decibel level when a family of forty-seven came in for a First Communion celebration lunch. I relocate to the News Café on the beach, on Ocean Drive. I order a mojito and watch this couple, Anglos, drinking some quart-size cocktails that mimic the colors of the sunset.

It's still early and quiet enough to eavesdrop. They're talking about this story in the *New York Times.* South Florida is overrun with weird exotic fauna: giant angry lizards that can tear your dog's head off, gangs of monkeys stealing the oranges off your trees, swarms of parakeets hell-bent on messing up your cable TV line. The guy, dressed in Banana Republic linen, reads to the pink-Tod's-shod woman swizzling her cocktail—which matches her shoes—next to him.

"This is in the Everglades," he says. *"It is more likely that pythons could eventually displace native snakes. Mr. Snow said he had been heartened by reports that an alligator recently swallowed a python in the park—a bone-chilling battle captured on film by stunned retirees from Wisconsin—because it suggests that pythons, which have few predators, could perhaps be controlled."*

"That's fucking awesome," says the woman.

The guy keeps reading out what he thinks are the good parts, about the Nile monitor lizard, a creature that starts out small and cute in the pet shop but soon gets seven feet long, hungry and irascible, about the vervet monkeys, unemployed since their roadside attraction shut down, who insist on hanging out at a car lot in Fort Lauderdale, about the Cuban tree frogs, eating native frogs every chance they get: *"'This stuff doesn't happen in New Jersey, it doesn't happen in Ohio, but in South Florida it happens constantly,' said Todd Hardwick, whose trapping business, Pesky Critters, gets 60 calls a day from people with peacocks on their roofs, caymans in their driveways and iguanas in their tool sheds."*

"That," says the woman, "is just fucking wild."

In 1992 Hurricane Andrew hit Miami like a sixteen-ton anvil dropped from the top of the Acme Building. One of the newspapers quoted a smarty-pants who said of the 1926 hurricane, the herald of the land-boom collapse, the breaker of the Lake Okeechobee dike, "It shows what a soothing tropic wind could do when it gets a good running start from the West Indies."

By the time Andrew was up to sprint speed, it was a Category 4, with winds of 135 miles per hour, chewing up South Florida and spitting it out, yanking up palms and swing sets, trailers and pickup trucks, slamming them down again somewhere in the next zip code.

The city was full of hollow-eyed people, faces ashy cold with shock, looking for their pets, looking for their cars, looking for their houses, looking for one another. The city was also full of creatures, hollow-eyed, wet-furred or feathered, scared. Cats clung to the cracked branches of banyans. Roosters, freed from certain death as Santería sacrifices, perched on bent pine trunks above the floodwaters. Even dogs had got into trees somehow, trying to stay balanced and howling in distress. The Miami Zoo had been breached and thousands of baboons, wallabies, birds, and barrel-size aquatic rodents from South America called capybaras liberated themselves. Andrew opened the cage doors at pet shops, research facilities, and farms, and thousands of geckos, rats, capuchin monkeys, parrots, and cockatiels took to the streets. Miami looked like Noah's Ark had hit a reef and everybody abandoned ship.

Thank God Flipper, Ben, and Clarence didn't live to see this.

Now the animals have joined the other exiles and refugees, the Haitians, Nicaraguans, Guatemalans, Salvadorans, Cubans, Venezuelans, Colombians, Panamanians, the *olla podrida,* the varied and unlikely stew, of South Florida.

One day I drove over to Coral Gables to look for the street my mother and father had lived on when they were part of the Miami mix. There's not really any coral here, nor gables, either. But the Massachusetts-derived Merrick family, whose farm this was in 1910, mistook the limestone for coral, and maybe they missed New England architecture. The Merricks used to sell their produce a few miles down the road over at the Royal Palm, Henry Flagler's swish hotel. Maybe Young George, whose daddy made him go to law school, even though he wanted to write romantic novels, looked at Flagler's fantasy palace and thought he, too, could make something fine (and profitable) out of South Florida.

When George Merrick inherited the farm, he hired a bunch of architects to create what he billed as "the city beautiful." He made the Venetian Pool out of an old quarry. It resembles nothing in Venice, Italy, but looks a bit like the pool at Hugh Hefner's Playboy Mansion. Merrick sold a lot of Mediterranean-fusion houses. He gave land for the University of Miami in the mid-1920s. Then the boom burst and

Merrick went bankrupt. He ended up running a little fishing camp in the Keys.

Coral Gables is still pretty, like an Italian village designed by Spaniards who'd been educated in France and Morocco. You can still swim in the Venetian Pool. My mother would go there some days in her turquoise-and-black Catalina and rhinestoned sunglasses to read a Thomas B. Costain novel under the palms. You can still take tea at the Biltmore. But the little street my parents lived on seems to have been swallowed by a sleek "town home" development in the Andalusian style (only with huge central AC units purring outside and New Guinea impatiens in alternating oranges and magentas under the double-thick windows). There is no trace of where my mother concocted those dinners my father couldn't eat out of her shower-present cookbooks, no trace of where she hung her pale cotton dresses, or where Daddy would sit with his graph paper and his slide rule.

This is normal, expected, in Florida: a place is there, then it's gone. It's built, then it's torn down. Petticoat Junction is now a Wal-Mart Superstore. The Miracle Strip Amusement Park closed on Labor Day 2004. Somebody wants the land for condos. Reptileland has disappeared without a trace into the pine thickets of Taylor County. The Goofy Golf hangs on as a kind of postmodern comment on the Redneck Riviera, the Sphinx looking older all the time.

Riding around South Florida, looking for the past in my red Honda covered with yellow North Florida pollen, I imagine another Category 4 hurricane, or maybe a 5, crashing into a city that's grown even since Andrew, scattering the polyglot nation of Greater Miami once again, liberating all kinds of fabulous beasts, till the macaques take up residence in the Biltmore bar, the capybaras swim laps in the Venetian Pool, and the Cuban tree frogs drown out all the other frogs, then eat them.

12

Looking-Glass Land

THE GOVERNOR BROUGHT A BLONDE to the 1967 Inaugural Ball. Not just *a* blonde: The papers called her the "Blitz Blonde." She didn't seem to have a name. He introduced her as "Madame X." No relation to the Madame X in John Singer Sargent's portrait. No relation to Malcolm X, either. The governor was Claude Roy Kirk, Jr. He had come from Alabama. He was an insurance salesman. He'd been a marine. He'd been chairman of Floridians for Nixon in 1960. He was divorced and would, reportedly, screw anything in frosted lipstick. The story in Tallahassee was that he had actually asked another woman to accompany him to the ball. She had bought a dress and everything. Then he ditched her for the Blitz Blonde. Madame X wore a jeweled evening gown and long white gloves. She looked like a Scandinavian actress with an unspellable name.

My mother and her friend Mary Cecilia, the 1950 May Queen,

raised their penciled eyebrows. What did you expect? The man was a *Republican*.

Republicans were like ivory-billed woodpeckers or Soviet spies: We believed they existed, we'd seen pictures, but we'd never actually met one. Kirk was the first Republican elected governor since Reconstruction. He'd beaten Democrat Robert King High, the mayor of Miami, by suggesting that High was basically Bobby Kennedy, Earl Warren, and Stokeley Carmichael in unholy alliance to force Florida into socialism and interracial dating. Kirk's campaign manager was named Robert E. Lee. Kirk claimed that High did not comprehend "the wealth-producing genius of the free-enterprise system."

Kirk had all kinds of sparky plans to unleash the wealth-producing genius of the free enterprise system in Florida. Some of that dynamism would go toward modernizing what was still a slow-walking, slow-talking extra-humid peninsula hanging off the tail end of the Deep South. Some would be channeled into doing eccentric things, like trying to preserve the Everglades and Biscayne Bay from destruction by developers who understood all too well the wealth-producing genius of the free enterprise system.

Jeb Bush would like you to believe he invented public-private partnerships in Florida government. But really, it was Claude Kirk. He decided Florida needed a War on Crime. (To hell with Johnson's War on Poverty: it was the goddamned poor people who committed the goddamned crimes in the first place.) So Kirk put the guy who owned the Wackenhut Detective Agency, the largest statewide crime-spotting organ and a nice little earner, too, in charge. Kirk and Wackenhut were going after the bad guys, the racketeers, the sleazebags. They were going after Meyer Lansky, one of Miami's better-known residents (Capone was dead of syphilis by now). They were going after corrupt politicians. Democrats about fainted: *Police state!* they gasped. Most politicians in Florida, corrupt or otherwise, were Democrats. The War on Crime announced its first big catch in 1967: A school superintendent was indicted for grand larceny. He stole a washer-dryer.

Kirk acquired nicknames within five minutes of taking the oath of office: "Governor A-Go-Go," "Kirk-Jerk," "Kissing Claude." He made a headline a day. But what the citizens of the state really wanted to know was: What about the Blitz Blonde?

Madame X had slipped away from the Inaugural Ball like Cinderella at 11:59 P.M. She resurfaced, with Governor A-Go-Go, sunning herself on the yacht *Security Risk*. The yacht was owned by the governor's crime tsar, George Wackenhut. It turned out she was Erika Mattfeld, a German clotheshorse with a young daughter named Adriana who was *almost* divorced from a Brazilian. Just a couple of months after the ball, Madame X shed her husband and married Claude Kirk. Richard Nixon crashed the reception.

Back in Tallahassee the First Lady of Florida failed to join the Garden Club. She didn't go to tea with the Junior League. She did not hang with the women who were on a mission to protect the live oaks or raise money for musical education. The likes of my mother and her friend the May Queen were a trifle miffed. This foreign glamour puss often didn't answer the invitations she was sent. Not so much as a "Mrs. Claude R. Kirk, Jr., regrets . . ." She preferred their house in Palm Beach.

The only parties at the mansion Tallahasseeans seemed to be invited to were children's parties. Since I was a child, that was okay by me. I remember one in about 1968. There was a chocolate cake with chocolate ice cream in the middle. There was white cake, too, with yellow icing roses. And three flavors of Kool-Aid. Erika was there, in what my mother and the May Queen would have recognized as a Pucci print. The governor was there, too (I don't remember what he was wearing), playing with the children. He liked children. He liked cake and ice cream. Maybe he had a little something extra in his cup of cherry Kool-Aid.

The Governor's Mullet

Florida State University was conducting experiments on me and my brother—all the kids at our school. The school was supposed to be a laboratory, a "demonstration" school where the future teachers of

Florida could get in-the-trenches experience and professors in the College of Education and the Department of Psychology could publish learned articles based on what they observed through that two-way mirror in the kindergarten classroom.

In reality, the University School was a highly selective prep school, bait to bring in faculty from Yale or Michigan who didn't want their little darlings shoved into the segregated educational desert that was the Leon County school system. I was signed up on the school waiting list about two hours after my parents gave me a name. The University School charged tuition, but most of its money came from an appropriation by the state legislature. This could be tricky sometimes.

Years before Ronald Reagan warned the nation that the Reds in Nicaragua could hop in the station wagon, drive through Honduras and Guatemala, gas up in Villahermosa or Veracruz, and invade the United States of America at Brownsville, Texas, in less time than your average spring break road trip, the Florida legislature passed a law that Florida schoolchildren had to take and pass a course called "Americanism versus Communism" in which "Americanism" must, by statute, win.

I don't think we had that class at the University School, or if we did, I don't remember it, and it wouldn't have worked anyway. We once reduced a teacher to tears by asking pointed questions about racism, imperialism, and genocide. We had a textbook called *La Florida* (the teacher pronounced it *Laff Loreeda*), which purported to unfold the history of the state to us, its future citizens. We noticed right away (we were eighth-graders of staggering sophistication) that Hernando de Soto and Andrew Jackson came out looking good, like it was okay for them to go kill a bunch of people then take their land. And why? because de Soto and Jackson were *white guys*? And while we're on the subject, what about Estévan, the African who'd been hanging out in the swamp with Cabeza de Vaca? We got Frederick Douglass and Sojourner Truth in the sixth grade, but that was with Mrs. Esposito, a known cool person, and we haven't heard slavery mentioned since. Or Chief Osceola, for that matter. This just illustrates the ideological bias in favor of conquest and capitalism that retards the American educational system. If we lived in Sweden, instead of Tallahassee, this wouldn't be happening.

The teacher fled to the principal's office. We got yelled at. But she retired at the end of the year.

Most of the other teachers were young, a lot of them working on Ph.D.s at FSU. They wore dashikis and home-made tie-dye and embroidered jeans. One of them had an Afro, which we admired very much. That Afro must have been hard work because her hair was blond and very fine. They gave us Salinger and LeRoi Jones to read. If class got rowdy, the Spanish teacher would do this imitation of Marlon Brando in *Streetcar Named Desire* to make us shut up. He'd scream "Stella!" and knock all the stuff off his desk. Then he'd go back to explaining the Mexican Revolution and why it was in the interest of developed nations to keep the Third World impoverished.

Sometimes somebody in the legislature would notice that the seventh-grade social studies class had gone on a march to protest the war in Vietnam (it was a field trip) or that we didn't say the Pledge of Allegiance every morning or that our football team was nicknamed "the Demons" and the mascot was a person in a maroon devil suit with horns and a spiky tail. The senator or representative or whoever it was would deliver an angry floor speech demanding to know what them hippies over yonder was up to, *probably teaching the young 'uns godless communism,* and recommend the school be "zero funded" in the appropriations bill.

Then someone would quietly point out to the senator or representative that several cabinet members and senators and lobbyists and occasionally the governor himself had children at the school, and we'd survive to subvert Florida another year.

One day—I was in the sixth grade, so this was in 1969 or 1970—we heard that Governor Claude Roy Kirk, Jr., was coming for a visit. Despite the school's apparent commitment to challenging the dominant paradigm, we were exhorted to behave or *else*. Our home room teachers warned us to call the governor "sir." We heard (but it might not have been true) that the principal held assembly for the high school kids to tell them no micro-minis, keep the beads to a minimum *please,* and anybody caught sitting in the magnolia trees smoking grass would be in deep shit and we *mean it* this time—Jesus, they could bust everybody, close us down, and your parents would have to send you to Christian school where the cheerleaders wear skirts down to their knees and *The Catcher in the Rye* is kept in a locked cabinet.

Anyway, the governor didn't just want to hang around with some kids—he could do that at his house. He was selling something. He was selling mullet.

Mullet, *Mugil cephalus,* translates literally, if inelegantly, as "sucker-head." Unlike your pompano, your snapper, your swordfish, your marlin, mullet is not a Florida glamour fish, not a fish sportsmen pay big bucks to snag. Poor people eat mullet. There's this story that one time some guys were arrested for catching fish out of season. It was an open-and-shut case. But their lawyer got a biologist to testify in court that since mullet have gizzards (they live on hard-shelled algae and need to grind off the top layer to get at the nice gooey stuff inside), mullet are, ipso facto, chickens.

In these days of retro chic, the mullet has become the Cracker poster fish. The Flora-Bama Lounge, which bestrides the border between Florida and Alabama like a drunken Colossus, holds a competitive mullet toss. People consume a lot of Jack Daniel's and throw dead fish on the beach. Mullet roe is also much sought after by the Taiwanese, who say it's an aphrodisiac.

When Kirk was governor, mullet was an "underutilized resource," maybe a way to make fast money. Just process it, can it, and call it *lisa*. Why should tuna get all the attention? They told us at the University School that not only was the governor coming to visit us, he was having lunch with us. Not only was he having lunch with us, the school would be serving a *special treat: Lisa Pizza.*

"Lisa" is the Spanish name for mullet. It's more euphonious than mullet. No one would want to toss a lisa. Rednecks would not sport a haircut called a lisa. In the University School cafeteria, the lunch ladies smiled at us like the prison guards in *Cool Hand Luke* as they gave us extra-large helpings. It was our usual Wednesday pizza—Wonder bread slathered with tomato paste, covered in grated Velveeta, and grilled—only topped with mullet.

The governor sat up at the teachers' table, moon-faced and sport-coated. He cut up his pizza with a knife and fork and never stopped smiling. The kids took about one bite. The word "barf" went whispered around the grade school tables. Lisa pizza smelled like an old metal garbage can. It had a slight butane aftertaste. We noticed that the governor ate all of his.

My father called Claude Kirk "Claudius Maximus."

Lisa didn't work out as a brand. Kirk was more worried that *he* wasn't working out as a brand. The governor hired a New York PR man named William Safire (the one who would later become a Nixon speechwriter and distinguished right-wing columnist) to help him hone his political message. Kirk planned on becoming president someday. Safire's salary was $90,000 a year. Kirk's was $36,000.

Kirk had accidentally invented state-sponsored environmentalism in Florida by hiring a young Republican named Nathaniel Reed, a rich boy from Jupiter Island, a self-confessed "bird-watcher and butterfly-catcher," who proceeded to stop the dumping of industrial waste and raw sewage into every river and lake in Florida and saved Biscayne Bay for the nation. Reed turned out to be a bargain compared to Safire: He worked for $1 a year.

Despite his administration's cutting-edge environmentalism, the Claude Kirk Experience went through the looking glass in 1967, and never quite returned to the everyday world. The governor took a submarine ride to plant a state flag beneath the Gulf Stream and claim the territory for Florida. He suggested a state militia in sharp uniforms, shiny boots, and red berets that would make a Paraguyan *generalissimo* proud. He personally intervened when the Health Department shut down a Brevard County kid's lemonade stand. He presided over a teacher's strike, a slush fund scandal, and race riots in Tampa and Miami. He had state employees addressing 50,000 Christmas cards for him on state time.

Florida didn't appreciate him properly. So maybe he felt perfectly justified in spending tens of thousands of Florida Development Commission dollars on second (and third and fourth) honeymoons with Erika in Germany and Brazil and Colorado. Soon after getting elected governor, Kirk had let it be known that he would accept the Republican nomination for president. In a pinch he'd take vice president. He couldn't believe "that little man" Spiro T. Agnew beat him out. At the Republican Governors' Conference in Palm Beach, he described himself as "a tree-shakin' son of a bitch."

A lot of strange fruit came down when Kirk shook the tree. He loved getting his picture made with Coach Jake Gaither and the Florida A&M Rattlers football team. He refused to take his stand with the Dixiecrat white supremacist governors of Mississippi, Alabama, and Georgia. But when H. Rap Brown of the Student Nonviolent Coordinating Committee came to Jacksonville (fondly described as the most racist city in the South) to speak in August 1967, Kirk acted like a plantation master dealing with an uppity hand.

Brown, who had mostly moved on from the nonviolent thing and was heading toward the Black Panther thing, planned to speechify at a Jacksonville baseball stadium. His message: Since white people have guns, and white cops especially have guns, then black people had better get guns, too. Kirk showed up with a black National Guard officer, hopped the fence at the field, walked up to the pitcher's mound where Brown was getting warmed up to start testifying about the fire next time, and tried to shake his hand. He took the microphone away from Brown (uncharacteristically struck dumb), welcoming him to Florida and, grinning like a jackass, saying that he *sure hoped* Brown wasn't there to cause trouble.

In 1970 Kirk tried to block the court-ordered desegregation of schools in the counties of Dade, Volusia, and Manatee. When those pesky judges of the federal and state courts didn't do what he wanted them to (that is, stop messing with the decent, white, increasingly Republican voters who hated school busing), Kirk took ninety state troopers and deputy sheriffs to Bradenton. The governor evicted the school board and sat himself down at the superintendent's desk: Claudius Maximus to the max. The lawmen took over the schools.

Kirk hung around for a couple of days, getting in all the newspapers, then left orders that it would be okay for troopers to shoot in self-defense. He had to get back to Tallahassee. The missus (or the Madame) had produced a new baby, a son called Erik. Their daughter Claudia had been born a couple of years before.

By 1971 Governor A-Go-Go, Madame X, all the little Xes were gone. A lot of the Republicans were gone—or had at least gone quiet. Reuben Askew, a calm, progressive Presbyterian Pensacola lawyer who'd been student body president at Florida State, a man more beige than rainbow-hued, whipped Kirk in the 1970 gubernatorial election, 57 to 43 percent. After four years of psychedelic governmental storms, Florida started crawling out from under the collapsed walls to look at the new world and found that the sun, thank God, was still in the sky.

The next time Florida had a Republican governor (it was 1986, his name was Bob Martinez, and he wasn't such a bad fellow even if he was dull, a one-termer who did his best but looked like Gomez Addams without the panache), the sentiments of the entire state were distilled onto a bumper sticker. It said: "At Least Kirk Was Funny."

Kirk still inhabits his alternative universe. He's changed political parties a few times (nobody seems sure if he's currently a Democrat or a Republican or LaRoucheiste or what). He says that when he dies, he'd like to be buried in the Capitol, under the floor.

Where You Live Is Who You Are

I see this place in the taxi on the way from the airport to the hotel. It will be a tall building. There'll be views of Biscayne Bay, the Port of Miami, the Intracoastal Waterway, the Straits of Florida stretching out to the Great Bahama Bank. The real estate people will tell you that on a good day you can see the Keys, but that is a lie.

It's condos, of course, though the real estate people prefer to call them "luxury apartments" or "exclusive residences." Condominiums, which were fashionable twenty years ago, are now where old people live, old people with saggy skin who complain about waiting half an hour to see the doctor, complain that those dogs have pooped on the path again, complain that the grandchildren never call, complain that somebody messed up their ballot in the last election. This place isn't for them. It's for the tight-skinned, loose-shirted young people who sit out under the stars on Lincoln Avenue eating sage risotto, the ones draped in front of the Clevelander Hotel on Miami Beach, the ones who'll be going on to a party later on, say, midnight, where they'll dance to a disco jam mix of the Fifth Dimension doing "Let the Sun Shine In." Ironically, of course.

Miami is a city of assertive texts. The hotels put their names giant-sized on their sides, lest you mistake a Fountainebleu for a Mandarin Oriental. The *Miami Herald* declares ownership of its headquarters in bright blue and bilingually. Two huge cruise ships parked in the Intracoastal, squat and graceless as a couple of hippos at the water hole, proclaim themselves *Imagination* and *Inspiration*. On the boards around this new, tall building they've painted in bold, big letters, WHERE YOU LIVE IS WHO YOU ARE.

Janet Reno, the former attorney general of the United States, has a coquina house in Kendall—Kendall is not an elegant section of Miami. Her mother, a journalist, built the house herself, and when I say *built,* I don't mean she stood around being the white lady telling the laborers what to nail where. She did much of the work herself. The designer Gianni Versace used to live on Ocean Drive in South Beach, not far from the singer Gloria Estefan's hotel. His place, Casa Casuarina, looked like it had wandered off from Umbria or Arcos de la Frontéra and got lost in the tropics. You imagine mildly pornographic Roman sculpture inside, a "Leda and the Swan" presiding over a courtyard with a fountain. Versace was shot right there in front in 1997.

The movie star Sylvester Stallone had a mansion in Miami for a while, then unloaded it. Madonna had a mansion in Miami for a while, too. She sold hers in 2000 to a dog. The dog paid $7.5 million. He's a German shepherd named Gunther. He has people to handle his fortune, which was bequeathed to him by some countess. When Gunther and his entourage moved in, he got Madonna's bedroom.

The dog probably bought the place as an investment property. Chances are, he'll sell up when the market looks right or when he gets bored with the beach. Florida, said Senator Bob Graham back when he was Governor Bob Graham, "is a mistress state."

As opposed to a wife state. You come to Florida for some fun, you spend some money, you stay a little while, then you go back to your real life. You don't make a commitment. Even if you live in Florida, work in Florida, buy a house in Florida, bring up children in Florida, somehow the relationship between you and Florida just isn't serious enough to take it to the next level—that is, pay grown-up taxes.

Go to Disney World; you'll hear little kids asking why they can't just live there, in the Swiss Family Robinson's tree house or in Cinderella's Castle. I wanted to live in the Haunted Mansion myself. Sometimes the adults ask themselves: Why *can't* we live here where the weather is warm and the streets are clean and the taxes are a joke and everything seems to happen, as the Disney workers are taught to say, *automagically*?

They relocate, work in the service industries that have almost replaced citrus as the non-touristic economic engine along the I-4 corridor. They buy a house in Maitland or Altamonte Springs; or, if they wish upon a star very hard, swear to Tinkerbell that they *do,* they *do* believe in fairies, and show the nice lady at the Celebration Company office that they can afford a $300,000 mortgage, then they can go live in Celebration, Disney's Cartoon Utopia in Osceola County.

Celebration, Florida ("Est. 1994" as the city seal says), is high-calorie cute, a gingerbread village built on spare land Disney snagged in the 1960s so that trailer parks and tar-paper shacks and concrete-block *barrios* would never crop up like crabgrass near the combed lawns of the Magic Kingdom, lowering the tone, lowering the property value. Celebration is not a town, it's an epiphany. The website intones, "The founders of CELEBRATION started down a path of research, study, discovery and enlightenment."

The Mouselords who run the place insist that you have a front porch, but they frown if you put up a plastic hanging pot from the sale table at Home Depot or that homemade macrame your roommate at Michigan State gave you as a birthday present in 1975. They want you to "celebrate" your individuality, but not if it makes your house look different from other people's. The lady who put up scarlet curtains instead of beige ones, the man who parked a preowned automobile out front, found themselves treated like denizens of Salem circa 1692, who had demonstrated an excessive fondness for black cats.

You don't mess with the Mouse.

If you're really rich, NBA-star rich, platinum-record rich, you can live your Florida fantasy at Isleworth. Under Florida law if you go bankrupt, however fancy and huge and pricey your house, they can't take it away from you.

The cheapest house in Isleworth, which must be one of those focus-group-derived names designed to sound vaguely English and therefore classy, sells for $850,000. Isleworth has twenty-seven security guards who do not smile. Isleworth has a lake and a golf course designed by Arnold Palmer. Isleworth has resident movie stars and princes of basketball and hockey. Michael Jackson decamped from his California ranch and rented a seven-bedroom plantation-style pile with a swimming pool edged in 14-carat gold. It's said that Michael Jackson likes to hang out at the theme parks, Disney World, and Universal Studios. It's said he came to Florida looking for some peace and quiet before he goes on trial for child molesting.

His California house is called Neverland; his Florida house is called Elysium.

Where you live is who you are. I saw a sign in the Palm Beach airport recently. It exhorted people to check out a new development, "Florida's Newest Hometown." The name of the place is "Tradition."

Here's my Disney dream: a two-story Celebration house, the sort of place Pollyanna might retire to—picket fence, swing hanging from the old palm tree in the front yard. I would paint the front door fuchsia and the shutters tangerine; I'd stick 144 pink plastic lawn flamingoes into the dainty grass on one side of the sidewalk; I'd put a wheel-less Dodge Dart up on blocks on the other; I'd pull on my best FUBU tank top and sit on my porch step drinking Jim Beam out of the bottle, calling out a neighborly "Hey, Dawg!" to everyone passing by. Make my Celebration truly Floridian. At least until the Disney "hosts" and "hostesses" come and take me away and charge me with crimes against corporate taste.

I'm from the swamp, after all.

Fly High

In Florida the 1960s arrived in 1970. (We're Southern; we're slow.)

We had got to the point where we were no fun anymore. We had the bus boycotts and the lunch-counter sit-ins and the race riots and SNCC and CORE, and the white students getting a clue and sitting down, sometimes getting arrested, with the black students. We had marijuana and *Dr. Strangelove* and black-light posters of Minnie and Mickey Mouse performing several dozen greatest-hit positions from the *Kama Sutra*. We had head shops and co-ops. We just hadn't quite put the whole thing together yet: Summer of Love, Chicago, Angela Davis, Nixon, Vietnam, Kent State.

We had our chance to be ahead of the groove curve. Jim Morrison, an angel-headed hipster if there ever was one, came up from South Florida in 1964 to take art history classes at FSU. He read a lot of Aldous Huxley and drank a lot of beer. He hung out at the old Cherokee Hotel downtown, telling any girl that would listen that he was a shaman, and that he never wore underwear.

Jim Morrison hated Florida. At the 1969 Doors concert in Miami when he got arrested for "lewd and lascivious behavior by exposing his private parts and by simulating masturbation and oral copulation," he had called out, "Anybody here from Tallahassee?" And when a few little stoned voices cheered, he said, "The place is a shithole." Unless he said, "Well, it sucks." Accounts differ. He haunts the house he used to crash in on College Avenue. Frat guys at parties there still say they see him sometimes and he's still real, real good looking.

Jack Kerouac died in St. Petersburg, Florida, in 1969. He hated

Florida, too. By the late 1960s, he was a sick, bitter conservative, an old guy who'd go sit on one of the green benches and glare at the sun.

Still, there was cool. My mother had a pair of leather trousers, handmade for her by her German friend Erika. Not Madame X, another German Erika who was six feet tall. My mother was director of arts and crafts at the City of Tallahassee's Lafayette Park Center. That's how she knew Erika. There on the edge of the last little scrap of the land granted to the Marquis de la Fayette for his help in fighting the American Revolution, the site where he had intended to create a model community that would prove that slavery wasn't just immoral but unnecessary, where everybody worked for the common good as well as personal advancement in an atmosphere of peace, love, and good wine, the bourgeoisie of Tallahassee took ceramics classes and watercolor classes, weaving and leatherworking. It wasn't Haight Ashbury, but it wasn't the Junior League, either.

My father was dead. We were still in Tallahassee. In 1967, about the time Claude Kirk claimed the Gulf Stream for Florida, Daddy had gotten a new job. It was in Jacksonville, with a private engineering firm. He was going to make a lot more money. We were going to sell our peculiar handmade house in the woods and live in a suburb. We were going to be like other people. Only Daddy's internal organs started shutting down. My mother went to Jacksonville and sat in the hospital every day for nearly three months that summer. Daddy died there, only a few miles from where his great-great-great-great-grandfather François Brouard had settled with his children and his slaves and his mules.

Mama was a young widow, still trying to figure out just what the hell she was supposed to do: no money, two small children, a house, chickens, cats, dogs, and flower beds all in need of attention. She had quit the Garden Club. She had stopped worrying about getting her hats and gloves to match. She had pretty much given up hats and gloves altogether. By the 1970s she had a fondue pot and several psychedelic print hostess dresses. She and Charlotte Allen Williams used to go to drink espresso and listen to young men in black-framed glasses read earnest and oddly rhymed poetry in the cellar of an old house on

Calhoun Street, maybe the same house Jane Broward Tucker was having tea in when the Second Seminole War broke out. They'd buy scented candles and ethnic jewelry at Vardi's on College Avenue, which was a kind of head shop for people who drank daiquiris in lieu of dropping acid. They'd see others of their kind, bohemian white ladies who never jumped over into hippiedom (they refused to give up their perms and their $200 handbags) but wanted to check out the scene.

Jessie Conrad liked to weave. She kept a herd of sheep out at Millstone Plantation, grazing on an oaky hill between the big house and Lake McBride. Susan Bradford would recognize the place: She and her sisters and cousins would have picnics there in the 1850s. Pine Hill is just a mile away. Indeed, in her old age Susan Bradford had been a patient of Jessie Conrad's husband, a dentist. Jessie's son Jack assures me that somewhere, in the attics at Millstone, they've got Susan Bradford's dental records. I expect the United Daughters of the Confederacy would love to get their hands on them.

Jessie's friend Clifton Lewis, an ex–May Queen, fought to save the live oaks and preserve Florida's architectural heritage, too—when she wasn't agitating against Jim Crow. She used to gather up progressive white people to go sing freedom songs outside the Leon County Jail when black civil rights activists were locked up inside. She and her husband, chairman of the Lewis State Bank, would sometimes pay bails and jail fines.

By the time I hit the eleventh grade in 1975, the revolution began to look possible. David Schomberg, who graduated from the University School two years before, appeared on the cover of the *Florida Flambeau* buck naked. At least, we were pretty sure it was him, streaking with some other guys across Landis Green, pursued by stiff-mouthed cops. His sister was in my class. Their father was a dean at FSU.

There was a time in Tallahassee when the counterculture *was* the culture. Until 1947 Florida State had been a deceptively genteel women's liberal arts college with a secret mission to sabotage the patriarchy from within. Florida A&M been founded in 1887 adhering to the Booker T. Washington philosophy of teaching the Young Negro useful agricultural and mechanical skills (though how were you going to keep them down on the farm once they'd read W.E.B. DuBois?). By the early 1960s, both institutions were incubating peppery activists for SNCC and CORE, then Students for a Democratic Society and Black Power.

Aided and abetted by what irate deans called "sprout-eating, blouse-wearing, long-haired professors," the *Flambeau* had thrown off the shackles of university control. It declared itself independent in 1973 and commenced to breaking some national stories that sent the university administration into swivel-eyed hissy fits, such as the one about how FSU football coaches "trained" players by staging no-holds-barred, bare-knuckle fights in chicken-wire cages. Still, the paper wasn't above putting out an April Fools' Day issue that proclaimed the End of the World in 96-point type and featured an exit interview with God, who had taken the form of a dog—he thought it was fun to spell his name backward.

The reactionary president of the university (who now runs a reactionary think tank in Tallahassee) kept trying to censor their anti-Nixon, anti-Vietnam, anti-*him* reporting. The only slightly less reactionary state legislature kept trying to make the university close down the Center for Participant Education, the nation's first "free university." CPE taught classes in French cinema, Latin American history, organic gardening, and the overthrow of the United States government by any means necessary.

At the University School, all we wanted was to be *older,* so we could join in the Revolution, so we could liberate our black brothers and sisters, liberate women, get the U.S. out of Vietnam, get ourselves into Students for a Democratic Society, take the course at CPE where, we'd heard, required text was *The Anarchist's Cookbook,* and they taught you (this was the rumor) how to make an actual bomb.

We wanted to live at the Miccosukee Land Co-op, for all the wrong reasons, too. The boys heard that women out there went skinny-dipping in the creek. The girls had seen a picture of one of the founders, a doctor's son, in the newspaper and he was *so cute*. We wanted to be streakers, too, or at least be where we could see streakers, up close. Nakedness was power—or if it wasn't power exactly, it sure freaked the grown-ups.

We were dilettante bohos, most of us, like our parents. We were nerds masquerading as rebels. We sneaked off to a Tennessee Street bar to suck down Salty Dogs. We patronized the Co-op Record Store and bought Che T-shirts. We were confident we'd get the *fuck* out of Florida and end up in New York or Paris—after Wellesley or Duke. We smoked Kools and cheap marijuana out by the drainage ditch at school. We were secretly glad that Fidel Castro could still embarrass the United States, and we knew that Richard Nixon was to blame for everything that had ever gone wrong, even before he was president.

We stopped referring to our school as the University School, like our parents wanted us to, or even Florida High, which was its semi-official name. We called it "Fly High." We were striking a blow for individual enlightenment. We reveled in the knowledge that on Friday night, when we played football against North Florida Christian, the "Go Fly High!" banner some of the seniors painted on a sheet stolen from the school infirmary would drive the Christians out of their tiny minds. Our Demon mascot would waggle his horns and swing his tail while we cheered, "Unh! Ungowa! The Demons got the Power!"

It would be the beginning of the end of global capitalism. Everyone could streak or smoke or drink cheap wine or tie-dye his or her mother's best Irish linen tablecloth as much as he or she liked.

Our parents, however, would have skinned us alive if we'd been caught streaking in 1975. So, while waiting for the revolution to ignite in the Sunshine State, we did the next best thing; we agitated for the Equal Rights Amendment.

My cousin Donald Tucker, Speaker of the House of Representatives, was in favor of the ERA. Donald had gotten his consciousness raised. He wasn't a pathological fanny-patter like his father: Senator Luther Tucker was well known at the Silver Slipper, Angelo's, and other restaurants for tactile inspections of the outlines of young women's panty girdles. Donald didn't attend the more notorious porkchopper orgies: the Lil' Abner costume ball (where the Daisy Maes were all out-of-town girls) or the toga parties where legislators would show up in sheets from the Floridan Hotel with sumac wreaths on their heads.

Support for equal rights scandalized some of Donald's Tucker, Roberts, Broward, and Vause aunts. Did he not realize that the ERA would lead to homosexual marriage and unisex bathrooms and so to the fall of Western Civilization? Most of the family had come around to the idea of civil rights: You had to admit that the Middle Passage, the slave market, the whippings, the cotton fields, the lynchings, and the not being allowed to sit at the lunch counter in Woolworth's were a lousy way to treat people who went to church even more often than white Baptists. It was time to give them a chance.

Besides, Florida State and the University of Florida won a whole lot more football games with black guys on the team.

Feminists, now, were a different kettle of fish. Loud Yankee women with straggly hair demanding to be welders and brain surgeons and company presidents and contractors and taking jobs away from men? Bet not one of them could make a decent sponge cake.

Donald Tucker had a hard-core sense of fairness in those days, and if some of it emanated from what Papa Roberts said was a Tuckerish spirit of "pure devilment" (Wakulla County–speak for *épater la bourgeoisie*), so what? He also sponsored bills to increase welfare payments. He championed prison reform and collective bargaining for public employees. He favored open government—"sunshine"—which would later let everyone in the universe see exactly how Florida screwed up the presidential 2000 election. Best of all, he wanted to let eighteen-year-olds drink.

We'd been drinking since we were sixteen, of course. We'd drive to the Sing Store in Killearn Estates and, with great authority, buy a bottle of red Riunite, take it back to Suzy Corrie's house on Killearney Way, and get wasted while watching the ABC *Movie of the Week.* Still, since we believed in the rule of law, it would be better if we were legit.

Donald Tucker was hardly some tree-hugging, peace-symbol-sporting, bell-bottomed hippie. He abolished the state Environmental

Protection Committee. It's tough to embrace environmentalism when your roots are in the swamp and the environment was what kept your granddaddy poor. Donald had big hair. Not long hair: big, puffy hair like an overstuffed pillow. He wore three-piece suits with extravagant lapels, ties wide as the interstate highway in colors not found in nature, white belts, white shoes. He drove a Lincoln Continental Mark IV. He played "I Saw the Light" on the harmonica. He was like one of the TV preachers on *The Hour of Power.*

When the *Miami Herald,* never missing a chance to investigate Donald and his questionable business loans, called him a "provincial agrarian," he responded in a deadpan drawl, "I looked that up: it means *redneck*."

Donald's brother, Luther "Kit" Tucker, was, as political siblings go, up there with Billy Carter, Neil Bush, and Roger Clinton. For a while Kit seemed to be working for the music industry, making tapes, or that's what he told the *Miami Herald*. For a while Donald seemed to be working to kill a bill that would outlaw that kind of work as musical piracy, bootlegging. Donald brought Kit to a meeting in the House Speaker's office to talk over an amendment. The whole thing looked funny. A grand jury was convened and Kit started saying that he'd been misunderstood by the press: "I am in the brick business. That's the business I'm in."

So if Kit was in the brick business, not the music business, what, asked the *Herald,* "was he doing in the meeting to which his brother brought House Judiciary Chairman Talbot 'Sandy' D'Alemberte, D-Miami, and D'Alemberte's staff attorney, Janet Reno?"

Donald replied, "What my brother does with me is none of your damn business."

Later on Donald caught a *Miami Herald* reporter using the Speaker's office Xerox machine, marched into the House, and announced that the newspaper was stealing from the state. The reporter offered to write the state a check for five cents, but the Speaker refused to accept it. He said he was going to call Leon County Sheriff Raymond Hamlin, who happened to come from one of the founding families of Wakulla County.

In 1976 Donald looked like an emerging talent on the national Democratic Party farm team. He could be governor one day. U.S. Senator. Maybe he'd run for president. Jimmy Carter did it—a peanut farmer and a lay preacher from South Georgia. Donald was just as smart as Jimmy, just as ready with a reference to scripture, and had a larger repertoire of country songs. Jimmy Carter actually nominated Donald to become a member of the Civil Aeronautics Board, which might have been a stepping-stone to Washington doings, but, maybe because of Kit, maybe because of Donald's own complicated and perhaps dodgy deals, it never went anywhere. They couldn't take his harmonica from him, though.

The End of America

In 1998 Mary, Queen of Heaven, appeared in an office window in Clearwater. Then she showed up in an oil stain not far from the Orange Bowl, though you could only see her certain times of day when the sun was in the right place. When the cousins—the one who had been arrested on a felony firearms charge, the one who had been arrested for robbing a tourist in Little Havana, and the one who wanted to be a hairdresser—saw *Nuestra Señora* in *El Niño Milagro*'s bedroom mirror, no one was surprised. God was moving in Florida, moving fast, like a Colombian in a Crown Victoria on Alligator Alley in the middle of the night. God was laying his hand on Florida before the Millennium, and Florida had better wake up and smell the café con leche.

That goes double for Cuba. Fidel and the comrades scoffed in 1984 when Our Lady of Charity, patron saint of the island, took to hanging out in Havana. The Exiles in Miami said then that it was only a matter of time before the bearded usurper was sent to perdition, where devils with cat-o'-nine-tails would flog him every day for a hundred years, and that was just for starters.

The redemption of Cuba was taking a bit longer than the Exiles had hoped. But now in 1999, *El Niño Milagro* had come to be among them. The secular story was that his mother, Elizabeth Brotons, who was divorced from his father, Juan Miguel González, kidnapped him with her boyfriend and bundled him onto a raft headed north to Florida. He was picked up by a couple of guys out fishing on Thanksgiving Day, clinging to an inner tube in the Straits of Florida.

But that couldn't be all there was to it, not in Miami, not in Florida, where the miracles were stacking up like cars in rush-hour traffic, and where all stories involving Cubans and the sea become allegories. One of the men who scooped *El Niño Milagro* out of the sea claimed that the child was praying to the Holy Virgin as his mother had told him to do, just before she disappeared under the waves, and that he was protected by dolphins and guided by angels. He wasn't scratched, scarred, sunburned, or fish-bitten. He wasn't even dehydrated after two days at sea. He felt a little depressed about his mother drowning and everything, but he perked up when his great-uncle Lazaro and his cousin Marisleysis gave him chocolate milk, brand-new Nikes, and all the Mickey Mouse and McDonald's he could use. José Basulto, president of Brothers to the Rescue, said reverently, "There's no other explanation: This was an act of God."

Basulto and most of the other Exiles began referring to the kid, six-year-old Elián González, as the Child, pronounced in the same churchy tones as you'd say "the Messiah." The prophecies were already in place. Years ago a practitioner of Santeria supposedly told Castro that he could not be overthrown except by a holy child saved by the angels of the sea. Somebody said that Lazaro González had sent a letter to a nun insisting that Castro wanted Elián for a human sacrifice. The voodoo priestess who lived across the street from Lazaro González in Miami said Elián is a son of Eleggua, first of the *orishas* and holder of the Keys of Destiny. José Marmol, a columnist for one of the Cuban Exile newspapers, compared Elián to Moses, taken from the waters and destined to lead his people to the Promised Land. T-shirts appeared in Little Havana with Elián being Jesus or Jesus being Elián: it's hard to tell. He's not on the inner tube now but walking on the waves wearing a halo.

How about this: A *babalao,* a Santero priest, told the *New York Times* that Elián is "the chosen one," the one "who, in the Santero oracle for the year 2000, conquered death when he discovered that the representative of Evil owed his power to the suit he always wore. Therefore whoever possesses Elián possesses good protection against sickness and death."

So all Elián has to do is stay in Miami, where there will then be no more sickness and death, and all the CIA has to do (forget your exploding Cohibas) is bribe the official party dry cleaner in Havana to destroy Fidel's olive drab outfit. Communism will collapse, the Exiles will return, and peace, prosperity, Burger King, Microsoft, Coca-Cola, and Comcast shall rule the land.

From outside their little fenced house, the Miami Gonzálezes made daily appeals to the world: *Let Elián stay*. It's what Jesus would do. Elián may *be* Jesus, anyway. The Gonzálezes trusted in the Holy Virgin. They also hired a lawyer, Kendall Coffey, a Democrat, an Anglo, who understood Miami's rococo court system. After Elián, Coffey would score another well-known client: Vice President Al Gore.

To people living north of I-75, the Passion of Elián González appeared to be one of those periodic eruptions of Florida dementia, a shipwreck story with a villain and a hero, divine intervention and a moral, a story that has reared up every generation since Panfílo de Narváez came looking for emeralds and ended up eating horses while his co-conquistador Álvar Núñez Cabeza de Vaca wrote a best seller about being a shaman among *los Indios*. It turned out that Elián wasn't the wildest thing to happen in Florida in 2000. But at the time the kid looked hard to beat.

The wide, unstable fault line between the 40 percent of Miamians who call themselves Cubans and the 60 percent who describe themselves as Haitians, Jamaicans, Guatemalans, Salvadorans, Venezuelans, Bahamians, Born-Agains, Fashionistas, Yankees, Conchs, Crackers, Midwesterners, Jews (Reform and Orthodox), Seventh-Day Adventists, Plastic Surgeons, Professional Tanners, or some combination of the above started making ominous noises and breathing forth sulfurous fumes. For thirty-odd years, all the Cubans had to do was get their feet onto dry Florida sand and they could stay, while everybody else, even if they were fleeing the Ton Ton Macoutes or Salvadoran death squads (financed by U.S. tax dollars) had to sit in a detention cell filling out forms in triplicate.

No matter how outrageously the Cubans behaved, the U.S. government would write them a check and pat them on the head as if froth-mouthed anticommunism were some kind of divine dispensation. This collective American craziness started with the abortive Bay of Pigs "invasion" put on by the Exiles in 1961; it continues with Jeb Bush helping get Orlando Bosch out of jail. The Justice Department under President George H. W. Bush (that would be Jeb's daddy) figured Bosch had been involved in more than thirty terrorist acts, including a bazooka attack on a Polish freighter and the bombing of a Cuban passenger jet headed for Venezuela. Now the Exiles want to keep this little boy from his father just to spite Fidel Castro?

Elián attracted posturing politicos like a *Sports Illustrated* swimsuit issue shoot attracts frat boys. The candidate traffic was already bad, it being an election year, but now Florida governor Jeb Bush, Texas governor George W. Bush, Vice President Al Gore, and every senator, representative, and aspirant to office from dog catcher to tax assessor had something to say about the kid. Even if what they had to say was stupid, it was a testament to the clout the Exiles (who could win a gold medal if whining were an Olympic sport) wield in both parties. Texan congressman Tom DeLay went on *Larry King Live* to inform the nation that Elián was "a blessed child." Al Gore supported, sort of, his own administration's policy, then changed his mind and came out firmly in favor of giving Juan Miguel González, Elián's grandmother Maria González, Elián's mother's mother, the González aunts, uncles, and cousins, and, for all I know, Speedy González, too, U.S. residency whether they wanted it or not.

Gore's gymnastic pandering backfired. Miami mayor Alex Penélas, a Democrat who had raised money for Gore's campaign, informed President Bill Clinton and Attorney General Janet Reno that there could be riots if the Immigration and Naturalization Service didn't quit issuing dire threats to send Elián back home; and if there were riots, he, the mayor, wouldn't call out the cops to stop them.

If "blood is shed," said Penélas, it's all the federal government's fault—the federal government that just doesn't understand the special pain of the Exiles, so near (ninety miles) and yet so far from their old Land of Milk and Honey, their old source of cheap, but good, rum.

From the Feast Day of Saint Catherine in 1999 to Holy Saturday in 2000, through Advent, Christmas, Epiphany, Lent, and *almost* Easter, it was all Elián all the time in a fiesta of conspiracy theories, theological contortionism, shameless profiteering, and spectacular bullshit. I was working for the *St. Petersburg Times*. Our coverage of the Elián-o-rama and our editorials, some of which I wrote and all of which basically said pack up the kid, put a stamp on him, and ship him back to Cardenas, had generated a Dumpster full of angry letters and a few oblique death threats. I decided to ride down to Miami and check out the scene: take the temperature, read the mood, see if there were some really good Elián souvenirs to buy. There'd been rumors of posters with Elián as an updated Saint Iago Matamoros, wearing an American flag T-shirt, sitting on a pony with its hoof on Fidel Castro's neck, and T-shirts with Elián sitting on the lap of the enthroned Virgin.

Not too long before Elián came to walk among us, an ancient stone circle, built by the Tequestas maybe two thousand years ago, had been found where some developer wanted to put a high-rise. Debate over saving it raged: money or heritage? commerce or culture? Yeah, it's *old,* but do you have any idea what you can get per square foot of space in Miami? South Florida isn't about *old,* it's about *young*.

The old, the past, isn't exactly irrelevant to the Exiles. It's not just 1958 and the revolution, but the loss of the Spanish Empire in 1898 and farther back to the collision of Spanish and African culture when the first slaves were brought to the New World, and still farther back to the Reconquista when the world was tidily divided into Good and Evil, Christian and Heathen, Us and Them.

I took a taxi to Little Havana. Everybody said you couldn't park anywhere near the González house. You couldn't walk anywhere near the González house, either. The street was full of cops, cameramen, old ladies selling rosaries and key chains with Elián's face encased in plastic. There was a woman in Dior sunglasses handing out Xeroxes of selected quotations from Cuba's "Code of the Child." Article 3 says: "The communist formation of the young generation is a valued aspiration of the state, the family, the teachers, the political organizations and the mass organizations that act in order to foster in youth the ideological values of communism."

There were some T-shirts for sale, but they were dull, just the kid's face and an American flag, no sign of the Virgin Mary. The shirt was 50 percent polyester and the Anglo selling it ($25) swore that "half the proceeds go to support the family."

"The family" had come over all shy today, refusing to emerge from their bungalow to conduct the weird theatrics they've become famous for. A guy who I swear said his name was Batista kept blocking the path of anyone suspected of committing journalism and announcing "the family of González is not receiving today."

For all I knew, the family of González was at Disney riding the Mad Hatter's Tea Cups, sticking felt mouse ears on Elián, eating cotton candy, and taking in the Hall of Presidents. They've been all over the television for days, a reality (I guess that's the right word) *telenovela* trying to counter what they say are the vicious untruths, planted by agents of Fidel Castro, that they are not a model Christian family just trying to live a godly, righteous, and sober life despite their tragic banishment from the beloved homeland.

Marisleysis González, twenty-one, telegenic, big-eyed, and nicely manicured, cries a lot. Her crying has improved since the Clinton administration first started threatening to take Elián. Her eyes and nose used to get red and blotchy, but now she looks like a movie star crying, daintily brushing away crystalline tears, careful not to put her eye out with those nails. Her father, Lazaro González, has worked up a pretty good paterfamilias act he employs when ignoring questions he deems insulting, dignified yet fierce. Donato Dalrymple, one of the men who rescued Elián, takes on an expression of sanctity when crowds call out to him *"Pescador! Pescador!"* as if he were Simon Peter.

I bought a Niño Milagro key chain and left, ending up on Thirteenth Avenue at the Bay of Pigs Monument. It's a squat, square-sided column with an eternal flame. It's surrounded by shells—the kind you shoot, not the kind you pick up on the beach. I got to talking to a couple of *abuelitas* out for a stroll in the early spring air. They explained the whole thing to me. Elián is *El Niño de los Delfines,* the dolphin boy. Everyone knows that dolphins work for angels and angels work for the Holy Spirit. Elián isn't Jesus; that's blasphemous. He's more like the harbinger of the Messiah, like John. After all, his mother's name was Elizabeth, just like the mother of the Baptist in the Bible, and his father's name is Juan. He has come to prepare the way for the downfall of Castro. It's perfectly clear. Only the godless do not understand.

It *was* perfectly clear, all of a sudden. Floridians in the late 1950s thought of themselves as Southerners, much more than now, but they refused to see Cuban Exiles as fellow Southerners. Yet the Cubans came from a plantation society—a slave society—a mix of Europe and Africa. They had this baroque class system, this florid religiosity. They could hold a grudge for several hundred years at least. Did nobody in Gadsden County or Jefferson County or Jackson County notice the similarities? Cubans are obsessed with history, honor, purity, violence, ladyhood, land. This is Faulknerian. Somebody call Gabriel García Márquez. I got in the car and went back to Pinellas County.

Here's the secret: The Cubans are Florida's past come home to roost. Their presence in Florida seems to the English-speaking populace like an imposition, like guests who seem to feel as if they not only have a right to come to your house but to redecorate the place in gaudy colors, make you cook dinner spiced the way they like it, and speak a foreign language in front of you, right there in your own living room. I mean, communism is a terrible thing, but do they have to change the way our coffee tastes? And what about the *pope*? There used to be a bumper sticker (maybe there still is) that said: "Will the Last American to Leave Miami Please Turn Out the Light."

But the Cubans were here first, starting in the sixteenth century. Not in Miami; the Tequestas didn't want company. But in Pensacola and St. Augustine, up the Gulf coast and down the Atlantic. When Spanish governors got fed up with Florida recalcitrance, got a promotion, or retired, they went back to Cuba. The food was better there, and the wine; there were grand mansions and cathedrals and opera houses and no Apalachees trying to put an arrow through you. For 350 years, Florida was essentially a colony of Cuba. After 1898 Cuba became a colony of the United States. Teddy Roosevelt, Napoleon Bonaparte Broward, and the Big Stick press talked in misty tones about Cuban independence but expected the various be-medaled vassals who called themselves *el Presidente* to do as they were told, be nice to our corporations, be nice to our mafia, and everything would run smoothly.

It was a shock, then, when Fulgéncio Batista, a bastard (our bastard), was run out of Havana and off the island by the hirsute son of a sugar plantation owner, an Argentinian medical student, and a bunch of grubby cane-cutters who'd been hunkered down in the hills for years without shampoo. Batista hightailed it for Florida. His fellow plutocrats, plus a decent chunk of the middle class, went, too. Then came the Operation Pedro Pan children and later the Marielitos, and always the rafters. This wasn't an aberration, or some foreign element suddenly introduced to the body politic of Florida, it was just the closing of the circle. The Cubans are proof of the truth of the Southern Gothic—the return of the repressed.

As for the family of González, at least the Miami branch, they were the Little Havana Hillbillies. Faulkner's Snopeses had nothing on them. Great-Uncle Lazaro, always striving for gravitas, was a car mechanic with a drunk-driving conviction. He needed a job. Strangely enough, he got one once Elián was in the house, at a car dealership owned by a member of the Cuban American National Foundation. The *Sun-Sentinel* newspaper, however, reported that he rarely showed up for work.

Cousin José and Cousin Luís have an impressive number of arrests and parole violations between them. Rescuer Donato Dalrymple isn't, after all, a fisherman but a house cleaner who was talked into driving his cousin's boat that day. His cousin, unimpressed, calls Donato a phony and a liar. Those weren't dolphins in the water; they were swordfish. The people at the Joe DiMaggio Children's Hospital say that far from being in immaculate shape, Elián was treated for sunburn and dehydration.

As for Cousin Marisleysis, she's been taken to the hospital six times for nervous exhaustion and emotional collapse. She poses herself and Elián for the cameras to put you in mind of a Madonna and child, though once she dressed more like the other Madonna, the one with the recording career, in very short skirts and lots of eyeliner. The Calle Ocho gossip is that she's dating some high-up in the Cuban American National Foundation.

Even the González lawyer, Kendall Coffey, got yanked off his cloud. In 1996 Coffey, who'd just lost a big drug case for the U.S. Attorney's Office, needed—understandably—to unwind. He hit the Dixie Highway and drove to the Lipstik Adult Entertainment Club, where he ordered a magnum of Dom Pérignon and one of those, er, *private dances* from a stripper. There was some sort of scuffle. Coffey bit the stripper. But it wasn't that bad. The stripper's husband, a fair-minded fellow, supposedly said, "He bit her, but not like a crazy man."

For a while it looked like this spiritual and economic boom (there's talk of the Gonzálezes getting a TV deal, maybe a movie deal; the neighbors charged the satellite trucks and reporters at least 500 bucks a day to park on their lawns, the Santeria priests and priestesses have seen an upswing in business, while the souvenir-sellers are making out, too) would go on at least as long as Fidel Castro had breath to give seven-hour speeches and the American court system had some more layers to it. But finally the Gonzálezes lost. Janet Reno tried to cut a deal with Lazaro to take Elián to D.C. to be reunited with Juan Miguel. He told her she'd have to take *El Niño Milagro* by force.

So she did, or rather federal agents did, on the Saturday before Easter. Kendall Coffey was trying to sleep in the back room at the González house. Donato Dalrymple the not-fisherman was hiding in a closet with the kid. An agent in body armor took Elián away before dawn, even though the Exiles outside howled with rage and Marisleysis had strong hysterics, screaming that Bill Clinton and Janet Reno had betrayed America and that she *knew* that God would not let Elián be sent back to Cuba.

Elián was sent back to Cuba. Marisleysis stopped crying (except when on TV) and opened a hair salon. Kendall Coffey went to bat for Al Gore and lost (again), but had sense enough to stay out of strip clubs this time. Fidel Castro keeps on giving speeches that go on longer than transatlantic flights (he is obviously in league with the devil). His doctor has said that he will probably live to be 140.

The dolphins still dance in the warm sea, waiting for another saint to appear to redeem the Land of Flowers, where it's possible to believe many more than six impossible things before breakfast.

Epilogue: The Rules Are Different Here

AW, HELL. IT'S HAPPENING AGAIN.

In 2004 yet another Florida voter was disenfranchised. True, it was only a local election for a seat on the Longboat Key Town Commission. But democracy is democracy. We learned from the 2000 presidential train wreck that every vote counts. Some count more than others.

"Oh my goodness," said the voter, who filled out an absentee ballot then absentmindedly forgot to sign it, rendering it invalid. "I feel terrible."

The voter—you know her as Katherine Harris, former Florida secretary of state—went on, distraught: "It's a mistake. I regret it."

As karmic retribution goes, this is pretty lame.

Katherine Harris is now a member of the United States House of Representatives. Grateful Republicans in Washington compared her to Joan of Arc and Rosa Parks. Grateful Republicans in Tallahassee cut her a shapely congressional district around Sarasota, with its discreet scent of Hummer exhaust and its stratospheric pearl-to-person ratio. Her opponents included a couple of ungrateful Republicans, who said they were embarrassed by her, and a dog named Percy.

The race was closer than anyone expected, possibly because some people questioned whether her candidacy was even legal. Florida has a resign-to-run law: You have to leave one government gig to run for another. She just, kind of, *didn't*. First Harris, the cabinet officer in charge of elections law, admitted she never got around to actually reading the elections law. Then she claimed that she *had* resigned, only it was retroactive, sort of. Then she said she didn't think the statute applied to her. "As you know," she said, "I'm a stickler for the rule of law."

I was thinking about Katherine Harris the other day when I went to visit the carpet road. She always says she's interested in "Florida culture." This *is* Florida culture, one of the secret treasures of Florida, a dirt track in eastern Leon County (unless it's technically in Jefferson County, I'm not sure), about one lane wide, maybe half a mile long. It dead-ends at a scattering of block houses and single-wides, with hanging baskets of old-fashioned verbena out front and clotheslines of sheets and towels and socks and the kind of industrial underwear you can still get at Sears, flag-waving in the back. The road is entirely covered in pieces of carpet.

There's sculpted carpet in that distinctive 1967 blue-green that used to be called "Mediterranean," plush carpet samples in suburban taupes and creams and sage greens, orange shag carpet that looks like cheap pizza, about thirty-six square yards of that floral stuff that went out of fashion in the late 1950s, pieces of Astroturf, dust gray indoor-outdoor, hotel castoffs in maroon and teal, handmade rag rugs from the time of the Truman administration. The carpet must wear out and have to be replaced. Somebody keeps it up, a piece of folk art, performance art—a nice ride for your tires.

This is Florida: comfortable, piebald, eccentric down to its chromosomes; beholden to nobody.

Katherine Harris had recently come back to Tallahassee because the state finally fixed the fountain in back of the capitol. At the dedication, she said she'd been after them to do it *for absolute ever*.

Maybe the thought of all those reporters and lawyers and former secretaries of state—some of the same ones from the last Florida fiasco—coming back to see how we screwed up a presidential election this time, talking on television with that dried-up, pitiful, Third World–looking cement pond in the background, inspired them to take action. Maybe it was the million dollars the beer company gave them. In any case, the fountain now has water and an aluminum and steel sculpture of cavorting dolphins called *Stormsong.* There's also a plaque thanking Anheuser-Busch.

This is Florida: sponsored by Bud Lite, Disney, St. Joe, Carnival Cruise Lines, Tropicana, U.S. Sugar.

People keep asking me what's going to happen in the election. Come on, what do you think, who's going to win? Will Florida be a fifty-two-car, sudden-fog, semitruck-crossed-the-median pileup like last time? I'm not predicting anything. The state just spent $2 million on yet another list of ineligible voters. Then they tried to keep the list secret, even though it's public record. And sure enough, this "felon roll" is as messed up as the one from 2000. Lots of the "felons" aren't felons. Even if they were felons, they've had their rights restored in many cases. Lots of them seem to be black. None of them seems to be Latino. A cynical person might wonder if this has anything to do with the way African Americans tend to vote Democratic in Florida and Cubans Republican.

Now the state's thrown out the list, even though Jeb Bush spent another couple hundred grand in court trying to keep it hidden. Now we don't know who's really eligible to vote and who isn't. Maybe chaos is the natural condition of Florida democracy.

There are no more chads; there are no more butterflies. There are shiny new machines that take your vote off the tip of your finger. Your ballot is now virtual, like the images you see on the Internet. Your ballot is now an article of faith, like the Holy Spirit—there is nothing to see, so you must simply *believe*.

The state tourist board used to have this slogan: *Florida—the Rules Are Different Here.*

Acknowledgments

EVERYBODY HELPED. Sometimes they knew they were helping, and sometimes they didn't, but this book wouldn't have happened without the good humor, imagination, kindness, guidance, and talent of a lot of people in Tallahassee, Tuscaloosa, New York, London, Barnard Castle, County Durham, and Chipley, Florida. David McCormick read a little essay I wrote for the *New York Times* on Florida as the omphalos of American weirdness and saw a book in there. I am very grateful for his enthusiasm, determination, and prose-improving advice. At the Free Press, Maris Kreizman was always sunny-natured and helpful, no matter how many crazy writers she had to deal with that day, and Amy Scheibe has been a gem among editors: careful, creative, and tough. I lucked out when she took on this book.

Dream State really got started twenty years ago when I began writing about Florida politics for the *Florida Flambeau* newspaper. Various editors at papers and magazines in America and Britain, National Public Radio, and the BBC kept letting me do it. Thanks to Sidney Bedingfield, Michael Moline, Eileen Drennen, Moni Basu, Tom Hillstrom, Greg Smith, Stuart Seidel, Terry Tang, James Collard, and Mark Smirnoff for their indulgence and encouragement.

All the best stuff in the book comes from various members of my family who have allowed me to ransack their memories and their genealogical research, or who have, over the years, just told stories. Howard and Suzanne Gilbert of Orange Hill showed off Aunt Bankie's weaving and took me to the graves of Roxanne Bradford and

John Wesley Gilbert; Regina Gilbert Miller, Elizabeth Ann Williams, and Trudy Gilbert Green conjured up Big Mama, John Wesley, and Moses Gilbert, the Revolutionary War soldier, for me; Brenda Roberts Francis, Michael Roberts, Pete and Danica Winter, Maria Elizabeth (Betty) Roberts Folsom, and Thelma Roberts Meltsner helped me know my Roberts grandparents and great-grandparents better—Aunt Thelma, especially, has written sharp, moving reminiscences about life in the swamp in the 1930s. My wonderful cousin Mary Joan (Joann) Roberts Hadland shared her impressive and detailed research into the Roberts, Tucker, Broward, Vause, and McKenzie families—I couldn't have done this book without her. Charlotte Allen Williams and Ernest Williams aren't blood kin but—in the ways that matter—might as well be. They are walking storehouses of Old Florida, from the Tallahassee Capitals baseball team to the May Party (Charlotte was on the 1947 court) to the bus boycott to which woods were cut down to build what subdivision. My mother, Betty Gilbert Roberts, often a coconspirator with Charlotte, claims she doesn't remember anything, then turns around and sketches vivid pictures of the past. My brother Bradford Roberts, who never (unlike me) forgets anything really good, came up with all kinds of startling and detailed recollections of both his grandfathers.

I am fortunate in having a circle of friends in Florida and in Britain who have, over the years (decades, even), offered food, wine, moral support, and good lines for me to steal: Mark and Amy Hinson, whose families have been in Jackson and Calhoun Counties since the late Pleistocene; Pamela Ball and Gary White, splendid writers and cosmopolites; Deborah Jenkins and Ivor Stolliday, who let me borrow their beautiful County Durham house to write in; Bob Shacochis, who generously sent the *New York Times* my way; Mark and Jan Pudlow, who've been speaking truth to power for twenty-five years; Peter Wallsten, who knows all the best bad stories about Florida politicians; David Bedingfield, repository of *Flambeau* lore and keeper of the flame even from the grandeur of the Inner Temple; Sarah Jackson, Fred Ponsonby, Rebecca Jenkins, Susanna White, Oliver Grant, Bronwen Maddox, Alyson Coates, Ethan Hall, Deborah Postgate, Joe and Anne

Hornsby, Kathy Starbuck, Bruce Boehrer, Linda Hall, Tyler Turkle, and Jesslyn Krouskrop, all of whom provided hospitality, moral support, art, parrots, and incandescent conversation about everything from the monstrosity that was the 2000 election to when, exactly, the sea will come to cover Florida once again.

Carl Hiaasen famously said something on the order of there's nothing wrong with South Florida that a good Category 5 hurricane wouldn't cure. There are days when I feel that way about the whole state. Nonetheless, Florida is full of extraordinary people determined to stop the destruction of our environment, the erosion of our democracy, and the epidemic of stupidity that threatens to overwhelm us. Some of them I've already thanked (see above). Some of them work for the *St. Petersburg Times,* a newspaper I am proud to have an association with, others are rabble-rousers, lawyers, academics, writers. Many of them helped with this book, directly or indirectly. Thanks to Martin Dyckman, Dexter Douglass, Clifton Lewis, Stetson Kennedy, Rick and Martha Barnett, Senator Bob Graham, Adele Graham, Jack Conrad, Philip Gailey, Lucy Morgan, Joan Morris, Ben Wilcox, Julie Hauserman, Craig Pittman, David Guest, Barbara Petersen, Bill Maxwell, Robert Friedman, Robyn Blumner, Jon East, Sharon Bond, Robin Mitchell, Alisa Ulferts, and the *St. Petersburg Times* news researchers, especially Caryn Baird and Kitty Bennett.

My teacher and friend, the late Jerome Stern, loved Florida, from Sopchoppy worm-grunting to the Cypress Knee Museum. His book, *Florida Dreams,* testifies to how native he became. I hope he would like this book.

Note on Sources

You will have worked out by now that *Dream State* is not a traditional history. Some names have been changed to protect violators of Florida's open container laws or to shield those who hanker after a future political career. Nonetheless, I have done my best to be as accurate as possible, though accuracy, when you're dealing with oral history, competing family stories (and therefore competing agendas), plus the Southern habit of unintentional lying, can be tricky. In the South, what people think happened is always more important than what really happened. And anyway, as Thomas Pynchon says somewhere, history is mostly impersonation and dream.

I relied on letters, diaries, and other primary source papers whenever I could: Bradford Gilbert's World War I journal; the papers of Susan Bradford Eppes (in the Special Collections of the Robert Manning Strozier Library at Florida State University) as well as her published books, *Through Some Eventful Years* and *The Negro of the Old South;* letters, poems and reminiscences by Crandall Roberts, Vivienne Roberts Weaver, and Thelma Roberts Meltsner, as well as annotations in the Gilbert Bible and other bits and pieces. I also consulted a number of fine books, including (in no particular order) Michael D'Orso, *Like Judgment Day: The Ruin and Redemption of a Town Called Rosewood;* Samuel Proctor, *Napoleon Bonaparte Broward, Florida's Fighting Democrat;* Mark Derr, *Some Kind of Paradise;* Carl Hiaasen, *Team Rodent: How Disney Devours the World;* Marjorie Stoneman Douglas, *River of Grass;* Gloria Jahoda, *The Other Florida;* John McPhee, *Oranges;* Michael Gannon, ed., *The New History of Florida;* John T. Foster and Sarah Whitmer Foster, *Beechers, Stowes and Yankee Strangers: The Transformation of Florida;* years of Florida Handbooks put together by Joan and Allen Morris (these are indispensable to anyone who wants to understand Florida); everything by Stetson Kennedy; Clifton Paisley, *The Red Hills of Florida* and *From Cotton to Quail;* Ellen Call Long, *Florida Breezes;* June Wiaz and Kathryn Ziewitz, *Green Empire: The St. Joe Company and the Remaking of Florida's Panhandle;* Tracy E. Danese, *Claude Pepper and Ed Ball: Politics, Purpose and Power;* Tim Hollis, *Dixie Before Disney: 100 Years of Roadside Fun;* archives of the *St. Petersburg Times* and the *Tallahassee Democrat;* and the *WPA Guide to Florida*. I have ransacked the work of a number of distinguished Florida historians, including Allen Morris, Gary Mormino, William W. Rogers, Jerald T. Milanich, Michael Gannon, John K. Mahon, James W. Covington, Edmund Kallina, Dorothy Dodd, Daniel L. Schafer, Maxine Jones, Wayne Flynt, and E. R. Carswell. If I've got something wrong, it's my fault, not theirs.

Index

About the Author

Diane Roberts was educated at Florida State University and Oxford University. She is Professor of English at the University of Alabama and a commentator for NPR and the BBC, and she writes for the *St. Petersburg Times* and other newspapers. Diane Roberts divides her time between Tuscaloosa, London, and Tallahassee.